The Greening of America's Building Codes

A TIMELINE OF RESIDENTIAL AND ENVIRONMENTAL LEGISLATION WITH RELATED ARCHITECTURAL, ECOLOGICAL, AND SOCIOPOLITICAL EVENTS: 1840–2016

HOW TO READ THE TIMELINE

CHAPTER BAND (where?)

TYPE OF EVENT:

Legislation

Architecture, City, Technology

Environment, Ecology, Ecological Economics

Environmental

Residential

Environmental and Residential

(non-US or background events, marked lighter)

(natural disasters, marked lighter)

format (how?)

Clean Water Act | Public Law 92-500

title (what?)

1972

date (when?)

Zome House

name (what?)

1972

date (when?)

Steven Baer

author (who?)

Corrales, NM

location (where?)

United Nations Conference on the Human Environment

name (what?)

1972

date (when?)

LEGISLATION RELATED TO:

FG

act

authority (who?)

territorial

scale (where?)

environmental protection, water pollution, welfare, health

key issues (why?)

construction

format (how?)

environmental mgmt, passive strategies, lifestyle, spatial experience, arch design

key issues (why?)

United Nations

author (who?)

Stockholm, Sweden

location (where?)

conference

format (how?)

relations: environmental protection

key issues (why?)

AUTHORITY:

FG–federal, SG–state, MG–municipal, NGO–nongovernmental

E

R–residential, E–environmental

US Presidents

key sociopolitical events

1840

| | term *scientist* coined | William Whewell | UK | concept | method of inquiry |

1841 | A Treatise on Domestic Economy | Catherine Beecher | US | book | household mgmt

1845 | Cosmos, vol. 1 | Alexander von Humboldt | Germany | book | relations: scientific method, holism, harmony

1846 | A Report on the Trees and Shrubs Growing Naturally in the Forests of Massachusetts | George B. Emerson | US | report | relations: environmental conservation, environmental mgmt

1848 | The Octagon House: A Home for All, or A New, Cheap, Convenient, and Superior Mode of Building | Orson S. Fowler | US | book | model house, spatial experience, environmental efficiency

1840
1841
1842
1843
1844
1845
1846
1847
1848

John Tyler   James K. Polk

Mexican-American War 1846–40

California Gold R

1840–49

1850
Victoria Regia House
Joseph Paxton
Chatsworth, UK
construction
environmental mgmt

1854
Walden
Henry David Thoreau
US
book
relations: transcendentalism, pastoralism, holism, harmony

1855 the first model tenement
Association for Improving the Condition of the Poor
New York, NY
construction
model house, health, safety

1855 Haussmann's renovation of Paris
Georges-Eugène Haussmann
Paris, France
master plan
urban planning

1855 the first Atlantic–Pacific train
Panama Railroad
US
construction
mobility

1855 The World a Workshop, or the Physical Relation of Man to the Earth
Thomas Ewbank
UK
book
relations: environmental mgmt, economic dev

1849
1850
1851
1852
1853
1854
1855
1856
1857

Zachary Taylor   Millard Fillmore   Franklin Pierce   James Buchanan
*Financial Panic

ush 1948–55

1859

1859 Baltimore Building Code, MD — MG code — building — safety — construction — landscape design, recreation, beautification
1859 Frederick Law Olmsted, Calvert Vaux — New York, NY — laws: natural economy, evolution, natural history
1859 Central Park — UK — book
Charles Darwin — *On the Origin of Species*

1860
1860 "The Social Organism" — Herbert Spencer — UK — essay — concepts: social organism

1861

1862
1862 Homestead Act — FG act — territorial — economic dev, land use, population mgmt
1862 Ventilation and Warming of Buildings — Henry Ruttan — US — essay — environmental mgmt, mechanical services
"Walking" — Henry David Thoreau — US — relations: environmental preservation

1863
1863 *Man's Place in Nature* — Thomas Henry Huxley — UK — book — relations: subjugation of nature

1864
1864 *Man and Nature* — George Perkins Marsh — US — book — relations: environmental preservation

1865

1866
1866 *The Principles of Biology* — Herbert Spencer — UK — book — concepts: equilibrium, progress, cooperation
1866 term *oecologie* coined — Ernst Haeckel — Germany — concept — knowledge, method

Abraham Lincoln
American Civil War 1961–65

Andrew Johnson

*Lincoln Assassination

1860–69

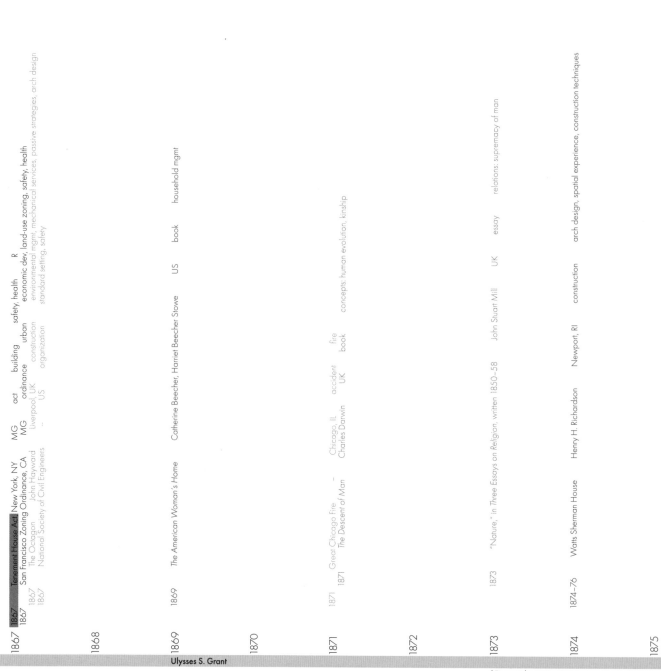

1867 | 1867 | **Tenement House Act** New York, NY | MG | | safety, health | R
1867 | San Francisco Zoning Ordinance, CA | MG | act | building | safety, health | economic dev, land-use zoning, safety, health
1867 | The Octagon | John Hayward | Liverpool, UK | MG | ordinance | urban | environmental mgmt, mechanical services, passive strategies, arch design
1867 | National Society of Civil Engineers | | US | | construction | standard setting, safety
| | | | | organization |

1868

1869 | The American Woman's Home | Catherine Beecher, Harriet Beecher Stowe | US | book | household mgmt

1870

1871 | Great Chicago Fire | Chicago, IL | accident | fire
1871 | The Descent of Man | Charles Darwin | UK | book | concepts: human evolution, kinship

1872

1873 | "Nature," in Three Essays on Religion, written 1850–58 | John Stuart Mill | UK | essay | relations: supremacy of man

1874 | Watts Sherman House | Henry H. Richardson | Newport, RI | construction | arch design, spatial experience, construction techniques
1874–76

1875

Ulysses S. Grant

*Financial Panic

1870–79

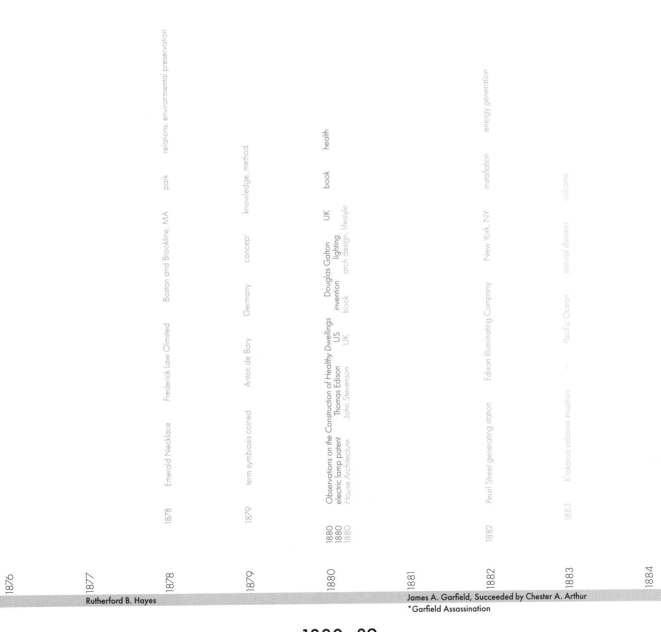

1876

1877

Rutherford B. Hayes

1878

Emerald Necklace · Frederick Law Olmsted · Boston and Brookline, MA · park · relations, environmental preservation

1879

term symbiosis coined · Anton de Bary · Germany · concept · knowledge, method

1880
1880
1880

Observations on the Construction of Healthy Dwellings · Douglas Galton · UK · book · health
electric lamp patent · Thomas Edison · invention · book
House Architecture · John Stevenson · UK · lighting · arch design, lifestyle

1881

James A. Garfield, Succeeded by Chester A. Arthur
*Garfield Assassination

1882

Pearl Street generating station · Edison Illuminating Company · New York, NY · installation · energy generation

1883

Krakatoa volcano eruption · Pacific Ocean · natural disaster · volcano

1884

1880–89

1885 1885

1886

1887

1888

1889

1890

1891

1892

1893

Modesto Zoning Ordinance, CA MG ordinance urban economic dev, land-use zoning, safety, health
Women, Plumbers, and Doctors: Or Household Sanitation Mrs. H. M. Plunkett US handbook household mgmt, health, mechanical services

Great Blizzard — East Coast, US natural disaster winter blizzard

Life Zones C. Hart Merriam US concept knowledge, method

Der Städtebau Josef Stübben Germany handbook urban design
Yosemite National Park Galen Clark, then John Muir, Robert Underwood US park relations: environmental protection

Sierra Club John Muir US NGO relations: environmental protection

Winslow House Frank Lloyd Wright River Forest, IL construction arch design, spatial experience, prairie style
World's Columbian Exposition Frederick Law Olmsted, Daniel Burnham Chicago, IL exhibition urban design, environmental integration
1893 The Psychic Factors of Civilization Lester Ward US book concepts: social progress, scientific mgmt, environmental mgmt
1893 Evolution and Ethics Thomas Huxley UK book concepts: supremacy of man, subjugation of nature, ethics, nature as evil

1885

1886

1887

1888

1889

1890

1891

1892

1893

Grover Cleveland

Benjamin Harrison

Grover Clevela

Progressive Era 1890–1920

1890–99

*Financial Pani

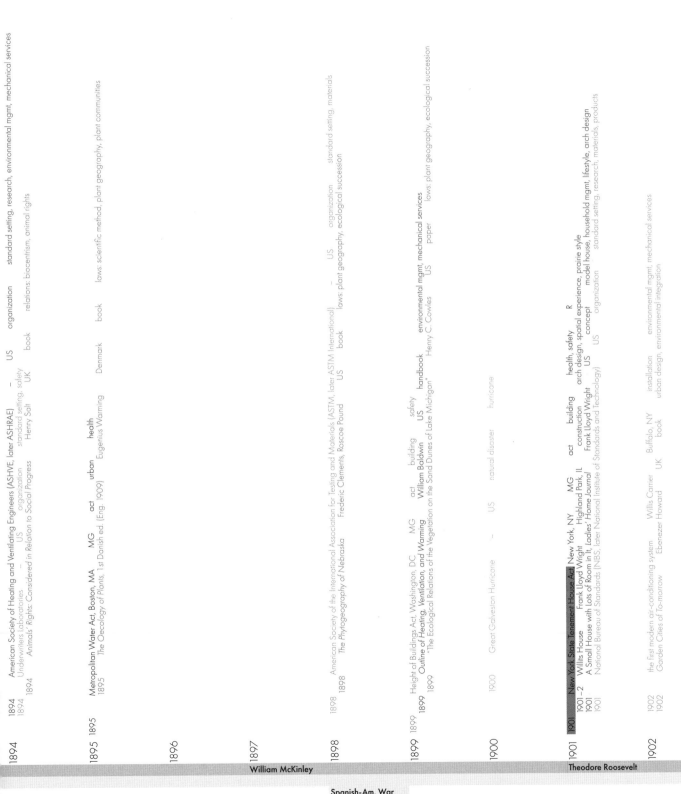

1894
1894 American Society of Heating and Ventilating Engineers (ASHVE, later ASHRAE) – US organization standard setting, research, environmental mgmt, mechanical services
1894 Underwriters Laboratories – US organization standard setting, safety
1894 Animals' Rights: Considered in Relation to Social Progress Henry Salt UK book relations: biocentrism, animal rights

1895
1895 Metropolitan Water Act, Boston, MA MG act urban health
1895 The Oecology of Plants, 1st Danish ed. (Eng. 1909) Eugenius Warming Denmark book laws: scientific method, plant geography, plant communities

1896

1897

1898
1898 American Society of the International Association for Testing and Materials (ASTM, later ASTM International) – US organization standard setting, materials
1898 The Phytogeography of Nebraska Frederic Clements, Roscoe Pound US book laws: plant geography, ecological succession

1899
1899 Height of Buildings Act, Washington, DC MG act building safety
1899 Outline of Heating, Ventilation, and Warming William Baldwin US handbook environmental mgmt, mechanical services
1899 "The Ecological Relations of the Vegetation on the Sand Dunes of Lake Michigan" Henry C. Cowles US paper laws: plant geography, ecological succession

1900
1900 Great Galveston Hurricane – US natural disaster hurricane

1901
1901 New York State Tenement House Act New York, NY MG act building health, safety
1901–2 Willits House Frank Lloyd Wright Highland Park, IL construction arch design, spatial experience, prairie style R
1901 A Small House with Lots of Room in It, Ladies' Home Journal Frank Lloyd Wright US concept model house, household mgmt, lifestyle, arch design
1901 National Bureau of Standards (NBS, later National Institute of Standards and Technology) US organization standard setting, research, materials, products

1902
1902 the first modern air-conditioning system Willis Carrier Buffalo, NY installation environmental mgmt, mechanical services
1902 Garden Cities of To-morrow Ebenezer Howard UK book urban design, environmental integration

William McKinley

Theodore Roosevelt

Spanish-Am. War

1903
- 1903 Royal Victoria Hospital Belfast — Belfast, UK — construction — environmental mgmt, mechanical services, arch design
- 1903 Iroquois Theatre fire — Herman and Cooper — Chicago, IL — accident / fire
- 1903 National Wildlife Reserve System — United States Fish Wildlife Service — US — program — relations: governance, environmental conservation

1904
- 1904 The Development and Structure of Vegetation — Frederic Clements — US — book — laws: ecological succession, plant communities

1905
- 1905 Building Code Recommended by the National Board of Fire Underwriters — NGO — model code — building — safety
- 1905 The Cost of Shelter — Ellen H. Richards — US — book — household mgmt
- 1905 Bureau of the Biological Survey — FG — US — governmental agency — relations: governance, environmental mgmt, predator control
- 1905 United States Forest Service — FG — US — governmental agency — relations: governance, environmental mgmt, subjugation of nature

1906
- 1906 Apparatus for Treating Air Patent — Willis Carrier — US — invention — environmental mgmt, mechanical services
- 1906 Larkin Administration Building — Frank Lloyd Wright — Buffalo, NY — construction — environmental mgmt, mechanical services, arch design
- 1906 San Francisco earthquake — US — natural disaster — earthquake

1907

1908
- 1908 Los Angeles Land Use Zoning Ordinance, CA — MG — Pasadena, CA — ordinance — urban — economic dev, land-use zoning
- 1908 Gamble House — Greene & Greene — company — construction — environmental mgmt, passive strategies, arch design, lifestyle, spatial experience
- 1908 Pacific Ready-Cut Homes — CA — kit house, assembly method, standardization
- 1908 Ford Model T — Henry Ford — US — invention — mobility

1909
- 1909 Baker House — Frank Lloyd Wright — Willamette, IL — construction — environmental mgmt, mechanical services, passive strategies, arch design, lifestyle, spatial experience
- 1909 Robie House — Frank Lloyd Wright — Chicago, IL — construction — environmental mgmt, mechanical services, passive strategies, lifestyle, spatial experience, arch design
- 1909 First National Conference on City Planning — Washington, DC — conference — urban planning
- 1909 Plan of Chicago — Daniel Burnham, Edward H. Bennett — Chicago, IL — master plan — urban planning
- 1909 Town Planning in Practice — Raymond Unwin — US — book — urban planning

1910
- 1910 Model Tenement House Law — FG — model law — building — code making, safety, health — R

1911
- 1911 Rational Psychrometric Formulae — Willis Carrier — US — report — environmental mgmt, comfort
- 1911 Principles of Scientific Management — Frederick Winslow Taylor — US — book — scientific mgmt

William Taft

1910–19

Nothing Gained by Overcrowding! How the Garden City Type of Development May Benefit Both Owner and Occupier — Raymond Unwin — US — book — urban planning

1912

1913
New Jersey Subdivision Regulation, NJ — SG — regulation — urban — land use
1913 — Chicago City Club competition — Chicago, IL — competition
1913 — the first moving assembly line — Henry Ford — Highland Park, MI — installation — industrial production, scientific mgmt
1913 — Owens Valley Aqueduct — — Los Angeles, CA — construction — aqueduct

1914
The New Housekeeping: Efficiency Studies in Home Management — Christine Frederick — US — handbook — household mgmt
1914 — American Sewerage Practice — Leonard Metcalf; Harrison Prescott Eddy — US — handbook — urban infrastructure, mechanical services

1915
Building Officials and Code Administrators International (BOCA) — NGO — organization — building — code making, property standards
1915 — Principles of Domestic Engineering: Or the What, Why, and How of a House — Mary Pattison — US — handbook — household mgmt
1915 — Cities in Evolution — Patrick Geddes — — US — book — urban planning, environmental integration
1915 — the first transcontinental telephone call — — — installation — telecommunication
1915 — The Ecological Society of America — — US — NGO — relations: environmental conservation, scientific research

1916
New York Zoning Ordinance, New York, NY — MG — ordinance — urban — land use
1916–21 — Hollyhock House — Frank Lloyd Wright — Los Angeles, CA — construction — arch design, spatial experience, water, construction techniques
1916 — Plant Succession: An Analysis of the Development of Vegetation — Frederic Clements — US — book — laws: plant succession, process, stability, monoclimax, complex organism
1916 — National Park Service — FG — US — governmental agency — relations: environmental preservation, recreation, beautification

1917
Neighborhoods of Small Homes — Thomas Adams — US — handbook — urban design
1917 — American City Planning Institute — — US — organization — urban planning
1917 — On Growth and Form — D'Arcy Wentworth Thompson — UK — book — laws: morphogenesis

1918
Emergency Fleet Corporation, United States Housing Corporation — FG — agency — urban — governance, economic dev, population mgmt, financial risk mgmt — R
1918 — Own Your Own Home campaign — Department of Labor, National Association of Real Estate Brokers — US — program — house ownership
1918 — American National Standards Institute (ANSI) — — US — organization — standard setting, materials, safety

1919

1920
Los Angeles City Planning Commission, CA — MG — agency — urban — governance, land-use zoning
1920 — Architects' Small House Service Bureau — — US — organization — standard setting, affordability, property standards
1920 — One Week — Buster Keaton — US — film — kit house, standardization
1920 — The Concept of Nature — Alfred North Whitehead — UK — book — concepts: natural philosophy

Woodrow Wilson

*Federal Reserve Act World War I 1914–18

Prohibition 1920–33
1920–29

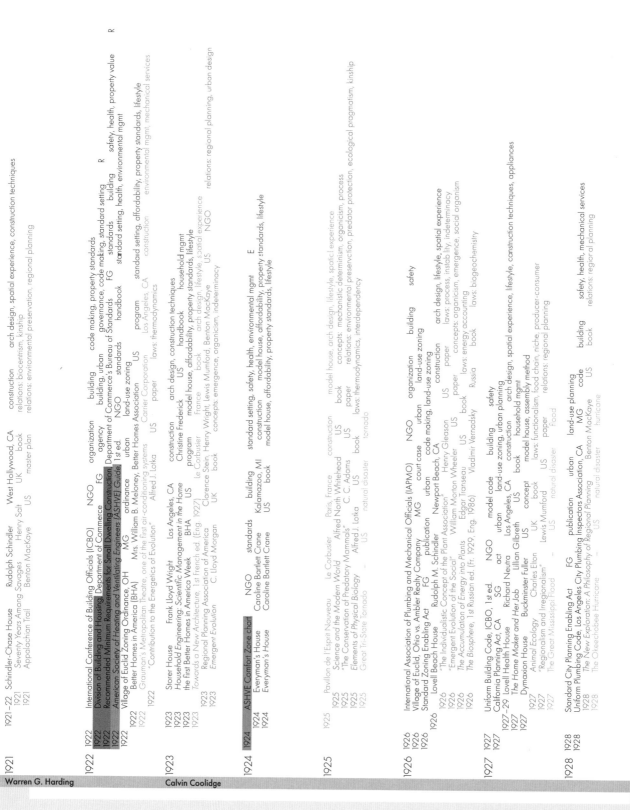

1921

- 1921–22 Schindler-Chase House · Rudolph Schindler · West Hollywood, CA · construction · arch design, spatial experience, construction techniques
- 1921 · Seventy Years Among Savages · Henry Salt · UK · book · relations: biocentrism, kinship
- 1921 · Appalachian Trail · Benton MacKaye · US · master plan · relations: environmental preservation, regional planning

1922

- 1922 · International Conference of Building Officials (ICBO) · NGO · organization
- 1922 · Division of Building and Housing, Department of Commerce · FG · agency · building
- 1922 · Recommended Minimum Requirements for Small Dwelling Construction, Department of Commerce's Bureau of Standards · FG · standards · building, urban · code making, standard setting · R
- 1922 · American Society of Heating and Ventilating Engineers (ASHVE) Guide, 1st ed. · NGO · handbook · standards · governance, code making, standard setting · safety, health, property value
- 1922 · Village of Euclid Zoning Ordinance, OH · MG · ordinance · urban · land-use zoning · standard setting, health, environmental mgmt
- 1922 · Better Homes in America (BHA) · Mrs. William B. Meloney · Better Homes Association · US · program · standard setting, affordability, property standards, lifestyle
- 1922 · Grauman's Metropolitan Theatre, one of the first air-conditioning systems · Carrier Corporation · Los Angeles, CA · construction · environmental mgmt, mechanical services
- 1922 · "Contribution to the Energetics of Evolution" · Alfred J. Lotka · US · paper · laws: thermodynamics

1923

- 1923 · Storer House · Frank Lloyd Wright · Los Angeles, CA · construction · arch design, construction techniques
- 1923 · Household Engineering: Scientific Management in the Home · Christine Frederick · US · handbook · household mgmt
- 1923 · the first Better Homes in America Week · BHA · US · program · model house, affordability, property standards, lifestyle
- 1923 · Towards a New Architecture, 1st French ed. [Eng. 1927] · Le Corbusier · France · book · arch design, lifestyle, spatial experience
- 1923 · Regional Planning Association of America · Clarence Stein, Henry Wright, Lewis Mumford, Benton MacKaye · US · NGO · relations: regional planning, urban design
- 1923 · Emergent Evolution · C. Lloyd Morgan · UK · book · concepts: emergence, organicism, indeterminacy

1924

- 1924 · ASHVE Comfort Zone chart · NGO · standards · standard setting, safety, health, environmental mgmt · E
- 1924 · Everyman's House · Caroline Bartlett Crane · Kalamazoo, MI · building · construction · model house, affordability, property standards, lifestyle
- 1924 · Everyman's House · Caroline Bartlett Crane · US · book · model house, affordability, property standards, lifestyle

1925

- 1925 · Pavillon de l'Esprit Nouveau · Le Corbusier · Paris, France · construction
- 1925 · Science and the Modern World · Alfred North Whitehead · US · book · model house, arch design, lifestyle, spatial experience
- 1925 · "The Conservation of Predatory Mammals" · C. C. Adams · US · paper · concepts: mechanistic determinism, organicism, process · relations: environmental preservation, predator protection, ecological pragmatism, kinship
- 1925 · Elements of Physical Biology · Alfred J. Lotka · US · book · laws: thermodynamics, interdependency
- 1925 · Great Tri-State Tornado · – · natural disaster · tornado

1926

- 1926 · International Association of Plumbing and Mechanical Officials (IAPMO) · NGO · organization
- 1926 · Village of Euclid, Ohio vs. Ambler Realty Company · MG · court case · urban · code making, land-use zoning · building
- 1926 · Standard Zoning Enabling Act · FG · publication · urban · code making, land-use zoning · safety
- 1926 · Lovell Beach House · Rudolph M. Schindler · Newport Beach, CA · construction · arch design, lifestyle, spatial experience
- 1926 · "The Individualistic Concept of the Plant Association" · Henry Gleason · US · paper · laws: process, instability, indeterminacy
- 1926 · "Emergent Evolution of the Social" · William Morton Wheeler · US · paper · concepts: organicism, emergence, social organism
- 1926 · The Accumulation of Energy into Plants · Edgar Transeau · US · book · laws: energy accounting
- 1926 · The Biosphere, 1st Russian ed. [Fr. 1929; Eng. 1986] · Vladimir Vernadsky · Russia · book · laws: biogeochemistry

1927

- 1927 · Uniform Building Code, ICBO, 1st ed. · NGO · model code · building · safety
- 1927–29 · California Planning Act, CA · SG · act · urban · land-use zoning, urban planning
- 1927 · Lovell Health House · Richard Neutra · Los Angeles, CA · construction · arch design, spatial experience, lifestyle, construction techniques, appliances
- 1927 · The Home Maker and Her Job · Lillian Gilbreth · US · book · household mgmt
- 1927 · Dymaxion House · Buckminster Fuller · UK · concept · model house, assembly method
- 1927 · Animal Ecology · Charles Elton · US · book · laws: functionalism, food chain, niche, producer-consumer
- 1927 · "Regionalism and Irregionalism" · Lewis Mumford · US · paper · relations: regional planning
- 1927 · The Great Mississippi Flood · – · US · natural disaster · flood

1928

- 1928 · Standard City Planning Enabling Act · FG · publication · urban · land-use planning
- 1928 · Uniform Plumbing Code, Los Angeles City Plumbing Inspectors Association, CA · MG · code · building · safety, health, mechanical services
- 1928 · The New Exploration: A Philosophy of Regional Planning · Benton MacKaye · US · book · relations: regional planning
- 1928 · The Okeechobee Hurricane · – · natural disaster · hurricane

1929

- 1929 · The Neighborhood Unit · Clarence Perry · US · book · urban design

Warren G. Harding · Calvin Coolidge · Herbert Hoover · *Wall Street

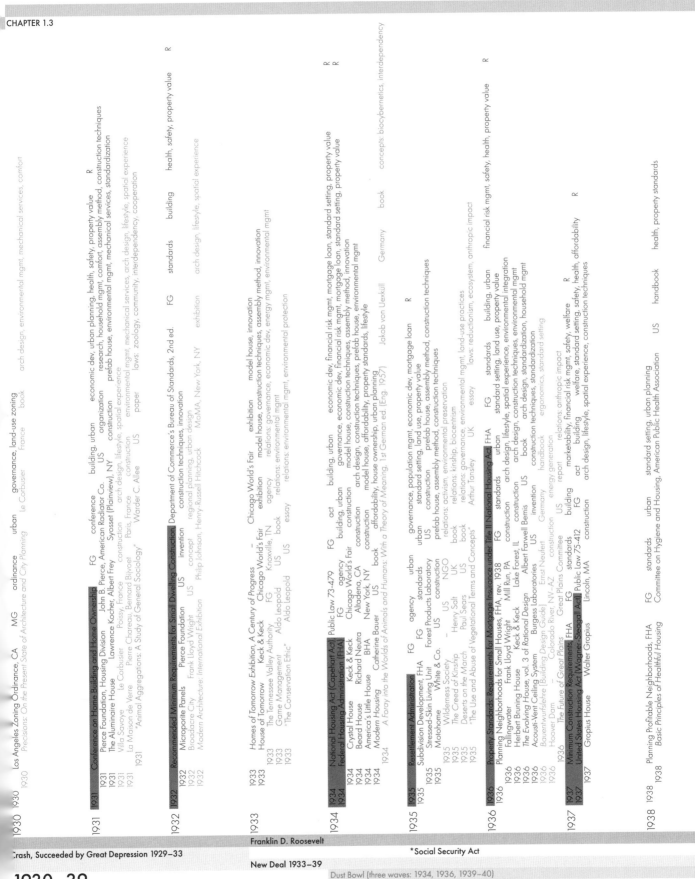

1930–39

- **1930** — Los Angeles Zoning Ordinance, CA — MG ordinance — urban — governance, land-use zoning
- **1930** — *Precisions: On the Present State of Architecture and City Planning* — Le Corbusier — France — book — arch design, environmental mgmt, mechanical services, comfort — R

- **1931** — Conference on Home Building and Home Ownership — FG conference — building, urban — economic dev, urban planning, health, safety, property value — R
- **1931** — Pierce Foundation, Housing Division — John B. Pierce, American Radiator Co. — US organization — research, household mgmt, comfort, assembly method, mechanical services, standardization
- **1931** — The Aluminaire House — Lawrence Kocher, Albert Frey — Syosset (Plainview), NY — construction — prefab house, environmental mgmt, mechanical services, standardization
- **1931** — Villa Savoye — Le Corbusier — Poissy, France — construction — arch design, lifestyle, spatial experience
- **1931** — La Maison de Verre — Pierre Chareau, Bernard Bijvoet — Paris, France — construction — environmental mgmt, mechanical services, arch design, lifestyle, spatial experience
- **1931** — "Animal Aggregations: A Study of General Sociology" — Warder C. Allee — US — paper — laws: zoology, community, interdependency, cooperation

- **1932** — Recommended Minimum Requirements for Small Dwelling Construction — Department of Commerce's Bureau of Standards, 2nd ed. — FG standards — building — health, safety, property value — R
- **1932** — Micoporite Panels — Pierce Foundation — US invention — construction techniques, innovation
- **1932** — Broadacre City — Frank Lloyd Wright — US concept — regional planning, urban design
- **1932** — Modern Architecture: International Exhibition — Philip Johnson, Henry-Russell Hitchcock — MoMA, New York, NY — exhibition — arch design, lifestyle, spatial experience

- **1933** — Homes of Tomorrow Exhibition, A Century of Progress — Chicago World's Fair — exhibition — model house, innovation
- **1933** — House of Tomorrow — Keck & Keck — Chicago World's Fair — FG exhibition — model house, construction techniques, assembly method, innovation
- **1933** — The Tennessee Valley Authority — BHA — Knoxville, TN — agency — relations: governance, economic dev, energy mgmt, environmental mgmt
- **1933** — Game Management — Aldo Leopold — US — book — relations: environmental mgmt
- **1933** — "The Conservation Ethic" — Aldo Leopold — US — essay — relations: environmental mgmt, environmental protection

- **1934** — National Housing Act (Capehart Act) — Public Law 73-479 — FG act — building, urban — economic dev, financial risk mgmt, mortgage loan, standard setting, property value — R
- **1934** — Federal Housing Administration (FHA) — FG agency — governance, economic dev, financial risk mgmt, mortgage loan, standard setting, property value — R
- **1934** — Crystal House — Keck & Keck — Chicago World's Fair — US construction — model house, construction techniques, assembly method, innovation
- **1934** — Beard House — Richard Neutra — Altadena, CA — construction — prefab house, construction techniques, prefab house, environmental mgmt
- **1934** — America's Little House — BHA — New York, NY — construction — model house, affordability, property standards, lifestyle
- **1934** — Modern Housing — Catherine Bauer — US — book — model house, affordability, house ownership, urban planning
- **1934** — A Foray into the Worlds of Animals and Humans: With a Theory of Meaning, 1st German ed. [Eng. 1957] — Jakob von Uexküll — Germany — book — concepts: biocybernetics, interdependency — R

- **1935** — Resettlement Administration — FG agency — governance, population mgmt, economic dev, mortgage loan — R
- **1935** — Subdivision Development, FHA — FG standards — standard setting, land use, property value
- **1935** — Stressed-Skin Living Unit — Forest Products Laboratory — Mill Run, PA — US construction — prefab house, assembly method, construction techniques
- **1935** — Motohome — White & Co. — Lake Forest, IL — US construction — construction techniques
- **1935** — Wilderness Society — US — NGO — relations: activism, environmental preservation
- **1935** — The Creed of Kinship — Henry Salt — UK — book — relations: kinship, biocentrism
- **1935** — Deserts on the March — Paul Sears — US — book — relations: governance, environmental mgmt, land-use practices
- **1935** — "The Use and Abuse of Vegetational Terms and Concepts" — Arthur Tansley — UK — essay — laws: reductionism, ecosystem, anthropic impact

- **1936** — Property Standards: Requirements for Mortgage Insurance under Title II National Housing Act, FHA — FG standards — building, urban — standard setting, land use, property value — R
- **1936** — Planning Neighborhoods for Small Houses, FHA, rev. 1938 — US construction — arch design, lifestyle, spatial experience, environmental integration
- **1936** — Fallingwater — Frank Lloyd Wright — Mill Run, PA — construction — arch design, construction techniques, environmental mgmt
- **1936** — Herbert Bruning House — Keck & Keck — Lake Forest, IL — construction — arch design, standardization, household mgmt
- **1936** — The Evolving House, vol. 3 of Rational Design — Albert Farwell Bemis — US invention — book — construction techniques, standardization
- **1936** — Acoust-Vent Ceiling System — Burgess Laboratories — US — construction
- **1936** — Bauentwurfslehre [Building Design Guide] — Ernst Neufert — Germany — handbook — ergonomics, standard setting
- **1936** — Hoover Dam — Colorado River, NV-AZ — US construction — energy generation
- **1936** — The Future of Great Plains — Great Plains Committee — US — report — relations: anthropic impact

- **1937** — Minimum Construction Requirements, FHA — FG standards — building — marketability, financial risk mgmt, safety, welfare — R
- **1937** — United States Housing Act (Wagner-Steagall Act) — Public Law 75-412 — FG act — welfare, standard setting, safety, health, affordability
- **1937** — Gropius House — Walter Gropius — Lincoln, MA — construction — arch design, lifestyle, spatial experience, construction techniques

- **1938** — Planning Profitable Neighborhoods, FHA — FG standards — urban — standard setting, urban planning
- **1938** — Basic Principles of Healthful Housing — Committee on Hygiene and Housing, American Public Health Association — US — handbook — health, property standards

Franklin D. Roosevelt

Crash, Succeeded by Great Depression 1929–33

New Deal 1933–39

*Social Security Act

Dust Bowl (three waves: 1934, 1936, 1939–40)

1939
- Housing for the Machine Age — Clarence A. Perry — US — book — urban planning, urban design, land dev, affordability, arch design
- East Lansing Usonian houses — Frank Lloyd Wright — East Lansing, MI — mortgage loan — construction
- Alan I. W. Frank House — Walter Gropius, Marcel Breuer — Pittsburgh, PA — construction — arch design, lifestyle, spatial experience
- Practical Standards for Modern Housing — National Association of Housing and Redevelopment Officials, American Public Health Association — US — handbook — health, property standards
- Westside Village — Marlow-Burns developer — Los Angeles, CA — community — urban design, land dev
- Land Subdivision — American Society of Civil Engineers, Committee of City Planning Division on Land Subdivision — US — handbook — urban design, land dev
- 1939 Bio-Ecology — Frederic Clements, Victor Shelford — US — book
- 1939 The Science of Life — H. G. Wells, Julian Huxley — US — book — relations: anthropic impact

1940 — First Census on Housing — FG — act — population mgmt — urban
- Successful Subdivisions, FHA — FG — standards — standard setting, urban planning, property value
- Southern Building Code Congress International (SBCCI) — FG — NGO — building — code making, property standards
- Census on Housing — FG — program — population mgmt
- Chamberlain Cottage — Marcel Breuer — Wayland, MA — territorial construction — assembly method, construction techniques
- 1940 "The Annual Energy Budget in an Inland Lake" — Chancey Juday — US — paper — relations: environmental mgmt, bioeconomics, new ecology

1941
- Westchester, Homes at Wholesale — Marlow-Burns developer — Westchester, CA — community — urban design, land dev

1942 — Minimum Property Requirements, FHA — FG — standards — building, urban — standard setting, property standards, property value — R
- 9 Ash Street House — Philip Johnson — Cambridge, MA — construction — arch design, spatial experience, construction techniques, assembly methods
- Traffic Engineering Handbook — U.S. Army Corps of Engineers, Institute of Traffic Engineers — Oak Ridge, TN — handbook — community — urban design, land dev
- Cocoanut Grove fire — – — Boston, MA — accident fire
- 1942 "The Trophic-Dynamic Aspect of Ecology" — Raymond L. Lindeman — US — paper — laws: trophic levels, metabolism, thermodynamics, relations: bioeconomics

1944
- Introduction to Studies of Family Living — John Hancock Callender, Pierce Foundation — US — handbook — household mgmt, property standards, arch design, lifestyle, spatial experience
- Case Study House (CSH) Program — John Entenza, Arts & Architecture — Los Angeles, CA — program — arch design, lifestyle, construction techniques, assembly method

1945
- Standard Building Code, SBCCI, 1st ed. — NGO — model code — building — code making, safety
- Uniform Plumbing Code, IAPMO, 1st ed. — NGO — model code — building — code making, mechanical services
- **Master Draft of Proposed Minimum Property Requirements for Properties of One or Two living Units, FHA** — FG — standards — standard setting, property standards, property value — R
- 1945–49 Eames House, CSH #8 — Charles Eames, Ray Eames — Los Angeles, CA — construction — building — model house, construction techniques, assembly method, arch design, lifestyle

1946
- Los Angeles Zoning Ordinance, CA — MG — ordinance — urban — land-use zoning, urban planning
- Thermo-Namel House — Higgins Incorporated of New Orleans — US — construction — prefab house, assembly method, construction techniques, standardization
- Airform (bubble) house — Wallace Neff — Pasadena, CA — construction — prefab house, assembly method, construction techniques, standardization
- 1946 The Ecologists' Union — US — NGO — relations: environmental conservation

1947 — Air Pollution Control Act — CA — SG — act — territorial — environmental mgmt, air pollution
- Significant Variations of the Minimum Property Requirements of FHA Insuring Offices, FHA — FG — standards — E — standard setting, safety, health, property value — R
- Lustrous House — Lustrous Corporation — US — construction — building — prefab house, assembly method, construction techniques, standardization
- Wichita House — Buckminster Fuller — Wichita, KS — construction — model house, economic dev, construction techniques, assembly method
- 1947 Glazer-Higgins-Woodward tornadoes — US — natural disaster — tornado

World War II 1939–45

Manhattan Project 1942–46

1940–49

Harry S. Truman
*First Nuclear Bomb   *First Bikini Atoll Nuclear Test
*The Charter of the United Nations
*ENIAC Computer

Cold War 1947–91

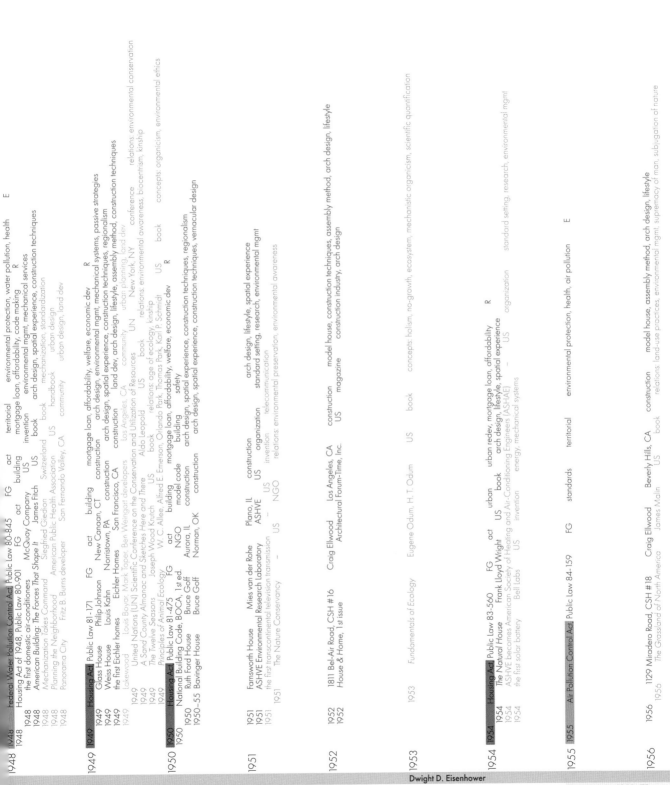

1950–59

Year	Entry	Author/Developer	Location	Type	Keywords
1948	Federal Water Pollution Control Act, Public Law 80-845		FG	act — territorial	environmental protection, water pollution, health — E
1948	Housing Act of 1948, Public Law 80-901	McQuay Company	US	act — building	mortgage loan, affordability, code making — R
1948	the first domestic air-conditioners	James Fitch		invention	environmental mgmt, mechanical services
1948	American Building: The Forces That Shape It	Siegfried Giedion		book	arch design, spatial experience, construction techniques
1948	Mechanization Takes Command	American Public Health Association	Switzerland	book	mechanization, standardization — relations: environmental conservation
1948	Planning the Neighborhood		US	handbook	urban design
1948	Panorama City	Fritz B. Burns developer	San Fernando Valley, CA	community	urban design, land dev
1949	Housing Act, Public Law 81-171		FG	act	mortgage loan, affordability, welfare, economic dev — R
1949	Glass House	Philip Johnson	New Canaan, CT	building — construction	arch design, environmental mgmt, mechanical systems, passive strategies
1949	Weiss House	Louis Kahn	Norristown, PA	construction	arch design, spatial experience, construction techniques, regionalism
1949	the first Eichler homes	Eichler Homes	San Francisco, CA	construction	land dev, arch design, lifestyle, assembly method, construction techniques
1949	Lakewood	Louis Boyar, Mark Taper, Ben Weingart developers	Los Angeles, CA	community	urban planning, land dev
1949	United Nations (UN) Scientific Conference on the Conservation and Utilization of Resources	UN	New York, NY	conference	
1949	A Sand County Almanac and Sketches Here and There	Aldo Leopold	US	book	relations: environmental awareness, biocentrism, kinship
1949	The Twelve Seasons	Joseph Wood Krutch	US	book	relations: age of ecology, kinship
1949	Principles of Animal Ecology	W. C. Allee, Alfred E. Emerson, Orlando Park, Thomas Park, Karl P. Schmidt	US	book	concepts: organicism, environmental ethics
1950	Housing Act, Public Law 81-475		FG	act — building	mortgage loan, affordability, welfare, economic dev — R
1950	National Building Code, BOCA, 1st ed.		NGO	model code	safety
1950	Ruth Ford House	Bruce Goff	Aurora, IL	construction	construction
1950–55	Bavinger House	Bruce Goff	Norman, OK	construction	arch design, spatial experience, construction techniques, vernacular design
1951	Farnsworth House	Mies van der Rohe	Plano, IL	construction	arch design, lifestyle, spatial experience
1951	ASHVE Environmental Research Laboratory	ASHVE	US	organization	standard setting, research, environmental mgmt
1951	the first transcontinental television transmission	–	US	invention	telecommunication
1951	The Nature Conservancy	–	NGO		relations: environmental preservation, environmental awareness
1952	1811 Bel-Air Road, CSH #16	Craig Ellwood	Los Angeles, CA	construction	model house, construction techniques, assembly method, arch design, lifestyle
1952	House & Home, 1st issue	Architectural Forum-Time, Inc.	US	magazine	construction industry, arch design
1953	Fundamentals of Ecology	Eugene Odum, H. T. Odum	US	book	concepts: holism, no-growth, ecosystem, mechanistic organism, scientific quantification
1954	Housing Act, Public Law 83-560		FG	act — urban	urban redev, mortgage loan, affordability, lifestyle, spatial experience — R
1954	The Natural House	Frank Lloyd Wright	US	book	arch design, lifestyle, spatial experience
1954	ASHVE becomes American Society of Heating and Air-Conditioning Engineers (ASHAE)	–	US	organization	standard setting, research, environmental mgmt
1954	the first solar battery	Bell Labs	US	invention	energy, mechanical systems
1955	Air Pollution Control Act, Public Law 84-159		FG	act — territorial	environmental protection, health, air pollution — E
1956	1129 Miradero Road, CSH #18	Craig Ellwood	Beverly Hills, CA	construction	model house, assembly method, arch design, lifestyle
1956	The Grassland of North America	James Malin	US	book	relations: land-use practices, environmental mgmt, supremacy of man, subjugation of nature

Dwight D. Eisenhower

*NATO

*First Nevada Desert Nuclear Test

Vietnam War 1955–75

Korean War 1950–53

1950–59

1957

1957	Mon Oncle	Jacques Tati	France	film	arch design, lifestyle, mechanization, progress
1957	Solar Do-Nothing Machine	Charles Eames, Ray Eames	US	construction	design; technology; toy; solar energy
1957	Urban Land Use Planning	Stuart Chapin	US	handbook	urban design

1958

1958	Minimum Property Standards for One and Two living Units	FHA		FG	US	book	standards	building	standard setting, property value, energy efficiency	R
1958	Pierre Koenig House, CSH #21	Pierre Koenig	Groff Conklin	Los Angeles, CA	construction	model house, assembly method, arch design, lifestyle, spatial experience
1958	The Weather-Conditioned House	Groff Conklin	US	book	environmental mgmt, mechanical services
1958	Committee for Nuclear Information	E. Gellhorn, B. Commoner, J. M. Fowler, R. C. Abele, A. S. Schwartz	St. Louis, MO	NGO	relations; public awareness, environmental ethics

1959

1959	Pierre Koenig House, CSH #22	Pierre Koenig	Los Angeles, CA	construction	model house, assembly method, arch design, lifestyle, spatial experience
1959	The Measure of Man	Henry Dreyfuss	US	handbook	ergonomics, standard setting
1959	ASHAE becomes American Society of Heating, Refrigerating and Air-Conditioning Engineers (ASHRAE)	US	organization	standard setting, environmental mgmt

1960

1960	Malin Residence (Chemosphere)	John Lautner	Los Angeles, CA	construction	technology, assembly techniques, arch design, lifestyle, spatial experience
1960-67	Fisher House	Louis Kahn	Hatboro, PA	construction	arch design, spatial experience, environmental mgmt, natural materials
1960	Recommended Practice for Subdivision Streets	Institute of Traffic Engineers	US	handbook	urban design, land dev

1961

1961	Quincy Jones and Frederick Emmons House, CSH #24	Jones & Emmons	Los Angeles, CA	concept	construction	model house, construction techniques, assembly method, lifestyle, spatial experience
1961	Esherick House	Louis Kahn	Philadelphia, PA	construction	arch design, spatial experience
1961	Prairie Chicken House	Herb Greene	Norman, OK	construction	arch design, lifestyle, spatial experience, natural materials, organicism
1961	The Death and Life of Great American Cities	Jane Jacobs	-	US	book	urban design, community, social ecology
1961	World Wildlife Fund	-	US	NGO	relations: environmental preservation, environmental awareness

1962

1962	Garcia House (Rainbow House)	John Lautner	Los Angeles, CA	construction	assembly techniques, arch design, lifestyle, spatial experience
1962	Moore House	Charles Moore	Orinda, CA	construction	arch design, spatial experience, vernacular design
1962	Our Synthetic Environment	Lewis Herbert (Murray Bookchin)	US	book	relations: environmental ethics, public awareness, pollution
1962	California. Going. Going.	Samuel E. Wood, Alfred E. Heller, California Tomorrow	US	report	relations: environmental ethics, public awareness, pollution
1962	Silent Spring	Rachel Carson	US	book	relations: environmental ethics, public awareness, pollution

1963

1963	Clean Air Act	Public Law 88-206	FG	act	territorial	environmental protection, health, air pollution	E
1963	Nuclear Test Ban Treaty	FG	treaty	territorial	environmental protection, health, safety	E
1963	Design with Climate	Victor Olgyay	US	book	environmental mgmt, passive strategies, arch design
1963	The Quiet Crisis	Stewart L. Udal	US	book	relations: environmental ethics, pollution, environmental policy
1963	"Deterministic Nonperiodic Flow"	Edward N. Lorenz	US	paper	laws: chaos theory, indeterminacy

1964

1964	Wilderness Act	Public Law 88-577	FG	act	territorial	environmental protection	E
1964	Vanna Venturi House (Mother's House)	Robert Venturi	Philadelphia, PA	construction	arch design, spatial experience
1964	Sea Ranch Condominium	Moore, Lydon, Turnbull, Whitaker	Sonoma County, CA	construction	spatial experience, site specificity, local materials

1965

1965	Solid Waste Disposal Act	Public Law 89-272	FG	act	territorial	environmental protection, waste mgmt	E
1965	Land and Water Conservation Fund Act	Public Law 88-578	FG	act	territorial	environmental mgmt, natural resources, health, welfare	E
1965	Act to Amend the Federal Water Pollution Control Act	Public Law 89-234	FG	act	territorial	environmental mgmt, water pollution	E
1965	Department of Housing and Urban Development Act	Public Law 89-174	FG	act	building, urban	governance	R

John F. Kennedy

Lyndon B. Johnson

*Civil Rights Act

*Kennedy Assassination

*Watts R

1965
- "Community Resource Land Studio" — Charles Gwathmey — Amagansett, NY — construction — arch design, spatial experience
- "A Home Is Not a House" — Reyner Banham — US — essay — arch design, environmental mgmt, mechanical services, lifestyle, spatial experience
- Cry California — California Tomorrow — US — magazine — relations: environmental protection, public awareness, environmental ethics
- The Destruction of California — Raymond Fredric Dasmann — US — book — relations: environmental ethics, public awareness, pollution
- "The Metabolism of Cities" — Abel Wolman — US — essay — relations: environmental mgmt

1966
- Endangered Species Preservation Act, Public Law 89-669 — FG — act — standard setting, environmental mgmt
- ASHRAE Standard 55-1966 Thermal Environmental Conditions for Human Occupancy, 1st ed. — NGO — standards — standard setting, environmental mgmt
- Uniform Mechanical Code, IAPMO, 1st ed. — NGO — model code — building, appliance
- Tack House — David Sellers — Prickly Mountain, VT — construction — design-build, arch design, local-resource use, site specificity
- "The Economics of the Coming Spaceship Earth" — Kenneth Boulding — US — paper — relations: ecological economics

1967
- Air Quality Act, National Air Emission Standards Act Public Law 90-148 — FG — act — territorial — environmental protection, environmental mgmt
- ASHRAE Handbook of Fundamentals, 1st ed. — NGO — standards — standard setting, environmental mgmt, mechanical services
- National Conference of States on Building Codes and Standards (NCSBCS) — NGO — organization — building — code making
- The Cost of Economic Growth — E.J. Mishan — UK — book — relations: ecological economics
- The Theory of Island Biogeography — Robert MacArthur, E. O. Wilson — US — book — laws: population ecology, reductionism
- "The Historical Roots of Our Ecological Crisis" — Lynne White Jr. — US — essay — concepts: ecology, religion

1968
- Fair Housing Act, Title VIII of Civil Rights Act Public Law 90-284 — FG — act — territorial — civil rights, social discrimination
- Housing and Urban Development Act Public Law 90-448 — FG — act — building, urban — relations: do-it-yourself, back-to-the-land movement
- Whole Earth Catalogue — Stewart Brand — US — magazine — concepts: ecology, self-interest, community
- "The Tragedy of the Commons" — Garrett Hardin — US — essay — concepts: ecology, self-interest, community
- Population Bomb — Paul Ehrlich, Anne Ehrlich — US — book — relations: population mgmt, economic dev

1969
- National Environmental Policy Act Public Law 91-190 — FG — act — territorial — environmental protection, natural resources, welfare, health
- The Architecture of the Well-Tempered Environment, 1st ed. — Reyner Banham — US — book — environmental mgmt, passive strategies, arch design
- Man, Climate and Architecture — Baruch Givoni — US — book — environmental mgmt, passive strategies, arch design
- New Alchemy Institute — John Todd, Nancy Todd, William McLarney — Hatchville, Cape Cod, MA — organization — organic agriculture, aquaculture, Biosheller
- "Gaia Hypothesis" — James Lovelock — UK — paper — concepts: superorganism, holism, symbiosis
- Design by Nature — Ian McHarg — US — book — relations: land classification, regional planning, landscape design, geographic information system
- Fire on the Cuyahoga River — various Industries — US — man-made hazard — water contamination
- Santa Barbara Oil spill — Union Oil — Santa Barbara, CA — man-made hazard — water contamination, oil spill

1970
- United States Environmental Protection Agency (EPA) — agency — territorial — environmental protection, natural resources, welfare, health
- Act to Amend the Clean Air Act Public Law 91-604 — FG — act — territorial — environmental protection, air pollution, welfare, health
- Environmental Bill of Rights, AB-2070 — SG — act — environmental protection, environmental mgmt
- Arcosanti — Paolo Soleri — Arizona desert — construction — on-site resources, density, social interaction
- Natural Resources Defense Council — J. Adams, R. Ayres, J. Bryson, E. Strobbehn, J.G. Speth — US — NGO — relations: environmental protection, resource mgmt
- JABOWA forest simulation model — Daniel B. Botkin, James F. Janak, James R. Wallis, IBM Thomas J. Watson Research Center — US — software — laws: ecosystem dynamics
- the first Earth Day — Senator Gaylord Nelson — Canada — NGO — celebratory event — relations: environmental preservation, environmental awareness

1971
- Council of American Building Officials (CABO) One- and Two-Family Dwelling Code, BOCA, ICBO, SBCCI — NGO — model code — building
- Lead-Based Paint Poisoning Prevention Act Public Law 91-695 — FG — act — building, health, toxic materials
- 1971–73 Korman House — Louis Kahn — Fort Washington, PA — construction — arch design, spatial experience, monumentality, craftsmanship
- The Closing Circle — Barry Commoner — US — book — relations: economic dev, environmental ethics, environmental awareness
- Environment, Power, Society — H. T. Odum — US — book — concepts: systems theory, thermodynamics, ecological economics
- Entropy Law and the Economic Process — Nicholas Georgescu-Roegen — US — book — relations: ecological economics
- Man and Biosphere Program — UNESCO — international — program — relations: biophysical and socioeconomic interconnectedness
- Greenpeace — Canada — NGO — relations: environmental activism, environmental protection, public awareness

1972
- Clean Water Act Public Law 92-500 — FG — act — territorial — environmental protection, water pollution, welfare, health
- DDT Ban, EPA — FG — act — environmental protection, toxic materials, welfare, health
- Marine Protection, Research, and Sanctuaries Act (Ocean Dumping Act) Public Law 92-532 — FG — act — territorial — environmental protection, welfare, health
- Noise Control Act Public Law 92-574 — FG — act — territorial — environmental protection, welfare, health, noise
- Zome House — Steven Baer — Corrales, NM — construction — arch design, spatial experience, lifestyle, spatial experience
- American Building: The Environmental Forces That Shape It — James Fitch — US — book — arch design, spatial experience, construction techniques, environmental mgmt
- UN Conference on the Human Environment — UN — Stockholm, Sweden — conference — relations: environmental protection
- Steps to an Ecology of Mind — Gregory Bateson — US — book — relations: ecology of mind
- The Limits to Growth — D. H. Meadows, D. L. Meadows, J. Randers, W. W. Behrens, Club of Rome — Switzerland — report — relations: demographics, economic dev, environmental mgmt

1973
- Endangered Species Act Public Law 93-205 — FG — act — territorial — environmental protection, biodiversity
- ASHRAE Standard 62-1973 Natural and Mechanical Ventilation — FG — NGO — standards — standard setting, environmental mgmt, mechanical services
- Douglas House — Richard Meier — Harbor Springs, MI — construction — arch design, lifestyle, spatial experience
- "Succession" — William Drury, Ian Nisbet — US — paper — laws: instability, indeterminacy, continuous flux
- "Resilience and Stability of Ecological Systems" — C. S. Holling — Canada — paper — laws: instability, indeterminacy, continuous flux
- "Energy, Ecology, and Economics" — H.T. Odum — US — paper — relations: energy mgmt, ecological economics
- Small Is Beautiful: Economics As If People Mattered — E. F. Schumacher — UK — book — relations: ecological economics

Richard Nixon
*Martin Luther King Jr. Assassination
*Apollo 11
*Watergate Scandal   *First Oil Crisis

1970–79

1974
- Safe Drinking Water Act, Public Law 93-523, FG, act, territorial, health, water pollution — E
- California Public Resources Code, Sections 25402 and 25402.1, SG, act, appliance, energy efficiency — R
- Solar Heating and Cooling Demonstration Act, Public Law 93-409, act, appliance, energy efficiency, research dev — R
- Solar Energy, Research, Development, and Demonstration Act, Public Law 93-473, FG, act, building, standard setting, environmental mgmt, mechanical services — E
- NBSIR 74-452: Design and Evaluation Criteria for Energy Conservation in New Buildings, US, NGO, standards, building, appliance — E
- ASHRAE Standard 55-1974 Thermal Environmental Conditions for Human Occupancy, 2nd ed.
- 1974 Energy and Form, Ralph L. Knowles, US, book, environmental mgmt, passive strategies, arch design
- 1974 "Biological Populations with Nonoverlapping Generations; Stable Points, Stable Cycles, Chaos" Robert May, UK, paper, laws: order, chaos theory, stability, disturbance
- 1974 Worldwatch Institute, Lester Brown, US, NGO

1975
- 1975 ASHRAE Standard 90-1975 Energy Conservation in New Building Design, NGO, standards, building, energy efficiency — E
- 1975 Energy Policy and Conservation Act, Public Law 94-163, FG, act, appliance, energy efficiency — E
- 1975 House VI, Peter Eisenman, Washington, CT, construction, arch design, lifestyle, spatial experience
- 1975 Integral Urban House, Farallones Institute, Sim Van der Ryn, Bill Olkowski, Helga Olkowski, Jan Kreider, Berkeley, CA, construction, environmental mgmt, self-sustenance, urban farming — R
- 1975 Solar Demonstration Program, HUD, Joint Venture Architects, Boulder, CO
- 1975 Terry House, David Wright, Santa Fe, NM, construction, arch design, passive solar design
- 1975 Ecology as Politics, 1st French ed. (Eng. 1980), André Gorz, France, book, relations: political ecology

1976
- 1976 Energy Conservation and Production Act, Public Law 94-385, FG, act, appliance, building — E
- 1976 Resource Conservation and Recovery Act, Public Law 94-580, FG, act, territorial, environmental mgmt, health, toxic materials, waste mgmt — E
- 1976 Toxic Substances Control Act, Public Law 94-469, FG, act, environmental protection, environmental mgmt; health, toxic materials — R
- 1976 Manufactured Home Construction and Safety Standards, Code of Federal Regulations, Title 24, Part 3280, FG, code, building, property standards, mortgage loan, affordability — R
- Housing Costs and Government Regulations: Confronting the Regulatory Maze, Stephen Seidel, Center for Urban Policy Research, US, NGO, handbook, urban, regulatory mechanisms
- 1976 Solar Dwelling Design Concepts, Michael Holtz, AIA Research Corporation, US, handbook, arch design, solar design
- 1976 Social Limits to Growth, Fred Hirsch, UK, book, relations: ecological economics
- 1976 Energy Basis for Man and Nature, H. T. Odum, Elisabeth C. Odum, US, book, relations: energy mgmt, ecological economics

1977
- 1977 California Energy Conservation Standards Code, SG, code, building, energy efficiency — E
- 1977 Model Code for Energy Conservation in New Buildings, BOCA, ICBO, SBCCI, NCSBCS, NGO, model code, building, energy efficiency — E
- 1977 National Energy Plan, FG, plan, territorial, governance, code making, energy efficiency — E
- 1977 Department of Energy (DOE) National Renewable Energy Laboratory, FG, agency, territorial, governance, code making, energy efficiency, research, standard setting — E
- Clean Water Act, Public Law 95-217, FG, act, environmental protection, water pollution, waste mgmt
- 1977-93 Graves House and Studio, Princeton, NJ, Michael Graves, construction, arch design, spatial experience, lifestyle
- 1977 A Pattern Language, Christopher Alexander, US, book, relations: ecological economics
- Steady-State Economics, Herman Daly, US, book, relations: ecological economics
- Soft Energy Paths: Towards a Durable Peace, Amory Lovins, US, book

1978
- 1978 National Energy Conservation Policy Act, Public Law 95-619, part of National Energy Act, FG, act, building, energy efficiency — R
- 1978 Energy Tax Act, part of National Energy Act, Public Law 95-618, FG, act, building, energy, efficiency, economic incentive — E
- 1978 National Energy Conservation Policy Act, Public Law 95-619, FG, act, building, energy, efficiency, property standards, mortgage loan — R
- Gehry Residence, Frank Gehry, Santa Monica, CA, Richard Crowther, Denver, CO, construction, arch design, passive solar design — E
- 1977 Sun Earth: How to Use Solar and Climatic Energies, arch design, spatial experience
- 1978 Alliance to Save Energy, –, US, NGO, relations: environmental conservation, energy conservation
- 1978 Love Canal disaster, various industries, US, man-made hazard, man-made hazard, water contamination

1979
- 1979 Bubble Policy, EPA, FG, act, territorial, environmental mgmt, air pollution — E
- 1979 Balcomb House, William Lumpkins, Santa Fe, NM, construction, arch design, passive solar design
- 1979 This Old House, PBS, Russell Morash, US, TV show, arch design, home improvement
- 1979 Mind and Nature: A Necessary Unity, Gregory Bateson, US, book, relations: ecology of mind
- 1979 "Catastrophic Disturbance & Steady State in Northern Hardwood Forests", H. Bormann, Gene Likens, US, paper, laws: stability, resilience, landscape ecology
- 1979 Gaia: A New look on Life on Earth, James Lovelock, UK, book, laws: superorganism, Gaia hypothesis
- 1979 the First World Climate Conference, World Meteorological Organization, Geneva, Switzerland, conference, relations: climate change
- 1979 Earth First!, Dave Foreman, Mike Roselle, Howie Wolke, Bart Koehler, Ron Kezar, US, NGO, relations: environmental preservation, environmental advocacy
- 1979 Three Mile Island nuclear accident, –, Harrisburg, PA, man-made hazard, nuclear meltdown

1980
- 1980 Comprehensive Environmental Response, Compensation, and Liability Act (Superfund Act), Public Law 96-510, FG, act, territorial, environmental mgmt, soil contamination, economic dev — E
- 1980 Solutions to Permit Compatible Use One and Two Family Code and the Min Property Standards, Nat. Assoc. of Home Builders Research Foundation, NGO, report, building, standardization — R
- 1980 Steel & Glass House, Krueck & Olsen, Chicago, IL, construction, arch design, spatial experience, lifestyle, minimalism, modular system, prefab house
- 1980 Carlisle House, the first all-solar residence, John Connell, Carlisle, MA, construction, environmental mgmt, active solar, photovoltaics
- 1980 Yestermorrow, John Connell, Waitsfield, VT, organization, design-build, sustainable design, local material use, site specificity, renewable energy
- 1980 "A Succession of Paradigms in Ecology", Daniel Simberloff, US, paper, laws: instability, indeterminacy, chance, complexity, probabilism
- 1980 World Conservation Strategy: Living Resource Conservation for Sustainable Development, initiative of World Bank, IUCN, report, relations: environmental conservation, sustainable dev
- 1980 North-South: A Program for Survival (Brandt Report), –, report, relations: environmental conservation, social equity, diversity, renewable resources
- 1980 Hurricane Allen, US, hurricane, natural disaster
- 1981 Building a Sustainable Society, Lester Brown, US, book, relations: sustainable dev, renewable energy, self-reliance
- 1981 Ocean Arks, John Todd, Nancy Todd, Harwich, MA, organization, environmental mgmt, natural wastewater treatment

1982
- 1982 Minimum Property Standards, One and Two Family Dwellings, FHA, last ed., FG, standards, building, standard setting, property standards, property value — R
- 1982 Nuclear Waste Policy Act, Public Law 97-425, FG, act, territorial, environmental protection, toxic materials, waste mgmt, health, natural resources — E
- 1982 Rocky Mountain Institute, Amory Lovins, US, organization, arch design, standard setting, energy efficiency

1974   1975   1976   1977   1978   1979   1980   1981   1982

Gerald Ford   Jimmy Carter   Ronald Reagan

*Second Oil Crisis   Iran-Iraq War 1980–88

*Reagan Assassination Attempt
*John Paul II Assassination Attempt

1980–89

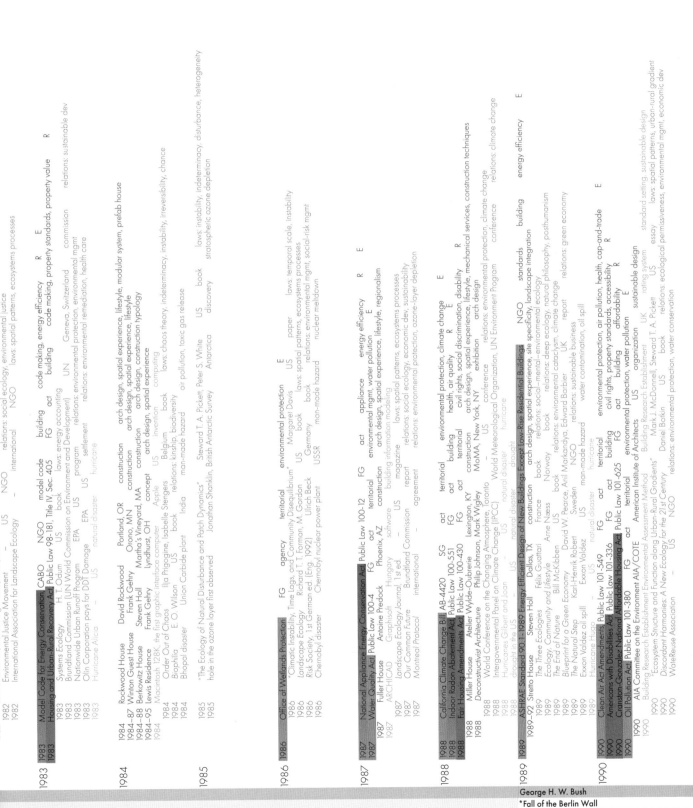

Commodore 64, best-selling desktop computer — — US invention computing
1982 Environmental Justice Movement — — US NGO relations: social ecology, environmental justice
1982 International Association for Landscape Ecology — — international NGO laws: spatial patterns, ecosystems processes

1983
1983 Model Code for Energy Conservation CABO NGO model code building code making, energy efficiency R E
1983 Housing and Urban-Rural Recovery Act Public Law 98-181, Title IV, Sec. 405 act FG code making, property standards, property value R
1983 Systems Ecology H.T. Odum US book laws: energy accounting
1983 Brundtland Commission (UN World Commission on Environment and Development) UN Geneva, Switzerland commission relations: sustainable dev
1983 Nationwide Urban Runoff Program EPA US program relations: environmental protection, environmental mgmt
1983 Olin Corporation pays for DDT Damage EPA US settlement relations: environmental remediation, health care
1983 Hurricane Alicia — US natural disaster hurricane

1984
1984 Rockwood House David Rockwood Portland, OR construction arch design, spatial experience, lifestyle, modular system, prefab house
1984-87 Winton Guest House Frank Gehry Orono, MN construction arch design, spatial experience, lifestyle
1984-88 Berkowitz House Steven Holl Martha's Vineyard, MA construction arch design, construction typology
1984-95 Lewis Residence Frank Gehry Lyndhurst, OH concept arch design, spatial experience
1984 Macintosh 128K, the first graphic interface computer Apple US invention computing
1984 Order Out of Chaos Ilya Prigogine, Isabelle Stengers Belgium book laws: chaos theory, indeterminacy, instability, irreversibility, chance
1984 Biophilia E.O. Wilson US book relations: kinship, biodiversity
1984 Bhopal disaster Union Carbide plant India man-made hazard air pollution, toxic gas release

1985
1985 "The Ecology of Natural Disturbance and Patch Dynamics" Steward T.A. Pickett, Peter S. White US book laws: instability, indeterminacy, disturbance, heterogeneity
1985 hole in the ozone layer first observed Jonathan Shanklin, British Antarctic Survey Antarctica discovery stratospheric ozone depletion

1986
1986 Office of Wetlands Protection FG agency territorial environmental protection E
1986 "Climatic Instability, Time Lags, and Community Disequilibrium" Margaret Davis US paper laws: temporal scale, instability
1986 Landscape Ecology Richard T.T. Forman, M. Gordon US book laws: spatial patterns, ecosystems processes
1986 Risk Society, 1st German ed. [Eng. 1992] Ulrich Beck Germany book relations: environmental mgmt; social-risk mgmt
1986 Chernobyl disaster Chernobyl nuclear power plant USSR man-made hazard nuclear meltdown

1987
1987 National Appliance Energy Conservation Act Public Law 100-12 FG act appliance energy efficiency R E
1987 Water Quality Act Public Law 100-4 FG act territorial environmental mgmt, water pollution E
1987 Fuller House Antoine Predock Phoenix, AZ construction arch design, spatial experience, lifestyle, regionalism
1987 ARCHICAD Graphisoft Hungary software building information modeling
1987 Landscape Ecology Journal, 1st ed. US magazine laws: spatial patterns, ecosystems processes
1987 Our Common Future Brundtland Commission US report relations: social ecology, economic dev, sustainability
1987 Montreal Protocol international agreement relations: environmental protection, ozone-layer depletion

1988
1988 California Climate Change Bill AB-4420 SG act territorial environmental protection, climate change E
1988 Indoor Radon Abatement Act Public Law 100-551 FG act building health, air quality R E
1988 Fair Housing Amendments Act Public Law 100-430 FG act territorial civil rights, social discrimination, disability R
1988 Miller House Atelier Wylde-Oubrerie Lexington, KY construction arch design, spatial experience, lifestyle, mechanical services, construction techniques
1988 Deconstructivist Architecture Philip Johnson, Mark Wigley MoMA, New York, NY exhibition arch design
1988 World Conference on the Changing Atmosphere, Toronto US conference relations: environmental protection, climate change
1988 Intergovernmental Panel on Climate Change (IPCC) World Meteorological Organization, UN Environment Program
1988 Hurricanes Gilbert and Joan — US natural disaster hurricane
1988 drought in the US US natural disaster drought

1989
1989 ASHRAE Standard 90.1-1989 Energy Efficient Design of New Buildings Except Low-Rise Residential Buildings NGO standards building energy efficiency E
1989-92 Stretto House Steven Holl Dallas, TX construction arch design, spatial experience, site specificity, landscape integration
1989 The Three Ecologies Félix Guattari France book relations: social–mental–environmental ecology
1989 Ecology, Community and Lifestyle Arne Næss Norway book relations: deep ecology, natural philosophy, posthumanism
1989 The End of Nature Bill McKibben US book relations: environmental cataclysm, climate change
1989 Blueprint for a Green Economy David W. Pearce, Anil Markandya, Edward Barbier UK report relations: green economy
1989 The Natural Step Karl-Henrik Robert Sweden NGO relations: sustainable business
1989 Exxon Valdez oil spill Exxon Valdez US man-made hazard water contamination, oil spill
1989 Hurricane Hugo — US natural disaster hurricane

1990
1990 Clean Air Act Amendments Public Law 101-549 FG act environmental protection, air pollution, health, cap-and-trade E
1990 Americans with Disabilities Act Public Law 101-336 FG act civil rights, property standards, accessibility R
1990 Cranston-Gonzalez National Affordable Housing Act Public Law 101-625 FG act building affordability E
1990 Oil Pollution Act Public Law 101-380 act territorial environmental protection, water pollution
1990 AIA Committee on the Environment AIA/COTE American Institute of Architects US organization sustainable design
1990 Building Research Establishment Environmental Assessment Method Building Research Establishment UK rating system standard setting, sustainable design
1990 Ecosystem Structure and Function along Urban-Rural Gradients" Mark J. McDonnell, Steward T.A. Pickett US essay laws: spatial patterns, urban-rural gradient
1990 Discordant Harmonies: A New Ecology for the 21st Century Daniel Botkin US book relations: ecological permissiveness, environmental mgmt, economic dev
1990 WateReuse Association — US NGO relations: environmental protection, water conservation

George H. W. Bush
*Fall of the Berlin Wall

Gulf War 1990–91
1990–99

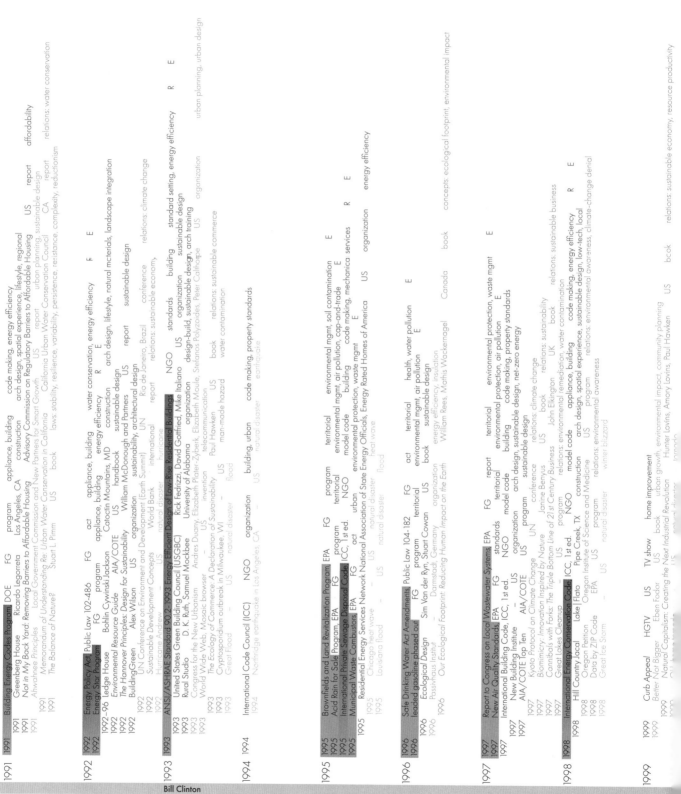

1991
- Building Energy Codes Program, DOE — FG — program — appliance, building — code making, energy efficiency
- 1991 Greenberg House — Ricardo Legorreta — Los Angeles, CA — construction — arch design, spatial experience, lifestyle, regional
- 1991 Not in My Back Yard: Removing Barriers to Affordable Housing — Advisory Commission on Regulatory Barriers to Affordable Housing — US — report — affordability
- 1991 Local Government Commission and New Partners for Smart Growth — US — report — urban planning, sustainable design
- 1991 Ahwahnee Principles
- 1991 Memorandum of Understanding Re: Urban Water Conservation in California — California Urban Water Conservation Council — CA — report — relations: water conservation
- 1991 The Balance of Nature? — Stuart L. Pimm — US — book — laws: stability, resilience, variability, persistence, resistance, complexity, reductionism

1992
- Energy Policy Act, Public Law 102-486 — FG — act — appliance, building — water conservation, energy efficiency
- Energy Star Program — FG — program — appliance, building — energy efficiency — R — E
- 1992–96 Ledge House — Bohlin Cywinski Jackson — Catoctin Mountains, MD — construction — arch design, lifestyle, natural materials, landscape integration
- 1992 Environmental Resource Guide — AIA/COTE — US — handbook — sustainable design
- 1992 The Hannover Principles: Design for Sustainability — William McDonough and Partners — US — report — sustainable design
- 1992 BuildingGreen — Alex Wilson — US — organization — sustainability, architectural design
- 1992 UN Conference on Environment and Development [Earth Summit] — UN — Rio de Janeiro, Brazil — conference — relations: climate change
- 1992 Sustainable Development Concepts — World Bank — international — relations: sustainable economy
- 1992 Hurricane Andrew — US — natural disaster — hurricane

1993
- ANSI/ASHRAE Standard 90.2, 1993 Energy Efficient Design of Low-Rise Residential Buildings — NGO — standards — building — standard setting, energy efficiency
- 1993 United States Green Building Council (USGBC) — Rick Fedrizzi, David Gottfried, Mike Italiano — US — organization — sustainable design
- 1993 Rural Studio — D.K. Ruth, Samuel Mockbee — University of Alabama — organization — design-build, sustainable design, arch training
- 1993 Congress for the New Urbanism — Andres Duany, Elizabeth Plater-Zyberk, Elizabeth Maule, Stefanos Polyzoides, Peter Calthorpe — US — organization — urban planning, urban design
- 1993 World Wide Web, Mosaic browser — US — invention — telecommunication
- 1993 The Ecology of Commerce: A Declaration of Sustainability — Paul Hawken — US — book — relations: sustainable commerce
- 1993 Cryptosporidium outbreak in Milwaukee, WI — US — water contamination
- 1993 Great Flood — US — natural disaster — flood

1994
- 1994 International Code Council (ICC) — NGO — organization — building, urban — code making, property standards
- 1994 Northridge earthquake in Los Angeles, CA — US — natural disaster — earthquake

1995
- Brownfields and Land Revitalization Program — EPA — FG — program — territorial — environmental mgmt, soil contamination — E
- Acid Rain for Sale Program, EPA — FG — program — territorial — environmental mgmt, air pollution, cap-and-trade — E
- International Private Sewage Disposal Code, ICC, 1st ed. — NGO — model code — building — code making — R — E
- Municipal Waste Combustors, EPA — FG — act — urban — environmental protection, waste mgmt — E
- 1995 Residential Energy Services Network, National Association of State Energy Officials, Energy Rated Homes of America — US — organization — energy efficiency
- 1995 Chicago heat wave — US — natural disaster — heat wave
- 1995 Louisiana flood — US — natural disaster — flood

1996
- Safe Drinking Water Act Amendments, Public Law 104-182 — FG — act — territorial — health, water pollution — E
- Leaded gasoline phased out — FG — territorial — environmental mgmt, air pollution — E
- 1996 Ecological Design — Sim Van der Ryn, Stuart Cowan — US — book — sustainable design
- 1996 Passivhaus Institut — Darmstadt, Germany — organization — energy efficiency, insulation
- 1996 Our Ecological Footprint: Reducing Human Impact on the Earth — William Rees, Mathis Wackernagel — Canada — book — concepts: ecological footprint, environmental impact

1997
- Report to Congress on Local Wastewater Systems, EPA — FG — report — territorial — environmental protection, waste mgmt — E
- New Air Quality Standards, EPA — FG — standards — territorial — environmental protection, air pollution — E
- International Building Code, ICC, 1st ed. — NGO — model code — building — code making, property standards
- 1997 New Building Institute — US — organization — US — program — arch design, sustainable design, net-zero energy
- 1997 AIA/COTE Top Ten — AIA/COTE — US — program — sustainable design
- 1997 Kyoto Protocol on Climate Change — UN — conference — relations: climate change
- 1997 Biomimicry: Innovation Inspired by Nature — Janine Benyus — US — book — relations: sustainability
- 1997 Cannibals with Forks: The Triple Bottom Line of 21st Century Business — John Elkington — UK — book — relations: sustainable business
- 1997 Great Lakes Cleanup — US — program — relations: environmental remediation, water contamination

1998
- International Energy Conservation Code, ICC, 1st ed. — NGO — model code — building — code making, building — R — E
- 1998 Hill Country Jacal — Lake | Flato — Pipe Creek, TX — construction — arch design, spatial experience, sustainable design, low-tech, local
- 1998 Oregon Petition — Oregon Institute of Science and Medicine — US — program — relations: environmental awareness, climate-change denial
- 1998 Data by ZIP Code — EPA — US — program — relations: environmental awareness
- 1998 Great Ice Storm — US — natural disaster — winter blizzard

1999
- 1999 Curb Appeal — HGTV — TV show — home improvement
- 1999 Better, Not Bigger — Eben Fodor — US — book — urban growth, environmental impact, community planning
- 1999 Natural Capitalism: Creating the Next Industrial Revolution — Hunter Lovins, Amory Lovins, Paul Hawken — US — book — relations: sustainable economy, resource productivity

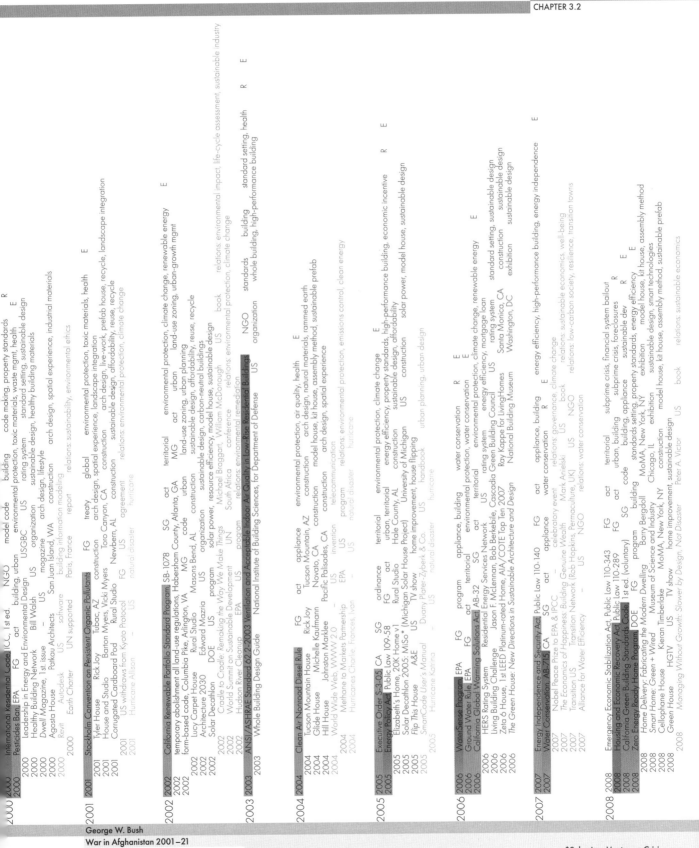

2000

- International Residential Code, ICC, 1st ed.
- **Pesticides Ban** — EPA — FG — act — code making, property standards — R
- Leadership in Energy and Environmental Design — USGBC — US — organization — rating system — standard setting, sustainable design — E
- Healthy Building Network — Bill Walsh — US — organization — environmental protection, toxic materials, waste mgmt, health
- Dwell Magazine, 1st issue — US — magazine — sustainable design, lifestyle
- Agosta House — Patkau Architects — San Juan Island, WA — US — construction — arch design, spatial experience, industrial materials
- Revit — Autodesk — US — software — building information modeling
- 2000 Earth Charter — UN supported — relations: sustainability, environmental ethics

2001

- **Stockholm Convention on Persistent Organic Pollutants** — FG — treaty — global — environmental protection, toxic materials, health — R
- 2001 Tyler House — Rick Joy — Tubac, AZ — construction — arch design, spatial experience, landscape integration
- 2001 House and Studio — Barton Myers, Vicki Myers — Toro Canyon, CA — construction — arch design, live-work, prefab house, recycle, landscape integration
- 2001 Corrugated Cardboard Pod — Rural Studio — Newbern, AL — construction — sustainable design, affordability, reuse, recycle
- 2001 US withdraws from Kyoto Protocol — FG — US — agreement — relations: environmental protection, climate change
- 2001 Hurricane Allison — US — natural disaster

2002

- **California Renewable Portfolio Standard Program** SB-1078 — SG — act — territorial — MG — environmental protection, climate change, renewable energy — E
- 2002 temporary abolishment all land-use regulations, Habersham County, Atlanta, GA — MG — urban — land-use zoning, urban-growth mgmt
- 2002 form-based code, Columbia Pike, Arlington, VA — MG — code — urban — land-use zoning, urban planning
- 2002 Lucy Carpet House — Rural Studio — Masons Bend, AL — construction — sustainable design, affordability, reuse, recycle
- 2002 Architecture 2030 — Edward Mazria — US — organization — sustainable design, carbon-neutral buildings
- 2002 Solar Decathlon — DOE — US — program — solar power, resource efficiency, model house, sustainable design
- 2002 Cradle to Cradle: Remaking the Way We Make Things — Michael Braggart, William McDonough — US — book
- 2002 World Summit on Sustainable Development — UN — South Africa — conference — relations: environmental protection, climate change
- 2002 Hudson River Cleanup — EPA — US — program — relations: environmental remediation

2003

- **ANSI/ASHRAE Standard 62.2-2003 Ventilation and Acceptable Indoor Air Quality in Low-Rise Residential Buildings** — NGO — standards — building — standard setting, health — R
- 2003 Whole Building Design Guide — National Institute of Building Sciences, for Department of Defense — US — organization — whole building, high-performance building

2004

- **Clean Air Nonroad Diesel Rule** — FG — environmental protection, air quality, health — E
- 2004 Tucson Mountain House — Rick Joy — Tucson Mountain, AZ — construction — arch design, natural materials, rammed earth
- 2004 Glide House — Michelle Kaufmann — Novato, CA — construction — model house, kit house, assembly method, sustainable prefab
- 2004 Hill House — Johnston Marklee — Pacific Palisades, CA — construction — arch design, spatial experience
- 2004 World Wide Web, WWW 2.0 — US — invention — telecommunication
- 2004 Methane to Markets Partnership — EPA — US — program — relations: environmental protection, emissions control, clean energy
- 2004 SmartCode User's Manual — A&E — US — handbook — urban planning, urban design
- 2004 Hurricane Katrina — US — natural disaster — hurricane

2005

- **Executive Order S-3-05** — CA — SG — ordinance — territorial — environmental protection, climate change — E
- **Energy Policy Act** Public Law 109-58 — FG — act — urban, territorial — environmental protection, energy efficiency, property standards, high-performance building, economic incentive — E
- 2005 Elizabeth's Home, 20K Home v1 — Rural Studio — Hale County, AL — construction — sustainable design, affordability
- 2005 Solar Decathlon 2005: MiSo* (Michigan Solar House Project) — University of Michigan — US — construction — solar power, model house, sustainable design
- 2005 Flip This House — A&E — US — TV show — home improvement, house flipping
- 2005 Hurricane Katrina — US — natural disaster — hurricane

2006

- **WaterSense Program** — EPA — FG — program — appliance, building — water conservation — E
- **Ground Water Rule** — EPA — FG — act — territorial — environmental protection, water conservation — E
- **California Global Warming Solutions Act** AB-32 — SG — act — US — rating system — energy efficiency, mortgage loan — R
- 2006 HERS Rating System — Residential Energy Services Council — US — rating system
- 2006 Living Building Challenge — Jason F. McLennan, Bob Berkebile, Cascadia Green Building Council — standard setting, sustainable design
- 2006 Zeta-0 House, 1st LEED Platinum-rated Home, AIA/COTE Top Ten 2007 — Ray Kappe for LivingHomes — Santa Monica, CA — construction — sustainable design
- 2006 The Green House: New Directions in Sustainable Architecture and Design — National Building Museum — Washington, DC — exhibition — sustainable design

2007

- **Energy Independence and Security Act** Public Law 110-140 — FG — act — appliance, building — energy efficiency, high-performance building, energy independence — E
- **Water Conservation, AB-715** — CA — SG — appliance — water conservation — R
- 2007 Nobel Peace Prize to EPA & IPCC — celebratory act — relations: governance, climate change — E
- 2007 The Economics of Happiness, Building Genuine Wealth — Mark Anielski — US — book — relations: sustainable economics, well-being
- 2007 Transition US — Transition Network (Rob Hopkins, Permaculture, UK) — US — NGO — relations: low-carbon society, resilience, transition towns
- 2007 Alliance for Water Efficiency — US — relations: water conservation

2008

- **Emergency Economic Stabilization Act**, Public Law 110-343 — FG — act — territorial — subprime crisis, financial system bailout
- **Housing and Economic Recovery Act**, Public Law 110-289 — FG — act — urban, building — subprime crisis, foreclosures — R
- **California Green Building Standards Code**, 1st ed. (voluntary) — SG — code — building, appliance — sustainable dev — E
- **Zero Energy Ready Home Program** — DOE — FG — program — standards setting, property standards, energy efficiency — R
- 2008 Home Delivery: Fabricating the Modern Dwelling — Barry Bergdoll — MoMA, New York, NY — exhibition — model house, kit house, assembly method
- 2008 Smart Home: Green + Wired — Museum of Science and Industry — Chicago, IL — exhibition — sustainable design, smart technologies
- 2008 Cellophane House — Kieran Timberlake — MoMA, New York, NY — construction — model house, kit house, assembly method, sustainable prefab
- 2008 Green House — HGTV — US — TV show — home improvement, sustainable design
- 2008 Managing Without Growth: Slower by Design, Nat Disaster — Peter A. Victor — US — book — relations: sustainable economics

George W. Bush
War in Afghanistan 2001–21
*9/11 Attacks
*China Enters WTO
Iraq War 2003–11
*Subprime Mortgage Crisis

2009

			R	E
American Recovery and Reinvestment Act, Stimulus Plan, Public Law 111-5	FG	act		
economic recovery, mortgage crisis, energy efficiency			R	E
Preventing Mortgage Foreclosures and Enhancing Mortgage Credit Public Law 111-22	FG			
financial risk mgmt			R	
Federal Leadership in Environmental, Energy, and Economic Performance	FG	program		
water conservation, energy efficiency			R	E
Energy Upgrade California	CA	SG	program	building
energy efficiency, economic incentive			R	

- 2009 Sustainability by Design: A Subversive Strategy for Transforming Our Consumer Culture — John R. Ehrenfeld — US — book — E
  relations: sustainable production, consumerism
- 2009 Prosperity without Growth — Tim Jackson — UN — book
  relations: sustainable economics
- 2009 Climate Change Conference — Copenhagen, Denmark — conference
  relations: climate change, greenhouse gas emissions

2010

- California Green Building Standards Code 2nd ed. (mandatory) — SG — code — building — sustainable dev — R — E
- 2010 Porch Houses — Lake Flato — Vanderpool, TX — construction — model house, kit house, assembly method, sustainable prefab
- 2010 BP's Deepwater Horizon oil spill — – — US — man-made hazard — water contamination, oil spill

2011

- ANSI/ASHRAE/ICC/USGBC Standard 189.1-2011 Standard for the Design of High-Performance Green Buildings — NGO — standards — building — sustainable dev — E
- National Standards for Mercury Pollution from Power Plants — EPA — FG — standards — territorial — environmental protection, air pollution — E
- 2011 Solar Decathlon 2011: CHIP House — SCI-Arc/Caltech — Los Angeles, CA — construction — US — solar power, model house, sustainable design
- 2011 Health Product Declaration® Open Standard — Health Product Declaration Collaborative — US — rating system — standard setting, sustainability, healthy building materials
  relations: ecological economics
- 2011 The End of Growth — Richard Heinberg — – — US — book
- 2011 Hurricane Irene — – — US — natural disaster — hurricane
- 2011 Super Outbreak — – — US — natural disaster — tornado

2012

- International Green Construction Code ICC 1st ed. — NGO — model code — building, appliance — code making, sustainable dev — R — E
- Air Pollution Standards for Oil and Natural Gas update, EPA — FG — act — territorial — environmental protection, air pollution — E
- 2012 Edgeland House — Bercy Chen Studio — Austin, TX — construction — spatial experience, sustainable design, pit house, green roof
- 2012 UN Conference on Sustainable Development — Rio de Janeiro, Brazil — UN — conference
  relations: environmental protection, climate change
- 2012 Hurricane Sandy — – — US — natural disaster — hurricane

2013

- Urban Agriculture Incentive Zones Act AB551 — SG — act — urban — land use, food production — R — E
- 2013 Vault House — Johnston Marklee — Oxnard, CA — construction — arch design, spatial experience
- 2013 Smart House — HGTV — US — TV show — home improvement, smart design
- 2013 Northeast US winter blizzard — – — US — natural disaster — winter blizzard

2014

- 2014 Tiny House, Big Living — HGTV — US — TV show — home construction, tiny house
- 2014 Tiny House Nation — FYI TV — US — TV show — home construction, tiny house

2015

- Executive Order B-30-15 — CA — SG — ordinance — territorial — environmental protection, climate change — E
- Clean Energy and Pollution Reduction Act SB-350, CA — SG — act — territorial — environmental protection, air pollution, energy efficiency, renewable energy — E
- 2015 Wing House — David Hertz — Malibu, CA — construction — arch design, spatial experience, reuse, recycle
- 2015 Architecture and Systems Ecology: Thermodynamic Principles of Environmental Building Design — William W. Braham — US — book — arch design, energy mgmt, environmental design
  relations: environmental mgmt, climate change
- 2015 Paris Climate Agreement — Paris, France — agreement
- 2015 This Changes Everything: Capitalism vs. the Climate — Naomi Klein — Canada — book
  relations: economic dev, environmental impact, capitalism

2016

- Community Resilience through Building Codes and Standards — President Obama — FG — program — building — standard setting, resilience, safety — R — E

The Greening of America's Building Codes

Promises and Paradoxes

ALEKSANDRA JAESCHKE

PRINCETON ARCHITECTURAL PRESS · NEW YORK

CONTENTS

2   A Timeline of Legislation with Related Events

27   Preface

Introduction

31   1. The Greening of America's House: Competing Agendas

34   2. Green Building Standards: Promises and Paradoxes

36   3. Beneath the Green Surface: Means and Methods

38   4. Predesign: Rethinking the Boundaries of Spatial Practice

41   PART ONE — AGENDAS

Chapter 1. From Welfare and Safety to Ecology: Before the 1970s

53   1.1. Standardizing Human Welfare: Before the 1920s

56   1.2. Building the Real-Estate Market: 1920s

59   1.3. Growing out of the Depression: 1930s–1945

62   1.4. Prospering by Expansion: 1945–1950s

65   1.5. Normalizing Environmental Welfare: 1960s

Chapter 2. Environmental Protection and Sustainable Development: 1970s–1980s

69   2.1. Regulating Environmental Degradation: 1970s

76   2.2. Aligning Sustainability with Global Economic Expansion: 1980s

Chapter 3. Green Economy and Green Building Standards: 1990s–Present

85   3.1. Greening the Markets: 1990s–mid-2000s

94   3.2. Offsetting Speculation with Green Standards: Mid-2000s–2010s

101 PART TWO — MEANS AND METHODS

Chapter 4. The Logics behind Green Technologies and Financial Incentives

111   4.1. Why These Artifacts and Techniques? Critiques

114   4.2. Persuade or Coerce? Questions

117   4.3. Incentivizing the Green Market. Solutions

124   4.4. Artifacts Versus Plants. Paradoxes

Chapter 5. The Structure and Form of Regulations

131   5.1. Who Protects the Environment?
Focus: Materials

137   5.2. Where Are the Rule Makers?
Focus: Water

143   5.3. Why Continue Stacking?
Focus: Air

149   5.4. What About Agency?
Focus: Vegetation

Chapter 6. The Power of Predesign in Four Conversations

158   6.1. Standardizing the Nonstandard
Focus: Straw-bale Construction
In Conversation with Martin Hammer

162   6.2. Normalizing the Alternatives
Focus: Waterless Toilet
In Conversation with Mathew Lippincott

166   6.3. Coding the Uncertain
Focus: Environmental Simulation Software
In Conversation with Michael Bruse

169   6.4. Certifying the Living
Focus: Live Moss Panel
In Conversation with Al Benner

Conclusion

173   1. Plotting the Regulatory Circuits: From Ideas to Standards

175   2. Recircuiting the Code Landscape: Topics for Predesign Research

176   3. Breaking the Green Circuit Open: Sustainable Morality versus Ecological Consciousness

178   Notes

201   Selected Bibliography

204   Index

To my parents, who taught me

how to live well without calling it *wellness*,

how to stay fit without calling it *fitness*,

how to sustain life without calling it *sustainability*.

PREFACE

This book is an attempt to think through a problem commonly ignored by architects advancing design from within academia. When I rejoined these circles after several years of running a small architectural practice to embark on a doctoral research project at the Harvard Graduate School of Design, I was struck by the fact that most design-driven conversations that addressed the *ecological question* focused on either developing new technologies or improving parametrically driven computational design techniques. Yet while we talked about constraint-driven design techniques, almost no attention was being paid to a constraint that—next to finance—imposes a major limitation on professional practice and, by consequence, environmentally driven design. There was an elephant in the room; no one was interested in building regulations and construction standards that constitute an integral part of what I refer to as the "predesign" phase of construction.

As I started to analyze how building codes responded to environmental concerns, I became more and more aware of the fact that recent green-building-code overlays were only the tip of an iceberg that would prove much harder to "green." Rather than assessing how well new parts of the code were regulating the environmental impact of construction (or figuring out how to bring the existence of the predesign phase to the attention of environmentally minded researcher-designers), I became concerned with understanding why building codes could not do what was promised by the green overlays. I focused on the forces that shaped the regulatory circuit and on its inner logics—the internal architecture and verbiage—forces that I intuitively sensed still inform the regulatory landscape and logics that continue to determine architecture's relationship with the environment to this day.

I am neither a historian nor a building-code expert, so the task was intimidating and risky.

Nonetheless, I decided to embrace the beginner's mindset, hoping that the fresh eye would help me make meaningful observations that would compensate for possible errors due to lack of expertise. I obviously strived for accuracy, but this book is not an objective account. It is a story meant to trigger thinking rather than provide answers. While the analyzed facts—all listed in the included timeline—span a period from the mid-nineteenth century when the first building codes appeared in the US to, approximately, the end of the Obama presidency, the analysis gets deeper as construction standards and environmental concerns start to proliferate in the late 1960s. I focused on residential construction and used the California Building Code since, in single-family construction, building regulations are a binding constraint due to mortgage loan requirements and California is the forerunner in environmental regulation. Still, the issues I am concerned with transcend typological and state boundaries. Although I updated the references to the originally analyzed 2016 edition of the code with those from the 2019 edition, unfortunately, this version will also become obsolete once this book has been published. Nonetheless, the issues that I raise are bigger than what is normally addressed during the regular, triennial building-code update. A significant change, if possible, at all, could only be triggered by a comprehensive—structural and linguistic—reform that would require a new political mindset.

In 1970, Charles A. Reich published a volume whose title inspired the title of this book: *The Greening of America*. Encouraged by the transformative events of 1968, Reich abandoned the original title, *The Coming of the Closed Society*, to focus on the positive change—reflected in the final title—that he joyfully observed in America's social landscape.[1] Fifty years later, what we might be witnessing is, unfortunately, a technocratic attempt to *green the closed society*

that came. And yet, to reopen our society, green Band-Aids won't do it. We need a total recircuiting of mindsets. Obviously, the story I tell in this book—one of the interactions of agendas and programs that inform the regulatory circuits and by consequence shape the built environment—is only a small subregion of a larger *closed-minded* circuit that determines how we think about and act upon the environment. I almost archived this research, fearful that it would be perceived as a superficial way to think about the ecological question, one that does not get to the very core of the problem, the modern mindset. What made me change my mind was the eye-opening effect that the content of this book had on the students who took the seminar entitled "Sustainability: Why This Way," which I teach at the University of Texas at Austin. And so my hope is that it will help others move away from the reductionist approach embedded in the green building standards and codes toward a more holistic ecological posture.

———————

This book is based on the dissertation for which I was awarded the Doctor of Design degree by the Harvard Graduate School of Design (GSD) in 2018. I started the research in Cambridge, Massachusetts, wrote the dissertation in Los Angeles, and turned it into this book in Austin, Texas, between 2020 and 2021.

My gratitude goes to my doctoral advisors. Iñaki Ábalos, former chair of the Department of Architecture at the GSD, for the freedom he granted me in this research and for his beautiful book *The Good Life* (2001), which reminded me of why we practice architecture when reading building codes and standards made me doubt it. Antoine Picon, for drawing my attention to crucial arguments at key moments and teaching me how to keep my work "up to standard." Jane

Hutton, whose then forthcoming book *Reciprocal Landscapes* (2019) was an inspiration in the early stages of this exploration. Our conversations, which gradually evolved into a friendship, helped me persist in this project.

A special thanks goes to Mohsen Mostafavi, former dean of the GSD, for his continuous support during my education, both at the Architectural Association and at the GSD. I also want to thank other GSD faculty members, among them: Martin Bechthold, former director of the Doctor of Design program, for his guidance during the initial phase of this project; Richard Peiser for helping me understand some of the inner workings of real estate; Pierre Bélanger for having helped me think telescopically and politically about the environment; Kiel Moe for his eye-opening lessons on energy; and Richard T. T. Forman for introducing me to the science of ecology. My immense gratitude goes to Sanford Kwinter for his astounding science of the environment, intellectual generosity, and friendship that continue to inspire my thinking.

In Los Angeles, I wish to thank my colleagues at the Woodbury School of Architecture, where I taught while writing my dissertation, and my friend Liz Falletta, whose appreciation for the real-world dynamics on which architecture depends has been an important inspiration.

In Austin, I wish to thank Dean Michelle Addington at the University of Texas School of Architecture (UTSOA) for her continuous support and Anthony Alofsin for his guidance in the book-proposal-development phase. I am also very grateful to the UTSOA students who participated in my seminar. Their enthusiasm toward the material contained in this book made me persist in this project when new ideas started to occupy my mind.

I also wish to thank Jan Hartman, former senior editor at Princeton Architectural Press, without whom this book would not have been born. Lucas Friedman for offering initial editorial remarks on my dissertation, which provided precious guidance as I embarked on the journey of transforming it into a book. And, of course, Abby Bussel, Holly La Due, and Kristen Hewitt, editors at Princeton Architectural Press, as well as project editor Linda Lee for their patience and editorial support.

My gratitude also goes to those who made the financial burden of this project more bearable: the GSD; the Kosciuszko Foundation, whose fellowship I received in 2014; Fundacja Ivy Poland, together with Inglot Poland, which gave me support in 2016; and the UTSOA for support during the final stages of this venture. This project would not be financially possible without the support from my parents and friends and the hospitality of the Baglioni family. It was in their Los Angeles home that the initial dissertation was written.

Last but not least, I thank my husband, Marcello Baglioni, for his unconditional support and contagious joy for life, which fed me throughout this journey, and my parents and sister for always standing by my side, even when it is unclear where I am heading.

INTRODUCTION

1. The Greening of America's House: Competing Agendas

Two basic threads inform this story of the "greening" of America's building codes. The first one focuses on the regulation of single-family construction; the second is an account of the rise of environmental awareness. Each is told from a number of perspectives: the former explores the agendas of domestic engineers, merchant builders, and realtors; the latter recounts the initiatives inspired by naturalists, informed by scientists, and put into action by environmental activists. My ambition in this book is to understand how these two threads got entangled throughout the twentieth century and how this entanglement was normalized by politicians, optimized by economists, and standardized in the circuits of code makers. Ultimately, the aim is to evaluate the outcome of this entanglement: the green building standards.

To better understand how America's houses—due to various policies, codes, and standards—assimilated the emerging ecological imperative, it is necessary to answer a chain of questions: 1) which interests informed building standards before they were subjected to the greening process; 2) what kinds of agendas shaped the ecological imperative itself; and 3) what forces captured the ecological imperative to transform them into green building standards? These are addressed in Part One – Agendas. The answer to these questions would remain incomplete if this study was only concerned with the development of ideas, programs, and the directives born from them. Inevitably, it has to pay attention to the geography of rule-making circuits, the structure of the building code, and the regulatory language itself, as, together, they are responsible for how knowledge is articulated, framed, and applied. It must also involve an investigation of economic forces, especially market instruments used to "prop" up the diffusion of new products. These issues are addressed in Part Two – Means and Methods, where I explore a heterogeneous set of codependent power strategies—an "apparatus," in philosopher Michel Foucault's words—that, among other mechanisms, relies on standards propagated across the circuits of code makers and on financial incentives that support market-preferred technologies to propel the growth of economy.[1] This book is a story of an old apparatus— capitalism's wicked success depends on its workings—but this time around, due to the urgent need to address the environmental emergency, there is a green twist to it.

The American house has served this apparatus well, and the opportunities to put it to work in favor of economic growth have been many. Today, the reason is to make the house resilient; the palpable consequences of climate change put personal safety and the protection of property again at the center of the general public's attention.[2] Mitigation of risk to humans rather than prevention of environmental disaster is again the main concern of code makers. In 2016, the Obama administration launched the first public-private initiative meant to improve community resilience by addressing building codes and standards. Undoubtedly, the term *resilience* will serve the market as well as the green building standards did when they were first launched. In 2008, when California became the first state in the US to adopt the Green Building Standards Code meant to reduce the environmental impact of construction, the market for green building products was experiencing a boom. When the housing bubble burst in the late 2000s, architects responded to the unsustainability of the housing market by symptomatically embracing technological innovation rather than simple restraint; they endorsed the "green prefab."

This reflected the fact that, while in part the effect of a genuine concern for the environment, green construction standards evolved in the 1990s as part of the green economy. They expressed the pragmatic idea of sustainable development and reflected the belief that it is possible to decouple economic productivity from environmental degradation. They did not attempt to correct the increasingly deregulated real-estate market, which considered financial rather than material obsolescence a reason for building more and bigger houses. This tendency was already visible in the 1980s when the need to renew the aging housing stock provided an excuse to build bigger rather than less impactful or more affordable houses.

Similarly, in the previous decade, the passive-solar-design methods failed to compete with off-the-shelf energy-conserving mechanical appliances promoted as a means to improve energy security after the 1973 oil crisis. This was inevitable considering that already in the 1960s, merchant builders focused on delivering quickly and cheaply built rather than custom-designed, climate-responsive, and site-specific houses. During the same period, although passive climate-control strategies attracted unparalleled interest, more market-friendly climate-control solutions were being defined by the American Society of Heating, Refrigerating and Air-Conditioning Engineers, commonly known as ASHRAE.

While the first energy-conservation standards were introduced in the 1970s, similar measures were already contained in the 1958 edition of the Minimum Property Standards for Properties of One or Two Living Units, published by the Federal Housing Administration (FHA). Adopted before the rise of environmental awareness, however, their rationale was clearly aligned with the economic interests. In fact, these standards embodied almost twenty-five years of efforts to standardize the American house, normalize its cost, and minimize financial risks while promoting economic growth. Already in 1922, Secretary Hoover's Department of Commerce started to promote uniform and cheap construction methods to increase homeownership among middle-class families, ultimately to reduce workforce instability and secure steady economic activity.

Although the purpose was novel, this, too, was a declination of an earlier project, the one undertaken by the first code makers in the early twentieth century. Their main concern was the basic safety, health, and welfare in tenements occupied by a poor (and highly unstable) workforce. The preoccupations embedded in the century-old triad of terms *health*, *safety*, and *welfare* still resonate in the current use of the term *resilience*. The difference is that back then, the threat came from industrialization and excessive urban growth; today, it comes from climate change and environmental disasters. It is deeply ingrained in the regulatory landscape for the code makers to be narrowly concerned with human safety and protection of property as opposed to caring more broadly for the natural environment. The ultimate goals remain unchanged: ensure community stability and economic growth or, in modern terms, increase community resilience and economic development.

If it is deeply ingrained in American culture to consider the housing industry as a vehicle for economic growth, it is equally well impressed in the cultural landscape to think about the environment in economic terms. In the early period when the American house was being "made" safe and healthy, environmental awareness manifested itself in the creation of urban parks, garden cities, and wildlife reserves—initiatives inspired by early environmental preservationists, such as John Muir. Although "nature" was abundant—as it was thought at the time—the utilitarian attitudes of the conservationists, among them forester and politician Gifford Pinchot, concerned with resource-use efficiency gradually came to the forefront.

At this determinative stage, environmental dynamics were still poorly understood, and, hence, it was impossible to apply scientific management methods to them. Even when regional planning emerged in the 1920s, ecology was still defining its key concepts, and the first impact-assessment methods would not be developed until the 1960s. It wasn't until the 1970s—and in reaction to the devastating impact of chemical industries as famously exposed by many scientists and activists in the 1960s, among them Rachel Carson in *Silent Spring*—that Americans witnessed the creation of the first comprehensive federal environmental-protection framework (i.e., the National Environmental Policy Act of 1970).[3]

It became evident that it was no longer possible to simply set aside green reserves to offset the impact of industrial development and that a more systemic action was required. Various events, conferences, and reports, among them the first Earth Day (1970), the Stockholm Conference on the Human Environment (1972), and the econometric report *The Limits to Growth* raised alarm about the state of the planet, but the second wave of environmental legislation (e.g., the Energy Policy and Conservation Act of 1975) was in large part also triggered by the 1973 oil crisis and the threat of energy scarcity.[4] Unfortunately, the voice of economist Herman Daly, who criticized the excessive focus on relative efficiency and advocated for setting absolute limits for the economy, remained largely ignored.

The Reagan administration brought a drastic revision of US legislation favoring economic growth over environmental protection. Similar attitudes marked the 1980s across the entire Western world, slowly deregulating most of the existing control mechanisms in favor of a free market and private property. The negative effects of this backlash, together with the growing scientific evidence of the global economy's impact on climate change and a series of major environmental disasters (e.g., Chernobyl) triggered the first wave of intergovernmental actions. The 1987 *Report of the World Commission on Environment and Development: Our Common Future*, published by the United Nations, introduced the concept of "sustainable development" into global politics, and the issue of emissions reduction was first discussed at the World Conference on the Changing Atmosphere held in Toronto in 1988.[5] The collapse of the Communist Bloc, yet again, pulled international attention toward issues of economic growth and triggered a new wave of expansion of capitalist markets.

Although major climate summits took place during the 1990s, it was free-trade agreements, such as NAFTA, and the entry of China into the World Trade Organization that determined the course of the global dynamics during the next two decades. Climate action suffered heavily from the increasing deregulation of global markets, and attention hypocritically shifted from the impact of global trade to the efficiency of products and sustainability of daily practices. Amid these dynamics, and thanks to an impressive set of regulatory mechanisms, America's natural and domestic environments continue to work (as source and vehicle) in service of the same—although apparently greener—market.

2. Green Building Standards: Promises and Paradoxes

It is abundantly clear by now—think of all the competing eco-labels—that the notion of sustainability has been hijacked by suppliers of products and services to generate new niche markets. This mechanism is so widely diffused that many free-market economists claim that we can only be sustainable in ways that generate profit. On the global scale, the argument that "the way to reduce pollution is to create a market for it" resulted in cap-and-trade mechanisms that triggered a wave of lucrative speculation, replacing previous policies that imposed simple limitations on individual polluters.[6]

On a more tangible scale, it created a market for solar panels, eco-cars, low-energy bulbs, and many other green consumer products. Even though mandatory green building regulations carry the risk of social exclusion—homes equipped with more and more green appliances become less and less affordable—as social activist and writer Naomi Klein highlights, "Policies based on encouraging people to consume less are far more difficult for our current political class to embrace than policies that are about encouraging people to consume green."[7] As a consequence, economic incentives coupled with mandatory green building standards address the environmental impact (or cost) of individual households in a very limited—if not inadequate—manner, diverting attention away from other, less tangible environmental issues. Also, our commodity-driven culture and long working hours mean that most people do not have the time to engage in voluntary environmental action or even do some gardening, which—if done thoughtfully—can bring environmental benefits.

Market-driven logics promoted by the media and supported by green building standards make an average owner of a McMansion believe that their home is sustainable—that is, it can *sustain* itself without imperiling the environment—if its daily operations are powered by solar panels and their water flows from an efficient faucet. Unfortunately, this conviction is not simply born of naivete or hypocrisy: a house that consumes less energy due to spatial solutions will not receive a tax write-off, while one that promises to cover predicted consumption with an array of solar panels will. In this context, there is no motivation to adopt environmentally friendly solutions that do not require a purchase, even though residential construction and domestic operations cannot possibly achieve a net-zero impact using solar panels alone.

Perhaps more importantly, the net-zero concept is simply not a valid answer to the ecological question since nothing (at least in our Western society) will result in a net-zero impact if the real system boundaries and all processes—not just energy consumption and carbon emissions—are considered. A result of a strategic manipulation of knowledge in support of the green apparatus, the net-zero quantity is one of the most deceptive market propositions successfully disseminated by the media. Additionally, many environmental issues cannot be quantified and therefore easily accounted for. Also, when the risks do not appear immediate and when the economic benefits of environmental action will surface in a poorly defined future, we lack the tools to address them.

Commonly, alternative solutions that look beyond the narrow system boundaries considered by policy makers are also either not sufficiently advertised or simply not allowed unless by special permission.[8] While, as discussed in Chapter 6, "The Power of Redesign in Four Conversations," to standardize an alternative technology—such as straw-bale construction or composting toilets—can take years of voluntary work, complying with the current green building standards by tweaking the efficiency of existing products is relatively easy, can help increase the sales, and can potentially act as a shield against environmental criticism.

And if criticism arrives, companies can join forces with professionals and citizens to form standard-setting nongovernmental organizations (NGOs) to indirectly bend the norms toward their own needs. As philosophers Michael Hardt and Antonio Negri observe in *Empire*: "NGOs extend far and wide in the humus of biopower; they are the capillary ends of the contemporary networks of power."[9] In the absence of governmental measures, many green nonprofit organizations, such as the U.S. Green Building Council (USGBC), emerged over the last two decades to promote sustainability among architects and builders and eventually develop voluntary green building certification programs, such as USGBC's Leadership in Energy and Environmental Design (LEED). The broad spectrum of social groups that support the USGBC offers unique opportunities. Neither directly representing industries and suppliers nor the state, NGOs offer a perfect structure to exert indirect influence. To use psychoanalyst and philosopher Félix Guattari's description, they are "best fitted to capture desire and harness it to the profit economy."[10]

Industries support NGOs to promote their products, real-estate developers comply with their standards to green their public image, and environmentalists, concerned citizens, teachers, and students turn them into a trustworthy third-party authority. Grassroots alternatives not aligned with the prevailing economic logics struggle to compete. In fact, organizations that pursue more ambitious environmental and social goals, such as the Living Future Institute, are forced to adopt the same certification-based formula to compete for members among architects and developers. Peer support becomes a form of discipline as organizations compete to impose and certify compliance with sustainable norms. Eventually, what could be a set of flexible guidelines becomes a form of self-inflicted "micro-fascism," again Guattari's term.[11]

Eventually, when the most successful set of voluntary guidelines gets adopted as an extension of the legally binding building regulations, a cultural norm—informed by the usage driven by environmental concerns shared by a like-minded community—becomes a legally imposed order, an *imperative*, as philosopher Georges

Canguilhem would describe it.[12] Many US states and cities made LEED guidelines a requirement for certain types of construction in the early days of green building standards. By adopting the criteria developed by USGBC, governments legitimized them as a national green building standard monopoly, despite (but, in reality, precisely because of) the fact that it represented a compromise between the interests of those advocating for sustainability, the construction industry, and real-estate developers. However, since obtaining a LEED certificate posed a financial challenge to smaller (especially residential) developers, these projects were initially exempted from the mandatory compliance with LEED standards. Despite the initial resentment, in 2008, California was the first state to develop and adopt its own mandatory standards—the California Green Building Standards Code (also known as CALGreen)—to almost all types of new construction.[13]

It is noteworthy that the USGBC, whose obvious interest is to maintain LEED certifications on the market, responded by granting points for compliance with the CALGreen Code to maintain its visibility and also to mark a clear distinction between the California baseline and its own ambition to set a higher standard. Ultimately, in 2012, the International Code Council (ICC), another powerful nongovernmental organization, introduced a new model code, the International Green Construction Code, to make baseline green building standards available to all states. With this latest addition, the ICC recognized the work done by, among others, the USGBC and the state of California as sufficient to prepare policy makers, the market, and the general public to accept an additional layer of restrictions. The greening of America's building codes is under way. The question that remains open is whether it can really curb the environmental impact of America's construction.

Clearly, green building standards impose some limitations on the housing industry, affecting its profitability and affordability, but the complicated nature of the green restrictions means that they ultimately support other forms of economic growth elsewhere. According to economist Ha-Joon Chang, even if "some markets look free, it is only because we so totally accept the regulations that are propping them up that they become invisible."[14] Paradoxically, it seems that the very visible—ostentatiously advertised—green building standards achieve a similar effect; rather than limiting the market, they invisibly prop up its freedom. The question is whether these standards promote the right to a healthy environment (or, better, the right of the environment to *be* healthy) or simply perpetuate the market-driven image of sustainability exploiting the regulatory apparatus.[15] Surely, the requirements meant to restrict the market support it at least in one way. The quantifiable nature of these (in most part) prescriptive and product-based regulations ensures that environmental solutions can be easily assessed in terms of their cost and compared in terms of financing risk. This mechanism was put in place when the American house became a standardized real-estate product financed with an FHA-insured mortgage, and it naturally continues as the housing construction industry evolves under the pressure of the environmental imperative.

3. Beneath the Green Surface: Means and Methods

When environmental agendas started to influence regulations in the 1970s, the building code was already a crystallized system of rigid prescriptions of often forgotten origin, criticized for excessive complexity.[16] Environmental regulations (e.g., the Energy Code, first intro-duced in 1978 by the state of California) were simply added to existing codes. Selective "band-aiding"—to use urban scholar Eran Ben-Joseph's term—rather than a comprehensive revision of the older regulations and underlying notions continues to characterize the code-development process as new green building standards are being introduced in response to newly emerging environmental pressures.[17] The tendency to focus on isolated issues is also driven by the fact that these issues—as discussed more than half a century ago by urban activist Jane Jacobs—are administered across a maze of independent governmental agencies, each responsible for an isolated aspect of the built environment.[18]

This reductionist approach is reflected in the regulatory language as well. While discuss-ing different ways of expressing norms, housing policy expert William Baer pointed out that the more common, prescriptive standards impose blueprints for product-based solutions, while performance-based criteria impose a result.[19] They require a capacity to develop new recipes and think in terms of—to use political scientist and economist Herbert Simon's distinction—process rather than state description.[20] Clearly, it is easier to analyze an issue *reduced* to a simple two-variable problem and evaluate a handful of potential product-based solutions rather than approach it in terms of organized complexity and be forced to accept that the results can only be loosely outlined. It is also easier to explain a simply defined issue to the public and convince it that the solution lies in a more efficient prod-uct rather than revise the entire system of codes and expect an immediate change in the public's habits. In other words, simple problems can be resolved by adopting a product-based solution, while complex issues must be acted upon by adopting process-based solutions that require a dramatic shift in behaviors while guaranteeing no clear outcome.

In recent years, to encourage innovation, some building codes (e.g., the California Energy Code) have become more flexible, gradually evolving into a complex mix of prescriptive and performance-based standards and criteria. Yet adopting performance-based, nonstandard solutions requires a team of well-prepared designers and consultants capable of developing and defending them, which inevitably increases soft costs and entails additional legal risks. Many potentially beneficial passive design strategies that take advantage of the local climate are rarely adopted, either because they create conflicts with preexisting regulations or require expensive per-formance tests.[21] Passive solutions (e.g., natural ventilation) and organic systems (e.g., vegetative shade) are penalized by prescriptive standards that prefer products with a manufacturer's warranty over custom-designed spatial config-urations or vegetation that undergoes seasonal changes.[22] Meanwhile, the fact that mechanical systems can be easily made unreliable by peo-ple's irrational behaviors is not perceived as a problem in a culture that prefers passive con-sumption over active involvement and that relies on product data sheets that guarantee lab-tested performance, even if the latter does not reflect the complexity of the real world.

In *The Science of the Artificial*, Simon observes, "As creatures of bounded rationality, incapable of dealing with the world in all of its complexity, we form a simplified picture of the world, view-ing it from our particular organizational van-tage point and our organization's interests and goals."[23] Green building standards are born from within this bounded rationality, yet this type of rationality—one that favors highly prescriptive standards—is a double-edged sword. While it protects from unpredictable effects of unverified solutions, it also limits our capacity to innovate in response to new conditions.

As Canguilhem remarks, "No fact termed normal, because expressed as such, can usurp the prestige of the norm of which it is the expression, starting from the moment when the conditions in which it has been referred to the norm are no longer given."[24] Informal norms and normative practices naturally evolve as cultures change. Fixed prescriptive standards inevitably inhibit (or at least delay) this evolution. Regulatory mechanisms that transform fluid systems of norms into rigid, legally binding structures will always struggle to keep pace with changing conditions and will often fail to reassess norms to respond to emerging needs. They will also inevitably limit "unbounded" expressions of ecological awareness to "bounded" forms of sustainability.

4. Predesign: Rethinking the Boundaries of Spatial Practice

Although certain authors have acknowledged the harmful side effects of some of the existing standards and have recognized the need for a comprehensive reassessment of the entire building code, most studies concerned with the recently introduced green building standards investigate their effects in isolation from the rest of the regulations.[25] For example, in *Green Buildings and the Law*, construction experts Tamera McCuen and Lee Fithian acknowledge that "legislation is typically passed for a particular component or a problem in the system, rather than addressing the entire system," but they then concentrate on the potentially harmful impact of selected green building standards.[26]

Meanwhile, a number of larger—transversal—issues that indirectly impact the environment without anyone taking notice of it calls for attention. Among them, I would list: 1) the influence of older—apparently not related

to the environmental cause—regulations; 2) the excessive reliance on prescriptive and product-based solutions; 3) the power of regulatory language to indirectly determine what is permissible; 4) the use of mandatory regulations to support market-preferred green products; and 5) the vulnerability of the regulatory language and the code-making process to political and economic pressures. The three chapters contained in Part Two – Means and Methods explore these issues through a transversal reading of the code's approach to a number of highlighted topics. By no means exhaustive, the themes that I explore include the status of solar panels versus trees, use of plastic foam as thermal insulation, repercussions of the current domestic water-management methods, and utilization of living systems for climate control.

Throughout this book, particularly in Part Two, where the above topics are explored, I refer to the regulations for single-family residential construction contained in the 2019 edition of the California Building Standards Code (California Code of Regulations, Title 24) as adopted by the City of Los Angeles. Since most single-family homes are financed with mortgages issued under strict conditions imposed by lenders and insurers to minimize financial risk, in residential construction, solutions that comply with prescriptive standards imposed by the code prevail over spatial and ecological innovation. Most of the time, the codes make up the sole mechanism responsible for the mitigation of the environmental impact of new houses in the United States, and this is why this study focuses on residential construction.

As mentioned previously, California has always been at the forefront of environmental legislation and was the first state to expand its code of regulations with a set of mandatory green building standards. When the discussed issue (e.g., water-use management) is in part regulated at the municipal level—in the zoning code, I reference the regulations adopted by the City of Los Angeles. Los Angeles seemed the right choice for a number of reasons. Its vast, and apparently uniform, fabric regulated by the same code extends over a territory characterized by many different Ecologies, as architectural critic Reyner Banham describes the different areas of Los Angeles: Surfurbia, Foothills, and the Plains of Id, all innerved by the highway system named Autopia.[27] Because of its thriving economy, and now also due to climate change, the Los Angeles basin suffers from excessive heat waves, extreme air pollution, and almost incessant water shortage. Simultaneously, its constantly irrigated greenery resembles a tropical garden. Obviously, although this research examines a specific jurisdiction and its regulations, the issue transcends state borders and municipal boundaries. While grounded in a specific context, it will hopefully contribute to a general discussion about the standards that predetermine our relationship with the environment, shape our notions of ecology, and practically represent the predesign phase of architectural—or more generally, spatial—practice.

Together with voluntary guidelines, mandatory codes standardize household operations and normalize the daily activities of their dwellers. They define minute details of the apparatuses in which we are all captured. Along with economic incentives and green technologies, building regulations determine the character of America's houses and the nature of its environmental awareness. The codes impose spatial organizations, determine design solutions, and limit material choices. They regiment construction practices to augment efficiency, reduce risks, and maintain preferred orders. They regulate how designers and developers act on the environment and affect their thinking about sustainability and ecology. It is this precise regulation of the most banal and seemingly insignificant details that determines the way we build and interact with the environment and constitutes the substrate of design. This substrate must be constantly questioned for the sake of our ecological well-being. If designers truly wish to minimize the environmental impact of buildings and stay relevant as a profession, they need to expand their definitions of design, start to interrogate the regulatory circuits, and recognize predesign, if we wish to call it that, as a critical aspect of spatial practice.

Part One — Agendas

INTRODUCTION

Ecology, in the widest sense, turns out to be the study of the interaction and survival of ideas and programs…in circuits.
—Gregory Bateson, *Steps to an Ecology of Mind*

Numerous past events and forgotten motivations shaped building regulations throughout their history and—as I argue in this book—influenced, albeit indirectly, the character of the contemporary standards of green construction. The chapters that make up the first part of this study examine how regulatory measures applied to single-family houses and those meant to curb environmental degradation in general evolved in relation to each other and in response to other sociopolitical and cultural events throughout the twentieth century. My ambition is twofold. The first objective is to simply analyze the regulatory activity that occurred before and after the first environmental legislation targeted residential construction, paying particular attention to the sociopolitical and economic agendas that influenced them. The second objective is to demonstrate how late the environmentally driven building regulations actually addressed the health of the environment as opposed to environmental-resource management or human climate comfort (an aspect of health and welfare).

The general aim, therefore, is to understand when the "circuits" of code making formed and what ideas and programs informed them. If ecology, as anthropologist and philosopher Gregory Bateson postulated, has to do with the understanding of "ideas and programs…in circuits," our understanding of construction ecology will remain incomplete without addressing the code-making circuits, since these circuits are an intrinsic part of ecological dynamics.[1]

The legislative acts, building regulations, and other relevant nonregulatory events discussed in this part of the book can be found in the comprehensive—although obviously not exhaustive—timeline that opens the book. The more concise timelines included below are meant to highlight the key regulatory events and suggest the agendas that shaped them. The first focuses on regulations related to residential construction, regardless of the underlying motivation. [Figure 1] The second lists the most important environmentally driven legislative acts that targeted a larger territorial scale. [Figure 2] The last timeline compares the residential and territorial-scale acts and illustrates the gradual emergence and accumulation of the driving agendas. [Figure 3]

The agendas are divided into two groups, and this is reflected in the way the abridged timelines are structured. The socioenvironmental motivations are listed on the left side of the central spine. They are: 1) health, safety, and welfare; 2) environmental-resource management; 3) environmental protection; and 4) civil rights. The agendas that are economically driven are listed on the right side of the spine, and they are: 1) real-estate market; and 2) economic growth. The central spine is divided in three to indicate the targeted scales: 1) territorial; 2) urban; and 3) building. The aim of these three chapters, as illustrated in the comparative timeline, is to convey as clearly as possible the impact of the many different motivations that shaped regulations before the advent of green building standards. My contention is that many long-forgotten decisions still actively shape the present-day codes, and this fact has important (even if indirect) environmental repercussions.

Chapter 1, "From Welfare and Safety to Ecology: Before the 1970s," concentrates on the events and ideas that shaped building regulations before the rise of environmentalism. It illustrates in five sections the gradual accumulation of regulatory measures that preceded the enactment of the first environmental acts. The first section focuses on the period before the 1920s, highlighting how scientific management affected the early health-, safety-, and welfare-driven regulations

and emphasizing the distance between health-driven climate control and the early environmental-protection movement. The second section emphasizes the market-driven motivations in a period of intense economic growth, the Roaring Twenties, and contrasts it with the agendas embraced by regional planners and first ecologists. Section three then follows up with the Great Depression. The objective is to highlight the impact of the New Deal programs on the future of the building codes and to simultaneously emphasize the distance between the agendas of code makers and the environmental emergencies that defined the Dirty Thirties. In the fourth section, the focus is on the growing importance of the Federal Housing Administration and its standards after World War II, specifically on its role in promoting suburban expansion as a means of achieving economic prosperity, despite the early signs of an impending environmental crisis. The final section focuses on the environmental action and legislation that, while still disconnected from building regulations, addressed the impact of environmental degradation on human health and welfare in the 1960s. By parsing out the driving agendas in these formative decades, this chapter highlights the distance between residential architecture and the environmental-protection movement during a period when both the science of ecology and building regulations were being defined.

Chapter 2, "Environmental Protection and Sustainable Development: 1970s–1980s," continues the analysis of the key events that shaped the environmental-protection movement and residential regulations as the two coincided in the energy-driven 1970s and then parted again in the development-focused 1980s. The objective in this chapter is twofold. In the first section, the aim is to explain the actual reasons for the adoption of the first environmental-resource-management measures that targeted energy conservation in residential construction and then highlight the specific character of the adopted measures. The second section reviews the conflicting interests that defined the 1980s: the disconnection between the agendas that drove residential construction and those that shaped the environmental movement, as well as the gap between the international environmental-protection efforts and the expanding global markets. The discussion explains the broader sociopolitical context in which the first energy-conservation measures were adopted and then analyzes how they were absorbed by the 1980s, a decade that saw a backlash against environmental regulations but prepared, even if quietly, the construction industry for the green 1990s.

Chapter 3, "Green Economy and Green Building Standards: 1990s–Present," focuses on the period in which green architecture and green building standards as we know them today were born. The first section discusses the context from which green construction standards emerged. The main issues addressed here are the international environmental action and US regulations in the context of the globalization of markets, and the green economy as a pragmatic response to the sustainable-development imperative. The discussion focuses on the multiple agendas that shaped the third-party rating systems (health and welfare, environmental-resource management, and environmental protection) before the adoption of the first state-level green building standards code in 2008. The second section, and the last in this historical overview, concentrates on the period defined by the subprime mortgage crisis, which happened to coincide with the introduction of the green building standards. The objective is to highlight the contrast between the agendas that drove the adoption of green building standards and the environmental impact of residential construction caused by the deregulated real-estate speculation.

While the environmental repercussions of the building code will be explored in more detail in the chapters that make up Part Two – Means and Methods, in this part I hope to demonstrate the general limitations of the premises that underlie green construction standards.

Figure 1 [pp. 46–47]
—
A timeline of selected residential legislation, with driving agendas

Figure 2 [pp. 48–49]
—
A timeline of selected environmental legislation, with driving agendas

Figure 3 [pp. 50–51]
—
A comparative timeline of selected environmental and residential legislation, with driving agendas

HOW TO READ THE TIMELINE

TYPE OF EVENT:

Legislation—key items

LEGISLATION RELATED TO:

Environmental | Residential | Environmental and Residential

AUTHORITY:

FG—federal, SG—state, MG—municipal, NGO—nongovernmental

1977 — Model Code for Energy Conservation in New Buildings

date (when?) | name (what?)

author (who?)

format (how?) — NGO — model code — FG

scale (where?) — building — code making, energy efficiency

key issues (why?)

INCLUDED / EXCLUDED

key sociopolitical events

---

agenda
- economic growth
- real-estate market

scale
- territorial
- urban
- **building**

agenda
- health safety welfare
- environmental resource mgmt
- environmental protection
- civil rights

Earlier local regulations:
1859 Baltimore Building Code, MD
1867 San Francisco Zoning Ordinance, CA

1905 — Building Code Recommended by the National Board of Fire Underwriters   NGO   model code   building   safety

1916 — New York Zoning Ordinance, New York, NY   MG   ordinance   urban   land use

1922 — Recommended Minimum Requirements for Small Dwelling Construction   FG   standards   building   safety, health, property value

1922 — *ASHVE Guide, 1st ed.   NGO   standards   handbook   standard setting, health, environmental mgmt

1927 — Uniform Building Code, ICBO, 1st ed.   NGO   model code   building   safety

1934 — Federal Housing Administration (FHA)   FG   agency   building, urban   governance, economic dev, financial risk mgmt, mortgage loans

1936 — Property Standards: Reqs for Mortgage Insurance, FHA   FG   standards   building, urban   financial risk mgmt, property value

---

1900
1910
1920
1930

*Progressive Era 1890–1920
World War I 1914–18
*Great Depression 1929–
*New Deal 1933–

1900-present

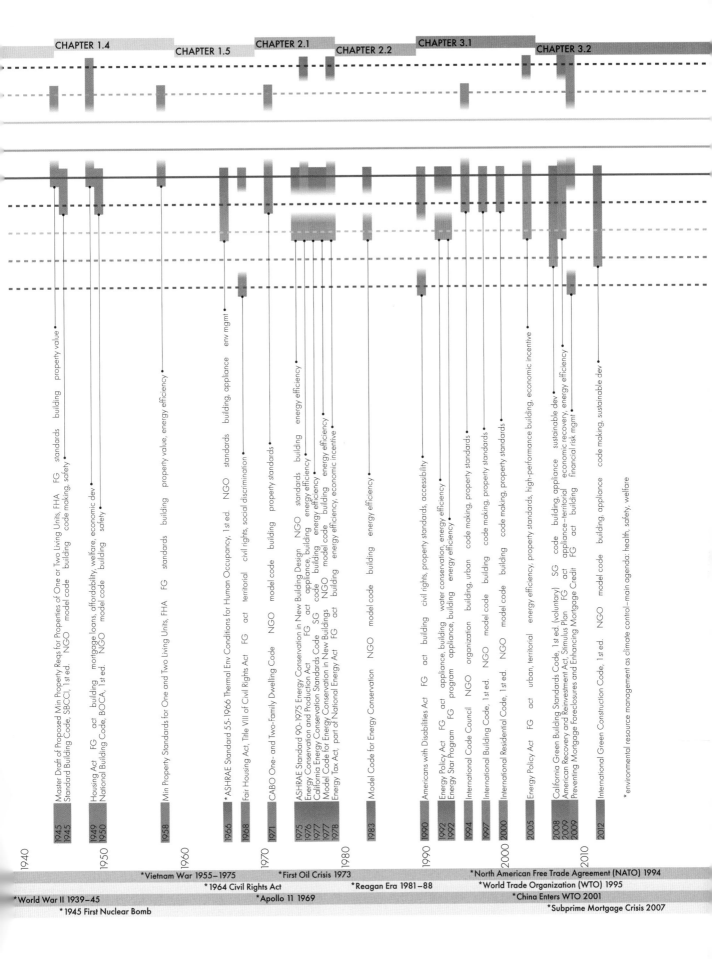

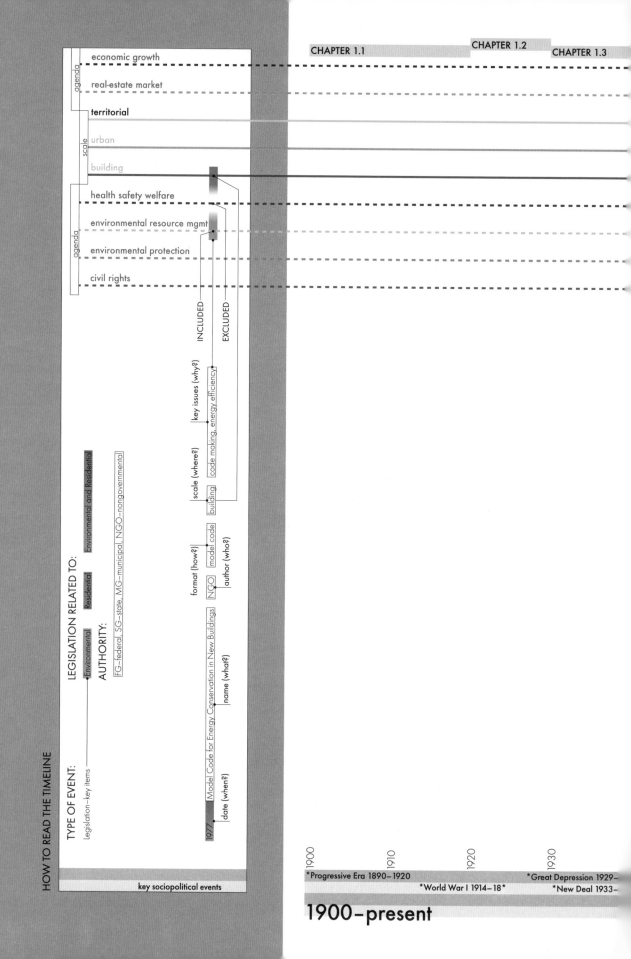

HOW TO READ THE TIMELINE

TYPE OF EVENT:

Legislation—key items

LEGISLATION RELATED TO:

Environmental   Residential   Environmental and Residential

AUTHORITY:

FG–federal, SG–state, MG–municipal, NGO–nongovernmental

date (when?) | name (what?) | format (how?) | scale (where?) | key issues (why?)

1977 | Model Code for Energy Conservation in New Buildings | NGO | model code | building | code making, energy efficiency

author (who?)

INCLUDED   EXCLUDED

agenda
economic growth
real-estate market

scale
territorial
urban
building

agenda
health safety welfare
environmental resource mgmt
environmental protection
civil rights

CHAPTER 1.1   CHAPTER 1.2   CHAPTER 1.3

key sociopolitical events

1900   1910   1920   1930

*Progressive Era 1890–1920
World War I 1914–18
*Great Depression 1929–
*New Deal 1933–

1900–present

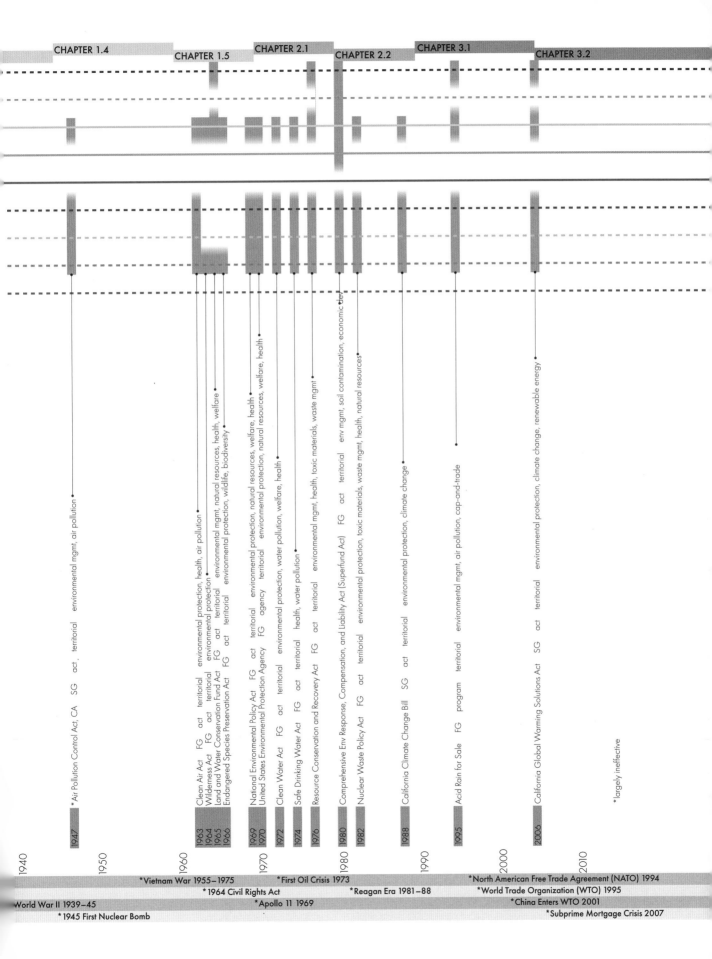

*Air Pollution Control Act, CA   SG   act.   territorial   environmental mgmt, air pollution

Clean Air Act   FG   act   territorial   environmental protection, health, air pollution
Wilderness Act   FG   act   territorial   environmental protection
Land and Water Conservation Fund Act   FG   act   territorial   environmental mgmt, natural resources, health, welfare
Endangered Species Preservation Act   FG   act   territorial   environmental protection, wildlife, biodiversity

National Environmental Policy Act   FG   act   territorial   environmental protection, natural resources, welfare, health
United States Environmental Protection Agency   FG   agency   territorial   environmental protection, natural resources, welfare, health
Clean Water Act   FG   act   territorial   environmental protection, water pollution, welfare, health
Safe Drinking Water Act   FG   act   territorial   health, water pollution
Resource Conservation and Recovery Act   FG   act   territorial   environmental mgmt, health, toxic materials, waste mgmt

Comprehensive Env Response, Compensation, and Liability Act (Superfund Act)   FG   act   territorial   env mgmt, soil contamination, economic dev
Nuclear Waste Policy Act   FG   act   territorial   environmental protection, toxic materials, waste mgmt, health, natural resources

California Climate Change Bill   SG   act   territorial   environmental protection, climate change

Acid Rain for Sale   FG   program   territorial   environmental mgmt, air pollution, cap-and-trade

California Global Warming Solutions Act   SG   act   territorial   environmental protection, climate change, renewable energy

*largely ineffective

1947

1963
1964
1965
1966

1969
1970

1972

1974

1976

1980

1982

1988

1995

2006

1940

1950

1960

1970

1980

1990

2000

2010

*Vietnam War 1955–1975   *First Oil Crisis 1973   *North American Free Trade Agreement (NATO) 1994
       *1964 Civil Rights Act   *Reagan Era 1981–88   *World Trade Organization (WTO) 1995
              *Apollo 11 1969   *China Enters WTO 2001
World War II 1939–45   *Subprime Mortgage Crisis 2007
       *1945 First Nuclear Bomb

HOW TO READ THE TIMELINE

TYPE OF EVENT: LEGISLATION RELATED TO:

Legislation—key items   Environmental   Residential   Environmental and Residential

1975   ASHRAE Standard 90-1975 Energy Conservation in New Building Design
          name (what?)
    date (when?)

FIRST INSTANCE when a new AGENDA affected the legislation

Earlier local regulations:
1867   San Francisco Zoning Ordinance
1859   Baltimore Building Code

economic growth

real-estate market

territorial

urban

building

health safety welfare

environmental resource mgmt

environmental protection

civil rights

1975 env resource mgmt

agenda

scale

agenda

CHAPTER 1.1   CHAPTER 1.2   CHAPTER 1.3

building scale

1905 health safety welfare   1916 real-estate market   1934 economic growth

Bldg Code Rec by Nat Board of Fire Underwriters

New York Zoning Ordinance

*ASHVE Guide

Federal Housing Administration

1905   1916   1922 1922   1927   1934 1935

territorial scale

1900   1910   1920   1930

*Progressive Era 1890–1920   *Great Depression 1929-

World War I 1914–18   *New Deal 1933-

key sociopolitical events

1900–present

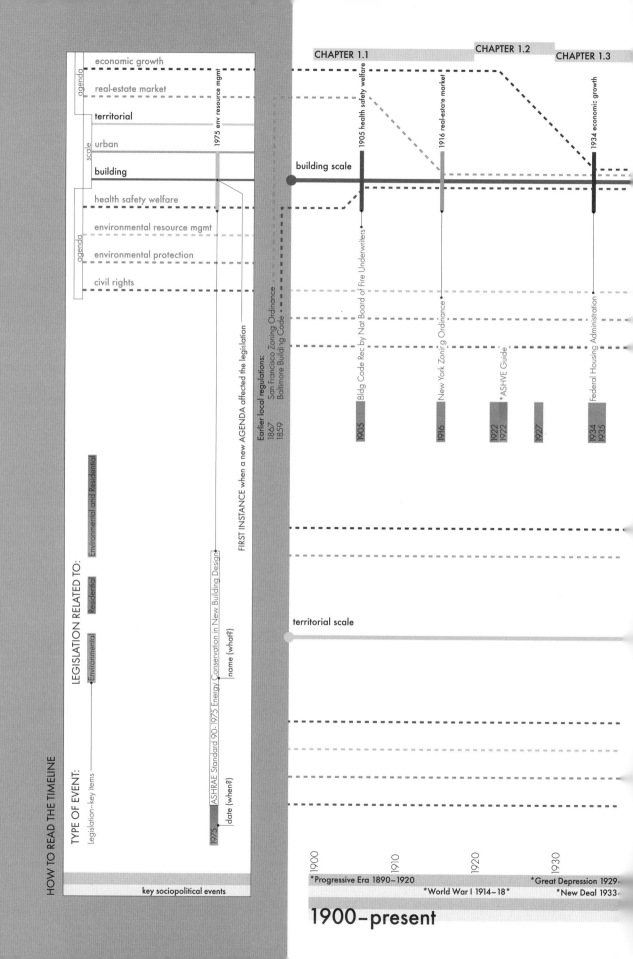

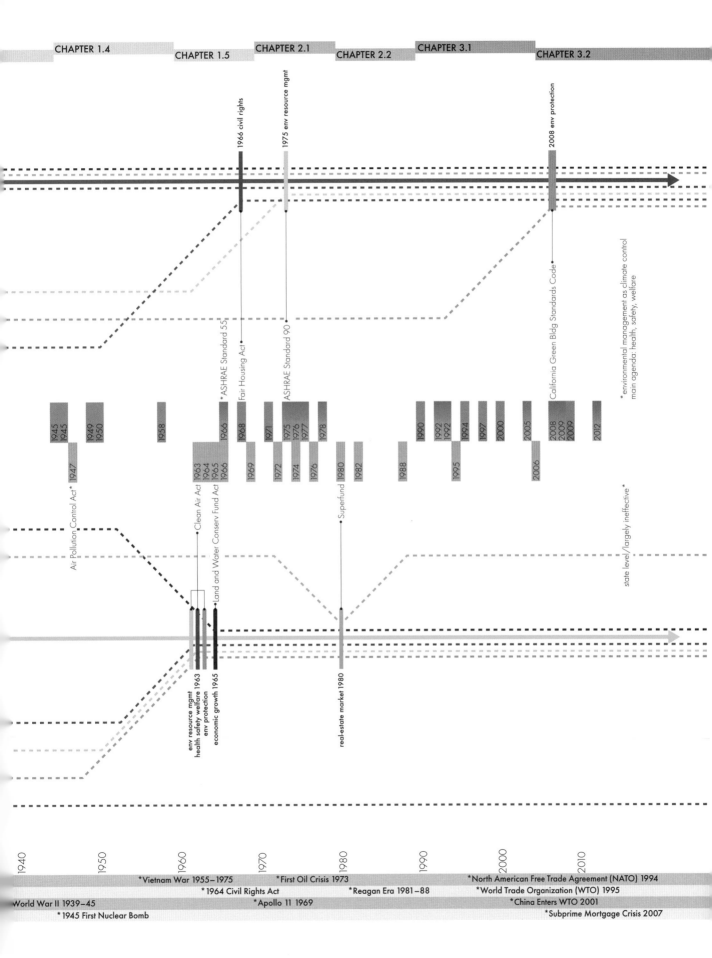

1966 civil rights

1975 env resource mgmt

2008 env protection

* ASHRAE Standard 55

Fair Housing Act

ASHRAE Standard 90

California Green Bldg Standards Code

* environmental management as climate control
main agenda: health, safety, welfare

1945
1945

1949
1950

1958

1966

1968

1971

1975
1976
1977

1978

1990

1992
1992

1994

1997

2000

2005

2008
2009
2009

2012

1947

1963
1964
1965
1966

1969

1972

1974

1976

1980

1982

1988

1995

2006

Air Pollution Control Act*

Clean Air Act

Land and Water Conserv Fund Act

Superfund

state level/largely ineffective*

env resource mgmt
health safety welfare 1963
env protection
economic growth 1965

real-estate market 1980

1940

1950

1960

1970

1980

1990

2000

2010

*Vietnam War 1955–1975   *First Oil Crisis 1973   *North American Free Trade Agreement (NATO) 1994

*1964 Civil Rights Act   *Reagan Era 1981–88   *World Trade Organization (WTO) 1995

World War II 1939–45   *Apollo 11 1969   *China Enters WTO 2001

*1945 First Nuclear Bomb   *Subprime Mortgage Crisis 2007

FROM WELFARE AND SAFETY TO ECOLOGY: BEFORE THE 1970S

1.1. Standardizing Human Welfare: Before the 1920s

The late nineteenth and early twentieth centuries were an intense period of standardization. Improvements in manufacturing methods and changes in workflow management transformed industrial production. Initially concerned with currency, weights, and measures, standards laboratories gradually evolved into research bodies charged with the task of improving (and later certifying) the safety, quality, and uniformity of materials, products, services, and eventually standards themselves. In 1901, the U.S. Department of Commerce established the National Bureau of Standards, recognizing that standardization was a fundamental step toward social and economic progress.[1] One of the

—
Framing residential construction—dimensional lumber

symbols of the Progressive Era, the Ford Model T, the first automobile affordable to an average American, started being produced in 1908. Its immediate commercial success and eventual impact on American society were in part due to the first moving assembly line introduced at Ford's Highland Park Michigan plant in 1913, yet, the ultimate success of these improvements hinged on the efficiency of manual workers, both during and outside of the working hours.

First efforts to standardize workflow were made by Frederick Winslow Taylor, the founder of scientific (or as he initially called it, "shop") management. His influential ideas were eventually summarized in *Principles of Scientific Management*.[2] Yet while these efforts improved efficiency and contributed to a rapid development of industries, they also accelerated the growth of dense working-class neighborhoods clustered around factories. This trend amplified the already existing concerns about the order, safety, health, and welfare of worker communities and triggered an interest in the potential application of scientific management to workers' lives outside factories. Most of the urban-scale regulatory efforts during the Progressive Era addressed such issues as congestion and compatibility of land uses. Long before the famous New York Zoning Resolution introduced the first citywide code in 1916, zoning ordinances were enacted in California; Washington, DC, pioneered regulation of building heights; and New Jersey introduced the first subdivision regulations.[3] Drinking water provision was first regulated in Boston in An Act to Provide for A Metropolitan Water Supply (1895). By 1915, the United States produced its first sewage manual, which provided indispensable knowledge for cities expanding their water supply infrastructures.[4]

A highly influential urban-reform idea was popularized in 1893, during the World's Columbian Exposition in Chicago, which was designed by, among others, landscape architect Frederick Law Olmsted. The City Beautiful movement advocated for urban renewal through beautification and promoted the presence of nature in the city, construction of civic centers, public parks, and tree-lined boulevards. The movement, and urban planner Ebenezer Howard's book *Garden Cities of To-morrow*, greatly influenced the First National Conference on City Planning that took place in 1909, the year in which the most ambitious City Beautiful plan, the Plan of Chicago, was also unveiled.[5]

Another influential event, the 1913 Chicago City Club competition, attracted both garden-city proponents and urban reformers, but the jury seemed to favor optimum ratios of density to cost over new organizational protocols. What was to shape the American residential suburbs was the idea expressed by town planner Raymond Unwin, who claimed that a smaller number of houses surrounded by open space was more economical and could also provide badly needed green space—and space in general was still plentiful.[6] From its establishment in 1917, the American City Planning Institute launched a dedicated program to analyze and compare different urban schemes and to gradually develop standards and recommendations for the new American middle classes escaping congested tenements.[7] Industrial standardization not only indirectly triggered the need for urban planning, but it also influenced the planning methods themselves.

While American urban planners and designers were experimenting with optimal subdivision patterns for low-density green residential neighborhoods, building regulations were already quite commonly (although unsystematically) used to curb unsafe construction practices and prevent fires. Individual municipalities officially adopted general building codes in the 1850s. Baltimore, for example, had its first code in 1859. The first model tenement, the New York Workmen's Home, was built in 1855, and the first building act to specifically address living conditions in the tenements housing the poorest workers was passed in 1867 as the New York Tenement House Act. In 1901, the New York State Tenement House Act imposed the first statewide measures: fire escapes, windows facing a source of fresh air and light in each room, privies, running water, maximum lot coverage, and, in a later edition, garbage removal, outward-facing windows, and additional fire safeguards. A decade later, the National Housing Association authored the 1910 Model Tenement House Law.

In 1905, an early form of a model building code was proposed by a nongovernmental organization, the National Board of Fire Underwriters.[8] The code addressed a wide range of issues in relation to different building classes. It differentiated between residences (one- and two-family dwellings, apartments, tenements, and other, temporary types of lodgings), offices, and public buildings. It discussed basic provisions, such as minimum amount of living space, means of egress, natural light, and ventilation. It addressed aspects of building techniques, such as quality of materials, structural loads, and fire resistance of different construction systems. Details concerning heating, plumbing, and drainage systems were also included. Most of the aspects addressed by our contemporary building codes were already contained in these early recommendations. The document consisted of 263 pages and referred to a list of more specific technical standards that had been developed by the same National Board of Fire Underwriters since its creation in 1866. Ten years later, in 1915, the first private organization dedicated to code making, the Building Officials and Code Administrators International, was established to collect local knowledge and promote uniformity in building regulations, an objective only achieved some eighty years later, when the first International Building Code was published by the International Code Council.

While planners were modernizing cities and early code makers were imposing minimum safety requirements on housing, philanthropists, housewives, engineers, and architects were reforming the idea of the house itself. In *The Natural House*, Frank Lloyd Wright asked, recalling his early years: "What was the matter with the typical American house? Well, just for an honest beginning, it lied about everything."[9] Yet while Wright complained about the absolute reign of joinery and lack of unity or "sense of earth," household reformers focused on efficiency.

The genealogy of domestic efficiency can be traced back to Catherine Beecher, recognized as the forerunner of studies of efficiency and comfort in housework.[10] Concerned with domestic economy rather than aesthetics, Beecher's dynamic vision of the household paved the way for the pragmatic house in which most of the American suburbanites now live. It inspired the early twentieth-century studies and publications promoting efficient homes in the spirit of

positivism of the Progressive Era and those influenced by scientific management.[11] In the meantime, efforts were made to render efficient and standardized house plans available to the masses; Americans were moving into the first Pacific Ready-Cut Homes.[12]

In these early efforts, an attempt was made to examine natural processes with scientific precision in order to provide optimal management of environmental comfort and to legitimate the choices. Climate control was perceived as an aspect of household efficiency, and environmental technology was promoted as a means to improve levels of sanitation and health. The opportunity to define the meaning of environmental comfort was, however, snubbed by most architects and interior decorators, and the task was ultimately left to engineers and their methods.[13] Moreover, environmental technology arrived in households relatively late, and when it did, it was inserted rather than integrated into the design.[14]

There were exceptions to this tendency, however. Recognizing that "bowels, circulation, and nerves were new in buildings," Wright accepted that "they had come to stay and a building could no longer remain a mere shell in which life was somehow to make shift as it might."[15] He developed some of the most innovative ways to integrate environmental control with architectural design, for example, in his 1909 Baker and Robie Houses. Whether inserted as an afterthought or skillfully integrated, climate-management technology was to transform households forever. It assumed the role of a mediator between the house and nature (or at least the weather), permanently influencing ideas of domestic comfort and our daily relationship with natural elements.

First attempts to address the well-being of the natural environment itself concentrated on large-scale territorial dynamics, far beyond the scope of individual households. Early natural preservation projects, among them the creation of the National Park Service in 1916, were inspired by nineteenth-century naturalists, such as Henry David Thoreau, for whom man was "part and parcel of Nature," and possible thanks to the subsequent efforts of such preservationists as John Muir.[16] However, utilitarian attitudes of conservationists, best represented by forester and politician Gifford Pinchot and mainly interested in efficient use of resources and sustainable yield, would increasingly take over.[17] The managerial attitude manifested itself in the creation of the National Wildlife Reserve System in 1903 and the United States Forest Service created in 1905. Nature was increasingly perceived as an external entity (or an "externalized" source of resources), which could be controlled—preserved or conserved, but always managed—by man and his increasingly complex technologies.

Scientists, yet to be called ecologists, were only starting to comprehend natural dynamics that politicians, planners, and legislators were tinkering with.[18] Most of them ignored diplomat and conservationist George Perkins Marsh, who extensively wrote about land management, and, as one of the first, called for (ecological) caution, warning in 1864 that "our limited faculties are at present, perhaps forever, incapable of weighing their immediate, still more their ultimate consequences."[19] Long before the term *Anthropocene* gained currency, Marsh was fully aware of the fact that, even if limited, these faculties were making man—like fires, floods, or storms— "a geographic agency."[20]

1.2. Building the Real-Estate Market: 1920s

By the 1920s, the risks posed by unconstrained urban and industrial development were becoming clear. Most urban planners continued to work on zoning regulations to internally manage growth. The decade was an important period in the history of urban codes: the Village of Euclid Zoning Ordinance was passed in 1922, and in 1926, the Supreme Court defended its contested constitutionality. The case gave name to the oldest form of land-use control, Euclidean zoning, which prescribed permitted land uses, setbacks, and maximum heights of buildings and controlled means of egress and access to light.[21] Since zoning was considered an important component of the urban reform, the federal government encouraged it by publishing two sets of independent legislative guidelines, one suggesting rules relative to zoning-code adoption and the other to urban planning. However, since zoning and planning were not bound together, in many cities, zoning regulations are in place to this day despite the absence of an official development plan, whether local or regional.[22]

Alarmed by the shrinking gap between expanding human settlements and protected wilderness, some planners did, however, focus on the larger picture. Historian and philosopher of technology Lewis Mumford warned: "In the very act of seizing all the habitable parts of the earth, we have systematically misused and neglected our possession."[23] Mumford was an active supporter of the Regional Planning Association of America (RPAA), founded in 1923, whose members strived to combine lessons learned from garden-city planners, wilderness preservationists, and resource conservationists to develop decentralized forms of networked settlements organically interacting with natural dynamics. Their projects were also inspired by pioneering urban planner Patrick Geddes, who understood cities and human systems to be intrinsically related to larger regions and dependent on their biogeographies and geomorphologies.[24] Members of the RPAA contributed to the creation of state-level land-use plans; however, implementation of interstate projects proved problematic without some form of governmental coordination (which Herbert Hoover as president fiercely opposed), and many of them eventually dedicated themselves to smaller urban-development projects.[25]

The Tennessee Valley Authority (TVA), established in 1933 (and possible thanks to a changed political climate during President Roosevelt's New Deal era), stands out as a unique example of a regional economic-development agency that holistically considered preservation and management of natural resources as part of a successful regional-planning strategy. The team included planner and conservationist Benton MacKaye, famous for his 1921 Appalachian Trail and for his campaigns against unplanned regional sprawl. For MacKaye, the TVA project was a rare opportunity to test ideas in practice. The strategy he adopted was to develop open-ended protocols and flexible frameworks—neither aesthetically pleasing landscape patterns nor rigidly engineered plans—for an inevitably indeterminate future economic development.[26]

Members of the RPAA were clearly aware of, and inspired by, new scientific theories and developments in ecology. Notions of emergence, aspects of evolution, and process-based organicist thinking influenced their most innovative concepts and proposals. Although philosopher Alfred North Whitehead's 1925 Lowell lectures entitled *Science and the Modern World* offered perhaps the most precise critique of mechanistic thought, many other thinkers and natural scientists embraced a form of organicist approach in

that period.[27] Geddes, Mumford, and MacKaye embraced the indeterminate and interdependent nature of ecological systems and believed in the efficacy of natural systems of checks and balances. However, the future generations of planners would see more promise in the emerging New Ecology, which embraced the managerial ethos of the era and the precision of mathematical models.[28] The fascination with evolution and process was gradually supplanted by an interest in circumscribed dynamics that could be reduced to concrete quantities, modeled more precisely, and eventually applied to achieve specific outcomes. It was the tangibility of bioeconomics developed by zoologist and ecologist Charles Elton in his studies of community structures that would lay the foundations for systems ecology.[29] These ideas would eventually also shape environmental-resource management and legislation in the decades to come.

In architecture, organicist thought found its best expression in the work of Wright, who exclaimed, "Conceive now that an entire building might grow up out of conditions as a plant grows up out of soil and yet be free to be itself, to 'live its own life according to Man's Nature.'"[30] Yet it was the same managerial ethos that pervaded New Ecology that would shape the organization and climate management of American homes through new regulations and standards. The second of the three principal code-making organizations, the International Conference of Building Officials (ICBO), was created in 1922. In 1927, the ICBO authored the Uniform Building Code, which would remain in use on the West Coast and across most of the Midwest until the introduction of the International Building Code in 1997.

In 1922, the American Society of Heating and Ventilating Engineers (ASHVE) published the first edition of its guide, which contained data and instructions pertaining to design and construction of heating and ventilating installations, as well as many regulatory recommendations.[31] Unfortunately, although it was emphasized in the preface that the guide was directed toward "the engineer, the architects and the contractor alike," it was written in a language that most architects must have found simply inaccessible. Two years later, the ASHVE produced the first version of the Comfort Zone diagram, the result of a study of physiological reaction of (unclothed) humans (in front of a fan) to temperature, humidity, and air movement. Adjusted over the years (with more and more quantitative data pertaining to, for example, metabolic rates and impact of clothing), the diagram became a fundamental component of the American Society of Heating, Refrigerating and Air-Conditioning Engineers (ASHRAE) Standard 55 Thermal Comfort Conditions for Human Occupancy (first published in 1966). The diagram standardized the idea of comfort representing it as a well-demarcated region in a field defined by varying temperatures and humidity levels.

The quest for efficiency and standardization that was shaping codes and standards of climate management continued to define the tone of household manuals as well. Yet although healthy lifestyle determined the character of the celebrated houses that Dr. Philip Lovell commissioned Rudolf Schindler and Richard Neutra to build in the Los Angeles area, the motivations among the general public were shifting from health and welfare to a new set of underlying agendas: consumption of household appliances and homeownership.[32]

In 1923, American home economist Christine Frederick published another popular household manual.[33] Although many of the promoted methods (e.g., precise inventories and schedules) did not enter average households, as architectural scholar Witold Rybczynski observes, domestic engineering affected their physical organization, especially the efficiency of

kitchens, and had a tremendous impact on the market of household appliances.[34] While some reformists, such as Charlotte Perkins Gilman, were calling for a complete revision of domestic roles, Frederick was interested in rendering homemaking more efficient without disrupting the traditional family structure and its importance for the economy. In *Selling Mrs. Consumer*, Frederick aligned herself even further with the emerging economic reality, focusing on the spending power of housewives.[35] Recognizing women (and children) as an important but previously ignored consumer type was crucial in the context of the overall economy increasingly relying on single-family households as an important source of growth and social stability. The house was becoming a commodity, and its efficiency and durability were fundamental prerequisites for its marketability.

The federal administration actively endorsed private initiatives that promoted home ownership and provided technical support to future homeowners.[36] In 1923, the Better Homes in America (BHA) campaign initiated its Better Homes Week program, which promoted the construction of demonstration houses across the country and distributed information about homeownership. The BHA was to become an important privately developed model for the federal campaigns to promote standardization and efficiency in the housing industry during the 1930s.[37]

While leveraging private initiatives, the federal government was also developing its own programs to address housing shortage. In 1922, the Department of Commerce released the first federal Recommended Minimum Requirements for Small Dwelling Construction. In contrast to the 1905 Building Code Recommended by the National Board of Fire Underwriters, the aim of the Recommended Minimums—as explained in the introduction—was to simplify and standardize the codes in order to conserve resources in the face of "high cost and inactivity in building industries."[38] While professional bodies and municipal governments were working to improve the safety of buildings in general, the intention of the federal government was to streamline construction and delivery of small privately built and owned dwellings. In fact, the report expressed the need to differentiate between rules applied to complex buildings and regulations applicable to simple dwellings. By promoting a simplified set of standards for small dwellings, it indirectly determined the future character of the American houses. The aim of the report was, of course, also to reduce low-grade construction and improve the quality of housing stock, but the principal reason for these concerns was to control investment risks.

It was clear that the future of American housing depended on a skillful combination of public and private endeavors and had to satisfy both government's goals and private interests of the builders and realtors.[39] The private and federal efforts of the 1920s culminated in the second edition of Recommended Minimum Requirements for Small Dwelling Construction, published in 1932.[40] A year earlier, President Hoover's Conference on Home Building and Home Ownership addressed city planning and subdivision methods in the style of the 1913 Chicago City Club competition. While the Recommended Minimums were shaping the house itself, the outcomes of the conference would greatly influence the shape of urban developments and provide support to the community builders active in the postcrisis period.[41]

While most voices prized homeownership for its positive impact on economic growth and social stability, the dark side of the everyman's dream home (and life) was exposed by artists. Describing the Everyman's House, one of the demonstration cottages built by the BHA, reformer Caroline Bartlett Crane emphasized the role of homeownership as a means of control of migrating masses of workers.[42] Meanwhile, in his 1920 film One Week, Buster Keaton mocked the emerging standards of building practices for their impact on domestic life. As architect Iñaki Ábalos notes, "Keaton has no alternatives to hand, no other model of thinking to oppose to that of the manual, and will blindly proceed to mechanically assemble what turns out to be a cruel metaphor of the destiny of the couple and the institutional family of our times."[43] A cruel metaphor for both "home" and "house" indeed. The homemaking standards that even such keen domestic engineers as Lillian Gilbreth saw as an individual choice of each family were to become recommendations, then minimum requirements, and eventually legally binding code.[44] From what might have initially been a creative—to echo Georges Canguilhem—"normative intention," in a short span of time crystallized into a conservative imperative reflecting the sociopolitical demands that emerged in the 1920s.[45]

1.3. Growing out of the Depression: 1930s–1945

The Roaring Twenties culminated in a spectacular market crash and the bankruptcy of thousands of banks. Still, the efforts initiated by the Hoover administration in the 1920s laid the foundations for the New Deal programs. Launched to offset the effects of the Great Depression, President Roosevelt's initiatives dedicated to residential construction supported construction of affordable housing, improving mortgage-financing mechanisms, and promoting homeownership. The National Housing Act of 1934, also known as the Capehart Act, established the Federal Housing Administration (FHA), an agency authorized to provide insurance to private lending institutions that would then offer low-interest, long-term loans to individual homebuyers. The authors of the National Housing Act and the creators of the FHA were not architects, planners, or philanthropists. The FHA was created by representatives of real-estate, finance, and insurance companies, who together crafted a mixed-economy system that supported private entrepreneurship by guaranteeing low-risk investments and securing returns to the real-estate industry. By doing so, it provided access to cheap housing to low-wage workers and the emerging middle class. As architect and historian Jonathan Massey observes, "Instead of socializing housing production, as Ackerman and others had advocated, the National Housing Act socialized risk."[46] Housing was to become an industry, and to function well the product had to be made as predictable and controllable as Ford's Model T. Efficiency and comfort became selling points and quality of construction a guarantee both for the lenders and the borrowers. Increasingly perceived as a commodity and a site of consumption, the home ultimately turned into a loan security.

It became clear that the protocols of production and delivery needed to be further standardized to reduce risks. Based on the knowledge accumulated by President Hoover's Bureau of Commerce and the successful campaigns of the BHA, the FHA gradually developed and popularized its own criteria of assessment, influencing the shape of individual homes and that of subdivisions and neighborhoods. As planning expert Marc Weiss points out, realtors, distrusting local politicians and planning commissions, actively supported the FHA standards to defend their own interests.[47] The mortgage conditions were so beneficial that both lenders and borrowers were happy to adopt the FHA standards. Eventually, developers started applying for simultaneous approval of large numbers of identical homes, a practice that was well received by the FHA since it improved coordination and helped reduce risks.[48]

In 1936, the FHA published the first Property Standards (focused mainly on neighborhood design and planning), and in 1937, it released the Minimum Construction Requirements for New Dwellings (which addressed construction methods).[49] In 1942, the content of both documents was combined into the Property Standards and Minimum Construction Requirements, but the publication was rarely used until after World War II, when the FHA significantly updated it. By the end of the war, the foundations for a parallel regulatory system were in place. When it came to one- or two-living-unit dwellings, the FHA standards just about replaced local building regulations where they were either still missing or less stringent.[50]

Initially, the FHA subdivision guidelines greatly improved construction standards. Larger, forward-looking community builders contributed to it by testing new subdivision patterns and experimenting with private deed restrictions to ensure long-term quality.[51] With time, the FHA guidelines crystallized into a perfect regulatory system. However, while minimizing risks and ensuring smooth operations, they also greatly limited architects and stopped innovation in urban design for decades. Wright deplored the situation, referring to the influence exerted by the FHA in the following words: "Our government forces the homemaker into the real estate business if he wants a home at all."[52] In 1939, his East Lansing Usonian houses failed to meet the underwriting criteria and were denied the FHA-insured mortgage. The design remained on paper.[53] Wright's own minimum standard proved incompatible with the early FHA ideals, although the principles he developed for the middle-income Americans in his 1930s Usonian houses would greatly influence the spatial organization of many suburban houses in the postwar period, defining the spirit of the contemporary ranch-type house in general.

Such architectural visionaries as Buckminster Fuller, Neutra, and Keck & Keck dedicated efforts to redefining the future of the American household. These innovators often integrated structural experimentation with concerns related to climate management. In the 1934 Beard House, Neutra experimented with a hollow metal load-bearing paneling wall system, which, in theory, also distributed conditioned air. Keck & Keck's houses, built with modern materials, featured various climate-control strategies and mechanisms, including movable external blinds and evaporative cooling roofs. Yet only those inventions that helped streamline construction and lower costs influenced the shape of the average house. Eventually, even Neutra accepted that wood framing was the way Americans wanted to build their houses.[54] Walter Gropius, too, "framed" his own "modern" house near Cambridge.

Meanwhile, such organizations as the Housing Division of the Pierce Foundation, Bemis Industries, or the U.S. Housing Authority led some of the most important experiments in modular construction technologies. While architect Ernst Neufert was publishing his famous design norms in Germany, Albert Bemis, engineer, businessman, and inventor of the Cubical Module Method of design, was summarizing his efforts to codify the construction of small, affordable dwellings in *Rational Design*, the third volume of *The Evolving House*.[55] Rationalization, however, quickly produced side effects. As observed by Reyner Banham, with the emergence of modular building components, "a dimensional inertia was built up, which resists variations of the tile sizes, and constrains the dimensions of any new technologies."[56]

Researchers also continued to study household efficiency. Still, as historian Greg Hise explains, in contrast to the Taylorist pursuit of specialization, the aim of these "laboratories for living" was to develop flexible multipurpose spatial arrangements in order to reduce the need for many separate rooms dedicated to specialized tasks. Eventually, private and federal efforts toward "degadgeting" the house created new standards. A combined cooking and dining space and the absence of basements became common. Although the aim was to eliminate substandard housing, critics described the American version of *Existenzminimum* as "*reductio ad absurdum*."[57] The effect was far from the "interior spaciousness" that Wright achieved in his designs, although he was equally critical of domestic functions translated into separate boxes.[58] A "minimum" became the "optimum," and by the end of World War II, the United States had a dwelling norm and a perfect product. All of this took place with little contribution from renowned architects. Wright's East Lansing Usonian houses were denied mortgage.

While human existence was being condensed to a minimum, the earth, as Mumford warned back in 1927, was being reduced to flat rectangles, and…dust.[59] If Fallingwater—Wright's masterpiece of landscape integration—had little impact on the way average houses would fit in with the environment, ecologists were more preoccupied with dust storms, insect plagues, and the alarming effects of the modern farming methods used in the Midwest. These were the Dirty Thirties. Unfortunately, scientists were still debating about what exactly should be protected, and even the little and imprecise existing knowledge was only starting to be considered as relevant to land-use planning. In his influential 1935 book *Deserts on the March*, ecologist Paul Sears deplored this situation, speaking against "a system which tolerates private privilege in utter disregard of public policy, and which as yet does not understand how science may be made to help in the determining of policy."[60]

In the meantime, the problems discussed by ecologists were the nature of ecological relationships and the role of man. While some scientists were eager to follow American plant ecologist Frederic Clements's natural climax theories and protect the grass-bison biome, others agreed with British pioneer ecologist Arthur G. Tansley, who pointed out that the modern man could no longer be isolated from ecological studies, as there was little land that he left untouched. Strikingly, while some experts were simply acknowledging the devastating effects of farming and advocating for a more conservative land use, others were suggesting that there was no ideal natural climax state and man was free to manipulate the environmental dynamics in function of his needs. Humans could simply redesign the world in search of an ideal anthropic climax state. It was hard to accept that man was an invasive species characterized by a managerial attitude and equipped with a powerful technology. Although these disagreements would keep on dividing ecologists in the future and often served as a justification for invasive land-use policies, one of the important results of the Dirty Thirties, as pointed out by environmental historian Donald Worster, was the fact that "the new profession of ecologists found themselves for the first time serving as land-use advisers to an entire nation."[61] Even if still timidly, ecology entered planning.

1.4. Prospering by Expansion: 1945–1950s

Following Charles Elton's bioeconomic vision of nature, many ecologists were gradually switching from Whitehead's organismic holism and MacKaye's flexible protocols to quantifiable systems models. Tansley's "ecosystem" concept suited the era of systems theory and operations research better than Clements's "superorganism."[62] Following biophysicist Alfred J. Lotka's work in the 1920s, the first energy budgets appeared in 1940s. An early study, which preceded ecologist Howard T. Odum's work, assessed the productivity of a natural lake. Yet, as Worster explains, "One cannot help but see in such research the agronomic influence at work: the concern for crops, productivity, yield, and efficiency now being translated into a broader ecological model."[63] The tendency to think about natural systems in managerial terms echoed Pinchot's Progressive Era conservationist methods, but it was also clearly inspired by the ongoing wartime research agendas.[64] Ecosystem ecology emerged from that context, and such prominent ecologists as Raymond L. Lindeman, G. Evelyn Hutchinson, and Eugene Odum all embraced quantity-based stock and flow models to study natural systems.[65]

Paradoxically, to comprehend these systems in their complexity, ecologists had to reduce them to more and more discrete and manageable physiochemical processes. The risk was that their management would remain equally disjointed. While the analytical approach of New Ecology equipped postwar conservationists with tangible tools, many environmentalists perceived it as a threat. For those who saw nature as a community rather than a resource, the managerial ethos—as clearly expressed in the title of the first UN Scientific Conference on the Conservation and Utilization of Resources held in 1949 in New York—was isolating humans from nature. Forester and conservationist Aldo Leopold's "The Land Ethic" provided a poignant expression of this disillusion with the modern approach to nature and marked an important moment of shift. Leopold's well-established scientific expertise combined with a newly acquired biocentric ethic helped launch the so-called Age of Ecology and inspired a new generation to appreciate nature again as a community rather than a commodity.[66] Regardless of the differences in methodological approach, many scientists actively supported conservation efforts. In 1946, the Ecologists' Union was formed by a group of scientists "to take 'direct action' to save threatened natural areas." The union evolved into a leading environmental organization and is now called the Nature Conservancy.[67]

These and other similar efforts resulted in the first (although little known) environmental acts. In 1947, in reaction to severe smog episodes, California passed the United States' first Air Pollution Control Act, and in 1955, the federal government, for the first time, recognized air pollution as a danger to public health and welfare.[68] However, despite numerous attempts to regulate the pollution in rivers and lakes—the Federal Water Pollution Control Act was enacted in 1948, and other congress bills allocated funds for important research and information campaigns—federal air- and water-pollution control would remain effectively nonexistent until the 1960s.[69]

Essentially disconnected from large-scale environmental concerns, urban areas were preparing for an era of dramatic expansion. The wartime experiments in mass-produced housing prepared the ground for the era of merchant builders. In 1946, Los Angeles passed a new zoning ordinance, which remapped most of the city and rezoned most of its agricultural land for residential use to comply with the FHA subdivision standards and to satisfy the demand for large tracts of land. The times of community-oriented developers were coming to an end, and the West Coast's version of Levittown—called Lakewood—was hastily being sketched onto a bean field. In *Holy Land*, essayist D. J. Waldie explains how Lakewood was designed:

Louis Boyar's wife told her husband to redesign the street plan he had sketched.

She wanted him to add parkway panels and parallel service roads to separate the residential streets from highway traffic. She told her husband that children like to play in the street, and how dangerous the streets were in Chicago where she grew up. When construction began in 1950, the *Los Angeles Daily* News said the new community was "scientifically planned."[70]

While American houses were inarguably becoming a perfectly standardized commodity, they were also an expression of an attainable American dream, a fact often denied by the critics of the postwar sprawl. To use Waldie's words again, "This pattern—of asphalt, grass, concrete, grass—is as regular as any thought of God's." And to that disillusioned wartime generation, what counted was precisely that: it was a thought of God's dedicated to them, the ex-GIs.[71] With thousands of families ready to move in, planning and design were stripped to a minimum. Predictability became a marketing tool and the key to deliverability. The merchant builders mastered the process of quickly assembling traditional cottages and ranch-style houses perfectly aligned with FHA standards. Although Joseph Eichler's fascination with modern design helped popularize the design and lifestyle associated with the Case Study houses, his firm Eichler Homes was a small niche.[72] Crude but tested technologies persisted against visions of a perfectly prefabricated future.[73] As architectural scholar Keller Easterling points out, "in many ways prefabrication techniques, ironically, served as a model for the regimentation of the assembly process in conventional stick construction."[74]

Innovation was selectively absorbed by the market, but the federal government made sure that the right regulatory structure was in place to support it. While the first postwar act, the Housing Act of 1948, continued to focus on the provision of credit for lower-cost homes, it also emphasized the need to standardize building codes and measurements in construction. The objective of President Truman's landmark Housing Act of 1949 was, on the other hand, "a decent home and a suitable living environment for every American family," and while it continued to address mortgage insurance, it also provided funding and mechanisms for slum clearance and urban redevelopment.[75] A year after the passage of this act, Building Officials and Code Administrators International published the first edition of its National Building Code, which remained in use on the East Coast and throughout the Midwest until the introduction of the International Building Code in 1997.

In the meantime, the FHA continued to define the shape of federally insured subdivisions and homes by refining its underwriting standards. In 1945, it released the Master Draft of Proposed Minimum Property Requirements for Properties of One or Two Living Units.[76] While individual states initially issued their own amended versions of the document, by the time the 1958 edition was released as the Minimum Property Standards for Properties of One or Two Living Units, all differences were erased to achieve a complete uniformity across the country. The Minimum Property Standards, now occupying 315 pages, became "a de facto building code," yet, since desirability was paramount, safety and welfare consideration were listed next to prescriptive descriptions of closets.[77]

It is worth also pointing out (based on research done by the Alliance to Save Energy) that "residential [energy] efficiency standards were first established in the 1950s…in response to mortgage defaults on federally insured loans on homes with high utility bills."[78] In fact, although air cooling was not yet regulated, as the first domestic air conditioners only started to be advertised around 1948, heating and insulation standards were addressed in multiple articles of the 1950s editions of the FHA Minimum

Property Standards.[79] However, the aim was purely economic: reduce operational costs of heating in order to improve the desirability of the property and ultimately minimize the financial risk for the mortgage lenders. However, since standardized postwar tracts equipped with energy- and water-demanding appliances catered to the perfect Mr. and Mrs. Consumer, energy conservation inevitably became a secondary problem. Profit and economic growth rather than the state of the environment motivated both the developers and the FHA.

The American postwar house, shaped by the positivist outlooks of domestic engineers of the Progressive Era and wartime ergonomists, became a perfect expression of the dream visualized by the federal government for the "men in the gray flannel suits."[80] In *The Good Life*, Iñaki Ábalos dedicates a chapter to Jacques Tati's 1957 film *Mon Oncle*, in which he contrasts the positivist ideals embodied in the life and the house of the Arpels with alternative ways of living of *mon oncle* (the old-fashioned uncle) and with alternative forms of, to use his words, "subjectivism or vitalism" that those models express.[81] Unlike the European Arpels, the American suburbanites did not embrace modern orthodoxy, but it would be an error to assume that they all instead inhabited the celebrated pragmatist houses depicted by David Hockney in his paintings.[82] The houses that the American men in the gray flannel suits would live in, were, yes, in some ways also modern and affordable, but they did not reflect the celebrated ideals of the Case Study houses that Eichler tried to popularize as an alternative to the cottages standardized by the FHA. Unlike Tati's European Arpels who engaged in a modernist spectacle, American Raths from Sloan Wilson's novel *The Man in the Gray Flannel Suit* (1955) and thousands of other nostalgic pragmatists across the continent enjoyed the coziness of a better home (in America) without noticing that their cottage—

maybe a guarantee of a relative wealth, surely an expression of a comfortable predictability and a longing for a bygone past—was little more than a perfectly standardized bank collateral, adorned to simulate the old ways of the American settler.

1.5. Normalizing Environmental Welfare: 1960s

According to Ned Eichler, Joseph's son, himself a developer and writer, the following decade brought little technological advance since delivering tracts of identical dream cottages required none.[83] By the end of the 1950s, the construction industry was efficiently ordered, and the postwar housing emergency was over; the early 1960s saw a recession. Gradually, the overall focus shifted from single-family tracts to higher-density products and to the planning of communities.[84] While the issue of density was perceived as an opportunity by developers, the focus on community became urgent for planners. This trend was famously epitomized in Jane Jacobs's 1961 book *The Death and Life of Great American Cities*, in which she defended public space, mixed-use developments, and sociocultural diversity.

Reflecting this changing climate, in 1961, the Case Study House Program included a community-oriented proposal designed by architects Quincy Jones and Frederick E. Emmons for Eichler Homes. However, although Case Study House #24 included greenbelts and communal recreation areas, and houses were located below grade to provide more greenery, due to rigid regulations and lacking strategies on how to maintain common areas, the zoning variance was not approved and the scheme was denied the permit.[85] By the mid-1960s, the economy was again booming, and satisfying the demand for dwelling units became once more the main focus. In 1965, the government created the Department of Housing and Urban Development, which absorbed the FHA, and although it continued to release its underwriting standards, the FHA's role slowly declined.[86]

Although the government, yet again, hoped to streamline construction by encouraging technological innovation through such efforts as Operation Breakthrough, launched in 1969, both merchant builders and architects lost faith in technology.[87] To echo Banham, the house became a stylized container for ducts, wires, pipes, and vents, "nothing but a hollow shell."[88] The perfectly rationalized stick frame became a scaffold both for the ducts and for postmodern stylistic explorations. In 1964, Robert Venturi's Mother's House launched an era of new possibilities and contradictions. Radical projects such as John Lautner's 1960 Chemosphere represented a potential, to use Banham's expression, "future of the recent past." David Sellers's Prickly Mountain (1966) design-built experiments and Paolo Soleri's Arcosanti (initiated in 1970) would influence experimental architecture of the 1970s, and, later, ecologically driven design-build initiatives such as the Vermont-based Yestermorrow (1980) and the Alabama-based Rural Studio (1993), yet they failed to influence mainstream residential construction. Less radical but carefully integrated into the landscape, Sea Ranch Condominium (1964) stands out as a singular example of a possible future in harmony with nature, an approach that became popular in the late 1980s in the form of (an apparently modest) "sustainable vernacular."[89]

Although important research around the topic of bioclimatic design was carried out in the late 1950s and 1960s by, among others, Victor and Aladar Olgyay at Princeton University, Baruch Givoni at the Technion in Israel and

University of California in Los Angeles, and, later, Ralph Knowles at University of Southern California, low-tech passive climate-management techniques struggled to compete with the ducts and wires and to influence the mainstream housing industry.[90] In 1966, the American Society of Heating, Refrigerating and Air-Conditioning Engineers (ASHRAE) published the first edition of its Standard 55, which included the 1924 Comfort Zone diagram and established performance criteria for thermal acceptability for people engaged in sedentary activities, such as office work.[91] A year later, in 1967, ASHRAE released its *Handbook of Fundamentals*, which replaced and expanded the 1922 *ASHVE Guide*.[92] The handbook now included all basic principles as well as issues separately covered by individual standards: indoor environmental quality, load and energy calculations, HVAC design, building envelope, and materials. Consolidated into a well-funded and thoroughly studied field of expertise, mechanical, electrical, and plumbing technologies took over passive low-tech design strategies developed by academic researchers that were tested unsystematically and with little funding by a few architects passionate about human health and comfort and about the environment.

The 1960s were obviously a period of intense civic and environmental activism. Among many victories of the civil rights movement, discrimination in access to housing was outlawed by the Fair Housing Provision, Title VIII of the Civil Rights Act of 1968, and the decade brought many social and environmental victories, which would shape the future of environmental policies and regulations in the United States. *Oikos* was still far from home—the focus of legislators was not yet on the individual shelter—but the attitudes toward the larger environment that we all share were changing.[93] Many important events shaped public awareness in the dozen years preceding the first Earth Day. In 1958, biologist Barry

Commoner coestablished the Committee for Nuclear Information to attract public opinion to the issue of nuclear tests and atomic fallout. Taking a clear political stance was becoming less and less unscientific.[94] Eventually, the US Senate passed the *Nuclear Test Ban Treaty* in 1963.

In 1962, a report entitled *California, Going, Going* was published by an influential environmental organization, California Tomorrow, to increase public awareness of the environmental implications of the growing population and economic development in California.[95] This and other little-known publications prepared the ground for Rachel Carson's *Silent Spring*, which became the best-heard cry against environmental devastation, passionate enough to trigger a nationwide ecological movement and precise enough to convince federal authorities to investigate further.[96] *Silent Spring* addressed the harmful effects of synthetized chlorinated hydrocarbon used in organic pesticides, exposing the environmental effects of the arrogance with which the chemical industry has shortsightedly manipulated certain, seemingly confined aspects of nature.

While Carson was reporting the vulnerability of the natural environment and demonstrating the general interconnectedness of apparently disconnected realities, mathematician and meteorologist Edward Lorenz was mathematically proving that the behavior of complex systems could not be predicted because apparently insignificant events could potentially trigger highly complex and unpredictable consequences.[97] While nature was appearing more and more sensitive and chaotic, and social ecologies were soon to reach states far from equilibrium, ecologist Howard T. Odum was perfecting his energy-based models of ecosystems, and computer engineer Jay Forrester was fine-tuning his system dynamics models at the Massachusetts Institute of Technology.[98] Preoccupied with different flows, both contributed to a vision of the world that described complex systems as well-defined circuits in a motherboard, providing tools to the emerging field of urban metabolism and for environmental policy making. While many ecologists who disagreed with Odum's unifying theories also opposed public involvement andchose to concentrate on specialized research, the majority supported the environmental movement, calling for a more comprehensive approach to conservation.[99]

It was in this context that the federal government initiated the era of modern environmental planning. Carson's battle had a tangible effect on the first wave of environmental policy making. Thanks to such progressive leaders as Stewart L. Udall, who, while serving as the Secretary of the Interior, published *The Quite Crisis*, the environmental movement became policy.[100] Air pollution was first addressed in the Clean Air Act of 1963 and then in the Air Quality Act of 1967. The Solid Waste Disposal Act and the Act to Amend the Federal Water Pollution Control Act were passed in 1965. Decades of land-conservation efforts were acknowledged in the Wilderness Act of 1964, the Land and Water Conservation Fund Act of 1965, and eventually in the Endangered Species Preservation Act of 1966. Fundamental in setting the stage for future legislation, these acts concentrated on defining key terms and methods, giving authority to special agencies and allocating funds. While the decade was crowned with the passage of the National Environmental Policy Act, which introduced environmental assessment as a prerequisite for all decision-making at the federal level, 1969 also brought the famous fire on the Cuyahoga River and the Santa Barbara oil spill, two man-made disasters that clearly confirmed the urgency of the environmental cause.

In parallel to criticism expressed by environmental scientists and activists, condemnatory statements started to emerge from economists who began to question the fundamental tenets of the growth-obsessed framework. They were saying that human *oikos* was suffering from an artificial separation of economics from ecology. Economist Ezra J. Mishan was among the first to point out the ecological side effects of the neoclassical economics.[101] He spoke out about the opportunism with which the inconvenient costs referred to as external diseconomies were regularly ignored. As observed by environmental historian Jeremy Caradonna, "the bad stuff was nudged out of the model even though it led to 'social conflict,' health problems, and eco-disasters."[102] Many other voices, all critical of the system that considered the natural environment as an external source of precious resources and a convenient sink for trash, were simply pointing at a specific (economic) instance of a more general epistemological fallacy.[103] Gregory Bateson described it superbly in the following parable:

> You decide that you want to get rid of the by-products of human life and that Lake Erie will be a good place to put them. You forget that the eco-mental system called Lake Erie is a part of your wider eco-mental system— and that if Lake Erie is driven insane, its insanity is incorporated in the larger system of your thought and experience.[104]

Paradoxically, most economists (and industrialists) refused to acknowledge that there was only one *outside* and that Lake Erie (or the planet Earth) was inevitably source, home, and sink. Ironically, in July 1969, Apollo 11 landed man on the moon and a new frontier emerged.

ENVIRONMENTAL PROTECTION AND SUSTAINABLE DEVELOPMENT: 1970S–1980S

2.1. Regulating Environmental Degradation: 1970s

By the end of the 1960s, everything was in turmoil. Attitudes were shifting and roles were being challenged. A handful of respected ecologists embraced environmental activism; a few prominent economists turned to ecology. Architects—focused on cultural heritage—left the environmental question up to engineers, but policy makers seemed to be listening. Gregory Bateson continued to expose epistemological errors hidden in the conventional ideas about the relationship between man and his environment. The very idea of nature was again in crisis. Scientists were challenging concepts of stability

—

Weatherizing economies—insulation foam

and order, questioning "the balance of nature," which Aldo Leopold had exposed as a common yet misleading "figure of speech" more than twenty years earlier.[1] Ecologists William Drury and Ian Nisbet criticized the idea of emergent order and predetermined direction in ecological succession. Ecologist Robert May emphasized the coexistence of order and chaos. Although supportive of the idea of stability, his colleagues Herbert Bormann and Gene Likens were also acknowledging irregularities in their exemplary Hubbard Brook studies, eventually describing nature as a "shifting-mosaic steady state." Biologist Daniel Simberloff adamantly criticized all superorganismic notions as deprived of material substance. For him, it was all driven by chance.[2] They all seemed to agree on one point at least: there was no such thing as one natural state.

Less concerned with whether the universe was a game of dice or the result of a grand scheme, the general public was seeing smog and polluted water. In 1970, the first Earth Day brought together millions of Americans disillusioned with the side effects of the American Dream and eager to reconnect with an expanded web of life, regardless of how ecologists described its nature. Two years later, the first United Nations Conference on the Human Environment, held in Stockholm, acknowledged the link between human well-being and the condition of the natural environment. Unfortunately, while the conference recognized that all nations equally depended on the overall health of our planet, the conversations were divided and the ultimate focus remained on the distribution, management, and conservation of resources rather than the well-being of "one Earth."[3] Principle 14 of the *Stockholm Declaration* stated, "Rational planning constitutes an essential tool for reconciling any conflict between the needs of development and the need to protect and improve the environment."[4] What remained unaddressed was the need to question the basic tenets: our dependence on continuous (economic) development.

In December of the same year, the celebrated Blue Marble photograph taken by the Apollo 17 crew pictured James Lovelock's Gaia in its awe-inspiring wholeness and undeniable instability.[5] The Earth appeared both fluid and in stark isolation from a larger, possibly infinite, thermodynamic universe. This powerful image became a symbol of the environmental movement, but rather than celebrating an expanded vision of the universe, it was used to communicate—perfectly in line with the overall spirit of those years—the idea of finiteness and scarcity. Scarcity triggered by excessive economic growth but also, as laid out in Paul Ehrlich's *The Population Bomb*, global overpopulation.[6]

The vision of the future became even more distressing once computationally simulated by the previously mentioned pioneering computer engineer and founder of system dynamics Jay

Forrester as support for *The Limits to Growth: A Report for the Club of Rome's Project on the Predicament of Mankind*. Although criticized both for the initial assumptions and concluding predictions, the general message attracted immediate attention from environmentalists.[7] While it did not halt growth, the report initiated an important debate and influenced policy making in the 1970s. It inquired into the causes and consequences of five trends: excessive industrialization, accelerating population growth, malnutrition, resource depletion, and environmental degradation. It warned against the ecological and social consequences of declining resource quality and industrial pollution. The message was that "the earth is finite."[8] Although erroneous from the thermodynamic point of view, the statement recognized the fact that the rate at which most material resources renew is simply too slow in comparison to the voracity with which we consume them. It became urgent to acknowledge these inconvenient "external" effects of rapid growth and consider them as diseconomies.

The natural way to address these environmental externalities was to attempt including them in the equations and models. In a sense, this is what the Club of Rome tested in some of the scenarios, but as economist Herman Daly observed in *Steady-State Economics*, control of relative prices was only acceptable as a way to "fine-tune" resource distribution. The only way to curb environmental degradation was to establish a coordinated program that would set absolute limits for the market.[9] Notably, in *The Limits to Growth*, only those scenarios that assumed a restricted industrial output promised a relative form of equilibrium.[10] One possible way to more effectively internalize external diseconomies— and this was proposed by E. F. Schumacher in his book *Small Is Beautiful*—was to reduce reliance on large, centralized economies managed by companies with little incentive to care for the land and resources that they managed from afar. His argument was that smaller-scale, decentralized systems were more likely to make people feel responsible for the land they exploited since it was the same land they inhabited. For Schumacher, however, modern economics needed to rethink fundamental values, not simply its modus operandi: "Just as a modern European economist would not consider it a great economic achievement if all European art treasures were sold to America at attractive prices, so the Buddhist economist would insist that a population basing its economic life on nonrenewable fuels is living parasitically, on capital instead of income."[11]

Clearly, while many economists and ecologists shared the fundamental message delivered by the Club of Rome, they often disagreed on the ontological plane or adopted different epistemological lenses. Economist Fred Hirsch warned that the biophysical limits emphasized by the Club of Rome may be less impending than the social ones.[12] To paraphrase Bateson, our ecomental system may well go insane first. Ezra J. Mishan also criticized the ethos of economic growth on a similar plane, saying that it disregarded not only the natural environment but also human well-being and happiness, factors that, to use his words "possibly not measurable but certainly meaningful, do not lend themselves easily to the number system."[13] He questioned "the cult of efficiency," which, in the spirit of scientific management and postwar technocracy, continued to disregard sociocultural values and myopically focused on short-term profits.

The same was criticized by Daly, who called for a more ethically driven economics and condemned the modern obsession with equations.[14] He criticized the ubiquitous use of indexes of growth such as the GDP, pointing out that they did not reflect the distribution of wealth or the ecological effects of its acquisition. This is how he expressed this paradox: "We devote more effort and resources to mining poorer mineral deposits and to cleaning up increased pollution, and we then count many of these extra expenses as an increase in GNP and congratulate ourselves on the extra growth!"[15]

Particularly significant in the era of oil shocks was the emphasis that Howard T. Odum put on the energetic basis of economics (and politics). Notably, his critique of Forrester's models developed for *The Limits to Growth* focused on the lack of an overarching energetic basis.[16] Odum's proposition sounded simple: "Power is a common denominator to all processes and materials."[17] In the 1973 paper "Energy, Ecology and Economics," Odum summarized twenty general energetic principles (in part following Alfred J. Lotka's work from the 1920s) to explain why he believed that our culture needed to gradually convert from growth to a steady state. He drew attention to the fundamental difference between gross and net available energy, which made many contemporary predictions regarding available energetic reserves overly optimistic. He also pointed out the importance of the scales of energy—the fact that potential work depended both on quantity and quality of available energy. For this reason, he doubted whether the diluted, low-quality solar energy could ever do significant work without being "subsidized" by high-quality energy obtained from highly concentrated fossil fuels.[18]

While Odum somewhat doubted that the future of our economy could depend on solar energy, physicist Amory Lovins (who later founded the Rocky Mountain Institute) was optimistic that new technologies would advance fast enough for solar energy to become a viable alternative. In the book titled *Soft Energy Paths*, he criticized "hard" energy sources, such as nuclear power and fossil fuels, and argued for a "soft" option based on renewable-energy sources.[19] His belief was that they would be not only more environmentally friendly but also more democratic due to their reliance on smaller-scale technologies and decentralized management systems. This position not only followed in on Schumacher's critique of large, centrally controlled systems in which responsibility was hard to locate but also reflected the general spirit of survivalism that characterized the era of oil crises and a nuclear arms race, pushing many communities and individuals to search for energetic self-sufficiency.

The overall verdict pronounced by all these voices was that the assumptions underlying our economy had to be reconsidered. And while the basic trend to promote economic growth continued relatively undisturbed—the early ecological economists did not manage to change the basic assumptions—the 1970s were a time of important environmental recircuiting. It was in the atmosphere of a peculiar mix of scientific questioning, passionate activism, sense of catastrophic urgency, and bioeconomic management that the United States witnessed the creation of the first comprehensive federal environmental-protection framework. Among many legislative victories are the 1970 amendment to the Clean Air Act, the 1972 Clean Water Act, the Endangered Species Act of 1973, and the 1974 Safe Drinking Water Act. It may sound inappropriate to question what was achieved in the 1970s, as it clearly slowed down environmental degradation by curbing harmful industrial practices. Still, it is worth pointing out that the precision of command and control that the government aspired to (and was expected to provide in order to justify the restrictions imposed on private entities) inevitably reduced a complex reality to a series of segregated (and inevitably quantifiable) issues. Not only was a qualitative approach not a part of the current epistemology, but an all-inclusive quantitative approach also proved unattainable even for such a comprehensive agency as the United States Environmental Protection Agency (EPA). Aggregation of interconnected issues is

something that would characterize approaches to sustainability in the 1980s and 1990s but was absent in the early period of environmental policy making.

As federal acts gradually targeted one problem at a time, one issue emerged as a concrete cause for an impending (economic) catastrophe in the mid-1970s and hence became the central concern for policy making: the lack of cheap energy that could sustain economic growth uninterrupted—a preoccupation and an attitude that still persists some fifty years later. Policy makers followed Odum's call to concentrate on energetics, but they failed to consider the Jevons paradox.[20] Their initial focus on energy conservation quickly shifted toward relative efficiency. They disregarded the warnings from Daly, who echoed British economist William Jevons and, unlike many others, agreed with the following observation made by Odum: "Most of our century of progress with increasing efficiencies of engines has really been spent developing mechanisms to subsidize a process with a second energy source. Many calculations of efficiency omit these energy inputs."[21]

The acts that focused on conservation of energy were the first environmental legislations to directly impact buildings. With few exceptions (e.g., the 1971 Lead-Based Paint Poisoning Prevention Act that addressed the use of toxic substances in households), conservation of energy was the only environmental issue that the early environmental legislation addressed in the case of individual dwellings. One could even risk saying that the reasons were economically rather than ecologically driven. A year after the 1973 oil crisis, the first federal acts were passed to encourage research programs for the development of solar energy systems and their application in residential dwellings.[22] In 1977, the Carter administration announced its National Energy Plan and established the Department of Energy (DOE), providing a consolidated framework for a comprehensive national energy-plan implementation. Thanks to these plans and programs, research centers, such as the National Renewable Energy Laboratory, were established to develop and assess renewable-energy and energy-efficiency technologies and practices. The DOE demonstration projects, such as Brookhaven House, continue forty years later under such names as Solar Decathlon and Zero Energy Ready Homes.[23] In 1975, the Energy Policy and Conservation Act was enacted by the federal government establishing a program that defined test procedures, labeling, energy targets for consumer products, and efficiency standards for major household appliances. The act also required all states to adopt energy standards for new buildings. This request was met a year earlier by the state of California, which created the first legislative framework for building energy conservation at the state level, requesting that the California Energy Commission adopt, implement, and periodically update energy-efficiency standards for both residential and nonresidential buildings.[24]

In the same period, the National Conference of States on Building Codes and Standards (NCSBCS)—established in the 1960s to improve the uniformity of building codes in the United States—commissioned the National Bureau of Standards (NBS) to develop guidelines for energy conservation in buildings. It was the first time that the code makers addressed an issue not directly related to life safety or welfare. It was, therefore, even more expected this time that the code makers would outsource the work to another nongovernmental agency with a long pedigree of standard-setting expertise in the field of mechanical systems and engineering. The resulting document produced by the NBS in 1974, entitled NBSIR 74-452 Design and Evaluation Criteria for Energy Conservation in New Buildings, provided the basis for the American Society of Heating, Refrigerating and Air-Conditioning Engineers (ASHRAE) Standard 90 Energy Conservation in New Building Design.[25] In 1977, code-development organizations jointly published the first Model Code for Energy Conservation in New Buildings, which referred to ASHRAE Standard 90, and California published its own energy-conservation standards (now California Energy Code).[26] Although the California code did not reference the ASHRAE Standard 90, it did refer to other ASHRAE norms, including the recently revised Standard 55-1974 Thermal Comfort Conditions for Human Occupancy. Eventually, in 1978, the National Energy Conservation Policy Act imposed the inclusion of new energy efficiency in the Federal Housing Administration's Minimum Property Standards, although as mentioned in the previous chapter, the standards did contain basic energy-conservation requirements meant to reduce maintenance costs already in 1950s.

To stimulate adoption of residential and industrial energy-efficiency measures, tax incentives started to be introduced in the late 1970s. The 1976 Energy Conservation and Production Act included loan guarantees for energy conservation in public and commercial buildings and a Weatherization Assistance Program for low-income homes. The Energy Tax Act of 1978 contained a tax credit for residential conservation and renewable-energy investments, and it supported such measures as weather stripping and insulation.[27] Regulations, which were increasingly standardized, coupled with energy codes and economic incentives, increasingly seemed a perfect solution to the United Nations Principle 14 dilemma: how to reconcile endless economic growth with environmental protection.[28] The effectiveness of this approach remained unverified at this initial stage: only 6 percent of US households participated in the Residential Conservation Service program during the following decade, as the Reagan administration opposed these measures and discontinued most of the energy-conservation programs in the go-go 1980s.

The housing industry experienced a boom in the first years of the 1970s and continued to thrive after the long-due recession of 1974, clearly exacerbated by the oil crisis. According to the Department of Housing and Urban Development (HUD), 26 million dwelling units were required to cater to the new generation coming of age.[29] Although the industry did face new challenges provoked by the energy crisis and environmental movement calling to limit growth, the demand was so high that the builders successfully adapted to the new conditions, and Americans absorbed the higher costs by working longer hours and sending women into waged work. In 1971, a first moratorium on development was imposed by the small town of Petaluma in Northern California, concerned with its capacity to provide adequate municipal services to new residents without compromising the quality of the environment.[30] Municipal standards were also changing, forcing developers to provide (and finance) more community services while building fewer dwelling units. Zoning restrictions, together with increasingly stringent and complicated building regulations, raised the cost of houses.

Regardless of these changes, from its recovery in 1975, the industry continued to generate high profits until the end of the decade due to favorable monetary policies, cheap credit, and the increasing demand for both basic housing units and material for real-estate speculation. Paradoxically, while local governments were limiting growth through various zoning provisions, the federal government was traditionally encouraging construction (read: economic growth) through specific financial mechanisms, such as the provision of easily available mortgage loans.[31] It is noteworthy that mortgage securitization, which, as urban studies scholar Dan Immergluck explains, led to the widespread

"vertical disintegration" of the lending process and was one of the causes of the subprime mortgage crisis, was introduced by the federal government and not, as many believe, by the private sector.[32]

Although burdened by the new energy codes imposing the use of expensive technologies, merchant builders were even less convinced by the alternative methods proposed by the architects and researchers fascinated with solar energy. A possible alternative to the ones promoted by governing bodies and code makers was proposed by, among others, architect Ralph Knowles, who, in 1974, published the results of a decade of design studies in his book *Energy and Form*. In the introduction, he called on his fellow architects to consider "long-term conservation of our natural resources a governing purpose for design." Following in biologist D'Arcy Thompson's steps, but decades before the "parametric turn," he and his students demonstrated how nonrenewable energy could be conserved (and renewable energy exploited) through a strategic manipulation of morphological (rather than technological) features of the built environment.[33] According to Knowles, "the low diversity of the [spatial] arrangement does not reflect the variety of environmental conditions that result from the cyclic forces of nature."[34]

The 1970s saw a wave of interest in active solar technologies and passive spatial techniques. Both institutes and independent architects contributed to this trend. Upon the invitation from HUD, in 1976, The American Institute of Architects Research Corporation published the *Solar Dwelling Design Concepts* to support designers and homeowners interested in the potential domestic applications of solar energy.[35] In 1977, the Colorado-based architect Richard Crowther published *Sun Earth: How to Use Solar and Climatic Energies*.[36] The Santa Fe Balcomb House by William Lumpkins was built in 1979. However, as more and more demonstration projects were successfully built and the performative effects were better understood, researchers started to point out that solar techniques and technologies applied to low-density single-family homes provided little saving in energy consumption and hardly affected the overall environmental impact. They provided autonomy and affordability, but to address environmental impact of inefficient land use, denser solar communities needed to be built.

Merchant builders, city planners, and traditionally oriented customers did little to support these independent efforts. If few passive solar homes were actually constructed (many of which were red-tagged for violation of building codes), even fewer solar communities were built.[37] Unfortunately, a decades-long process of optimization of construction protocols and increasing mechanization of climate control in buildings made it easier to focus on the efficiency of appliances rather than on spatial arrangements. Any merchant builder (or mortgage underwriter) would agree that formal (or morphological) diversity is squandered energy. Introduction of efficient appliances, on the other hand, will boost the economy.

In 1980, the first house powered by photovoltaics was built in Carlisle, Massachusetts. While the DOE would continue its "race to zero," projects such as architect Steven Baer's 1972 Zome House or the Integral Urban House experiment run by the Farallones Institute were to become examples of a potential future of the recent past—oddities conceived by the alternative desert culture of the Southwest and the progressive community of Berkeley, California.[38] Similarly, architects Victor and Aladar Olgyay's bioclimatic principles, Baruch Givoni's psychrometric chart, and Knowles's solar envelope method were rarely applied in mainstream projects, further distancing the architecture of American dwellings from a holistic approach to ecology.[39] According to

urban historian Dolores Hayden, adding efficient gadgets to a Victorian house not only boosted the economy but also helped maintain the old dream house and the model family structure untouched. While she argued that the Farallones Institute urban homesteading experiment in Berkeley "did not stress rethinking family life so much as the introduction of urban agriculture and ecosystem analysis," Reyner Banham worried that the heavy physical activity involved in the daily operations of a "passive" house like Zome would fall to the women.[40] The question turned out to be even more complicated: as prices swelled, women went to work to help maintain the family structure, and the efficient functioning of the American dream home fell back on technology.

Disillusioned with the positivism of the modernist era, critical of the reductive obsession with energy performance, and generally cynical about architecture's capacity as a problem-solving discipline, most architects questioned the modernist imperative that derived form from function. They withdrew into a world of semiotics and linguistics, searching for a "sense of place" in cultural (and natural) heritage. While in 1964, architect Christopher Alexander proposed a cybernetic method as to how to deal with complexity in design, by 1977 he was calling for a return to archetypal patterns.[41] Although symptomatic of a general shift in the field, his work was far from representative. It remained ignored by the postmodern architectural establishment, as it promoted the use of archetypal patterns to solve problems.[42] Alexander, on the other hand, criticized the "mannerist" attitude with which postmodern architects used architectural history and cultural heritage.[43] While deconstructing sociocultural norms embedded in form, postmodern architects also deconstructed our relationship with the environment. And so, the pure white volumes of Richard Meier's Douglas House (1973) celebrated nature by standing (classically) in stark contrast to it, Peter

Eisenman's House VI (1975) questioned the basic norms of domestic life by exploring the autonomy of universal formal principles, and Frank Gehry's Gehry Residence (1978) deconstructed the ubiquitous stick frame, deriding the very bones of the familiar body of American suburbs.

While questioning the modernist orthodoxy, most architects returned to what they knew best—the cultural production of meaning. Once again, they left ecological dilemmas and climate control in the hands of researchers, engineers, standard setters, and code makers. Ironically, their disregard for the environmental cause coincided with a change in the political climate: over the next decade, environmental regulations in the United States experienced a backlash, developers were encouraged to speculate, and architects were given a carte blanche to play.

2.2. Aligning Sustainability with Global Economic Expansion: 1980s

The 1988 MoMA exhibition *Deconstructivist Architecture*, curated by Philip Johnson and Mark Wigley, celebrated one—even if somewhat "disfigured"—face of architecture. Meanwhile, architecture of the 1980s was multifaceted. While, according to the curators, Gehry's Santa Monica Residence (1978) epitomized the deconstructivist house, his painterly Winton Guest House (1984–87) brilliantly exemplified the plurality of the decade. In general, Gehry's exploratory attitude was emblematic of the diversity with which the postmodern architects were breaking with the modernist past and dialoguing with cultural heritage.

In *American Masterworks*, architectural historian and critic Kenneth Frampton notes

the increasing heterogeneity of the American modern houses starting in the early 1980s.[44] Attitudes toward climate management and the environment in general were equally heterogeneous and predominantly symbolic. In Krueck & Olson's 1980 Steel & Glass House, Frampton recognizes traces of the Californian Case Study House tradition in addition to Miesian influences. In David Rockwood's 1984 Rockwood House in Portland, he notes a combination of the midcentury obsession with prefabrication and a neoplatonic minimalism in which purity of spatio-structural grids, which recall the architecture of Giuseppe Terrani, come together with impeccable resolution of technological detail. When discussing the 1988 Miller House by Atelier Wylde-Oubrerie, Frampton brings attention to the coexistence of Le Corbusier's *béton brut* and brise-soleil, with a quintessentially American stick frame and wood siding, next to Scarpian craftsmanship and technological "bowelism" in the exposed tubes and ducts.

A cosmic connection with the land and its natural and cultural history is celebrated in the regionalism of Antoine Predock's 1987 Fuller House in Phoenix, while Ricardo Legorreta's Greenberg House, built in Los Angeles in 1991, exemplifies Mexican minimalism. Due to their interest in the vernacular building traditions and environmental techniques of the Southwest, the last two projects continue (even if only symbolically) the ecological holism of the 1970s. Legorreta's use of volumes, colors, and light also announces the 1990s fascination with minimalism imbued with spirituality and a nostalgia for a lost connection with the universe.

As in previous decades, certain decontextualized features of these diverse masterworks influenced the character of the common houses built in the 1980s.[45] The postmodern fascination with cultural heritage and vernacular forms was, unsurprisingly, of particular appeal to the upper-aspiring middle classes. This tendency temporally brought architects and nostalgic suburban dwellers closer together. If one were to identify a house included in Frampton's collection that best exemplifies the homeowner's dream in the 1980s, it would probably be the neoclassicist antimodernism of Michael Graves's own House and Studio (1977–1993), with its complex spatial sequences, opulent upholsteries, and collector's objects.

The appeal of the old, both formal and vernacular, was successfully exploited by the early home improvement TV shows, most famously *This Old House*, which first aired in 1979 and is still on the air.[46] At first, the featured houses were relatively small, and the owners contributed "sweat equity" to reduce costs; with time, the show focused on luxury mansions renovated by tradespeople. Noteworthy is that the show has been generously underwritten by major manufacturers and distributors of construction materials and services (e.g., Home Depot). Also, homeowners whose property was featured on the show received donations from manufacturers eager to promote their merchandise. This inevitably impacted their choice of products and construction methods. As the early 1980s recession faded, "do-it-yourself" gave way to "hire," and "reuse and restore" turned into "replace." Budgets became unpredictable as ambitions fueled by free donations increased. In a truly postmodern way, replication of period detail went hand in hand with the promotion of the latest energy-efficient technologies. In line with postmodern trends, pluralism went hand in hand with contradictions: ecological benefits of "adaptive reuse" were counterbalanced by new additions. The early episode descriptions reflect the spirit: "Our host discusses plans for a new, historically compatible five-car garage…A solar energy expert recommends the best location for a solar collector." Another episode emphasizes the importance of technological upgrades: "It's time to insulate the house, remove the old

furnace, and replace it with a new energy-efficient heating system."[47]

The possible reasons for the initial success of this over-four-decade-old show are numerous. On one hand, the housing crisis of the late 1970s and early 1980s triggered interest in the idea of do-it-yourself and in-home improvements. The aging of postwar housing stock and the disillusionment with its poor quality and lack of identity further increased the popularity of *This Old House* in its early days. There was also the failure of the orthodox modern (mono) style to captivate culturally diverse American homeowners.[48] The historicizing decor was particularly appealing to the increasingly wealthy (but shrinking and more indebted) middle class desiring to exhibit new money as old. On the other hand, the continuous rise in house prices (often 20–30 percent a year) encouraged those who already owned a home to engage in micro-real-estate speculation through house flipping, which often involved improvements and additions. Those who did not dare or could not afford to do this simply enjoyed watching the Joneses flip on TV.

A gradual deregulation of the mortgage market, decreasing interest rates, and various property tax incentives created by the Economic Recovery Act of 1981 helped those willing to risk and speculate.[49] In this period, the importance of the mortgage circuits backed by the Federal Housing Administration (FHA) and the U.S. Department of Veterans Affairs dramatically decreased as other more accessible (but also riskier) products became available.[50] While FHA racial bias started to be openly criticized in the 1970s and 1980s, its negative impact on affordability of housing was criticized in a 1980 report to the HUD.[51] Ultimately, the FHA Minimum Property Standards for One and Two Family Dwellings saw its final edition in 1982, after having shaped American building regulations, practices, households, and dreams for almost fifty years. In 1990, in response to rising concerns regarding the cost of housing, the US Congress passed the Cranston-Gonzalez National Affordable Housing Act, in which it addressed funding of lower-cost homes and access to homeownership for low-income residents.[52] Another landmark act passed the same year—a sign of an increasing awareness of the importance of social justice—was the Americans with Disabilities Act. It prohibited discrimination on the basis of mental and physical disability and set standards that addressed both social and physical inclusion.[53]

While policy makers were addressing social inequalities, architects and the general public indulged in historicizing designs, and real estate was enjoying the first season of deregulation before the housing bubble would burst in 1989, standard-setting and research institutions continued to define how buildings should relate to the environment. Although ecologically driven groups, such as the New Alchemy Institute, continued to develop holistic solutions, the idealism of the 1970s was slowly giving way to the pragmatic art of the possible and profitable.[54]

The 1970s preoccupation with energy continued to shape these groups' agendas well into the 1980s. The Rocky Mountain Institute was established in 1982 by Amory Lovins. Despite a general backlash in federal attitude toward energy conservation, the institute was particularly successful. This was possibly due to a technologically and economically driven premise of "unlocking market-based solutions that can be replicated and implemented now."[55] Model energy codes continued to be perfected thanks to third-party efforts initiated in the 1970s. In 1983, the Council of American Building Officials published the first Model Energy Code, in part based on the previously mentioned 1977 Model Code for Energy Conservation in New Buildings.

No significant action toward energy conservation was taken at the federal level until 1987, when the National Appliance Energy Conservation Act established minimum efficiency standards for common household appliances (e.g., room air conditioners, refrigerators, and washers) by amending the National Energy Act of 1978, which directed the DOE to establish energy-efficiency standards but remained unimplemented under the Reagan administration, which did not consider it a priority.

Although due to its economic urgency in the post-oil-shock years, energy conservation received paramount attention from standard setters and policy makers, the adopted technological solutions (e.g., weatherization of building envelopes) quickly exposed unforeseen conflicts. The tightly sealed homes might have helped to conserve energy, but deprived of proper ventilation they trapped harmful concentrations of air pollutants indoors. This newly emerged problem triggered a national discussion, which dominated the first half of the decade.[56] While the controversial anti-pollution-policy experiments, such as the 1979 Bubble Policy, exposed many important issues—limitations of delocalized emission budgets, cost-effectiveness as a valid criterion, and economic incentives as an appropriate tool—the small scale and clear boundaries of highly controlled indoor environments simply made the pollution blatant.[57] It exposed the connection between outdoor pollution and indoor air quality and revealed the negative health impact of new and hardly understood materials—sources of previously neglected hazardous air contaminants.

A 1987 EPA report stated that indoor air pollution was one of the most important environmental risks to human health, and several important acts related to air pollution and toxic materials were gradually amended to provide technical support and funding for indoor-air-related research. In 1988, the Indoor Radon Abatement Act was added to the Toxic

Substances Control Act of 1976.[58] However, while of fundamental importance to human health, the issue of indoor air quality exposed yet a bigger epistemological problem: the limits of the reductionist method in the face of the unpredictability and complexity of the ecological relations that environmental health and our well-being depend on. While concerned with indoor air quality, the researchers demonstrated the need for a more comprehensive approach to environmental assessment. They also demonstrated how difficult it was to impose and maintain specific conditions, even in such a small and apparently closed environment as a "well-tempered" household, not to mention chaotic and boundless industrial landscapes that the government tried to address with the Bubble Policy.

Another important issue addressed in the 1980s was urban stormwater pollution. The U.S. National Urban Runoff Program carried out by the EPA between 1979 and 1983 recognized the importance of nonpoint-source water pollution (i.e., stormwater and snowmelt from agricultural fields, construction sites, parking lots, etc.), an issue neglected until then by legislators despite its recognized importance.[59] The program also analyzed the type of pollutants, their concentration, distribution, and impact on "receiving" water quality. Last but not least, it assessed various "best management" practices, promoting retention basins (wet basins) and suggesting need for more study of other potentially useful practices, such as detention and dual-purpose basins, grass swells, and wetlands. The program provided the basis for the 1987 amendment to the Clean Water Act and authorized local authorities to develop and implement runoff-management programs. The amendment made the disturbing nature of water pollution official: it came from everywhere and enveloped everything; it was ambient, like music, just more poisonous.

Other point-source toxic industrial wastes that time made ambient were addressed by the 1980 Superfund Program, established to manage the cleanup of contaminated industrial sites and coordinate response to future emergencies.[60] The most sinister of all was possibly the 1982 Nuclear Waste Policy Act meant to manage nuclear-waste disposal by designating an "outside," where it could be detained "safely" for at least ten thousand years. It is noteworthy that this managerial act was passed after two catastrophic events that occurred in 1979: the Three Mile nuclear meltdown and the Church Rock nuclear waste spill—two disasters that sociologist Charles Perrow called "normal accidents."[61] Normal because they resulted from, to use the author's expression, the inherent "interactive complexity" of systems; normal because they were triggered by local interactions between small technological or operational failures rather than deficiencies in design or violent natural phenomena, such as an earthquake.

Despite significant nuclear whistleblowing, the government focused on the management of the waste product without questioning the technology itself.[62] While some scientific alarmists question whether our civilization will still exist in the next century, the EPA's current standards address a one-million-year lifetime of toxic waste.[63] Regardless of the odds, those involved in the management of this artifact of human making are safe. As political theorist of technology Langdon Winner pointed out: "The closer you are, the more innocent; the farther away you are, the more innocent. It is a magnificent arrangement in which everyone is safe except the victims." This applies both to proximity in space and time; the geological timeframe will make the concept of responsibility in this case even more "slippery."[64]

If it is hard to think about a nuclear meltdown as a normal accident, it is even more difficult to consider a hurricane anything else than a natural disaster, even if we give the phenomenon a human name: Allen, Alicia,

Gilbert, Joan, Hugo, etc. Yet back in the 1980s, increasing numbers of scientists were realizing that next to wildfires, microbes, and predators, climatic fluctuations produce important—and "normal"—short- and long-term disturbances, which affect and periodically redefine ecosystems.[65] In 1986, Margaret Davis, an expert in palynology (the study of fossil pollen), contributed her geological-time perspective to claim that climatic changes were responsible for a general instability in nature. Her conclusion was that any judgment regarding the stability of natural processes on Earth depended on the spatiotemporal point of view of the observer.[66] At the same time, the chaos theory demonstrated that what we called disasters were events that normally occur in many highly complex dynamic systems. In his Nobel Prize–winning research, physical chemist Ilya Prigogine explained how dissipative structures, such as hurricanes and tornadoes, functioned far from equilibrium.[67] What was hard to accept was that such phenomena not only were normal but also could be triggered by human activity. In fact, climatologists were starting to agree that humans were propelling the environmental system into a state "far from equilibrium," and the consequences would possibly be magnificent but most likely catastrophic for humankind.

In 1979, the World Meteorological Organization hosted the World Climate Conference, which recognized climate change as a serious threat to humanity. One of the effects of this important conference was the establishment of the Intergovernmental Panel on Climate Change, which has been assessing and disseminating knowledge about climate, global warming, and possible response strategies and providing scientific basis for policies and defense for vulnerable policy makers since 1988. After decades of warnings from individual scientists, global warming finally attracted international attention. The same year and in the absence of a federal response during the Reagan presidency, California passed the first Climate Change Bill (AB 4420), directing its agencies to inventory greenhouse gas emissions, study their effects, and make recommendations to avoid, reduce, and address impacts. Faced with this new emergency, global warming eclipsed all other environmental issues and has dominated environmental legislation and regulatións until today.

It is a peculiar entanglement of the many monstrous phenomena of our own making— free-market economy, global warming, and nuclear power—that we are caught in. The hegemony of energy efficiency and carbon neutrality is legitimized by the need to fight global warming, which is, to use environmental theorist Eileen Crist's words, "endangering *the culprit*."[68] In the meantime, the risks carried by nuclear energy and a myriad of other environmental issues—deforestation, topsoil loss, and oceanic dead zones, to name just a few—are neglected, misinterpreted, or dealt with at scales and in ways that do not question the framework of the free-market-based economy.

In the essay titled "Beyond the Climate Crisis," Crist concentrates on the issue of biodepletion, following in the steps of biologist E. O. Wilson, for whom preserving biodiversity was an ecological imperative.[69] As she observes, what Wilson saw looming as the Era of Loneliness, or of Emptiness, we have welcomed with guilt (although tinted with a hint of pride) as the Era of Man—the Anthropocene. Since there is no quick techno-fix, no aerosol that one can spray, no magic wand to wave that will replay the process of biological evolution, we ignore the issue. Since we do not fully comprehend the importance of temporal processes and spatial patterns, we disregard their impact on biodiversity, a key aspect of ecological stability—our own as well.[70] We concentrate on problems that pose an immediate threat to our way of life and adopt solutions that do not question it.

Rather than leaving uranium underground, we spend billions looking for a repository to safely store the spent fuel. Rather than protecting old-growth forests, we plant "sustainable" mono-crop wood plantations because wood is renewable. Rather than sharing a vehicle, we buy a new electric car, despite the fact that the ecological footprint of the parking lot it will occupy most likely exceeds the environmental savings from its efficient technology.[71] Rather than building smaller and more durable houses, we flip them "green." In fact, the average square footage per person has almost doubled since the oil crisis, increasing from 551 square feet in 1973 to 1,058 in 2015, while household size has decreased from 3.01 to 2.54 persons.[72]

Although this upward trend in living standards of many Americans and the "good health" of the housing construction industry is clearly unsustainable, few seem to worry as long as housing technologies are energy efficient and keep utility bills low. As a matter of fact, building-scale environmental measures appear inadequate, if not simply offensive to common sense, when we think about the environmental perils that we face. Paradoxically, the global community came together to define the notions of sustainability that would influence the green building standards in the decades to come, while the globe was being "unified" by another doctrine: the neoliberal economy of the free market. And while the minds behind the notions were genuinely interested in environmental and ethical dimensions of sustainability, the hands charged with rendering them practicable were constrained by the market. While intergovernmental programs established in the 1980s were in part a reaction to the pressures of the accelerating economic development and its social and environmental consequences, they were inevitably shaped by it as well.[73]

In 1980, the International Union for Conservation of Nature, together with the United Nations Environment Program and the World Wildlife Fund, published *World Conservation Strategy*. The report established three interconnected objectives: 1) maintenance of essential ecological processes and life-support systems; 2) preservation of genetic diversity; and 3) sustainable utilization of species and ecosystems.[74] The report also defined two important terms. It described *development* as "the modification of the biosphere" dependent on social, ecological, and economic factors, and it defined *conservation* as "the management of the human use of the biosphere so that it may yield the greatest sustainable benefit to present generations while maintaining its potential to meet the needs and aspirations of future generations."[75] As environmental writer Ulrich Grober observed, it not only did anticipated the key principles of the *Brundtland Report (Our Common Future)*, but it also marked a change in our understanding of the term *conservation*.[76]

During the 1970s, the incompatibility of sustainability with economic development was questioned, and the term *sustainable development* emerged as an apparent solution to this fundamental conflict. In the introduction to *World Conservation Strategy*, one reads, "Conservation must…be combined with measures to meet short terms economic needs. This vicious circle by which poverty causes ecological degradation which in turn leads to more poverty can be broken only by development."[77] While it attempted to, in part, consider the need of underdeveloped countries to overcome poverty (as famously pointed out by Indian prime minister Indira Gandhi in Stockholm in 1972), it would soon be hijacked by the proponents of growth-based economics and criticized as contradictory by radical environmentalists.

While radical movements such as Earth First! called for uncompromising conservation of nature, often through civil disobedience, the meaning of development was forcefully questioned in *North-South: A Program for Survival*, a report published in 1980 and prepared under the leadership of the former West German Chancellor Willy Brandt.[78] While concentrating on the fundamental divide between the rich North and the poor global South, the report called for a culturally diverse, socially inclusive, and environmentally conscious international cooperation. It criticized the systemic dependence of the South on the rich North and rejected the Western model of development as an appropriate blueprint to be imposed on all nations and cultures. Brandt also forcefully urged the international community to question economic growth as the only satisfactory form of development. Instead, he envisioned it as a creative process of "unfolding of productive possibilities and of human potential."[79] Rather than concentrating on economic, social, or environmental perils, he emphasized the priority of the ethical lens. The *Brandt Report* addressed a vast array of interconnected issues from hunger and poverty, through energy and environment, to international trade and debt crisis, reiterating some of the perils listed in *The Limits to Growth*. However, his was a hopeful and truly inclusive vision of an equitable and sustainable development supported by a series of concrete recommendations. Unfortunately, it was doomed to fail during the 1980s; a decade shaped by aggressive economic measures promoted by President Reagan and Prime Minister Thatcher.

Twenty years later, James Quilligan, a member of the Brandt Commission, argued that the *North-South* report was still awaiting a response, while the social, economic, and environmental pressures continue to rise due to frictions triggered by global economic interdependences. In the closing paragraphs of *The Brandt Equation*, he speculated that "perhaps only a world crisis will refocus the issues of wealth and need, generating new dialogue and the opportunity for change."[80] An opportunity in the form of a crisis—a subprime mortgage crisis—indeed arrived in 2008, but it is hard to argue that it generated a new dialogue.

In 1983, the United Nations created the World Commission on Environment and Development to continue the work initiated by the Brandt Commission and to develop "a global agenda for change" to promote international cooperation driven by common environmental concerns. Presented in 1987, the final report, produced by a team led by Norwegian political leader Gro Harlem Brundtland and entitled *Our Common Future*, declared the need to consider sustainability as the guiding principle in global politics and economic planning—an ethical imperative. Initially meant to address environmental issues only, the *Brundtland Report* established its future legacy by forcefully emphasizing the intricate interdependences between economy, ecology, and equity, and in that, it echoed the *Brandt Report*. It also recognized the importance of complex interactions between seemingly unrelated policies and regulations by emphasizing the following:

> Environmental regulation must move beyond the usual menu of safety regulations, zoning laws, and pollution control enactments; environmental objectives must be built into taxation, prior approval procedures for investment and technology choice, foreign trade incentives, and all components of development policy.[81]

Last but not least, the report, stressed the importance of flexibility and capacity to self-correct, an issue poignantly illustrated by Bateson in his parable of the acrobat on the wire:

> For obvious reasons, it is difficult to control by law those basic ethical and abstract principles upon which the social system depends…On the other hand, it is rather

easy to write laws which shall fix the more episodic and superficial details of human behavior. In other words, as laws proliferate, our acrobat is progressively limited in his arm movement but is given free permission to fall off the wire.[82]

The decade that led to the Rio Earth Summit in 1992 produced a series of environmental reports, agendas, pledges, and some legally binding protocols. Especially worthy of mention due to its effectiveness was the 1987 *Montreal Protocol*, which initiated the international phase-out of ozone-depleting compounds, successfully reverting the problem observed by the international scientific community in the 1970s and confirmed by the NASA discovery of the ozone hole in Antarctica in 1985. Unfortunately, the 1980s also saw some of the most catastrophic man-made environmental disasters. A toxic cloud killed thousands in the 1984 gas leak at the Bhopal pesticide plant. Two years later, the Chernobyl nuclear power facility blast enveloped most of Europe with a radioactive cloud. While each of these "normal accidents" spurred an emergency response, accidents kept on coming. In 1989, the Exxon Valdez tanker spill covered thousands of square miles of ocean with crude oil, causing a collapse of the marine population. This environmental catastrophe caused by yet another unforeseen human mistake triggered the adoption of two more acts: the Oil Pollution Act and the Pollution Prevention Act, both passed in 1990.

A question arises: after how many normal accidents should we declare a system abnormal? In Brundtland's *Our Common Future*, everything was ecologically imbued and administered in a flexible way. In reality, when one considers technological systems, economic activities, and the social dynamics that affect the natural environment, the problem of sustainable development becomes tricky, if not—to use design theorists Horst Rittel and Melvin Webber's term—"wicked." We can address isolated aspects of the problem and attempt to regulate them with specific policies and standards to minimize risks, but this will not make sustainability a "tame" problem.[83] As a socioeconomic rather than environmental issue, sustainability is doomed to remain ill-defined and open, with no ultimate solution. As an imperative, it cannot be enforced. It can only be practiced—over and over again. It is not a task but a state of mind; it requires integrity before integration, attention before action, and ethics before efficiency. Indeed, a wicked problem in a world based on discretization, speed, and standardization.

GREEN ECONOMY AND GREEN BUILDING STANDARDS: 1990S—PRESENT

3.1. Greening the Markets: 1990s—mid-2000s

During the 1992 Rio Earth Summit, the countries of the South asked the North to rethink its lifestyle. President Bush responded that the American way of life was not negotiable.[1] Although the Rio *Agenda 21* reasserted sustainable development as "the global guiding principle for the 21st century," the concept matured in an era of unrestricted free-market growth. From a radical quest for a no-growth stability in *The Limits to Growth*, published in 1972, through a vision of nonmaterial cultural growth promoted in the Brandt Commission's 1980 *North-South* report, it evolved into a pragmatic principle of sustainable development expressed in *Our Common Future*, released in

—

Retrofitting construction standards—solar energy

1987. The environmental agreements signed afterward provided an increasingly flexible framework wherein the free-trade economy could flourish.

Although a 1992 World Bank report entitled *Sustainable Development Concepts* confirmed that the issue was on everyone's agenda, Herman Daly, who then worked for the World Bank, criticized the failure of the report to question the sustainability of unlimited economic growth.[2] Its vision was to maintain the status quo and work on "sustainable growth," a concept that he considered an oxymoron, given the size of the world economy in relation to the environment that hosts it.

While Daly warned against excessive globalization of trade, the World Trade Organization (WTO), established in 1995, continues to postulate—referring to various environmental summits—that "an open, equitable and non-discriminatory multilateral trading system has a key contribution to make to national and international efforts to better protect and conserve environmental resources and promote sustainable development."[3] Notwithstanding the plea to protect the planet and the 350-page-long guidelines on how to achieve it, the WTO built its mission on carefully selected messages contained in *Agenda 21*, specifically those that linked acceleration of sustainable development to the presence of robust international economic frameworks.[4] The WTO interpreted this as a call to accelerate economic growth. When the *Earth Charter* was signed in 2000, the speed of development was such that hardly anyone noticed its uncompromising plea: "We must realize that when basic needs have been met, human development is primarily about being more, not having more."[5] Unfortunately, "being more" escapes quantification and hence cannot be an "input" in an economic model.

While Daly was calling for a morally driven economy based on "values of enoughness, stewardship, humility, and holism," a more practical approach to environmental economics was being proposed by his British colleague David Pearce.[6] Pearce believed that in order to appreciate the value of the environment, it had to be somehow economically evaluated. He pragmatically claimed—against command-and-control measures and in favor of human liberties and preferences—that improvement required "policies that use selfishness rather than opposing it."[7] He admitted that some form of scientific cross-examination should be established to balance these preference-based measures, emphasizing that while he and his colleagues understood that the others may share other value systems, they only worked with the economic ones.[8] The ones that could be quantified.

Whether this was an instance of "the art of pragmatism" or a case of what philosopher Alfred North Whitehead called the "fallacy of misplaced concreteness," it provided practical solutions to governments.[9] Pearce believed that valuing natural capital and reflecting the social costs of its use in the price of products would help regulate demand and hence curb excessive depletion.[10] His pragmatic and practical "middle position," presented in a 1989 report entitled *Blueprint for a Green Economy*, was embraced by environmental policy makers across the globe, as it advocated for a "*complementarity* of growth and environment" and aimed at decoupling economic activity from environmental impact without drastically reducing the size or rate of economic growth.[11] Pearce believed that only market-based incentives (e.g., cap-and-trade) would encourage polluters to address environmental problems now rather than later, preventing the common phenomenon of "discounting the future."[12] Creation of pollution-trading markets and market-based incentives provided an anticipatory, preventive measure meant to reduce risks and future costs of adaptation to, for example, climate change, without directly curbing the freedom of individual polluters.

By the time the international community united to celebrate the twenty-fifth anniversary of the *Stockholm Declaration* and signed the *Kyoto Protocol on Climate Change*, US environmental planners had tested Pearce's methods and learned how to successfully trade in emissions. The cap-and-trade mechanisms gradually replaced previous policies, which imposed simple limitations on individual polluters. In 1990, the US Congress passed another amendment to the Clean Air Act that introduced a national cap-and-trade system to reduce sulfur-dioxide emissions. This strategy later served as a model for reduction of greenhouse gas emissions under the *Kyoto Protocol*. While the Acid Rain for Sale Program contributed to an overall reduction of national levels of sulfur dioxide and was tested at the state level to fight excessive greenhouse gas (including CO_2) emissions, the fairness of this scheme has been questioned.[13] One of the issues discussed is that the coarse resolution of the cap-and-trade model neglects the uneven spatial and temporal distribution of certain copollutants.[14] Some suggested the introduction of local ceilings in addition to the cap-and-trade method to offset this problem.[15] From a global perspective, it might also prove difficult to reach an agreement regarding the distribution of the right to pollute that is fair to underdeveloped countries.

Although major international climate summits took place during the 1990s, the collapse of the Communist Bloc pulled international attention further toward issues of economic growth and triggered a wave of capitalist-market expansions. What would determine the course of global dynamics over the next two decades was the North American Free Trade Agreement (NAFTA), signed during the Clinton presidency in 1994, and the establishment of the WTO in 1995 rather than Clinton's proenvironmental policies or any of the international environmental protocols signed in the same period. While natural disasters continued to hit the United States at an abnormal rate, climate-change deniers were publishing misleading reports meant to antagonize the scientific community and confuse the public.[16] This kept on undermining the credibility of the scientific community in the matter of climate change and simultaneously detracted attention from other pressing environmental issues requiring immediate action. In the meantime, in 2001, China entered the WTO, and the United States withdrew from the *Kyoto Protocol* and failed to ratify the *Stockholm Convention on Persistent Organic Pollutants* signed the same year.

While opinions about the socioeconomic benefits of free-trade treaties vary, many agree that both climate action and the climate itself have suffered from the increasing deregulation and opening of global markets. NAFTA opponents argued that it had been detrimental to local communities and environments.[17] They also warned that it should not serve as a model for future agreements.[18] Strikingly, as part of its fundamental principles, the WTO *permits* members to protect the environment, but "members must not use environmental protection measures as a means of disguising protectionist policies."[19] While environmental protection is permitted as long as it does not harm trade, it seems that many WTO regulations have indirectly blocked programs and policies that address climate change by supporting renewable energy. An example can be found in *This Changes Everything*, in which social activist and writer Naomi Klein discusses the detrimental impact of the nondiscrimination principle on the promotion of the local solar energy industry in Ontario, implying that the indirect effects of the WTO agreements are clearly hampering the main goals of the *Kyoto Protocol*.[20]

Next to market-based incentives (e.g., pollution charges and subsidies that promote environmentally friendly solutions), traditional command-and-control policies continued being adopted in order to set or tighten overall pollution standards (which could then be "traded").[21] Other measures were introduced to raise public awareness. In 1996, water suppliers were obliged to publish information about drinking water quality. Highly polluting technologies were gradually banned, and leaded gasoline was phased out in 1996 as a result of a twenty-five-year-long program. In 2004, the Clean Air Nonroad Diesel Rule of the Environmental Protection Agency (EPA) initiated a similar program meant to reduce emission levels by modernizing engines and reducing sulfur in nonroad diesel. These measures indirectly addressed pollution from equipment used by the construction industry. And in 2000, Dursban, the most widely used household pesticide posing a risk to children's health, was banned.

Regardless of the adoption of the abovementioned standards, the international success of the cap-and-trade method confirmed the free-market ethos of the era. In general, the focus of "sustainists" shifted from curbing trade to promoting efficient products and green services that could be traded. In 2004, under the Bush administration, fourteen countries created the Methane to Markets Partnership to advance recovery and use of this greenhouse gas as an energy source. A celebratory EPA press release perfectly reflected the spirit of the era, emphasizing "the double benefit of capturing the second-most abundant greenhouse gas and turning it to productive use as a clean-burning fuel."[22] Although, as Jeremy Caradonna points out, "in the 1990s, 'reduce, reuse, recycle' became a mantra for every school kid," recycling (or at least promising to do so) ever larger amounts of waste proved easier and more profitable than reusing or simply reducing.[23] In other words, consuming green proved easier than consuming less. And so the economy went green. While the *Earth Charter* pleaded for "a new reverence for life," free-market economists were claiming that we can only be sustainable in ways that generate profit. The decade was marked by a hopeful and operative approach to sustainable strategies, but since the economy was booming, sustainability needed to embrace this trend.

The green spirit spread across all scales of economy, from international trade to local commerce, and affected many different domains of economic life: manufacturing, agriculture, construction, and services. The economy was becoming eco-minded and highly efficient. At least in the wealthy North, it was the time of "natural capitalism." In the introduction to a book with the same title, *Natural Capitalism*, the authors, Paul Hawken, Amory Lovins, and L. Hunter Lovins, propose that natural capitalism "recognizes the critical interdependency between the production and use of human-made capital and the maintenance and supply of natural capital."[24] The scale of the challenge changed,

ecological knowledge advanced, and the accounting tools became more sophisticated, but the attitude toward natural "capital" remained almost unaffected since the times when Gifford Pinchot oversaw the U.S. Forest Service under President Theodore Roosevelt. Be it "maintenance and supply" today or "conservation and sustainable yield" in the early 1900s, the aim is the same: efficiency. And so the prosperity of the "natural capitalist" society was to be built—again disregarding the Jevons paradox—on higher productivity and improved efficiency. It seemed easy to accomplish considering the blatant inefficiencies that stifle all sectors of the economy. Explaining their agenda, Hawken and the Lovinses referred to Albert Einstein's dictum: "Problems can't be solved within the mindset that created them."[25] And yet we are trapped in the same efficiency-obsessed mindset.

As Michael Hardt and Antonio Negri point out, no matter how much we resist, capitalism captures our desires and reflexes and converts them into power.[26] It transforms its own insufficiencies and overreach (e.g., energy scarcity, global warming) into new markets. It turns what could be a useful feedback mechanism (e.g., sustainable indexes, ratings, and eco-labels) into a self-imposed discipline corset. All this to reemerge stronger under the green banner. Hence the greening of capitalism created new market opportunities: pollution, waste, low-energy bulbs, eco-cars, zero-mile diet, and solar panels. What was an alternative culture in the 1970s became a niche product suite in the 1990s. Thanks to a renewed interest in biomimicry, nature was again perceived as a source of invaluable (and now also profitable) knowledge.[27] Created to quantify unsustainability and certify sustainable efforts, measurement tools and rating systems reinvigorated the standard-setting market. Manufacturers improved life-cycle assessment methods.[28] Business adopted the triple bottom line to promote financial, social, and environmental performance.[29] Commerce created various types of eco-labels to certify the origin and impact of products.[30] By the year 2000, environmental accountants measured, indexed, rated, and labeled the greenness of just about everything, architecture included. And still, the Earth Overshoot Day, "the date when humanity's demand for ecological resources and services in a given year exceeds what Earth can regenerate in that year," falls each year slightly earlier.[31] It fell on December 7 in 1990; in 2020, we entered ecological deficit spending on August 22.[32] In 1977, Daly observed with a dose of sarcasm: "Some ecologists have defined an economist as a person who is seeking the optimal arrangement of deck chairs on the Titanic."[33] Admittedly, it would take a Herculean effort to initiate a change of course instead.

The green spirit obviously also affected the construction industry. The first assessment method applied to buildings was formulated in the United Kingdom in the late 1980s and, in 1990, launched as the Building Research Establishment Environmental Assessment Method (commonly known as BREEAM). Its US equivalent was not launched until ten years later. Nevertheless, the 1990s saw an explosion of green building initiatives, from *The Hannover Principles*, which aspired to lay "the foundations of a new design philosophy" through numerous practical guidelines, to proprietary rating systems and green certificates.[34] The success of these initiatives depended on their capacity to leverage their constituencies to spread the agenda among industry leaders, customers, and eventually policy makers.

The most powerful framework was established in 1993 when Rick Fedrizzi, David Gottfried, and Mike Italiano (a marketing specialist, a real-estate expert, and an environmental lawyer) joined together to launch the U.S. Green Building Council (USGBC). While the American Institute of Architects hosted the founding meeting, the USGBC owes its success to the support from the construction industry but also to environmentalists, corporations and nonprofits, authorities, educators and students, and concerned communities. Support from such a broad spectrum of social groups offered unique opportunities. Although the USGBC was launched by the construction industry (rather than, for example, a public advocacy organization), it did not directly represent it. Nor did it represent the government or a specific professional body. A nongovernmental organization like the USGBC was a perfect structure to exert indirect influence.

While undoubtedly the involved actors shared a concern for the environmental cause, they all agreed that the US construction industry needed a green standard that, while improving the quality of construction, would also protect their interests. Their initial goal was to develop the standard within the American Society for Testing and Materials (renamed ASTM International in 2001), but they eventually opted for an independent rating system, which afforded them a greater degree of control.[35] Industries got involved in the standard-setting effort to make sure that the new standards did not render their products obsolete; real-estate developers were eager to quickly standardize the greening efforts to ensure smooth operations and enable economic valuation. Environmentalists, researchers, and students brought in enthusiasm, expertise, and an unbiased mindset, which helped the USGBC to present itself as a trustworthy third-party authority. It was a perfect framework to turn an important cause into a well-standardized system that only would not be assimilated by the economy but also could create a new market as well.[36]

Ultimately, since the standards negotiated by a third party reflected the interests of various social groups, they could, therefore, be easily incorporated into legally binding codes without the risk of being rejected by the market. Although the USGBC's Leadership in Energy and Environmental Design (LEED) rating system was met with criticism, many US states and cities initially adopted LEED standards as mandatory for certain types of construction.[37] By endorsing the criteria developed by the USGBC, governments legitimized them as a national green-standard monopoly. And yet, as these green standards gradually gain acceptance (by blending in with the other older ones), we should not forget that they represent the values and interests of those who managed to dominate the field in order to dictate these standards in the first place. This is not dissimilar from what happened in the 1930s, when the idea of "home" was standardized as a real-estate product thanks to the Federal Housing Administration and its mortgage insurance.[38]

While the LEED rating system originally aimed at reducing inefficiencies during the operational phase of a building's life, a more ambitious agenda was adopted by its offspring, the Living Future Institute. In 2006, the institute launched the Living Building Challenge (LBC), which is, according to the organization's website, the most stringent green building standard in the world. Its idealism reflects the fact that it was developed by architects rather than real-estate experts.[39] In fact, it echoes the philosophy contained in *The Hannover Principles* more than any other certificate. Unlike LEED, the LBC offers little flexibility and does not accept promises— all imperatives are mandatory, and the certificate is awarded based on the actual performance tracked during the first year of operations. Yet what really distinguishes it from other methods is its restorative character. (A restorative LEED certificate was not launched until 2019, when the USGBC decided that it was possible to push the market further. It is called LEED Positive.[40]) Another notable (and slightly troubling) feature of the LBC method is that projects must score a

point for beauty and spirit. While the ambition to restore environments is undoubtedly admirable, rating beauty seems problematic. Still, a more pressing question that persists is whether it is realistic to think that such ambitious standards are attainable in an era of unprecedented urban explosion. Are LBC buildings not simply a luxury niche product accessible to the wealthiest? Is their positive ecological impact real or purely symbolic? Can one flower, full of green petals, transform a desolate land into a green meadow?[41]

An alternative to rating isolated buildings with a limited impact would be to rate entire cities. Technically, it is feasible. Based on models previously developed by systems ecologists and industrial ecologists, environmental impact (and vulnerability) of cities, regions, and countries can now be quantified in terms of ecological footprint.[42] Methods developed by urban ecologists—their metabolic models as well as mappings of spatial fragmentation and functional heterogeneity of urban regions—offer practical tools for tracking of urban processes.[43] Thanks to these methods and an ever-increasing quantity of data, we can now know how (un)sustainable cities are. Hence, while IBM is turning urban operations "smart," the USGBC has entered the market to certify how green they can be.[44] The question that arises is whether we should be rating everything. In theory, we can, but would Gregory Bateson think this is mentally sustainable? My guess is that the answer would be "no," but we will most likely continue on this path.

While most of the principles behind green building rating systems were available in prior environmental-design handbooks and technical manuals, what was missing was not only a comprehensive assessment of the energetic efficiency and environmental impact of strategies and technologies but also a clear indication of what particular mix of solutions constituted a sustainable building (rather than a comfortable one). What was needed was clear metrics and a universal, marketable protocol. Previous guidelines were presented in the form of traditional handbooks offering flexible design strategies that were location specific: the previously mentioned *Design with Climate* (1963) by the brothers Olgyay, *Man, Climate and Architecture* (1969) by Baruch Givoni, and *Sun, Wind and Light* (1985) by Mark DeKay and G. Z. Brown.[45] Although the structure of the last book resembled a set of instructions, it did not provide a standardized checklist. In 1976, the American Institute of Architects (AIA) Research Corporation published *Solar Dwelling Design Concepts*. Years later, in 1992, the EPA joined AIA/COTE (a branch of the AIA that promotes environmentally friendly design) to publish the *Environmental Resource Guide*, which provided sustainable guidelines for architects throughout the 1990s.

In 1992, green building expert Alex Wilson started publishing *Environmental Building News*, now a monthly report by BuildingGreen, a web-based source of knowledge on sustainable-design strategies, materials, products, ratings, and codes. Not supported by advertising, it was (and still is) highly trusted by designers. The problem is that it did not offer easily marketable "recipes." Probably for this reason, in 1997, the format was expanded, and the BuildingGreen Approved product database was created. Clearly, in order to be part of the green system, one must either certify or be certified. Sadly, Pearce was right—everything needs to be valuated to have currency in a market-based economy. And while ratings do not provide economic valuation, they do provide metrics that facilitate it. In fact, one of the first ratings was created by the Residential Energy Services Network (RESNET), established by the mortgage industry to "develop national standards for home energy ratings and to create a market for home energy rating systems and energy mortgages."[46]

Since the market is free, a significant amount of effort (energy) is dedicated to differentiating a good product from a bad one. For example, the Open Standard Health Product Declaration Collaborative reports building-product content and associated health information. The tool is incorporated into many rating methods, including LEED v4.[47] Standard setters compete to create sustainable standards to defend the interests of their constituencies, and ultimately, specific social groups acquire authority when their standards and ratings are incorporated into other, more comprehensive systems and when they are used in legally binding codes. RESNET's Home Energy Rating System Index (commonly known as HERS Index) is used to assess Energy Star–certified homes and the U.S. Department of Energy's Zero Energy Ready Homes. RESNET air-tightness-testing standards are incorporated into rating systems and codes. When the California Energy Commission incorporated one of its standards into the state energy code, RESNET referred to it as a milestone.[48]

While most green initiatives born in the 1990s came from nongovernmental organizations and standard setters, and eventually from progressive states, some of them were triggered and accompanied by federal legislation. In 1992, the US Congress enacted the Energy Policy Act (EPACT92), which called on states to consider a revision of their residential building codes to meet or exceed the Model Energy Code standards developed by the Council of American Building Officials.[49] It also gave impetus to the American Society of Heating, Refrigerating and Air-Conditioning Engineers (ASHRAE) to finalize the new ANSI/ASHRAE Standard 90.2 Energy Efficient Design of Low-Rise Residential Buildings by referring to it as a benchmark for efficiency of manufactured housing.[50]

EPACT92 also launched programs that introduced appliance efficiency standards. Initially only a voluntary rating and labeling system applied to office equipment, the Energy Star program (introduced by the EPA, run in partnership with the Department of Energy) became an industry standard for the energy efficiency of many household appliances.[51] Energy Star standards have been incorporated into the LEED rating system and many state energy codes. Although efforts to conserve water were initiated in 1990 by a public advocacy group called WateReuse, the first voluntary water-efficiency rating and labeling system was launched by the EPA only in 2006. The EPA's WaterSense standards were later incorporated into the LEED certification and state codes (e.g., the California Green Building Standards Code). Since the legally binding federal water-efficiency laws and regulations have not changed since EPACT92 was enacted, in 2007, the state of California adopted the nation's first high-efficiency standards, and many other state jurisdictions have followed since then.[52]

Most organizations and methods established in the 1990s were inspired by nongovernmental initiatives born in the 1980s, which were, in turn, sparked by the activism of the 1970s. Unfortunately, two decades of efforts to reestablish a healthier relationship with the natural environment were embraced by the mainstream construction industry during an era that prioritized economic growth through deregulated free trade and globalization. The focus on expanding markets encouraged further standardization of industrial practices, including construction and, hence, building codes.

In 1994, the three regional model-code groups merged to form the International Code Council (ICC).[53] This certainly simplified the regulatory system and allowed the code makers to improve building performance, distribute safety standards, and spread technical expertise more uniformly across the country at a reduced cost. It also helped large construction companies and corporate clients further standardize their practices across the country. However, while state codes share model principles, they do so in a piecemeal fashion. Although the ICC is the main code-development organization and its codes cover all aspects of building regulations, states can write their own regulations and are free to adopt codes from other code makers as well.[54] The best state-developed standards, at times, become examples for the model code makers. Eventually, investments made by progressive states benefit other smaller, poorer, or less progressive states.[55]

Individual states adopt model codes with extensive amendments to assure compliance with state laws and eliminate conflicts with other adopted model codes. Many state agencies, boards, commissions, and departments have the right to adopt, amend, add, and delete parts of the model text. Local jurisdictions can further amend state codes in response to climatic, geographic, and topographical conditions, provided that amendments are more stringent. The complications do not end there: if not stringent enough, state codes must be applied in conjunction with mandatory federal standards, such as the previously mentioned ADA Standards for Accessible Design. They are also often used in combination with optional guidelines provided by nongovernmental rating organizations, such as the USGBC's LEED.

While based on universal standards, codes (especially in large cities) are ultimately local and site specific. While too specific for large national and international construction companies and developers, they often seem too generic for environmentalists and local neighborhood communities. The latter group found a solution in the rules of common interest developments (CIDs), the private covenants, conditions, and restrictions built into the deeds of individual homes and enforced by homeowner associations and their boards. The former—large developers—supported the development of green building ratings, which make standards more stringent but arguably less site specific. While the local CIDs, as pointed out by the leading authority on homeowner associations Evan McKenzie in his book *Privatopia*, are a sign of what political commentator Robert Reich calls "secession of the successful," the risk is that rating isolated homes and neighborhoods will create another degree of social separation and environmental injustice.[56] CIDs and green ratings are corporate islands of affluence and archipelagos of voluntary environmental correctness—both potentially unsustainable.

In the 1990s, the interest in sustainability among architects increased dramatically but was far from universal or uniform. Many architects embraced the green building movement and expanded their expertise by becoming green consultants. The majority of architects, overwhelmed by the new rules, either hired these consultants or continued to design buildings the way they previously did. This, however, does not mean that the latter disregarded the relationship between buildings and their natural environment. Those who did not, often simply refused to measure the results. Though not manifestly green, those environmentally driven attitudes continued to evolve: some architects embraced the new regional vernacular, others continued to explore the modular prefab, and yet others saw an answer in the computer-generated (and at times performance-oriented) curvilinear forms inspired by nature. While Kenneth Frampton's selection in *American Masterworks* reflects some of this heterogeneity, none of the presented houses reflect the spirit of the new digital era. Never built, Frank Gehry's Lewis Residence is missing.[57]

While none of the projects appear ostentatiously green, Frampton's masterworks intimately engage with landscapes and natural dynamics in search of delight rather than efficiency. Steven Holl's Stretto House (1989–1992) frames an aqueous topography with stark simplicity and modulates light through a treatment of surface and color evocative of the architecture of Carlo Scarpa. The rustic Ledge House (1992–1996) by Bohlin Cywinski Jackson carves into the site with the brute strength of its own locally extracted materials. The weathered surfaces of the 2001 Tyler House by Rick Joy sink into the rusty desert to let its dwellers appreciate the stars of the Arizona sky. The 2000 Agosta House by Patkau Architects "dams" the energy of an open meadow with a galvanized-steel wall while protecting the house-reservoir from deer and wildfires. "Proto-ecological," according to Frampton, the 2001 House and Studio by Barton and Vicki Myers is a series of open (Eames-inspired) pavilions scattered across a chaparral-covered hill. Crossed by natural breeze and covered with a thin layer of cooling water, the prefabricated frames form indoor-outdoor environments that can easily be closed off thanks to a system of off-the-shelf garage doors. While intimately related to their landscapes, these masterworks do not tell us how green they are. The question of whether they do practice sustainability without displaying a green plaque remains open.

The greening of the housing construction industry took place in an era of vertical disintegration of the residential-mortgage industry.[58] In the 1980s, mortgage lending shifted from local savings and loans to national mortgage companies not subject to the same strict regulations. These companies benefited from securitization via government-sponsored enterprises (GSEs) and from access to an expanding secondary-mortgage market.[59] Not only did they provide a less regulated investment channel for new capital but also drew advantage from economies of scale due to expanded geographic scope. They became wholesale lenders of standardized products, and thanks to advances in technology—data mining, credit scoring, etc.—they were able to sell mortgage packages through a nationwide network of independent brokers.[60] This helped reduce operational costs but also shifted responsibility for the origination process onto the brokers. This structural disintegration provided a safety mechanism when highly profitable yet often abusive lending practices increased in the 2000s. As more and more capital flooded the US market in search of low-risk, high-return investments, "private-label" (non-GSE) residential-mortgage products proliferated to supply them.[61] Private borrowers became the perfect target, as Wall Street investment firms bundled residential mortgages into mortgage bonds and sold those to global investors.

Dynamics varied regionally. In California, house prices peaked in 1991, plunged to their lowest point in 1997, and returned to the previous values in 2001.[62] The trend that made them continue to peak until 2006 was fueled by extreme lending practices. Exotic loans proliferated both in prime and subprime markets, as capital continued to search for investments but borrowers (both creditworthy and high risk) became scarce.[63] High-risk subprime mortgage-backed securities gradually dominated in collateralized debt obligations. The distance between lenders and borrowers—to use Langdon Winner's expression—was so vast that responsibility, in the case of mortgage defaults, would be impossible to locate.

Most brokers, as reported in "The Giant Pool of Money," a 2008 episode of the radio program *This American Life*, followed the trend since "the software, the data, didn't seem worried at all." In fact, as the program authors point out, "It was the triumph of data over common sense." The rating agencies also contributed to the general misjudgment by underestimating the risks of highly engineered finance (now directly influencing homeowners' lives) and overrating the obligations.[64] The market was in a speculative bubble, access to "affordable" mortgages increased, but affordability of housing decreased as prices

continued to rise in response to high demand. Some built poorly, some built greenly, houses sprung up everywhere. Since realtors, lenders, and homeowners benefited from swelling prices, the vertiginous spiral of premature teardowns, renovations, expansions, and new constructions continued. As pointed out by Jonathan Massey, "Prompted as they were by financial rather than physical obsolescence, such teardowns highlighted the centrality of financing to the architecture of American houses."[65] The fever was further fueled by media as TV programs— *Flip This House, Flip That House*, and the like— glorified speculation.

3.2. Offsetting Speculation with Green Standards: Mid-2000s–2010s

The hypercomplex architecture of the financial market successfully connected impatient investors—via dishonest arrangers and issuers, greedy brokers, and "generous" appraisers—with inexperienced house flippers and, most worryingly, with uninformed or desperate would-be homeowners. As borrowers defaulted, foreclosed properties were put back on the market. Seventeen percent of subprime mortgage homes were foreclosed in 2008.[66] The crisis left house-flippers with worthless properties and local lenders with unsold mortgages. Suddenly, priceless tulips became ordinary flowers.[67] While the subprime crisis affected many different people, who had hoped to make a profit as the money trickled through the system, most actors only temporarily took risks while briefly handling capital owned by others. Although investors and end borrowers paid a high price, the homeowners-occupiers who already owned very little—the greedy ones, the uninformed ones, and the underprivileged—were the ones to lose everything.[68]

Although highly complex, the mortgage-backed securities system itself included no safety mechanism to mitigate the impact of foreclosures. Unlike the traditional savings and loans, mortgage companies were unable to restructure the loans (which they did not own) to prevent foreclosures. Bundled, pooled, sliced up, and bonded back together into toxic pools, mortgages translated into strings of monthly payments—abstract data on a spreadsheet. Since homeowners were no longer concrete entities, their integrity was not protected. The risks and profits assigned to particular investor tranches were sacred. Perfectly engineered, the system collapsed. Although the US Congress passed the Housing and Economic Recovery Act in 2008, as foreclosures continued, the bailout measures to protect the investment bankers came quicker and were more comprehensive than the steps undertaken by the federal government to save low- to average-income (and often minority) homeowner-occupants.[69]

While not central to the subprime crisis, developers, construction companies, and architects were instrumental in the process. They were financially rewarded for developing new land and building bigger homes to satisfy the market's need for attractive loan collaterals. Efforts toward sustainable development were offset by an increase in house size and frequency of premature home improvements. The centrality of financial speculation challenged the underlying premises of the green building movement that promoted energy and resource conservation in individual homes but disregarded the impact of overbuilding and environmental consequences of potential foreclosures. One could risk saying that it was the same speculative construction boom that financed the emergence of green

standards that generated an ever greater need for them.

The wave of subprime crisis foreclosures damaged individual lives, disrupted social ecologies, and scarred urban landscapes.[70] Ghost houses were abandoned before anyone got a chance to inhabit them. Homes built to satisfy financial rather than existential demand devoured land, destroyed vegetation and soils, and wasted power, water, and materials before anyone could even assess their overall greenness or their operational energy efficiency. Thousands were eventually demolished to mitigate their negative impact on neighborhoods and to reduce maintenance costs to cities.[71] In a spectacular way, the subprime crisis reminded us of the common etymological roots of *ecology* and *economy*. The sustainability of housing construction is first a matter of honest finance and only then environmental sensibility.

Although rising prices and the poor quality of quickly built houses and McMansions could hardly be blamed on lack of advanced technology or green spirit, most architects underestimated the centrality of financial speculation. While it was the excessive demand and the value of scarce land (especially in urban areas) rather than construction costs that priced ordinary people out of the housing market, they addressed the issue by promoting more architectural and technological innovation. The pragmatic aesthetic of modern prefabricated houses experienced a revival in the 2000s and enjoyed popularity among a broader public, even after prefabrication was abandoned and only the aesthetics remained. The success of Michelle Kaufmann's prefabricated Glide House (2004) was officially confirmed when, in 2006, its full-scale replica was exhibited at *The Green House: New Directions in Sustainable Architecture and Design* show at the Washington National Building Museum.

Prefabrication was also recognized as an important trend in the 2008 MoMA exhibition *Home Delivery: Fabricating the Modern Dwelling*. In the spirit of the Better Homes demonstration projects, MoMA sponsored the design and construction of five prefabricated houses. Among them were the high-tech, SmartWrap-sealed, no-waste Cellophane House by Kieran Timberlake and the highly ornamented Digitally Fabricated House for New Orleans by Lawrence Sass from MIT—the latter a truly American combination of nostalgia and technology embodied in a shotgun house.[72] Still, none of the recent prefabricated green homes found their place among Frampton's *American Masterworks*—not even the winner of the 2007 AIA/COTE Top Ten Award for sustainable design, Ray Kappe's LEED Platinum-rated Zeta 6 House (2006) designed for LivingHomes. Prefabrication was also deployed as a signifier of *ecological*, and after the crisis, *economic restraint* in many Solar Decathlon demonstration projects.[73] Still, as in the previously discussed decades, prefabrication did not manage to threaten the stick-frame-construction market this time either.[74] While prefab green was launched as an antidote to environmentally and economically unsustainable housing, it once again failed to provide an affordable alternative to the rising prices of traditional homes or to compete with the price of home kits sold online. It created a new, green niche market instead. In fact, despite the financial meltdown, Kaufmann's assets were acquired in 2008 by Blu Homes, a luxury prefabricated green home manufacturer.[75]

Another phenomenon that emerged as a result of the economic and environmental unsustainability of available housing was the tiny-house movement. For context, in 2011, less than 1 percent of Americans purchased a house smaller than 1,000 square feet.[76] A typical tiny house is approximately 150–300 square feet, but tiny-house village activists are building even smaller units, hoping to provide "transitional micro-housing" and an address for otherwise homeless people.[77] Acceptable according to the ICC model building code, the tiniest of tiny houses (approximately 90 square feet) are too small to be considered an independent dwelling unit in many states.[78] The California Health and Safety Code (17958.1) defines efficiency dwelling units (for no more than two persons) as having a minimum floor area of 150 square feet (not including a mandatory closet and bathroom). Still, even the biggest of the tiny houses (the ones that comply with these standards) are at least ten times smaller than an average American home. The median house was 2,467 square feet in 2015; the 1,525-square-foot home considered median in 1973 is, today, considered a small house.[79]

It would be a considerable achievement to return to those standards, if one has to pursue the American dream of owning a detached cottage. As often happens with reactionary opposition, the tiny-house counterreaction to spatial and financial gluttony was radical, yet the prohibitive cost of available housing, even the small ones, was extreme as well. While tiny houses were seen by many as a sustainable alternative to scarce (and still unaffordable) low-income housing, for many others, they were an embodiment of the romantic Walden dream.[80] Not surprisingly, this fringe phenomenon attracted enough attention among viewers and potential homeowners to justify the launch of more TV shows. In 2014, HGTV released *Tiny House, Big Living*, and FYI TV launched *Tiny House Nation*.

A locally rooted, and hence less spectacular yet highly admirable counterreaction to generic prefabricated green homes (and romanticized green tiny trailers), has been explored by Rural Studio, a design-build program based at the University of Auburn and founded by the late Samuel Mockbee and D. K. Ruth in 1993. While Frampton had no place for such "minor" masterworks as the Rural Studio's 2001 Corrugated Cardboard Pod or the 2002 Lucy Carpet House, these projects explore and respect cultural, economic, and environmental constraints without neglecting the aesthetic dimension of architecture. In 2005, Rural Studio launched 20K, an affordable housing program, which continues today.[81] The main premise of the 20K project is to provide a locally built alternative to the generic homes found in trailer parks. Far from spectacular, Rural Studio projects are both pragmatic and delightfully inventive. What makes them unique is the recognition of the fact that true sustainability, if we want to still use this term, is local rather than universal and that the financial architecture of the house must also be designed locally rather than speculated upon globally. To be sustainable, American houses must be financially sound.

In the last decade, architects have explored sustainability in many different ways, with or without concern for green metrics—from the (tiny) LEED-certified prefabricated Porch Houses designed in 2010 by the Texas-based firm Lake|Flato and the 2012 modern version of an Earthship, the Edgeland House by Bercy Chen Studio, to the 2015 Wing House by David Hertz. The range of houses recognized with the AIA/ COTE Top Ten Award also confirms that sustainability does not entail a specific aesthetic.[82] No longer only an expression of an alternative culture (as it was in the 1970s), in the 1990s, green architecture got absorbed by the market. By the mid-2000s, it was elegant enough to be featured on the sleek pages of *Dwell* and marketable enough to be effectively flipped on TV. Despite the crisis, in 2007, *This Old House* turned green, and in 2008, HGTV launched a new series entitled *Green House*, in 2013 renamed *Smart House*.[83] In fact, when, in 2008, Kaufmann built a prefab green house on the grounds of the Chicago Museum of Science and Industry, it was part of the *Smart Home: Green + Wired* exhibition. Smart is the new green.

Consumed by the media, the greening of architecture was eventually incorporated into mandatory building codes. The first green building standards code was introduced in California in 2008 and was spurred by a series of state and federal acts addressing, again, energy independence and, now, also global warming. In 2006, once more a national first, California enacted the previously mentioned Global Warming Solutions Act (Assembly Bill 32), which required the state to reduce its emissions by approximately 15 percent.[84] The 2005 Energy Policy Act, the Energy Independence and Security Act of 2007, and the American Recovery and Reinvestment Act (ARRA) of 2009 introduced more stringent standards, appliance efficiency rebates, provisions for energy-efficient-home tax incentives, and weatherization assistance programs. The ARRA, specifically, incentivized states to adopt energy codes, making it a prerequisite for receiving federal stimulus funding.[85]

Since obtaining a private-label green building certificate posed a financial challenge and brought few advantages to smaller residential developers and homeowners, these groups were initially excluded from the mandatory compliance with LEED standards that was imposed onto federal and commercial buildings by many state building codes. Eventually, in response to the objectives set in the 2006 Global Warming Solutions Act, the California Building Standards Commission developed its own Green Building Standards Code (CALGreen Code) and, in 2008, adopted it as Part 11 of the California Building Standards Code (California Code of Regulations, Title 24). Initially a voluntary option, the measures became mandatory for almost all types of new constructions in 2010. The main objectives of the CALGreen Code are to: "(1) reduce GHG from buildings; (2) promote environmentally responsible, cost-effective, healthier places to live and work; (3) reduce energy and water consumption."[86] In somewhat awkward language, article 101.2 states its purpose:

> The purpose of this code is to improve public health, safety and general welfare by enhancing the design and construction of buildings through the use of building concepts having a reduced negative impact or positive environmental impact and encouraging sustainable construction practices.[87]

Even in this environmentally driven code, the goal is again to improve human health, safety, and welfare. The well-being of the environment is again instrumentalized.

Ultimately, in 2012, the ICC introduced a new overlay code, the International Green Construction Code (IgCC), to standardize the minimum requirements for sustainable construction. While the IgCC does not apply to low-rise residential buildings, its release signaled an important fact. The ICC recognized that the USGBC (next to ASHRAE and the progressive state of California) had sufficiently prepared developers, policy makers, and real-estate owners to accept an additional layer of mandatory restrictions. And yet, as of October 2020, less than twenty (out of several thousand) jurisdictions in a dozen states adopted one of the previous versions of the IgCC, while its heavily reworked 2018 edition has so far been adopted by one jurisdiction only, Montgomery County, Maryland, and even there only partially.[88]

The greening of building codes might be under way, but its national success will depend on the quality of available model codes and, most importantly, on the level of federal involvement. What will most likely be required is an equivalent of the abovementioned ARRA that used a financial incentive to convince states to adopt energy codes. It will also depend on the urgency of other, mostly safety-related, side effects linked to climate change. Of note is that, in 2016, the Obama administration launched a public-private initiative focused on resilience. The press note explained that the purpose was to "highlight the critical role of building codes in furthering community resilience and the importance of incorporating resilience and the future impacts of climate change in the codes and standards development process."[89]

The next set of practices to be standardized will most likely focus on the prevention of damage triggered by climate change (effects of flooding, tornadoes, etc.)—in other words, on resilient construction, which, if we continue on the current path, will provide yet another managerial solution to a problem that we have failed to prevent. The problem is in part triggered by the fact that we have been operating and building—to put it crudely—too wastefully, too big, and too much.

Twenty-five years after the *Kyoto Protocol* was signed, environmentalists continue to fight against the politics supporting the economy of "extractionism" and to denounce the impact of free trade on natural ecosystems and social ecologies.[90] Although critics of standard—growth-driven—economics are in the minority, they persist and return to the same questions in moments of acute crisis. In 2007, at the height of a period of apparent economic prosperity, just before the collapse of the financial market and forty years after the original publication of Daly's *Steady-State Economics*, economist Mark Anielski asked again: "Why do economists, financial analysts, politicians, and media fixate on growth measures (e.g., the GDP or gross domestic product) as the key indicator of human progress?"[91] At the same time, economist Peter Victor was completing his book *Managing without Growth*, in which he explained how growth only recently became the main economic objective of government policies and why developed countries should be transitioning out of it.[92] Among other issues, he emphasized (again after Daly) that the absolute throughput of materials and energy had to be reduced, that decoupling economic growth from environmental impact did not work, and that technology (and relative efficiency) should not be perceived as the ultimate solution to social and environmental dilemmas.

In 2010, in *Prosperity without Growth*, economist Tim Jackson also questioned economic growth and the meaning we, as a society, give to technological progress by writing, "Our technologies, our economy, and our social aspirations are all badly aligned with any meaningful expression of prosperity."[93] In *The End of Growth*, journalist Richard Heinberg returned to the scenarios from 1972's *The Limits to Growth*. Its authors predicted the end of growth as some time between 2010 and 2050. Although similar simulations have been run since then, the results remain almost the same regardless of advances in software and updates in data.[94] While many have tried to discredit the message contained in *The Limits to Growth*, it offered a plausible scenario for the future. A 2016 *Los Angeles Times* article reported that house prices in the Los Angeles area had again reached the record levels of 2007 and would continue to rise beyond the previous peak, as they "normally" do.[95] Our society and the systems that it relies on cannot function without growth.

Many important standards and policies were introduced during the Obama administration, but sustainability kept on being perceived in terms of efficient low-carbon technologies and smart cities, cities that continue to grow, pollute, and consume more and more land, water, and materials.[96] When talking about the misinterpretation of the concept of sustainable development set out in the 1987 *Brundtland Report (Our Common Future)*, Victor quoted Jim MacNeill, one of the main authors of the report: "Only in a Humpty Dumpty world of Orwellian doublespeak could the concept be read in the way that some suggest."[97]

What the green building standards have surely achieved is to bring this doublespeak home into American households. And if, as designer and theorist Christopher Hight says, "ecology is the central administrative knowledge for the ordering of things within an age of biopower," one could paraphrase Félix Guattari and say that the household is the smallest arena for "miniaturized instruments of coercion," a perfectly standardized market for green products.[98] As will be discussed in the following two chapters, the focus on economic incentives for efficient technological artifacts and on building regulations that support them achieves one goal for sure: it guarantees demand for green products and services. Thanks to these ingenious—both voluntary and coercive—techniques, economic development can continue undisturbed, validated—if not vindicated—by the qualifying adjective that precedes it. The adjective being *sustainable*.

Part Two —
Means and Methods

INTRODUCTION

The old adage *a posse ad esse non valet consequential*. (I take this to mean: just because something can be, it does not follow that it should be.)
—George Parkin Grant, "Thinking about Technology"

A surgical operation which was formerly not feasible but can now be performed is not an object of choice. *It simply is.* Here we see the prime aspect of technical automatism. Technique itself, ipso facto and without indulgence or possible discussion, selects among the means to be employed.
—Jacques Ellul, *The Technological Society*

A wide range of interactions between social, economic, and environmental ideas and programs have shaped present-day building regulations. As demonstrated in Part One – Agendas, the gradual accumulation or, better, legitimization of different motivations informed the code-making circuits and, as a consequence, determined the character of the American residential construction. The complicated system of codes formed slowly in response to changing socioeconomic realities. Today, however, it is rarely questioned and is applied as an indivisible (though expandable) device. Environmental concerns affected residential regulations relatively late in comparison with legislation that targeted territorial dynamics, and environmentally driven standards were the last ones to be added to the existing "stack" of residential codes. While the greening of construction standards and regulations was, in part, a reaction to excessive economic growth and its detrimental impact on the natural environment, the market quickly leveraged the commercial potential of green building standards. Incentivized in a number of stimulus acts, energy-efficient appliances and green construction systems were ultimately promoted to boost the waning economy while improving energy security.

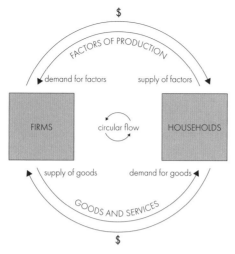

a. CIRCULAR FLOW OF ECONOMY
conceived as an isolated system

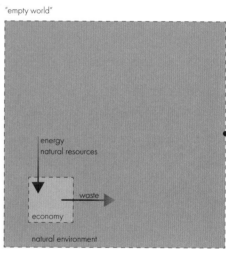

"empty world"

b. SMALL ECONOMY
conceived as an independent system
in an infinite natural environment*

c. NATURAL ENVIRONMENT
perceived as a subsystem
subservient to the economy*

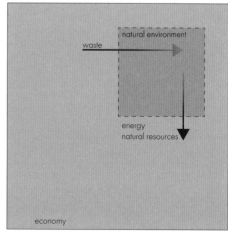

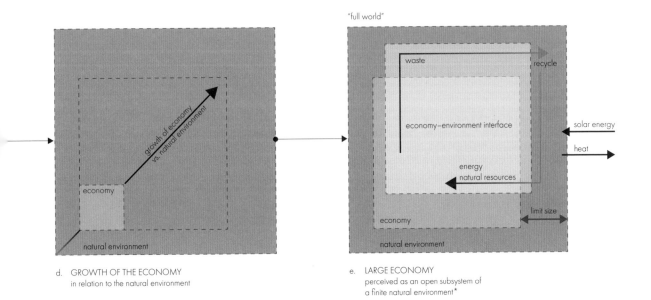

"full world"

growth of economy
vs. natural environment

economy

natural environment

economy–environment interface

waste

recycle

solar energy

heat

energy
natural resources

limit size

economy

natural environment

d. GROWTH OF THE ECONOMY
    in relation to the natural environment

e. LARGE ECONOMY
    perceived as an open subsystem of
    a finite natural environment*

Most economists represent the circular flow of an economy as a process suspended in a void. [Figure 4a] The consequence is that they either assume that it exists in an infinite land of bounty, [Figure 4b] or that somehow nature is a bottomless mine, a system subservient to our economies. [Figure 4c] These unspoken assumptions underpin economic models, and since neoliberal economists have been promoting these models as recipes for reality, they do eventually determine its shape. While such a way of conceiving of the environment was understandable when our economies were comparatively small, [Figure 4d] economies, due to their exponential expansion, should now be drawn—as advocated by Herman Daly—in a "tight" box. [Figure 4e] A partial realization of this fact has, of course, affected the measures promoted by the proponents of the green economy and green building standards. Yet, as explained by Daly, what is required is not just relative efficiency (i.e., better technologies and recycling) but also absolute limits imposed on the economic flow, which is not a closed circular loop. These limits have yet to be established, and we continue to focus on the relative efficiency of the interface that connects the economy with the environment—technology. Philosopher George Parkin Grant once observed,

The very American neologism brings before us our novelty. When "technology" is used to describe the actual means of making events happen, and not simply the systematic study of these means, the word reveals to us the fact that these new events happen because we westerners willed to develop a new and unique co-penetration of the arts and sciences, a co-penetration which has never before existed.[1]

The events and ideas described in Part One Part One - Agendas gradually connected the knowing of nature—the science of ecology—

with the making of domestic architecture—the art of building. Technology, as broadly defined by Grant, was omnipresent in this process, if not explicitly as artifacts, then implicitly either as techniques in their support or as science at their service.[2] Architecture absorbed certain ways of thinking about and acting on the environment into its own "means of making events happen," creating a unique technological interface. Not only were these ideas incorporated into artifacts (appliances, equipment, construction materials, and systems), but they were also reflected in the techniques that support the social acceptance, diffusion, and use of these artifacts: techniques of organization (from informal practices to bureaucratic management); forms of coercion (unwritten norms and legislation); and incentivization (cultural motivation and economic incentives, such as rebates). [Figure 5] Thus, as knowing and making were merging, a particular paradigm of ecological knowledge and environmental awareness was also being embedded in the techniques of coercion (laws, codes, and standards); and later on, techniques of incentivization (various discounts, refunds, and nonfinancial rewards). The latter, while encouraging homeowners to purchase products to comply with green standards, also generate economic activity.

Chapter 4, "The Logics behind Green Technologies and Financial Incentives," focuses on technological artifacts, and on the techniques

Figure 4 [previous]

—

The human economy in the natural environment.
*Inspired by Herman Daly and Joshua Farley, *Ecological Economics: Principles and Applications* (Washington, DC: Island Press, 2004), 18, Fig. 2.1, "From Empty World to Full World."

Figure 5 [opposite]

—

Artifacts, means, and methods: technology as an interface between human economy and the natural environment

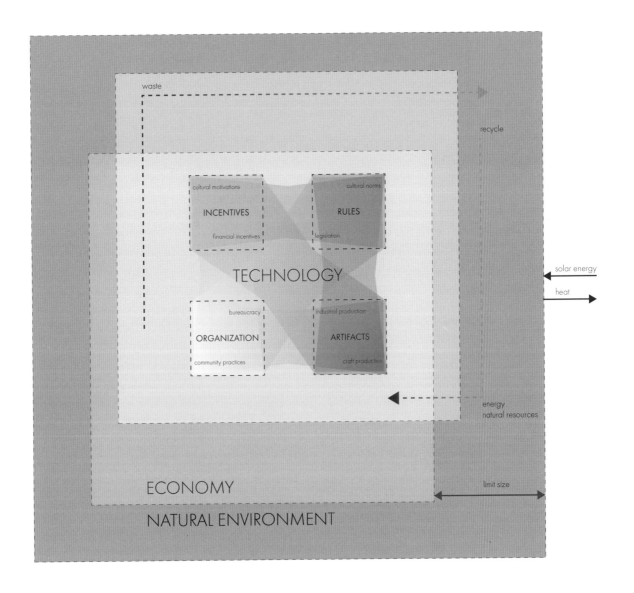

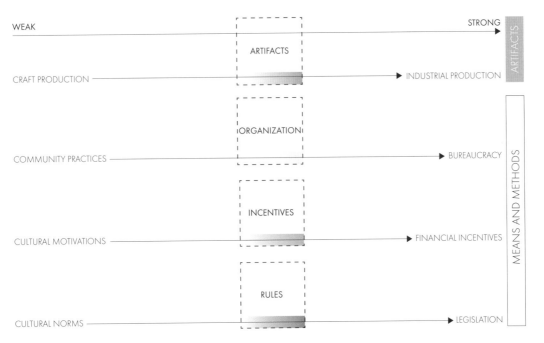

of incentivization used to promote them. In four sections, it explores the role of economic incentives in encouraging certain types of environmental solutions and products. The first section returns to the original critique of the progrowth economy and consumerism fueled by technological innovation. The objective is to better understand how the impact of technology was theorized in the postwar period, how it affected environmental action in the 1970s, and what alternative avenues were rejected by the market. The aim in the second section is to understand when and why governments choose market-driven techniques of incentivization rather than those of coercion when they decide to intervene to correct a market failure—in this case, its incapacity to recognize environmental limitations. The third section provides an overview of environmentally driven incentives available in the state of California to highlight the type of alternative solutions that are promoted and to understand how specific financial instruments and channels of distribution influence outcomes. The focus here is on the tension between the environmental agendas and the energy-security discourse. The last section explores the paradoxes hidden in these techniques, concentrating on the way in which building regulations promote solar technologies. While this last section also demonstrates that building regulations, and their internal grammar, play an important role in promoting technological artifacts—a topic further explored in the next chapter—the main objective is to expose the dangerous consequences of a system that prefers, to use priest and philosopher Ivan Illich's expression, an "overefficient" technological artifact to an efficient yet less predictable tree.

The second chapter of this part focuses on the core of the regulatory system, the legally binding code of building regulations. Chapter 5, "The Structure and Form of Regulations," investigates the environmental repercussions of its own

architecture. It examines the "geography" of the rule-making network, the internal structure of the code, and the grammar of the language used to express particular regulations. The ambition is to understand how these so-called technicalities affect the approach to environmental issues in residential construction and why they should matter to more than just the experts involved in code development. In this chapter, each section investigates one particular aspect of code architecture by means of an example of an environmentally challenging aspect of construction. The first section provides an overview of the different aspects of the architecture of the code. Standards applied to materials used for thermal insulation, specifically foam plastic, are discussed to examine the overall structure of the regulations and to interrogate the environmental implications of the adopted system. The second section of this chapter questions the rule-making matrix, addressing both the hierarchy of regulators and the boundaries of their jurisdictions, to understand how the geography of the regulatory network impacts the regulated environmental dynamics. Since man-made geographic divisions fail to reflect the boundaries of watersheds, this section uses the regulations that target use of water as an example. The third section of this chapter examines the multipart organization of the code and the multilayered structure of the individual parts. It uses air-related regulations to assess the purpose of the different parts and the reasons for internal cross-referencing. The aim is to understand how the structure of the code reflects and safeguards the agency of different authors and authorities. The fourth and final section addresses the internal grammar of the regulations. It explores how the way in which standards are expressed shapes the way we tackle the previously addressed issues. It asks how one is allowed to insulate, provide shade, purify air, and treat water and ultimately demonstrates that the range of accepted solutions does not include vegetation and that this exclusion is deeply embedded in the regulatory language. Ultimately, the final section highlights how the "meta-code" determines what is acceptable and emphasizes the importance of the apparently insignificant inner workings of the regulatory apparatus for the way we practice sustainability and think about ecology.

Chapter 6, "The Power of Predesign in Four Conversations," provides an overview of game-changing initiatives that address some of the issues discussed in the previous chapter. It recounts the experiences of four experts who operate in the predesign phase of construction, during which they prepare the ground for developers, architects, and builders. In the first conversation, code-development advocate and architect Martin Hammer talks about his work on model codes and their impact on the utilization and diffusion of nonstandard construction systems that use minimally processed natural materials, such as straw or earth. In the second conversation, code developer Mathew Lippincott recounts his work on standards for composting and urine-diversion toilets and discusses the impact of the regulatory language on the permissibility of alternative techniques and technologies. In the third conversation, geographer and developer of the ENVI-met software Michael Bruse discusses the current state of digital modeling of plants and their living processes. He speculates about which missing software functionalities are preventing vegetation from being considered as a permissible alternative to building components and mechanical systems currently used for climate control. In the closing conversation, entrepreneur Al Benner talks about the obstacles that hamper the commercialization of living moss walls as a solution to indoor and outdoor air-quality problems. This chapter reflects on what knowledge, digital tools, and laboratory tests are still needed to allow plant-based systems to gain acceptance as a credible alternative and what kind of service and maintenance infrastructure is required for these and other alternative solutions to compete with commonly serviced systems, such as heating, ventilation, and air-conditioning equipment. We also explore why it is so difficult to develop a new standard or model code and who has a better chance of succeeding in the code-development word.

Combating climate change and environmental destruction depends, only in a small part, on the work done by architects. Standards, regulations, building technologies, and digital tools together represent the predesign stage of architectural practice and construction. The recognition of this fact is a fundamental prerequisite for a meaningful change in the way we address the environmental impact of construction. If architects want to stay relevant, they must expand the way they think about construction and look beyond the boundaries of their discipline.

THE LOGICS BEHIND GREEN TECHNOLOGIES AND FINANCIAL INCENTIVES

4.1. Why These Artifacts and Techniques? Critiques

The Limits to Growth report on the "predicament of mankind" enjoyed instant fame and received fierce criticisms after its publication in the early 1970s, none more poignant than the one voiced by philosopher André Gorz. While most critics tried to attack the authors for their imprecise assumptions, approximate modeling methods, or inaccurate predictions out of hopeful incredulity or calculated interest to silence this ecological debate, Gorz agreed with the report. Yet he criticized the ones who commissioned it, the industrialists, scientists, and diplomats who, in 1968, founded the Club of Rome to address the "problematique"—as one of the founders,

—

Generating (green) economy through construction—
the solar panel

industrialist Aurelio Peccei, referred to the existential problems of humankind.[1] With well-founded pessimism, Gorz saw in the report a pragmatic attempt to prepare the economy simply for an epochal shift rather than willingly admit to limits and voluntarily surrender to some form of ecologically oriented socialism. Potential common-sense remedies, such as prioritizing the durability and repair of products, contradicted the basic premises of the capitalist system dependent on planned obsolescence and relentless technological innovation. Rapid deterioration of goods next to artificially stimulated scarcities and consumer needs were at the very heart of the growth-based economy. Gorz perceived any form of counterideology formulated by the leaders of the progrowth economy as an even greater peril, a form of "ecofascism," which posed a threat to both sociopolitical and psychic environments.[2]

The basic functioning of a growth-based economic system depends to a large extent on technology, or, to use the term preferred by Ivan Illich, *tools*. For Illich, tools are both material objects and immaterial devices used to organize, regulate, and incentivize their consumption—they are material and immaterial "means of making events happen," in George Parkin Grant's terms. In his *Ecology as Politics*, Gorz poignantly defined *technology* as "the matrix in which the distribution of power, the social relations of production, and the hierarchical division of labor are embedded."[3] He argued that, although often disguised as technical, societal choices hidden in this matrix are neither optimal nor without alternative. Illich, and Gorz after him, called for a "reversal" of tools from "manipulatory" to "convivial," celebrating a creative and free exchange between humans and their environment and criticizing "the radical monopoly" of certain products that impose compulsory consumption.[4] A radical anarchist, Illich saw an urgent need to inform, involve, and equip people with political and legal tools for a total reversal toward a more autonomous and environmentally respectful use of tools as means rather than ultimate ends. Others, driven by less radical but eventually—and unfortunately—just as utopian ideals, searched for ecological alternatives through adjustment rather than subversion of the sociopolitical regime.

Publicized by economist E. F. Schumacher in his book *Small Is Beautiful*, the Appropriate Technology (AT) movement applied its ecologically driven ideas in isolated counterculture communes scattered across wealthy areas of California and exported them as an "appropriate" or "intermediate" option to developing countries aspiring to reach Western standards without losing their autonomy. Regardless of good intentions and many successful applications, AT advocates, in most cases, fell victim to a series of fallacies. First, believing that one can isolate a community from the dominant global system and its techniques without bringing about atrophy.

Second, assuming that small size always guarantees autonomy and reduced environmental impact.[5] Third, hoping to define once and for all what the appropriate technologies and scales are. As Schumacher himself warned (but nuances often get forgotten), there can never be a final solution; the "idolatry of giantism" was not to be replaced by an "idolatry of smallness."[6] Fourth, AT proponents erred by concentrating on technological artifacts and underestimating the importance of institutional structures and information strategies.[7] And last but not least, they failed to acknowledge that labor-intensive, do-it-yourself solutions can only temporarily compete with the totalizing efficiency of the ready-made alternatives offered by the mainstream market.

"Appropriateness" is not permanent; for many AT followers, the interest in passive solar heating faded away when energy prices fell again at the end of the oil crisis. The alternative communities brought up on issues of the *Whole Earth Catalog* and living in Buckminster Fuller–inspired geodesic domes scattered across Drop City and the like gradually declined. Eventually, most of the young AT advocates grew up, gave up their autonomy, and accepted the Mumfordian "magnificent bribe"—instant gratifications of an apparently effortless lifestyle offered by the modern "megatechnics"—as an appropriate bargain.[8] In a truly Western spirit, some will still occasionally consult an issue of the *Whole Earth Catalog* to enjoy a do-it-yourself Sunday before returning to their fully wired smart home on Monday.

Often categorized as a pessimist and a technological determinist, philosopher Jacques Ellul believed that the success of *technique* hinged on one principle above all: "efficient ordering."[9] As such, the technique autonomously self-directs toward the most *appropriate* arrangement. Since, when using the term *technique*, Ellul had in mind a heterogeneous arrangement of immaterial techniques and material artifacts, it is fundamental to note that the efficiency of one artifact (or system of artifacts) will neither necessarily guarantee nor obstruct the efficient ordering of the overall arrangement.

The most diffused construction method used by the US residential construction industry—the stick frame—provides a simple example. The fact that this technically antiquated construction method persists means that all the techniques that support it are efficiently ordered. Ellul was correct when he said that "financial capitalism checks technical progress that produces no profit."[10] Although in itself the stick frame could be perceived as a "reverse salient"—as historian of technology Thomas P. Hughes refers to an outdated part of a larger system—the momentum of the entire industry is such that no radical innovation has so far managed to replace it.[11] It has been conservatively improved for decades, and the stick frame "scaffold" functions in relative harmony with the most advanced green technologies, smart devices, and mortgage products. While this does not mean that the homeownership system or houses themselves are efficient, the industry does seem efficiently ordered to generate profit.

Sadly, it is hard to agree with Ellul when he says that "capitalism, in spite of all its power, will be crushed by this automatism."[12] On the contrary, technique and its automatism have been so far absorbed by it, at least in the Western world. Ellul was right (although possibly for the wrong reasons), however, when he claimed that decentralization and technical progress could not coexist.[13] This might initially seem wrong—we are immersed in decentralized systems powered by solar panels scattered across private roofs. Yet the technical progress in this sector continues because those decentralized, and apparently democratic, systems are themselves embedded in, and dependent on, larger and increasingly unintelligible centralized systems. These systems

guarantee a performance that is, if not optimal, at least "satisficing," to use Herbert Simon's term. It is that cunning nature of capitalism that assures that technical progress persists in a way that is profitable and grants us an illusion of autonomy while assuring coherent functioning of the entire arrangement. Most importantly, as Lewis Mumford pointed out, "the center now lies in the system itself, invisible but omnipresent."[14] No single actor (possibly with the exception of the atomic bomb) has sufficient power to significantly alter this system.[15]

Never as pessimistic about the reign of technique as Ellul, Mumford had embraced the *machine* in the 1930s but lost some of this optimism when he returned to the topic thirty years later. This change in attitude was inevitable considering the historical events that occurred in the meantime: the Nazi regime and the atomic bomb are the two most significant incarnations of the monstrous megamachine. Yet the shift was also due to the fact that in his earlier writings he decoupled the "young" machine (technological artifact) from the more "mature" mechanisms of regimentation:

> If mechanical thinking and ingenious experiment produced the machine, regimentation gave it a soil to grow in: the social process worked hand in hand with the new ideology and the new technics. Long before the peoples of the Western World turned to the machine, mechanism as an element in social life had come into existence.[16]

If Ellul was pessimistic *tout court*, it is because he always saw this two-headed monster as one indivisible entity; the machine and regimentation, or machine and mechanism, together formed technique. While symptomatic of it, Ellul emphasized that "machine represents only a small part of technique."[17] In *The Pentagon of*

Power, Mumford came closer to Ellul by giving this assemblage of artifacts and mechanisms of regimentation a telling name: megatechnics. It is thanks to various forms of regimentation, both voluntary (incentives) and coercive (regulations), that technological artifacts penetrate the society to maintain—automatically, if not autonomously—a given technopolitical arrangement.

4.2. Persuade or Coerce? Questions

If a particular technopolitical program and the artifacts it depends on—in our case, sustainable development supported by green construction technologies—cannot function successfully without the support of some type of mechanism of regimentation, what drives the selection of one support mechanism over another? How do governments decide whether to persuade or coerce—in other words, incentivize or regulate? In a 2008 paper, expert in construction law Carl Circo discussed the economic reasons for which governments should intervene to correct unsustainable construction practices and promote green building methods.[18] After having reviewed a series of optimistic studies arguing for the economic advantages of green building standards, he pointed out:

> It is one thing to conclude that savings in operations justify increased construction costs to improve energy efficiency during a building's useful life, but it is a far different matter to prove the business case for the whole range of eco-friendly building practices that the sustainability movement advocates.[19]

He then asked whether the industry could be depended on to deliver this promise or if the government should intervene to correct the market failure in order to reach what he defined as noncontroversial objectives: a more efficient use of raw materials and energy and a decrease in pollution.[20] According to Circo, it was justifiable for the government to intervene and, as discussed in the previous chapter, authorities have been intervening in various ways for quite some time. Yet policy makers have a variety of methods to choose from—from corrective economic instruments to command-and-control regulations. Despite the fact that a command-and-control approach often improves economic efficiency, subsidizing alternative solutions, while not necessarily economically efficient, has become incredibly popular.[21] Before examining what is currently promoted through financial incentives (the topic of the next section in this chapter), it is worth asking when and why policy makers use mechanisms of incentivization instead of directly mandating green building standards.

Although the limits of what can be imposed by law are being pushed further as society absorbs more environmental standards in response to concrete threats and apparent risks, the economic cost of green building standards remains of paramount concern.[22] The end users will only accept so much financial responsibility for the consequences of modernization. Indeed, financial incentives are adopted when economic costs can no longer (or not yet) be shifted onto the consumers. This happens mainly when the threats are not perceived as concrete and immediate. Since the acceptance of mandatory restrictions is most commonly driven by fear, incentives are adopted when the threat is not considered imminent enough to be feared.

In *World at Risk*, sociologist Ulrich Beck talks about "fear business" in relation to personal security: "The tightening of laws, a seemingly rational 'totalitarianism of defense against threats'" affects all domains of life, and next to fear of terrorism, the tightening is accepted out of fear of, for example, an ecological catastrophe. Real and "staged" risks drive us to exchange freedom for security and make us "buy into" certain ideologies.[23] Although green standards are promoted as an antidote against real risks associated with climate change, most environmental threats (e.g., loss of biodiversity or bioaccumulation of toxic substances) appear so distant that they are not feared enough to trigger acceptance of tightened rules. Even those that are perceived as directly affecting human life and are feared (e.g., water scarcity) still often fail to attract attention because they do not appear to be sufficiently imminent. Green building standards are a young and contested agenda, and the connection between environmental protection and human welfare is not considered to be direct or immediate enough. Most people prefer to address it later and tend to discount the future. It is, in part, for these reasons that green standards are subsidized. Yet it remains an open question as to whether the subsidies really support what is urgently needed (for the environment) but is financially inconvenient for the customers and the market.

Buying into the ideology acquires a literal meaning when, instead of being forced to embrace a new standard, homeowners follow it voluntarily, and, rather than reducing consumption, they purchase partly subsidized energy-efficient appliances. The fact that consumers are disposed to literally buy into buying their freedom is a fact that policy makers capitalize on when they choose to convince the public by using economic instruments rather than by coercing them through legislation. Green construction incentives serve multiple purposes. They are a paradoxical "tool," to use Illich's term, which simultaneously protects against and promotes unsustainable consumption. This

approach emerged in the 1990s when economists successfully promoted the idea that a market failure is best fixed with market instruments.

Similar to cap-and-trade, end-user incentives are a market's proper instrument. They can supposedly correct a market failure—in this case negative environmental externalities of economic growth—while enhancing market performance and stimulating nothing other than the same growth by promoting purchase of green products. Subsidizing alternative green solutions that can be commercialized is then a preferred choice as it brings this important additional advantage. Moreover, unlike punitive taxes on negative actions, subsidies that promote positive alternatives will also make future prescriptive mandates easier to absorb if not simply unnecessary.[24] Once absorbed by the market and accepted by consumers, the winning alternative naturally becomes a standard or a norm. Often, there is no longer a need to impose it using coercive measures. Sadly, David Pearce was accurate when he pragmatically claimed that environmental improvement depended on whether we managed to capitalize human selfishness. Policy makers have been literally incentivizing this selfishness by providing subsidies for solutions that do not require a renegotiation of our way of life. The current economic system cannot subsidize restraint; instead, it rewards efficient waste. In this lies its cunningness.[25]

A challenging question persists, however: which existing (but economically inconvenient) alternative should be subsidized? If one decides not to curb individual freedom and, instead of taxing the negative effects, incentivizes a positive solution, one has to define what this positive alternative is. But defining an artifact is more challenging than describing performance. The definition must not repress innovation and allow the market to develop competitive solutions in the future; at the same time, it must also prevent misuse of public funds.[26] The former risk occurs when the alternative solution is defined too precisely; the latter when the definition is too broad. While it was possible to create a market for pollution and allow industries to search for innovative ways to reduce it by broadly describing performance objectives (maximum levels of emissions), it would be more difficult (if not absurd) to introduce a similar system in households hoping to spur an open-ended innovation among individual homeowners. This would also be supremely difficult to track.

The short life of the AT movement in California proves that lasting technological inventions require more than enthusiasm and ingenuity. Their penetration into society depends on "politics," "publicity," and simple "horsepower"; they must also guarantee "productivity" and "profit." In other words, they depend, in Mumford's terms, on a "pentagon of power." Since this pentagon is only accessible to large organizations rather than end users who work full-time, the incentivized solutions tend to be defined in exact terms. Rather than incentivizing environmental innovation by setting performance standards, end-user subsidies inevitably support the diffusion of specific technological artifacts—easy to buy and use consumer products.

At the expense of further innovation, subsidies are directed toward "safe winners." Policy makers incentivize the use of those technologies that have been recognized as valid by a broad constituency, once the "technological drama" of their social assimilation has been enacted and a general consensus has been reached.[27] While the most ambitious voluntary rating systems (e.g., the Living Building Challenge) go beyond operational efficiency, achieving such ambitious standards outside a small niche market has been so far perceived as too demanding by the mainstream construction industry. Although policy makers should be directing public funds toward financial incentives that promote the more

ambitious measures that cannot be imposed due to excessive cost, as it will hopefully become evident later in the discussion, most incentives still focus on the operational efficiency of appliances.

This is, in part, because many homeowners still struggle to recognize the benefits of basic operational efficiency. It is also, if not mainly, because these technological artifacts are not distributed for free; they are only partially subsidized. Most end users are only willing to spend money on those appliances that fulfill their own economic objectives rather than larger environmental goals.[28] Although renewable-energy sources and energy-efficient appliances are positive developments—policy makers are, this time, intervening at the right end with the right policy tool, to paraphrase Daly—they are insufficient. These measures should be combined with a mechanism equivalent to Daly's "depletion quota," meant to limit the overall use of natural resources such as minerals and fossil fuels, but this would require curbing consumption, which is not what a market instrument, such as a financial incentive, is made for. As stated in the previously cited *Energy Tax Policy* report: "Subsidizing renewable energy…reduces the average price of energy, which increases demand and ultimately consumption."[29] In fact, although household appliances continue to become more efficient, houses have grown bigger and more technology dependent. In the end, the paradox is that these technological artifacts and the incentives that support them make us consume, waste, and pollute more.

4.3. Incentivizing the Green Market. Solutions

In spring 2017, the Funding Wizard, a searchable database supported by the Environmental Protection Agency, listed more than six hundred incentives and funding programs for sustainable projects available in the state of California.[30] More than three hundred of these programs were applicable to the residential sector. The database categorizes programs according to various aspects of sustainability. [Figure 6] Energy-oriented funding was available through 243 programs in the residential sector. Other aspects of sustainability were addressed with the following frequency: Transportation: 9; Air Quality and Climate: 6; Water: 4; Agriculture and Forestry: 1; Public Health: 1; Waste Management: 0; Community Development and Land Use: 1; Natural Resources: 0; Business and Commerce: 0; Education and Outreach: 0.

Energy-related projects were clearly the most subsidized ones, but after having examined the remaining twenty-three non-energy-related residential incentives, it became clear to me that the majority of them also, even if indirectly, targeted energy efficiency. In the Transportation category, seven of the nine available programs were energy efficiency related, as they subsidized clean-energy vehicles and charging stations. The remaining two (vehicle retrofits) addressed Air Quality and Climate. Under Air Quality and Climate, five (out of six) were energy related (clean-energy vehicles and efficient appliances) and one was water related (conservation through turf replacement). In the Water category, out of four options, one targeted energy (efficient appliances) and the remaining three concentrated on water conservation (efficient appliances and turf replacement). The only program listed under Agriculture and Forestry was energy related, and it offered shade trees as part of a packet of energy-efficiency rebates. The only Public Health incentive available to residential and individual applicants also clearly addressed energy efficiency—it promoted weatherization. The only incentive listed under Community Development and Land Use concerned energy and water conservation as well. Only four programs related exclusively to water conservation and two to air pollution (although they were still indirectly promoting clean-energy vehicles, which also pollute less). Vegetation was mentioned in three programs, in each case serving another purpose, either water conservation through turf replacement or energy conservation through planting of shade trees. No funding was offered to promote biodiversity.

Since energy was the prevailing agenda, another internet source, the Database of State Incentives for Renewables & Efficiency (DSIRE), considered the most comprehensive national database dedicated to energy-efficiency (EE) and renewable-energy (RE) financing programs, was used to understand the specific types of energy-related solutions that were incentivized.[31] In spring 2017, DSIRE listed 214 programs in California, 114 of which were applicable to the residential sector. [Figure 7] While thirty of them related to regulatory policies, eighty-four were financial incentives available to end users. Most of the DSIRE programs included RE incentives: the database listed at least one of the ten different methods for generation of renewable energy eighty-eight times, which includes forty-three incentives for solar photovoltaics and sixteen related to solar water-heating equipment. Most programs also contained multiple EE incentives: the DSIRE database mentioned twenty-three

Figure 6 [overleaf]

—

Grants, rebates, and incentives for sustainable projects. Data source: The Funding Wizard, collected on March 8, 2017.

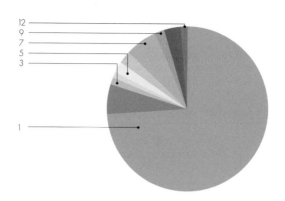

RESIDENTIAL: CATEGORY

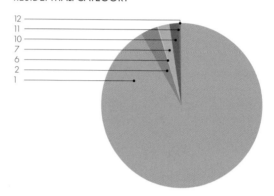

RESIDENTIAL: FINANCING TOOL TYPE

Loan 9
Loan (PACE) 7
Other 10
Tax Incentive 1
Rebates 302

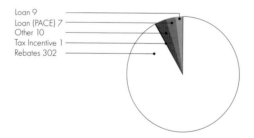

RESIDENTIAL: FUNDING ENTITY

Federal 1
State 26
Local 14
Utilities 291

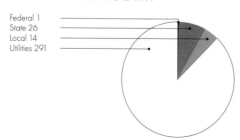

CATEGORY	All Applicants	Residential/Individual
1 Energy	392	243
Appliances		
Equipment		
Heating and Cooling		
Lighting		
Building Envelope		
Whole Building Systems		
Services		
Demand Response		
2 Transportation	31	9
Clean-Air Vehicle		
Public Transportation		
Alternative Fueling/Charging Stations		
Vehicle Retrofits		
Infrastructure		
Demand Reduction		
3 Natural Resources	8	
Habitat Restoration		
Land Conservation		
Wildlife Research and Preservation		
Recreation		
4 Education and Outreach	5	
Environmental Education		
Scholarships or Internships		
Teacher Training		
5 Business and Commerce	13	
Small Business		
Economic Development		
Special Technical Service		
6 Agriculture and Forestry	12	1
Organic Farming		
Resource Conservation and Development		
Urban Forestry		
Agriculture Conservation		
Forestry		
Technical Assistance/Information Services		
7 Air Quality and Climate	24	6
Air-Quality Improvement		
Air-Pollution Control		
Greenhouse Gas Emission Reduction		
California Climate Investments (GGRF)		
Disadvantaged Communities		
Climate-Change Mitigation		
Climate-Action Planning		
Climate Adaptation		
8 Waste Management	10	
Recycling and Composting		
Source Reduction and Reuse		
Pollution Prevention		
Hazardous-Waste Recycling		
9 Other	10	
10 Water	12	4
Water Conservation		
Wastewater Treatment		
Water Pollution Control		
Coastal Water Quality		
Water Recycling		
Community Water-Supply Services		
11 Community Development and Land Use	8	1
Green Building		
Land Acquisition/Facilities/Construction		
Planning and Technical Assistance		
Infrastructure		
Transit-Oriented Development		
Affordable Housing		
Economic Development		
Infill Development		
12 Public Health	7	1
Environmental Health		
Community Health		

CATEGORY			Total Count

		Heat Pumps	25
		Air Conditioners	24
		Water Heaters	20
		Pool Pumps	18
	EE.1	Ceiling Fans	8
	Heating,	Furnaces	7
	Cooling, and	Motor VFDs	6
	Ventilating	Geothermal Heat Pumps	6
	Devices	Fuel Cells Using Renewable Fuels	5
		Motors (Pool)	3
		Programmable Thermostats	3
		Fuel Cells Using Nonrenewable Fuels	2
		Total	127
	EE.2	Building Insulation	21
	Construction	Windows	18
	Materials and	Duct/Air Sealing	12
	Systems	Roofs/Reflective Roofs	11
		Caulking/Weatherstripping	3
		Total	65
ENERGY EFFICENCY / EE	EE.3	Clothes Washers	20
	Household	Refrigerators/Freezers	20
	Appliances	Dishwashers	12
		Total	52
	EE.4	Lighting/LED Lighting	21
	Lighting	Lighting Controls/Sensors	2
		Daylighting	1
		Total	24
		Total	268

	RE.1	Solar Photovoltaics	43
	RE.2	Solar Water Heat	16
	Everything	Solar Space Heat	7
	BUT	Wind (Small)	5
RENEWABLE ENERGY / RE	Solar PV	Solar Thermal Electric	5
		Biomass	4
		Solar Pool Heating	3
		Geothermal Electric	2
		Solar Thermal Process Heat	2
		Solar–Passive	1
		Total	45
		Total	88

CATEGORY			Total Count

RESIDENTIAL: CATEGORY

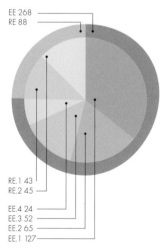

EE 268
RE 88

RE.1 43
RE.2 45

EE.4 24
EE.3 52
EE.2 65
EE.1 127

different energy-efficiency-related technological artifacts 268 times—127 of these incentives related to various types of heating, cooling, and ventilating devices (HVAC), sixty-five to construction materials and systems, fifty-two to household appliances, and twenty-four specifically to artificial lighting.

While the initial overview of the funding programs listed on the Funding Wizard website indicated that most financial incentives supported energy-related projects, the above analysis of energy-related funding listed on the DSIRE website confirmed that the promoted methods were either energy-efficient technological artifacts, such as household appliances, HVAC equipment, materials and construction systems, or renewable-energy generation devices, predominantly solar panels. With a single exception—daylighting and solar-passive heating mentioned once—passive design methods were not subsidized. It is impossible to receive a rebate to pay an architect for their environmentally driven design ingenuity.

While the assessment of the effectiveness of environmental programs is very difficult, what influences it, in addition to the choice of targeted issues and promoted solutions, are the tools and channels used to distribute funding. The energy-efficiency and renewable-energy (EE/RE) programs employ a variety of financing tools that not only influence the results in terms of the primary environmental goals but also raise questions regarding social equity. As explained in *State Support for Clean Energy Deployment: Lessons Learned for Potential Future Policy*, a 2011 report prepared for the National Renewable Energy Laboratory (NREL), the majority of

previously described programs used rebates and tax-based incentives.[32] Among the eighty-four residential programs listed on the DSIRE website, sixty-six offered rebates, which are the simplest financing tool, as they provide direct cash subsidies. Unlike tax credits and exemptions, which are only accessible to middle- and upper-income taxpayers, rebates do not depend on income.[33]

The simplicity and apparent fairness of rebates are positive points, but they also have social drawbacks. As explained in the same report for NREL, "uniform rebate levels can create an economically inefficient level of support, over-subsidizing some purchasers of EE/RE equipment and under-supporting others."[34] The Weatherization Assistance Program, run by the Department of Energy, is one of only a few programs designed to help low-income households retrofit their existing homes and pay energy bills free of charge. Based on an energy audit, authorized contractors install insulation, seal ducts, mitigate air infiltration, and repair or replace heating and cooling systems in order to improve operational efficiency.[35] In many cases federal, state, and utility-distributed subsidies can be combined to improve the diffusion of promoted solutions.

The effectiveness of incentives is assessed both in terms of their environmental and market performance. A common drawback of all direct tools (i.e., rebates) is that while they do guarantee a purchase, they do not always guarantee environmental performance. This is particularly true when it comes to the generation of renewable energy—for example, it is easy to imagine a photovoltaic system installed in an area excessively shaded by trees. Although rare in the residential sector, performance-based incentives and feed-in tariffs address this issue by adopting a different method to distribute renewable-energy funds: subsidies and revenues are guaranteed but are proportional to generated energy.

An important market-related issue recognized in the previously mentioned NREL report is that "the rebates will not help to build a market if potential customers face other significant barriers."[36] While the expression "build a market" is in itself noteworthy—it confirms the principal agenda behind the incentives—the point is that many additional mechanisms support incentives to ensure that regulatory or organizational issues do not create impediments. While some of these technology-friendly policies address systemic issues related to utility companies, others directly affect builders and homeowners.[37] Nonfinancial incentives are, for example, used to grant priority in building-permit issuance or to offer additional zoning rights. An example of a regulatory incentive that was once implemented through the Los Angeles zoning code was the green building floor-area bonus. Paradoxically, it allowed homeowners to build a bigger house as long as it followed the basic Leadership in Energy and Environmental Design (LEED) green building standards. This bonus was eliminated as part of the "anti-mansionization" measures.[38] As anticipated later in this chapter and discussed in the following one, building standards and codes are also used to support the diffusion of incentivized technologies through prohibitive measures (e.g., to prevent excessive shading of solar panels from adjacent trees). Codes are meant to assure performance, but they also indirectly help build the market.

Due to the overwhelming prevalence of energy-related subsidies, funding for the residential incentives is mainly channeled through the Department of Energy (DOE).[39] DOE funding is distributed through two programs to local water and power utilities, which eventually distribute it to their customers in the form of simple cash rebates or direct assistance. The State Energy Program (originally authorized by the Energy Policy and Conservation Act of 1975) provides funding to states, which then distribute them to local utilities.[40] The previously mentioned Weatherization Assistance Program (enabled through the Energy Conservation and Production Act of 1976) provides direct local grants to utilities and authorized contractors.[41]

The second channel is provided by the Department of the Treasury, which is responsible for tax-based incentives. The original energy-efficiency tax incentives (authorized by the Energy Tax Act of 1978) provided a 15 percent tax credit for residential energy-conservation measures and renewable-energy investments between 1977 and 1985, but as previously mentioned, it had little overall effect.[42] The Energy Policy Act of 1992 rendered residential EE/RE subsidies nontaxable.[43] The most comprehensive set of measures was introduced in the Energy Policy Act of 2005 in the form of energy-efficiency and renewable-energy tax credits.[44] These provisions were renewed and expanded as part of President Obama's stimulus package, the American Recovery and Reinvestment Act of 2009 (ARRA), and were available until 2016. The following example illustrates their scale: "Research by ACEEE and ASE (2011) estimates that about 90 percent of windows sold in 2010 and 2011 qualified for the tax credit, a level that indicates a high number of free riders."[45] The ARRA tax credits for energy efficiency have expired, possibly because the market has been assessed as sufficiently built. The tax credits for solar technologies were scheduled to expire in 2021 but were extended to 2023 (although gradually diminishing in value). The assumption is that the solar market is almost built and will require less and less subsidies.

Finally, the specter of mortgage defaults caused by high energy bills continues to drive various forms of regulatory and financial initiatives underwritten by the federal government. As mentioned before, financial risks associated with operational energy efficiency (or rather inefficiency) were already explicitly inscribed into the

Federal Housing Administration (FHA) Minimum Property Standards in 1958.[46] Not surprisingly, the Department of Housing and Urban Development (HUD) also provides funding. Incentives available through HUD are the Energy Efficient Mortgages through FHA and VA lending programs and the FHA PowerSaver Loans.[47] The above-described channels delegate distribution of funds to utilities, authorized contractors, and lenders. Architects are once again absent.

If the financial incentives described so far are not concerned with a broader vision of environmental protection, it is simply because protection of the environment has not been, historically, the primary agenda behind the diffusion of these incentives. While obviously welcomed and supported by environmentalists, the incentives developed in the 1970s were first and foremost a response to a threat to national energy security; the objective was to reduce the reliance on imported oil and encourage domestic investments.

The preponderance of energy security over environmental concerns is evident in the fact that these first energy tax incentives introduced immediately after the 1973 oil embargo supported national oil and gas industries rather than renewable-energy sources. According to the Energy Tax Policy report: "In the late 1970s nearly all revenue losses associated with energy tax provisions were the result of two tax preferences given to the oil and gas industry."[48] Not only did environmental concerns not trigger the introduction of these credits, but it is also unlikely that policy makers, at that time, would have considered an environmental issue as a market failure to be addressed using financial instruments such as tax credits. This approach was adopted in the 1990s, while in the 1960s and 1970s, environmental concerns were only starting to be addressed using old-fashioned command-and-control instruments. In any case, energy productivity was paramount and most

economists did not perceive environmental degradation as a negative externality worth their attention. The voices of economists Ezra J. Mishan and Herman Daly were hardly heard.

The situation gradually changed as cheap oil and gas became more difficult to extract and global warming turned from a concern into a national security threat. The preoccupation with climate change triggered a wave of subsidies meant to encourage the adoption of renewable-energy and energy-efficiency technologies: "By 2010, revenue losses associated with tax incentives for renewables exceeded revenue losses associated with fossil fuels."[49] While energy conservation and efficiency were initially promoted mainly to help reduce dependence on foreign sources of energy, they gradually acquired more environmental significance and gained more impetus when reduction of greenhouse gas emissions became a more widely discussed concern. Even then, the promotion of renewable-energy sources was only in part environmentally driven. The environmental discourse was co-opted to support efforts driven by the same initial agenda: energy security. The difficulty in extracting oil cheaply meant that new sources of energy were urgently needed rather than simply preferred because they are greener.

The result of all these efforts has been a clear increase in energy productivity. While the US economic output has tripled since 1970, the demand for energy has increased by *only* 50 percent. Unfortunately, environmental gains have been less clear. The absolute energy consumption has obviously not decreased, and the reduction in per capita use is relative and only significant considering the tripled size of the economy.[50] The 2011 NREL report estimates that the rate of saving is more than three times lower than the rate of growth in energy demand.[51] The picture becomes even more troubling when one considers outsourcing of industrial production. Externalities are clearly *external* to energy security concerns if heavy industries polluting a foreign country are considered a sign of increased productivity.[52] When national security encounters environmental concerns, system boundaries acquire an uncanny significance. As Ulrich Beck taught us, "there is a systematic 'attraction' between extreme poverty and extreme risk."[53] Yet while poverty is more likely to accept the risks inherent in modernization, risk ultimately has no boundaries. It has become global: "Nuclear contamination…is egalitarian and in that sense 'democratic.' Nitrates in the groundwater do not stop at the general director's water faucet."[54] A reflux of negative externalities is inevitable in the long run.

According to the abovementioned NREL report, the DOE uses five performance metrics to evaluate the effectiveness of the initiatives funded through its State Energy Program: energy saved or generated, greenhouse gas emissions reduction, energy cost savings, funds leveraged, and job creation.[55] According to the same report, in 2011, the cost of renewable-energy incentives that support the diffusion of solar panels still exceeded the average cost of procuring conventional energy supply in most regions, although it might have been below the price at peak hours, when energy is very expensive. On the positive side, however, "an evaluation of the California Solar Initiative estimated that each megawatt of grid-connected solar installed with program support through 2008 represents an estimated annual CO_2 reduction of 885 tons."[56]

It was also estimated that the results were clearly positive in the case of energy-efficiency incentives: "Federal cost of $0.02–2.33 per million Btu of energy saved is far less than the approximately $10 per million Btu we now pay for energy."[57] While we could clearly conserve a lot of energy by simply using common-sense measures, costly repairs receive no incentives in the United States, something that has been tested in Scandinavia.[58] Similarly, passive design

methods cannot be credited for leveraging funds or creating jobs (not counting unpaid housework required to actively manage passive systems— e.g., opening and closing windows). Equally, as discussed at length below, no tree can absorb as much CO_2 as a replacement megawatt of solar energy can prevent. Incentives do not spread sustainability; they assist the market on its path toward the most efficient ordering. Technology, its mechanisms, and its artifacts are used to propagate the paradox of sustainable growth.

4.4. Artifacts Versus Plants. Paradoxes

Shortly after the 1973 oil crisis, when the first energy tax incentives were being introduced, architect Ralph Knowles published *Energy and Form*.[59] The result of more than a decade-long study developed with his students, the book suggested an alternative path toward the conservation of nonrenewable energy and the use of renewable sources through the control of the built form and the command of spatial design strategies rather than through active mechanical equipment. It also constituted the basis for Knowles's "solar envelope" project, which, he hoped, would provide the foundations for an alternative regulatory instrument for urban zoning. Knowles's solar envelope was meant not only to regulate the right to solar access but also to generate the three-dimensional form of an urban fabric in response to the cyclic rhythms of the sun. Unfortunately, urban forms respond better to the rhythms of the market. With little concern for environmental dynamics, extrusion-based zoning envelopes have persisted, maximizing potential profits for the real-estate market. In the meantime, conservation of energy has been delegated to expensive technological artifacts—the engine of another market.

Not without limitations in the era of increasing urban densities, which limit access to daylight, the idea of an adaptive solar envelope has gradually lost to that of the productive solar roof and the technology of the solar panel, leaving the envelope to the real-estate market.[60] The media and the market managed to convince average homeowners that their house was sustainable if its daily operations were powered with solar panels.[61] Unfortunately, as the above discussion of available financial incentives demonstrates, a well-designed building envelope will not receive a subsidy, while a project that promises to compensate for the predicted consumption of energy with solar panels can count on one. Until recently, that house could even be designed bigger (and consume more resources); as mentioned above, the Los Angeles Zoning Code contained a green building bonus applicable to most single-family residential areas. This nonfinancial incentive offered an additional 20 percent of the maximum residential floor area if the new construction was in substantial compliance with the basic requirements for the LEED for Homes program. In part, it meant installing solar panels.

Once a health and welfare concern, the right to solar access has become a quantifiable commodity. Although the efficiency of solar technologies has gradually improved and continues to do so, shade remains a crucial problem.[62] This immaterial yet very concrete issue, which once limited the application of Knowles's passive solar method in dense urban environments, continues to pose a challenge to active solar technologies, as the economy directly couples solar exposure with energy productivity and financial profits. Solar productivity and profitability simply rely on the availability of unobstructed sunlit surfaces, best if horizontal.[63] Not surprisingly, Google's Project Sunroof

works in plan (similar to many municipal tools that assess solar potential)—it is quasi two-dimensional in nature.[64]

As solar technologies improve, they continue to decouple the three-dimensional form of structures from their environmental performance, liberating the economic and aesthetic potential of building volumes. Nonetheless, the power of active technologies is manifested not only in their disconnection from the actual three-dimensional form of the building but also in their spatial mobility. Unlike Knowles's solar envelope, which refers to the actual form of a building, the solar panel is an object that can be located somewhere else. If a newly built structure is doomed to always be in shade, a photovoltaic system can be installed on the roof of the adjacent building that deprives the new construction of its solar access. If one was concerned that, like many experiments in architecture that explored the ecological potential of parametrically controlled patterns, the solar trend also risked being consumed as a surface effect, the risk is no longer there. As long as a sunlit and a relatively flat surface is available for use somewhere, not only is the volume free to deliver maximum profit but also the surface, once an environmental mediator, again becomes a medium perfectly poised to express cultural meaning. It is free to express itself.

As economic incentives coupled with legally binding regulations focus two-dimensionally on operational energy efficiency and greenhouse gas emissions, flatness acquires yet another meaning. These mechanisms of regimentation create a "radical monopoly": they detract attention from other issues, distant places, and longer time scales and fail to clearly communicate ecological trade-offs of the current concentration on low-carbon and net-zero-energy strategies. Ivan Illich once criticized the selectiveness with which environmentalists approached the crisis, saying, "One-dimensional dispute is futile."[65] He

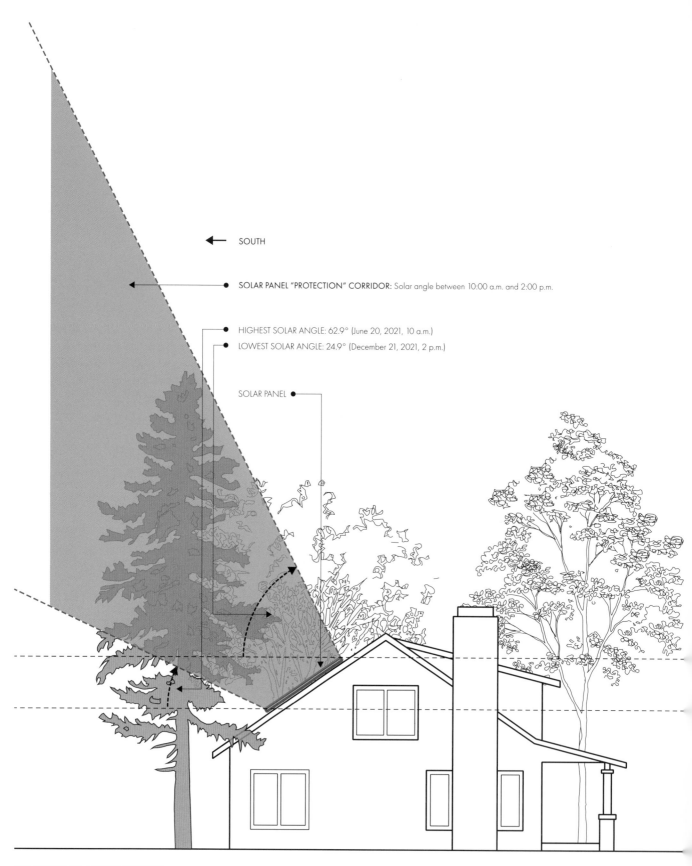

← SOUTH

● SOLAR PANEL "PROTECTION" CORRIDOR: Solar angle between 10:00 a.m. and 2:00 p.m.

● HIGHEST SOLAR ANGLE: 62.9° (June 20, 2021, 10 a.m.)
● LOWEST SOLAR ANGLE: 24.9° (December 21, 2021, 2 p.m.)

SOLAR PANEL ●

LOS ANGELES, CA–LATITUDE: 34.052° N

probably did not expect that the search for solutions would not open up to include multidimensional agendas or that it would also be almost exclusively addressed using what he feared most, "overefficient tools."[66] Surely, building codes and available incentives are not what define the dimensions of ecological awareness among architects, but most homes are built without involvement of an architect. They are built by right, in compliance with the minimum prescribed standards and in response to available financial incentives that prefer technological artifacts to environmentally responsive design.

Perhaps it is worth asking whether the green regime formed by coercive measures and financial rewards represents a positive non-zero-sum game that benefits both the net-zero-energy economy and the natural environment. Can one assume that the parameters are clear and, to use game-theory terminology, the "pay-off" table can be easily drawn up and filled in with quantifiable data and that both the economy and the environment are winners? Admittedly, the Los Angeles Zoning Code promotes a series of integrated methods for the conservation of energy that simultaneously encourage the use of vegetation. In order to mitigate urban temperatures and reduce energy consumption, its Section 12.42, for example, requires a tree-planting plan and a proposal for shading of walls of structures.[67] However, this and other municipal codes also list numerous exceptions from various requirements for solar energy technologies and support structures. Put another way, none of these codes associate the term *solar* with the word *envelope*. The envelope is a shell that dissipates energy, and solar panels are one of the technological artifacts

that are there to fix it. Reyner Banham's "technological scaffold" has acquired notable legislative immunity since he first thought of the house as an ensemble of technological gadgetry in the stunning essay "A Home Is Not a House."[68]

A reference to a minor yet striking provision appears in the Green Building Standards Code. Similarly to the zoning code, the CALGreen Code imposes tree planting as a measure against the heat island effect. Numerous (each reasonable on its own) considerations are listed:

> Tree selection and placement should consider location and size of areas to be shaded, location of utilities, views from the structure, distance to sidewalks and foundations, overhangs onto adjacent properties and streets; other infrastructure and adjacent to landscaping.[69]

One notable exemption affects the "rights" of trees: "In addition, *shading shall not cast a shadow* [my italics], as specified, on any neighboring solar collectors pursuant to Public Resources Code Section 25981, et seq. (Solar Shade Control Act)."[70] The Solar Shade Control Act of 1978 reads:

> 25982. After the installation of a solar collector, a person owning or in control of another property shall not allow a tree or shrub to be placed or, if placed, to grow on that property so as to cast a shadow greater than 10 percent of the collector absorption area upon that solar collector surface at any one time between the hours of 10 a.m. and 2 p.m., local standard time.[71]

Even in California, this means solar elevation angles as low as 24.9 degrees on December 21 at 2 p.m. [Figure 8] One feels urged to ask what a neighborhood would look like if trees that fall into this range were consistently prohibited in the future. Would ornamental bushes replace

Figure 8 [opposite]
—
Solar panel "protection" corridor according to the Solar Shade Control Act of 1978

them to protect solar panels? And if the common interest developments, criticized—rightly so—for exacerbating social divisions and urban injustice, seem perfectly poised to restrict the special rights granted by codes to solar panels, this option has been ruled out from the very outset. Among its many important provisions related to the right to sunlight, another piece of California state legislation from 1978, the Solar Rights Act (AB 3250), famously protects solar technologies against the private covenants, conditions, and restrictions that regulate these exclusive developments by simply ruling them void.[72]

In "Thinking about Technology," George Parkin Grant observes, "The coming to be of technology has required changes in what we think is good, what we think good is, how we conceive sanity and madness, justice and injustice, rationality and irrationality, beauty and ugliness."[73] Those who doubt whether it is right (good or beautiful) to remove a tree to gain solar power can be quickly reassured that the carbon math is clearly on the side of the solar technology: the environment will—according to this math—gain more from a solar panel than from a tree! An article entitled "Should You Cut Down Trees to Go Solar?" found on EnergySage's website provides a version of this troublesome math. The authors recognize a number of other factors to consider, among them the cost of removing the tree that casts the unwanted shadow, displacement of wildlife relying on it for food and shelter, removal of the beneficial shade provided by that tree during summer months, and other quality-of-life benefits. They conclude: "Depending on your *personal preferences* [my italics], this may or may not change your decision."[74] The statement expresses a kind of common sense, but, as Grant once said, "it is a common sense from within the very technology we are attempting to represent."[75] From within

our technopolitical order, this common sense comes almost automatically. Ellul writes,

> When everything has been measured and calculated mathematically so that the method which has been decided upon is satisfactory from the rational point of view, and when, from the practical point of view, the method is manifestly the most efficient of those hitherto employed or those in competition with it, then the technical movement becomes self-directing. I call this process automatism.[76]

It may well be that distributed solar power embodies the future and that an individual tree is not efficient enough to be given precedence over a solar panel and hence does not deserve to be supported with tax money. But a question persists: What are the environmental, bioethical, and cultural repercussions and limitations of this bioeconomic attitude that prefers an overefficient tool—a tool claimed democratic by many just because it is distributed—to a tree?[77]

Trees are glorious machines (although not an artifact of human making). The list of functions they perform and services that they deliver is long. According to ecologists, trees improve air quality by absorbing particulates and pollutants, removing carbon dioxide, preventing soil erosion, purifying stormwater, providing habitat, limiting noise, and regulating the microclimate.[78] Although large patches of urban forest are required to substantially reduce the urban heat island effect, trees reduce temperatures by shading buildings and paved surfaces. Keeping impervious surfaces cooler reduces the amount of energy used for indoor cooling in summer and consequently minimizes the amount of heat emitted by the mechanical systems. Studies demonstrate that trees can reduce energy used for cooling up to 40 percent when positioned, considering local winds, temperatures, and sun path.

Even if the capacity of trees to store carbon is not comparable to that of a solar panel (which does not store it but indirectly minimizes its release), trees emit oxygen, which the solar panels cannot yet do. According to the American Forestry Association, an average-sized tree releases enough oxygen for a family of four. Trees are also capable of trapping particulates and capturing other air pollutants, such as nitrogen oxides, sulfur oxides, particulate matter, and ozone. Trees use solar energy to evaporate water, which brings a double benefit: while reducing the amount of energy that would otherwise heat up surfaces, they improve air moisture levels. They also protect humans from ultraviolet light. During a rainstorm, they reduce stormwater runoff as they capture substantial amounts of water and process it through evapotranspiration. They have a significant influence on the soil properties and the organisms that occupy the rhizosphere. Soil properties and soil organisms help maintain a balanced water cycle and contribute to the decomposition of organic litter, which constitutes the main source of soil nitrogen, indispensable for plant growth and health. Trees play a key function in the overall urban metabolism and support biodiversity by providing habitat and nutrients for other organisms. Individual trees do not provide stable habitats, but they can form connective corridors and provide stepping-stones for animals.

The reason for listing so many details about the ecological function of trees (drastically simplified here) is that these facts cannot be omitted if we are to fully comprehend the ecological trade-offs of a "flattening" culture centered around the solar panel. And even if scientists were able to assess the exact value of the ecosystem services rendered by trees using bioeconomic methods, not everything can be expressed as a quantity to be then listed in a pay-off table and assessed using the federal assessment metrics. The presence of vegetation, especially in residential neighborhoods, fosters a sense of extended community of living beings and intensifies our involvement with the ultimate otherness—the world of plants.

Clearly, these aspects are impossible to quantify. As David Pearce points out, they are not something that economists work with. Maybe, after all, it is better this way. Otherwise, the risk of what Gorz called "ecofascism" and Beck referred to as "ecocracy" would be even greater.[79] And while Illich warned that the reestablishment of "an ecological balance depends on the ability of society to counteract the progressive materialization of values," for now, unfortunately, "there is nothing left to do but wonder at a mechanism that functions so well and, apparently, so tirelessly."[80] A mechanism that supports green technologies using voluntary incentives and legally binding regulations. Regulations whose very structure and form—as discussed in the following chapter—are designed to support market-driven and product-oriented strategies while precluding other means and methods that could help humans achieve a greater syntony with the natural environment.

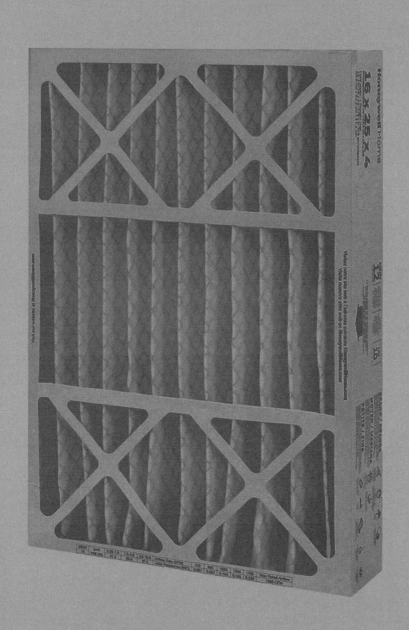

THE STRUCTURE AND FORM OF REGULATIONS

5.1. Who Protects the Environment? Focus: Materials

By selectively endorsing certain construction methods over other existing options, code makers and standard setters have the power to determine the fate of new technologies. Not surprisingly, building codes have been used as an alternative to or in combination with financial incentives to promote choices deemed more desirable. In this chapter, I argue that the way in which the codes are developed, organized, and phrased is as important as the prescriptions they contain. In other words, the structure of building regulations and the language used to express

—

Modulating the built environment with regulations— the HVAC filter

them carry hidden environmental consequences that are—even if unintentional—almost certainly more permanent than the messages they communicate. In this opening section, I examine how the residential code, specifically the 2019 California Residential Code, by regulating the boundaries of the indoor environments that must be safeguarded, implicitly also sets the boundaries of what is outside of the code's protection— the unconfined natural environment.[1]

The purpose of the Residential Code, part of the California Building Standards Code (California Code of Regulations, Title 24), is to "safeguard the public health, safety and general welfare" by protecting dwelling units from natural and man-made hazards.[2] According to the code, a "dwelling unit" revolves around a more strictly protected and regulated interior core consisting of "habitable spaces."[3] The term *habitable* appears in numerous sections of the code, and those sections that define the main attributes of "habitable rooms" reflect the core values embedded in the code. Section R303 specifies how habitable interiors should be illuminated, ventilated, and heated to satisfy basic health and comfort requirements. Sections R304 and R305 determine the minimum room dimensions to assure general welfare. Safety, in case of emergency, is regulated in Sections R310 and R311, which define means of escape and egress. Many other sections define the specific material and spatial attributes of the elements that demarcate the habitable interiors.

A quick analysis of how the term *interior* is employed in relation to various objectives of the code can, by consequence, provide a quick way to understand how the code defines the boundaries of the safeguarded environment. This type of reading is clearly partial, yet it is also transversal due to the many ways in which the term is used. The distinction, for example, between the interior and exterior face of a wall is, of course, of great importance when it comes to protecting the core of a dwelling unit—its interior. In fact, the term often appears in the Residential Code; by the time one reaches page 651, the interior of a habitable room is structurally stable, accessible, protected against fires, floods, termites, speculation, and weather. After 183 pages of the Energy Code and 217 pages of the Green Building Standards Code (CALGreen Code), the interior is also energy efficient and environmentally well tempered.[4]

Thermal Barrier Against the Insulation

Two cross-referenced sections trigger a particular curiosity, as their purposes appears paradoxical: they seem to be protecting the interior environment from the very means that protect it from the natural elements. The first section is part of a larger set of prescriptions regulating interior wall coverings and reads:

> R702.3.4 Insulating Concrete Form Walls. Foam plastics for insulating concrete form walls constructed in accordance with Sections R404.1.2 and R608 on the interior of habitable spaces shall be protected in accordance with Section R316.4.[5]

Section R316.4 is a part of a set of prescriptions that concentrate on the use of one family of products only: foam plastics. It specifies how this type of insulation should be protected and indirectly explains why it needs such protection:

> R316.4 Thermal Barrier. Unless otherwise allowed in Section R316.5, foam plastic shall be separated from the interior of a building by an approved thermal barrier of not less than 1/2-inch (12.7 mm) gypsum wallboard, 23/32-inch (18.2 mm) wood structural panel or a material that is tested in accordance with and meets the acceptance criteria of both the Temperature Transmission Fire Test and the Integrity Fire Test of NFPA 275.[6]

If in linguistic doubt, the term *thermal barrier* refers to fire resistance, not protection from excessive heat. A half inch of gypsum or less than an inch-thick space of wood will generate enough time—fifteen minutes to be precise—for the person in a habitable interior to escape in case the plastic foam catches fire. Foam is highly flammable, but aren't flame retardants there to provide a sufficient thermal barrier? A quick search on the website of Home Depot (the leading US home-improvement retailer) might not explain why the use of plastic foam is so tightly regulated in the building code, but it does explain other reasons why foam should be separated from the habitable interior, or better, why both the interior and the exterior environment should be protected from this material.

Foam Plastic Insulation

Most rigid foam-insulation products available at Home Depot appear benign; only those with a deep interest in environmental issues know the hidden risks of common expanded polystyrene (EPS) and extruded polystyrene (XPS) boards.[7] Not only do they apparently decompose in a dangerous way when in contact with seawater, but the brominated flame retardant hexabromo-cyclododecane (HBCD) that they contain has also been banned by many countries as part of the *Stockholm Convention on Persistent Organic Pollutants*.[8] Still, the risks embedded in other products advertised by Home Depot are more immediately visible. While apparently nontoxic to humans after it has cured, Touch 'n Foam polyurethane spray foam comes with a long safety data sheet, a clear warning that hazards exceed accepted levels of risk. Harmful, sensitizing irritants prior to, and during application, the components of this polyurethane foam are also hazardous to aquatic life.[9] Once cured and eventually disposed of, polyurethane is difficult to decompose in landfills, it releases poisonous gases when incinerated, and its chemical recycling is risky due to by-products.[10]

Unlike steel, aluminum, or glass, plastics cannot be physically recycled forever. They eventually end up in landfills. The distance between a landfill and groundwater is often a "short leach." Another highly efficient option available through Home Depot, the Rmax Thermasheath-3, is "made of environmentally sound, closed cell, polyisocyanurate foam."[11] While it remains unclear what "environmental soundness" means, polyisocyanurate (abbreviated as polyiso, or PIR), does offer the greatest R-value per inch, if we still consider that to be an indication of superior performance.[12] It is also often listed as an alternative to EPS and XPS, since it does not use brominated flame retardant HBCD. However, the chlorinated flame retardant TCPP (trisphosphate) typically used in polyiso panels as a replacement for HBCD is by many considered equally risky (just less understood and tested).[13]

Meanwhile, the Environmental Protection Agency warns against other ingredients used in this material that are either considered a hazard or have not been sufficiently tested yet.[14] The composition of this highly energy-efficient—if we are to rely on its R-value—foam raises doubts, and since it is similar to polyurethane, its end of life is most likely far from being environmentally sound.[15] Unfortunately, since it is hard to test all aspects of new materials, they are considered innocent until proven guilty. One more product, the Kerdi-Board tile substrate, draws attention as its description comes with a warning: "California residents: see Proposition 65," which warns, "Cancer and Reproductive Harm."[16] A type of XPS board, it most likely also contains brominated flame retardant HBCD, although the manufacturer does not provide this information. Yet, according to the Residential Code, as long as one acts "in accordance with the code and the manufacturer's instructions," one will stay safe, healthy, and generally well.[17] Would Gregory Bateson qualify it as a "double bind"?

Unwarranted Ecotoxicity

The plastic foam is here to protect humans from extreme elements. Although some studies point out that they are redundant and environmentally unsound, the flame retardants in the foam and Section R316.4 of the building code protect the interior (and the humans in it) from flames.[18] Or could it be that the above section protects the interior from the flame retardants? In any case, no article in the Residential Code protects the exterior environment from the weatherproofing foam, whether the ecotoxicity of its ingredients or simply from its sheer, nonbiodegradable bulk.

The product of a nationwide effort undertaken in the 1990s, the Residential Code has become more universal, but it still reflects the original triple-purpose of code making: public health, safety, and welfare. Its anthropocentricity appears socially just, but it is also ecologically shortsighted. One would hope that due to its sustainable agenda, the CALGreen Code would extend the boundary of the protected bubble beyond the walls of the interior of one's habitable room into a larger, exterior environment. Yet again, the code recognizes the importance of the natural environment, but it fundamentally describes it as a means and not an end in itself:

> 101.2 Purpose. The purpose of this code is to improve public health, safety and general welfare by enhancing the design and construction of buildings through the use of building concepts having a reduced negative impact or positive environmental impact and encouraging sustainable construction practices.[19]

After a quick search for "foam," one finds the following prescription:

> A5.205.3.2. Installation of Urea Formaldehyde Foam Insulation. Urea formaldehyde foam insulation may be applied or installed only if: 1. It is installed in exterior side walls; and 2. A four-mil-thick plastic polyethylene vapor barrier or equivalent plastic sheathing vapor barrier is installed between the urea formaldehyde foam insulation and the interior space in all applications.[20]

The greenest part of the code, the CALGreen Code, does not restrict the use of a number of commonly specified yet dangerous foams discussed above (of course, it would be an internal contradiction to prohibit them—after all, the CALGreen Code is just another part of the larger set of regulations), and it also names and regulates urea formaldehyde, a foam judged unsafe as a carcinogen by California's own Proposition 65 and banned by many jurisdictions in the 1980s.[21] Many, since then, have claimed

that the precaution was excessive, and similar products exist today under new names (with reduced formaldehyde off-gassing), but to be sold, a product must be regulated.[22] By regulating it, the code internalizes, or better, interiorizes it. By norming, it normalizes.

Who Protects the Exterior?

As specified in Section R316.3 of the Residential Code, ASTM E84, a third-party fire standard developed by ASTM International (formerly known as the American Society for Testing and Materials), protects the foam from flames by imposing a certain level of flammability, hence the use of flame retardants.[23] In reference to another national standard developed by the National Fire Protection Association, the NFPA 275, the previously cited Section R316.4 imposes a half-inch layer of gypsum board to prevent flames (and toxins) from spreading into a habitable interior. Article A5.205.3.2 of the CALGreen Code protects interiors from urea formaldehyde foam by imposing an extra layer of an apparently harmless polyethylene barrier.

No article or jurisdiction protects the exterior from either of them—from brominated flame retardants, urea formaldehyde, EPS, XPS, polyiso, polyurethane, or from the tons of polyethylene that we dump into the oceans and landfills each year.[24] [Figure 9] Even if the interior of the habitable room in which one resides seems oppressively small, if not toxic, at least it is safe and healthy according to the California Building Standards Code. Still, the interface that separates the interior from the environment is a fuzzy space that protects and harms at the same time. Not only does the code fail to protect our health from a multitude of poorly understood materials,

Figure 9 [opposite]
—
Thermal insulation of "habitable" interiors: climate control versus environmental protection

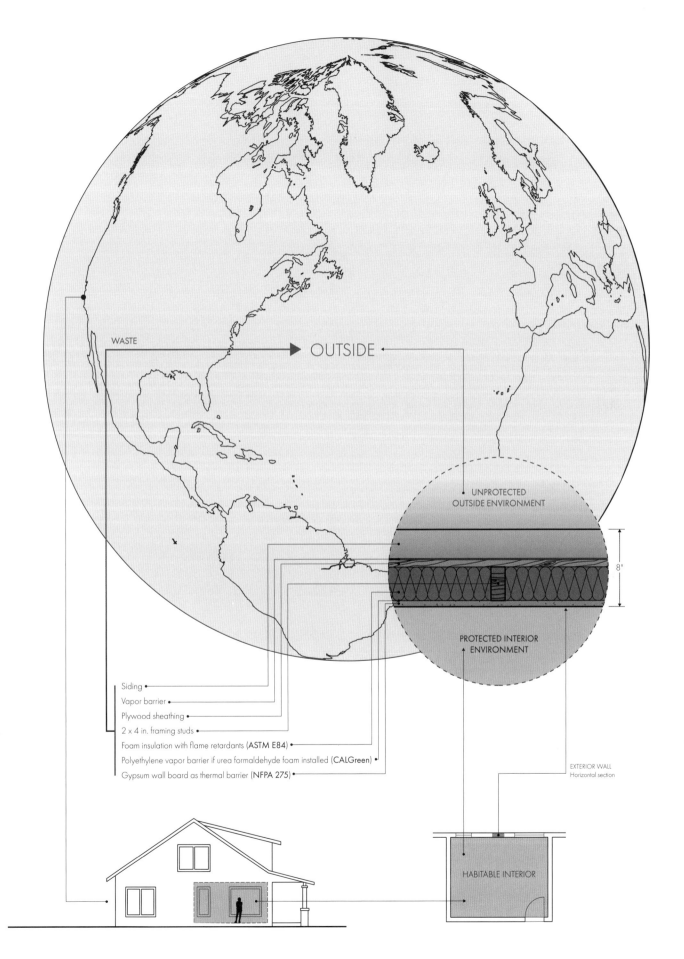

WASTE

OUTSIDE

UNPROTECTED
OUTSIDE ENVIRONMENT

8"

PROTECTED INTERIOR
ENVIRONMENT

Siding
Vapor barrier
Plywood sheathing
2 x 4 in. framing studs
Foam insulation with flame retardants (ASTM E84)
Polyethylene vapor barrier if urea formaldehyde foam installed (CALGreen)
Gypsum wall board as thermal barrier (NFPA 275)

EXTERIOR WALL
Horizontal section

HABITABLE INTERIOR

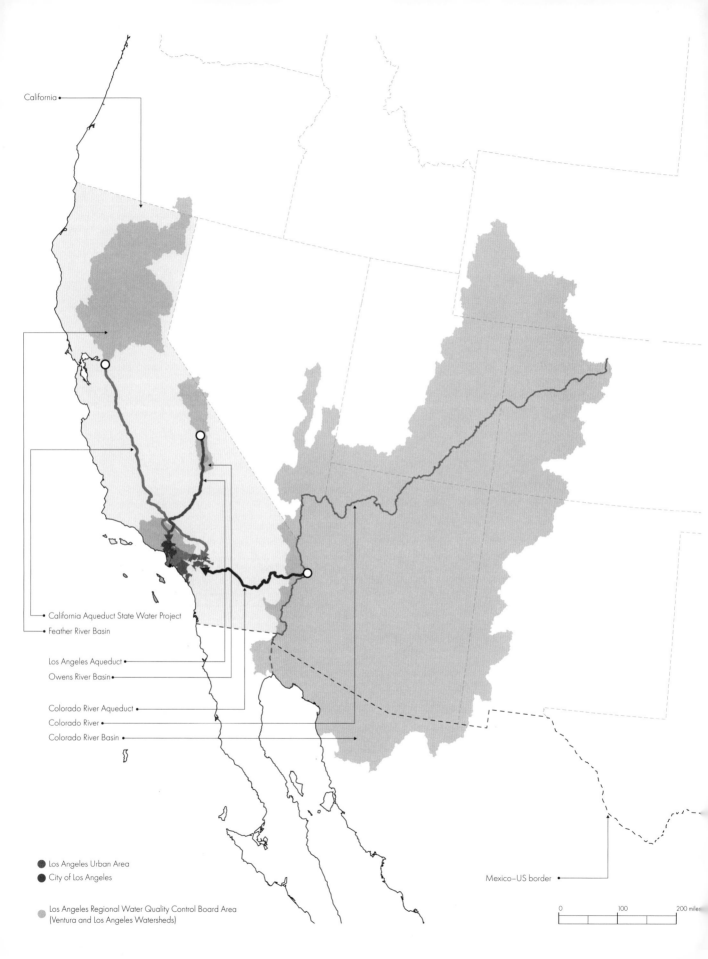

California

California Aqueduct State Water Project
Feather River Basin

Los Angeles Aqueduct
Owens River Basin

Colorado River Aqueduct
Colorado River
Colorado River Basin

Mexico–US border

Los Angeles Urban Area
City of Los Angeles

Los Angeles Regional Water Quality Control Board Area
(Ventura and Los Angeles Watersheds)

0   100   200 miles

it does even less to protect the environment from them. It is clearly beyond its scope to regulate the market—it can only regulate the way available products are used. A building code is only as green as the economy that created it. Perhaps Home Depot might be able to do more for the environment than the building code.

5.2. Where Are the Rule Makers? Focus: Water

Water, more than any other aspect of the environment, is a matrix. It is the substance from which life originates and on which it depends.[25] Human dwellings rely on a constant and strictly regulated provision of running water for personal hygiene, food preparation, climate control, fire protection, and gardening. Domestic effluents are taken care of in an equally invisible and apparently effortless way. The "blue gold" becomes "black medium" as used water, bodily waste, and food leftovers are piped down the drain. Although a small percentage of rainwater is collected, most of it, instead of seeping into the ground, is "safely" piped away through another network of invisible drains to rivers, lakes, and oceans. Depending on whether it is called supply, sewage, runoff, flood, or excessive moisture, water assumes the role of resource or risk. Opportunities, hazards, regulations, and

Figure 10 [overleaf]
—
The geography of rule making: from global treaties, through federal laws and state regulations, to municipal ordinances

Figure 11 [opposite]
—
The geography of Los Angeles water supplies. Data sources: State of California, United States Geological Survey

regulators change accordingly. Since every aspect of water use and handling is regulated, and the geographies of these man-made hydrologic systems are vast and complex, it seems appropriate to examine water-related regulations in relation to the regulatory matrix. [Figure 10] In urban areas located on the coast of Southern California, the sources of clean water and the final destination of contaminated effluents are rarely located within the same watershed. Both treated wastewater and polluted stormwater are piped to the ocean, while potable water is transported from distant places, affecting the ecology of other watersheds. Unlike natural hydrologic systems, water supply and drainage networks are wide open. They disregard the geography of water, as do the rules that govern these networks.

Supplies

Although federal laws provide a framework for state and local regulations pertaining to the use and management of most resources, no federal act regulates the allocation of water supplies.[26] The issue is regulated by state laws and managed at state, regional, and municipal levels. In California, as in the other arid states of the American Southwest, the regulatory compromise between riparian and appropriative rights reflects an epic tale of appropriations and acquisitions possible thanks to borderline legality, fraud, and graft.[27] No matter how the economic output of the Los Angeles region is accounted for to justify its water consumption, the situation feels far from sustainable if one stands in the dusty Owens Valley or the dry Colorado River delta.[28] While the question of water rights goes beyond the scope of this project, it is fundamental to remember that Los Angeles relies on water "grabbed" from elsewhere. [Figure 11] Only one-tenth of its water is extracted locally, and instead of replenishing groundwater supplies, most of the rainfall is dumped into the ocean. According to the Los

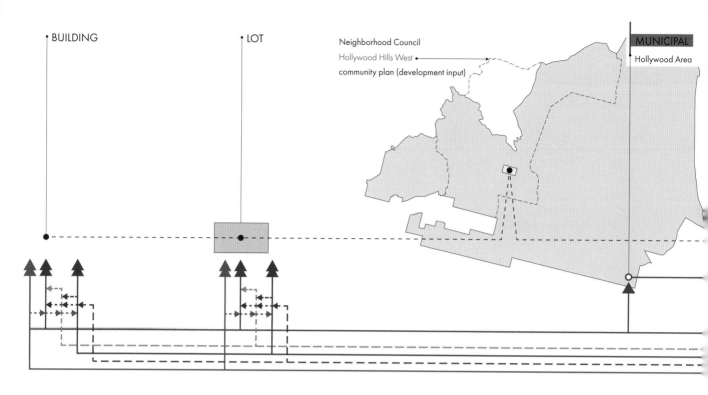

BUILDING

LOT

Neighborhood Council
Hollywood Hills West •
community plan (development input)

MUNICIPAL

Hollywood Area

model building codes, e.g., International Building Code
standards, e.g., ASHRAE 55
third-party certifications, e.g., USGBC's LEED

NATIONAL NGC

Washington, D

treaties, e.g., *Stockholm Convention on Persistent Organic Pollutants*
protocols, e.g., *Kyoto Protocol*

GLOBAL

acts, e.g., Clean Air Act
regulations, e.g., ADA Guidelines

FEDERAL

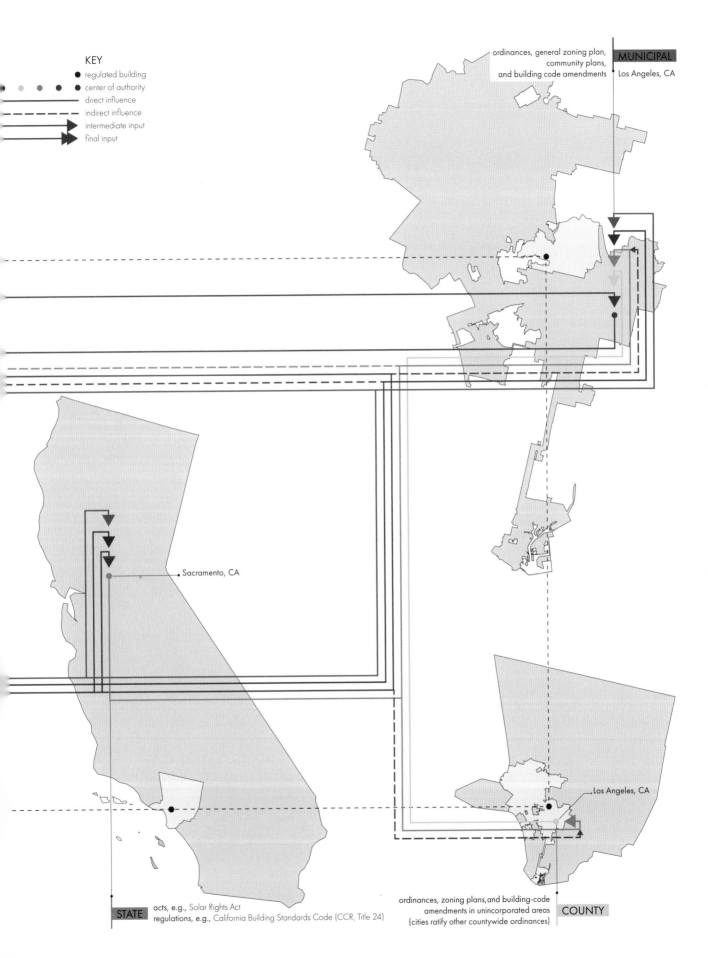

KEY
● regulated building
● center of authority
—— direct influence
----- indirect influence
⟶ intermediate input
⟹ final input

ordinances, general zoning plan,
community plans,
and building code amendments
MUNICIPAL
Los Angeles, CA

Sacramento, CA

Los Angeles, CA

STATE
acts, e.g., Solar Rights Act
regulations, e.g., California Building Standards Code (CCR, Title 24)

ordinances, zoning plans, and building-code
amendments in unincorporated areas
(cities ratify other countywide ordinances)
COUNTY

Angeles County Flood Control District, "the same infrastructure that protects the region from large-scale flooding pours out into the ocean roughly one-third of the region's total annual water demand."[29]

While no federal act impedes such waste of rainwater, the state—driven by increasing water scarcity—has ordered municipalities to develop water-management plans and adopt water-efficient landscape ordinances by enacting the Water Conservation in Landscaping Act of 2006 (AB 1881), all in order to reduce runoff and improve infiltration.[30] As stated in the municipal Stormwater Capture Master Plan, in the highly impervious—almost watertight—city of Los Angeles, only 6 percent of incoming flow is captured.[31] In 2015, the annual incoming flow was estimated to be 831,000 acre-feet, an amount that exceeds the Los Angeles Water Demand Target for 2035 (estimated to be 551,000) by one-third.[32] Although the state has also launched rainwater collection incentives, the projected two thousand acre-feet captured in rain barrels combined with a bioswale for every household will not undo a century of tropical gardening.[33] It will also not revert decades of real-estate speculation.[34] In fact, the Los Angeles Department of Water and Power is launching a new era of water projects, only this time they will be less spectacular. Rather than impressive dams and aqueducts, it will take a lot of apparently fallow land for surface spreading, some surgical precision to position recharge wells, and a dose of unglamorous restraint to allow the rest of it to simply seep into the soil, replenishing the groundwater for the sake of a distant future.[35]

Stormwater Discharge
If the geography of water regulations is getting closer to that of the watersheds, it is because in the face of water shortage, regions act like city-states to limit their reliance on imports. While it is the scarcity that drives the local

authorities to consider capturing stormwater runoff worthwhile, it was the environmental concerns triggered by Rachel Carson's *Silent Spring* that made the federal government scrutinize the pollutants in the uncaptured portion of that same runoff. Unlike the Safe Drinking Water Act, which regulates the levels of contaminants in drinking water, the Clean Water Act of 1972 (CWA) goes beyond the issue of human health as it regulates contaminants in all waste discharged into US waters.[36] Since 1987, it has included nonpoint sources of pollution, such as urban runoff. Thanks to this amendment, discharging runoff requires a National Pollutant Discharge Elimination System (NPDES) permit. The federal government delegates the task of issuing these permits to the states.[37]

Since the geography of hybrid hydrologic systems (in part natural watersheds, and in part artificially created and managed stormwater drain systems) does not overlap with administrative areas, stormwater runoff is managed by parallel but cross-boundary authorities, water-quality control boards, and flood-control districts. Additionally, since the states (and various boards and districts) have no right to interfere with land-use control, they release permits but leave the mechanics to cities and counties.[38] To meet the requirements listed in the permit, the City of Los Angeles adopted the Stormwater Low Impact Development (LID) Ordinance, which applies to projects that add more than five hundred square feet of impervious area.[39] It requires them to capture and mitigate urban runoff on-site by increasing infiltration, evapotranspiration, bioretention, phyto-purification, and use of stormwater. Although the Stormwater LID Ordinance and the Model Water Efficient Landscape Ordinance (MWELO) both address infiltration and use of stormwater, they are driven by different agendas promoted by different authorities. The former, imposed by a federal act, the CWA, is clearly environmentally driven; the nature of the latter, imposed by a state act (AB 1881) in drought emergency, is conservationist and managerial. While in some way they complement each other and express a healthy system of checks and balances, they evince the lack of coordination between the geography of the rule-making matrix and that of the watershed. Although eighty-four municipalities (including Los Angeles) share one watershed and one runoff discharge permit, each municipality is free to choose and implement its own mitigation measures. The watershed, the permit-issuing body, and the authority that implements the measures all have different geographic boundaries. Heavily managed, the watershed remains nobody's *oikos*.

Sanitary Sewage

Within less than a mile's distance from the outlet of the Ballona Creek flood-protection channel, where the stormwater from the Los Angeles Basin is released, the Hyperion treatment plant discharges wastewater collected from a slightly different area. Less than the watershed, more than the Los Angeles municipality, the area served by the plant reflects cross-municipal contracts rather than a geography. In the CWA, sanitary sewage generated by individual house-holds is considered "point source pollution," since it is collected and disposed of by a treat-ment plant. It is the plant, rather than individual residents, that is responsible for respecting the federal provisions contained in another NPDES permit issued by the same regional branch of the California Water Quality Control Board.[40]

In single-family households, approximately half of the freshwater consumption is used indoors, and most of it—once used—is eventu-ally piped to a treatment plant.[41] The largest single indoor use of water (more than 21 percent) is to flush toilets; a significant portion of the second largest use (18 percent via faucets) takes place in kitchens, in part to dispose of food waste.[42]

Neither of them can be recycled as gray water. Although waterborne disposal of waste is an act of extravagant luxury, unlike distributed stormwater management or energy production, decentralized sewage treatment has yet to capture the public imagination. Although at-home kitchen-waste composters are becoming increasingly popular, composting toilets—as discussed in Chapter 6, "The Power of Predesign in Four Conversations"— are still waiting to be properly marketed as a green technology. Centralized treatment of human waste is not only a waste of water. Even an award-wining plant, such as Hyperion, relies on an extensive network of pipes susceptible to leakage and overflow during wet weather.[43] Even if all gray water and stormwater were to be captured and reused locally, these pipes would still have to be maintained to dispose of the bodily waste and food leftovers. While waterborne disposal of kitchen waste is not a problem for the treatment plant, the Los Angeles Department of Public Works warns not to dispose of food scraps in the drain to minimize clogging and breakage of pipes, which this authority maintains. Nevertheless, since in-sink garbage disposal seems not to significantly increase water consumption and reduces the amount of waste transported to landfills, it is a market standard normed (and therefore normalized) in the state-approved building code.[44]

The issue of waterless toilets is more problem-atic. Clearly, composting human waste on-site requires occasional work, it can constitute a health hazard if not handled properly, and the end product needs to be used or disposed of appropriately.[45] However, judging by the regula-tory language, the problem might be mainly cultural. According to the Residential Code, one of the provisions that makes a dwelling is the presence of a toilet, or, more precisely, a "water closet":

R306.1 Toilet Facilities. Every dwelling unit shall be provided with a water closet, lavatory, and a bathtub or shower.[46]

Individual parts of the building code are based on model codes developed by various nongovernmental organizations. These model codes also refer to a multitude of technical standards. Consequently, nongovernmental standard-setting organizations exert a tremendous influence on the environment by defining the rules hidden in the code. If the mention in the model code or a reference to an existing standard is lacking, the issue will likely also be poorly regulated by the state. In fact, the state-written CALGreen Code mentions composting toilets in Section A4.303.4, "Nonwater Urinals and Waterless Toilets," one of the residential voluntary measures pertaining to indoor water use, yet it fails to define the technicalities.[47] No part of the code defines what a composting toilet is or how it should be installed. In the Plumbing Code, the terms *toilet* and *water closet* are used interchangeably:

Water Closet. A fixture with a water-containing receptor that receives liquid and solid body waste and on actuation conveys the waste through an exposed integral trap into a drainage system. Also referred to as a toilet.[48]

The Plumbing Code does not mention composting toilets, and waterless toilets are prohibited:

405.3 Miscellaneous Fixtures…No dry or chemical closet (toilet) shall be installed in a building used for human habitation, unless first approved by the Health Officer.[49]

A measure listed as a standard of sustainability in the CALGreen Code requires, according to the Plumbing Code, special approval from a health officer. In the absence of clear regulations, lack of technical knowledge, or willingness to take risk, officers refer to precedents or to existing standards. Many standards regulate the type and installation of water closets, and while the Residential Code does not mention composting toilets, it does list a relevant standard developed by NSF International (formerly National Sanitation Foundation).[50] However, while the NSF standard 41–2011 Nonliquid Saturated Treatment Systems (Composting Toilets) is used in the 2018 International Residential Code, in California, Part VII, "Plumbing" (where the standard is mentioned), has not been adopted.[51] This is because in California, the Plumbing Code is based on the model code developed by the International Association of Plumbing and Mechanical Officials (IAPMO).

In any case, what is clear is that the ICC model code only allows NSF-compliant manufactured toilets, indirectly prohibiting those built on-site.[52] Meanwhile, thanks to an initiative launched by the Oregon-based Recode, the IAPMO developed a new standard called Water Efficiency and Sanitation Standard (WE·Stand), which, among other issues, includes the requirements for site-built composting toilets.[53] As discussed in the next chapter in a conversation with Mathew Lippincott, a member of Recode and the lead author of the WE·Stand code, one state has adopted the provisions so far. It is still to be seen whether California decides to follow in Oregon's footsteps. When a nonstandard practice conquers the popular imagination, standard setters are eventually forced to standardize it. Yet it is always easier to add a new standard than to amend or delete an old one. In fact, some standards persist and oppose a particular inertia. The issue of waterborne waste disposal will remain unresolved if composting toilets are only allowed once the first water closet has been installed and connected to a public sewer system as specified in the following section:

R306.3 Sewage Disposal. Plumbing fixtures shall be connected to a sanitary sewer or to an approved private sewage disposal system.[54]

One may hope that California will once again lead the nation by amending the above section.[55] This would allow any household—not just a rural dwelling—to install a waterless toilet and do without sewage pipes.[56]

Water Consumption

Waterborne sewage disposal is so enmeshed in modern society that it might be impossible to ever eliminate it. Hence, the specter of water scarcity makes most regulations and economic instruments concentrate on minimizing water use. In fact, sewer-service charges are based on the amount of water used. State building codes, municipal ordinances, and federal incentives impose high-efficiency, low-flow water appliances.[57]

But indoor water use is just the tip of the iceberg. Firstly, water evaporates on its way to Los Angeles, and the Colorado River never reaches Mexico due to overextraction. Secondly, American households waste one-fifth of food, which is full of "hidden water": approximately 35 gallons in a cup of coffee and 460 gallons in a quarter-pound of bovine meat.[58] One-fifth of this "embodied" water goes wasted, which corresponds to 25 percent of all water used in agriculture. While the water footprint of domestic activities (not to mention construction materials or household appliances) is largely ignored, the focus on conservation makes residents underestimate the importance of such distant environmental issues as ocean pollution or disrupted nutrient cycles.[59]

Still, although passive water conservation measures might be a perfect example of "seeking the optimal arrangement of deck chairs on the Titanic," other measures are either unavailable to the rule makers or simply not economically viable.[60] No federal law can undo a century of local appropriation deals written into the landscape with concrete channels. No state act can force municipalities to reuse stormwater that falls on the land they are entitled to use and control. No municipal act can possibly stop residents from buying too much food; such a tax revenue loss would be against market logics. Yet, as discussed above, the rule-making matrix does contain a measure of last resort: the CWA and the Ocean Dumping Act can deny states and cities the possibility of discharging waste into US and international waters.[61] As outlandish as it may sound, the vicious cycle could be stopped, maybe even made more virtuous in the very end, by denying the right to use rivers and the ocean as sinks for food leftovers and bodily waste.

5.3. Why Continue Stacking? Focus: Air

Air is another matrix, just more intangible and hence less controllable than water. While we do not respect watershed boundaries, the wind does not respect ours, carrying pollutants across borders.[62] Similar to indoor air, ambient (or outdoor) air quality was initially the responsibility of individual states. Although California passed the nation's first air-pollution act in 1947, in response to smog, the importance of air quality for public health was not acknowledged until the passage of the first federal Air Pollution Act in 1955 and fully recognized in the Clean Air Act (CAA) of 1963 and subsequent amendments.[63] In response to the CAA standards for automobiles, and the more stringent state Zero Emission Vehicle program, the building code, specifically its CALGreen portion, includes provisions that indirectly address ambient air quality by imposing mandatory and voluntary measures to "facilitate future installation and use of EV chargers" in new residential buildings and by promoting the use of bicycles.[64]

Unable to control local land use since it is controlled by municipalities, the building code (enacted by the state) can only regulate construction practices. It cannot, as an example, stop the City of Los Angeles from approving residential developments within one thousand feet of a freeway—a fact so commonly recognized as an extreme health hazard that the municipality releases an advisory notice together with building permits.[65] The structure of the CALGreen Code, nonetheless, suggests that this might change in the future. While land-use practices are included among voluntary measures in the form of recommendations and the section entitled "Outdoor Air Quality" is a "reserved" placeholder, we know from previous editions that what is now voluntary is meant to become mandatory in the future, and what is reserved will one day contain new provisions.[66]

Indoor Air

While of relatively little influence on ambient air, the CALGreen Code and other parts of the California Building Standards Code are extensively used to regulate air quality indoors, which remains outside the jurisdiction of the federal government.[67] After all, ventilation has been one of the initial objects of code makers' attention, and the current Residential Code (Section 1.1.2, "Purpose") continues to list it as one of the fundamental aspects of public health and welfare.[68] Yet while ventilation has been regulated for more than a century, indoor air quality emerged as a side effect of the post-oil-crisis wave of weatherization, which made buildings warmer but also overly airtight.[69] Ironically, while Ulrich Beck was warning that "privileged ways of living

may still provide a refuge from air and noise pollution, but the waters will soon be polluted everywhere, and we will be equal before more than just the bomb," researchers were proving that there was nowhere to escape from the volatile effects of industrialization.[70] Homes, too, were poisoned. Indoor contaminants, such as volatile organic compounds (VOCs), were everywhere—not just in cleaning products handled by domestic workers, but in carpets, sofas, and wallpapers, the very embodiments of home comfort. While the buildings were too airtight to remove these indoor pollutants, they were not airtight enough to block excessive cold, heat, or, more importantly, the outdoor-generated contaminants that transform ambient air into smog. They were also not tight enough to keep the natural yet carcinogenic radon outdoors. Although in 1988 the federal government passed the Radon Abatement Act to provide funding for research for the colorless, odorless gas and the issue is now addressed in the building code, the local adoption of this act depends on the level of risk assessed locally of the elusive gas.[71]

The Structure of the Stack

The building code regulates indoor air, but for historical and practical reasons, it regulates it in different parts, in different ways, and for different reasons. When new environmental imperatives emerge but the Constitution of the United States is silent about them (as it is about all aspects of environmental protection), the individual states and their code makers are free to impose new rules based on custom-written or third-party standards.[72] When the environmental discourse started to influence regulations in the 1970s, the building code was already a crystallized system of complicated (and often forgotten) origins. For example, when the Energy Conservation Standards were first introduced by the State of California in the mid-1970s, they were added to the existing set of codes as a separate part, like an emergency Band-Aid.[73] Because states still have the right to decide whether to impose energy-conservation measures, even when new model codes were born in the green 1990s, the International Code Council was forced to keep the energy code separate from the residential model code to allow for selective adoption.[74] Similarly, when California adopted the Green Building Standards Code in 2008, it was introduced as another overlay, Part 11 of California Building Standards Code, Title 24.

As a result of this gradual expansion of building regulations, California's building code consists of eleven books. It is composed of three state-developed parts, four parts based on the International Code Council (ICC) model codes, two parts based on models developed by the IAPMO and one on a model published by the National Fire Protection Association. Although the Residential Code is meant to be a "complete cookbook" for common residential construction methods, its California edition adopts its chapters and sections selectively and refers to other codes for more technical provisions. In fact, one must consult Parts 3, 4, and 5 for prescriptions pertaining to electrical, mechanical, and plumbing systems; Part 6 for energy-efficiency standards; Part 8 for specific provisions applied to historical buildings; Part 9 for minimum fire-safety requirements; Part 10 for regulations that govern existing buildings; and Part 11 for green building standards. As a consequence, ventilation and air quality are regulated in four different volumes: the Residential Code, the Mechanical Code, the Energy Code, and the CALGreen Code. [Figure 12]

Ventilation

Ventilation is addressed in the central chapter of the Residential Code, Chapter 3, "Building and Planning." Section R303, "Light, Ventilation and Heating," contains the following prescriptions:

R303.1 Habitable Rooms…Natural ventilation shall be through windows, skylights, doors, louvers or other approved openings to the outdoor air. Such openings shall be provided with ready access or shall otherwise be readily controllable by the building occupants. The openable area to the outdoors shall be not less than 4 percent of the floor area being ventilated.

Not only after having provided 4 percent of openable area are spatial considerations complete and one no longer requires architectural expertise to manage ventilation, but there is also an exception that reads:

The glazed areas need not be openable where the opening is not required by Section R310 and a whole-house mechanical ventilation system is installed in accordance with the California Mechanical Code.[75]

While according to Section R310, "Emergency Escape and Rescue Openings," openable areas are not required in kitchens and bathrooms, it is hard to justify why one would want to avoid having the option of opening a window once it is there.[76] While such a choice might be, in fact, rare, mechanical ventilation is in any case almost always obligatory for other reasons. The state-added Section R303.3.1, "Bathroom Exhaust Fans," imposes mechanical ventilation for humidity control and excludes an openable window as an acceptable alternative.[77] Mechanical ventilation is practically compulsory also because of the following provisions included in the Mechanical Code:

402.2 Natural Ventilation. Natural ventilation systems shall be designed in accordance with this section and shall include mechanical ventilation systems designed in accordance with Section 403.0, Section 404.0, or both.[78]

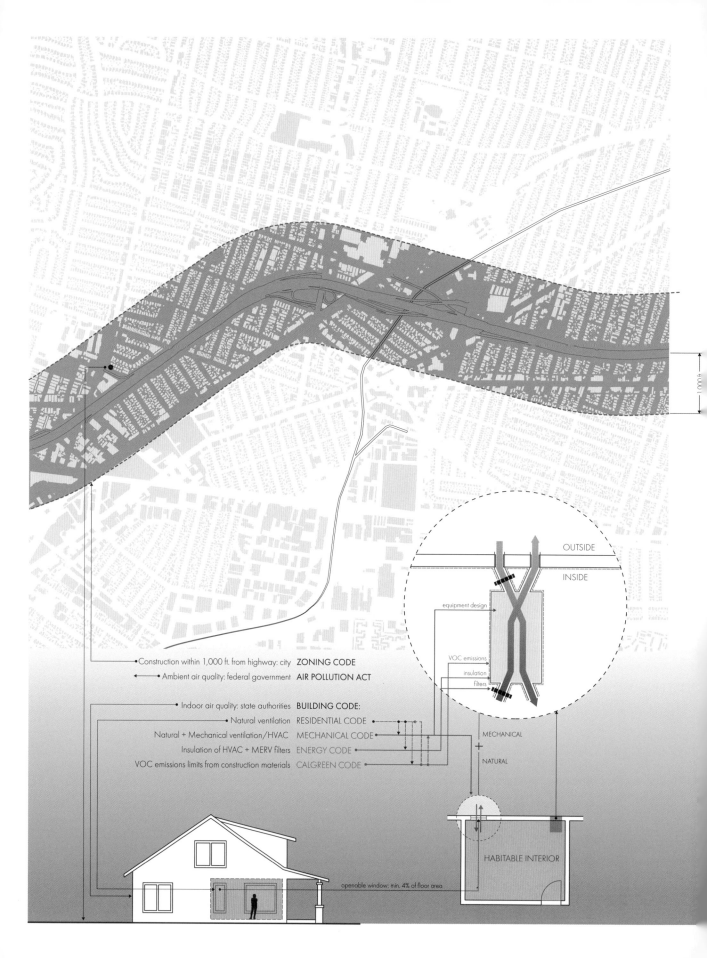

100 ft.

OUTSIDE

INSIDE

equipment design

VOC emissions

insulation

filters

• Construction within 1,000 ft. from highway: city **ZONING CODE**

◀──▶ Ambient air quality: federal government **AIR POLLUTION ACT**

• Indoor air quality: state authorities **BUILDING CODE:**

      • Natural ventilation **RESIDENTIAL CODE**

      Natural + Mechanical ventilation/HVAC **MECHANICAL CODE**

      Insulation of HVAC + MERV filters **ENERGY CODE**

      VOC emissions limits from construction materials **CALGREEN CODE**

MECHANICAL

+

NATURAL

HABITABLE INTERIOR

openable window: min. 4% of floor area

Although one of the exceptions to the above prescription is that mechanical ventilation is not required if "the zone is not served by heating or cooling equipment," most American homes must be provided with at least the heating system in the habitable zones and hence cannot avoid installing mechanical ventilation.[79] The Residential Code defines *ventilation* as "the natural or mechanical process of supplying conditioned or unconditioned air to, or removing such air from, any space."[80] Since air does not simply circulate but is supplied, a mechanical standard is surely required. Section R303.4, "Ventilation," refers to the Mechanical Code, which then refers to the American Society of Heating, Refrigerating and Air-Conditioning Engineers (ASHRAE) Standard 62.2.[81] Although at this point almost superfluous, the provisions (however basic) related to natural ventilation are also contained in the Mechanical Code, even if it is here that one would expect to consult an architect rather than a mechanical engineer. Yet since architects rarely understand the mechanics of "thermal, wind, or diffusion effects" responsible for natural ventilation, this ASHRAE definition of the term is reported in the Mechanical Code, meant for mechanical engineers.[82] Section 402.2.1, "Floor Area To Be Ventilated," specifies where operable openings should be positioned, depending on whether they are single-sided, double-sided, or corner openings.[83]

More than a complete cookbook, the Residential Code is an annotated index, only with the hyperlinks missing.[84] It acts as a textual map that helps in the hiring of the right consultants. In fact, once the ventilation rates and the size and location of openings have been specified

by a mechanical engineer, one still needs to consult an energy expert to comply with the efficiency standards contained in yet another book, the Energy Code. The requirements related to ventilation, albeit indirect, can be found in Section 110.7, "Mandatory Requirements to Limit Air Leakage."[85] More compulsory provisions are contained in Section 150.0, especially letter (m) "Air-Distribution and Ventilation System Ducts, Plenums and Fans" (e.g., Point 4, "Duct Insulation R-value Ratings," and Point 5, "Duct Insulation Thickness").[86] The Energy Code guarantees that the ventilation system is efficiently sealed, airtight. Both codes ensure that the provisions included in the ANSI/ASHRAE Standard 62.2 Ventilation and Acceptable Indoor Air Quality in Residential Buildings are observed.

Indoor Air Quality

Surprisingly, the abovementioned Section 150.0 (m) contained in the Energy Code also addresses the quality of air. Point 12, "Air Filtration," defines which mechanical systems that supply air to occupiable spaces require an air-filtering device.[87] One wonders whether it is to protect the human respiratory system or the equipment. The Residential Code addresses indoor air quality only once, to acknowledge the issue, and again, in this state-added Section 150.0, refers the reader to another part of the code:

> R340.1 Finish Material Pollutant Control. Finish materials including adhesives, sealants, caulks, paints and coatings, aerosol paints and coatings, carpet systems, carpet cushion, carpet adhesive, resilient flooring systems and composite wood products shall meet the volatile organic compound (VOC) emission limits in accordance with the California Green Building Standards Code, Chapter 4, Division 4.5.[88]

Figure 12 [opposite]
—
The building-code stack: cross-referencing across parts, thematic overlays, and regulatory limits

Once the ventilation system is made sufficiently airtight, thanks to sealants and caulks, one must refer to the CALGreen Code to protect the home and its inhabitants from VOCs trapped in the very same materials used to seal it from the outside, materials, which, to use Beck's words, "provide a refuge" from air pollution. Reducing excessive quantity of air contaminants is regulated under Division 4.5, "Environmental Quality," but what is not clearly acknowledged in this section is that construction materials allowed in other parts of the code are responsible for emitting them. The mandatory Section 4.504.2 lists them all: adhesives, sealants, and caulks; paints and coatings, carpet systems, flooring systems, and composite wood products.[89] Another voluntary section addresses pollutants emitted by insulation materials, a source unmentioned in the Residential Code.[90] It would be easier to simply ban the production of these materials, but since this would be against the spirit of the free market and customer choice, the only thing that the state-written CALGreen Code can do is to impose state rules to be observed "unless more stringent local limits apply."[91]

The remaining sections of Division 4.5, "Environmental Quality," repeat or slightly expand provisions included in other codes. Section 4.506 "Indoor Air Quality and Exhaust" and Section 4.507, "Environmental Comfort," both address issues already regulated in the Mechanical Code, confirming the authority of the Energy Code with respect to lighting efficiency and Energy Star as a standard of fan efficiency and also referring the reader to ASHRAE for standards related to heating and air-conditioning.[92] Section 4.505, "Interior Moisture Control," expands two measures already contained in the Residential Code. One of them includes the following prohibition:

> 4.505.3 Moisture Content of Building Materials. Building materials with visible signs of water damage shall not be installed. Wall and floor framing shall not be enclosed when the framing members exceed 19-percent moisture content.[93]

One wonders why this provision is not simply added to those chapters in the Residential Code that regulate wood-framing practices and the grade of lumber.[94] There it would be simply addressing an aspect of structural soundness. Listed in the CALGreen Code, the same provision improves air quality; it becomes a sign of sustainability. CALGreen, like the Residential Code, is mostly an annotated guide to other sources of expertise and other authorities having jurisdiction. The difference is that here the search filter is green.

Why Continue Stacking?
The Residential Code specifies what needs to be regulated; it is thanks to this code that habitable rooms receive air. The Mechanical, Plumbing, Electrical, and the Energy Codes provide the answers to the how questions. The Mechanical Code defines airflow rates and lays out how and where pipes and vents should move the air in and out. The Energy Code efficiently insulates them. The CALGreen Code specifies how to use the methods and materials regulated elsewhere in a more environmentally friendly way.

Beyond addressing questions of sustainability and health, an objective achievable through possible amendments to the other parts, the CALGreen Code provides a way to emphasize, or better advertise, the green why. The length, fragmentation, and repetitiveness of the building code are all effects of the extreme standardization of various aspects of planning, design, construction, and occupation of buildings, which in turn triggers excessive professional specialization, proliferation of licensed consultants and contractors, and, ultimately, the need for clearly compartmentalized regulations accessible to narrowly defined trades and experts. Multiple standard-setting and model-code companies combined with different authorities having jurisdiction over different occupancies results in many inevitably poorly coordinated efforts. And while these are the reasons for the existence of many technical parts, the more recent additions to the stack reveal yet another motivation: the growing stack is a reflection of the political necessity to "package" each new set of solutions in a way that is clearly visible to the citizens and signals the importance of the agenda in focus.[95] This was the why behind the adoption of the Energy Code in the age of weatherization, and this is the why behind the very existence of California's Green Building Standards Code. It will not be surprising, considering the growing concern about climate change, if the California Building Standards Code welcomes yet another part: the Resilient Building Code.

5.4. What About Agency? Focus: Vegetation

In an overview of regulatory practices used to govern construction, housing policy expert William Baer pointed out (building upon Herbert Simon's ideas) that "rules are merely human devices to translate between desired ends and possible means." Like other devices, rules—especially when formalized as professional standards or government-enacted regulations—function according to an inner protocol. As Baer puts it, they "have an internal organization or grammar and meta-rules for its organization."[96] While some rules are prohibitive (i.e., proscriptive) and concentrate on avoiding negative effects, most of them tend to be formulated as positive prescriptions, even if in practice they still simply prohibit what is not permitted.[97] They promote positive outcomes either by imposing a method tested to be beneficial or at least safe or by indicating a desired performance without defining specific means. The former approach reduces the risk but does not necessarily promote optimal solutions or encourage innovation. The latter performance-based approach attempts to maximize the benefits by accepting an elevated level of risk.

The specificity of regulations can also vary: they can impose exact standards or, whenever such degree of absolute precision is impossible, more relative criteria requiring specialized knowledge and professional judgment. **[Figure 13]** At the latter, softer end of the spectrum, performance-based, process-oriented criteria only signal desired results and vaguely suggest means. For example:

> Provide clean indoor air [performance] by venting air to the outside [process] to carry out harmful pollutants [relative criterion].

In such a prescription, neither the means nor the effects are clearly defined; designers, plan-checkers, and users are all entrusted with a significant amount of responsibility.

Not surprisingly, it is difficult to find rules like this in the current building code. I was forced to make the example up. What is more common is what one finds at the other end of the spectrum: prescriptive, product-oriented standards that impose precise outcomes, leave little freedom to designers, plan-checkers, and users, and shift responsibility onto manufacturers and

Figure 13 [overleaf]
—
The form of regulations. Redrawn from William C. Baer, "Customs, Norms, Rules, Regulations and Standards in Design Practice," in *Companion to Urban Design*, ed. Tridib Banerjee and Anastasia Loukaitou-Sideris (New York: Routledge, 2011), 281, 283, Figure 21.2, "Differences between Criteria and Standards," and Figure 21.3, "Eight Permutations of Rule Forms."

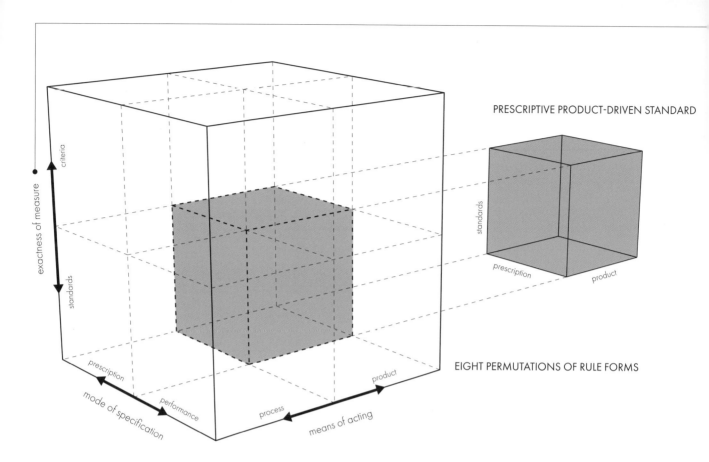

PRESCRIPTIVE PRODUCT-DRIVEN STANDARD

standards

prescription   product

EIGHT PERMUTATIONS OF RULE FORMS

exactness of measure

criteria

standards

mode of specification

prescription

performance

process

means of acting

product

EXACTNESS OF MEASURE

CRITERIA   STANDARDS

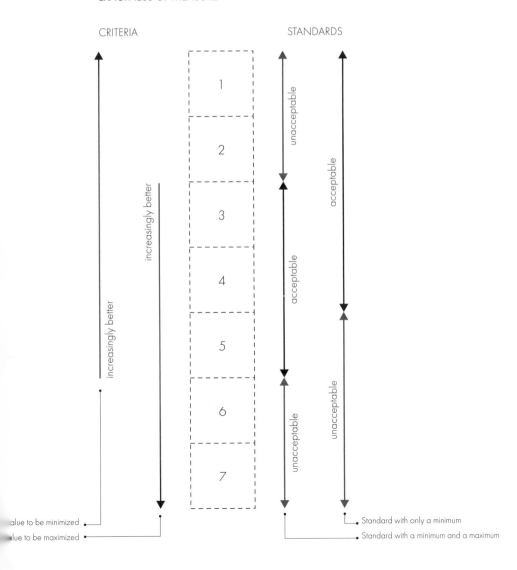

installers. The following regulation contained in the CALGreen Code serves as an example:

> A4.506.2 Construction Filter…Provide [prescription] filters on return air openings rated at MERV 8 [exact quantitative standard] or higher during construction.[98]

This level of precision is preferred by code makers as it reduces the need for specialized knowledge and minimizes legal liability. As will become evident in the rest of this section, the way of expressing standards and regulations determines how we practice sustainability as a society. The freedoms and responsibilities assigned to each of us — manufacturers and certifiers, users, plan-checkers, architects, and nowadays simulation software—are embedded in these metarules. They define our relationship with the environment.

Vegetative Shade: The Simulation Engine and Its Agency

Historically, US building codes have been either prohibitive or, when expressed in a positive way, prescriptive, granting little freedom to designers and trust to users. While over the last decades performance-based rules have occasionally been woven into the existing prescriptions, the California-written Energy Code appears very progressive, as it explicitly offers two options: a prescriptive compliance path and a performance-oriented approach.[99] While the choice reflects, in part, the increasing acceptance of digital simulation as a way to assess untested solutions and a need to encourage technological innovation, there is a twofold caveat. Performance must be computed by compliance software certified for this use by the California Energy Commission, and the software only accepts a limited range of "compliance options" (or inputs), all itemized in additional reference volumes.[100] Rather than granting complete freedom, the software engine

assesses the effects of combinations that, while finite and quite limited, exceed the capacities of a human brain. A quick look at how shading is outlined in Section 3.5.8.4, "Fixed Permanent Shading Devices," illustrates how those options are defined:

> Overhangs or sidefins that are attached to the building or shading from the building itself are compliance options for which credit is offered through the performance approach. *However, no credit is offered for shading from trees, adjacent buildings, or terrain* [my italics]."

Further in the same section one reads:

> Shading is more challenging on the east and west sides of the house…Vertical fins can be effective, but they degrade the quality of the view from the window and limit the natural light that can enter. In cooling-dominated climates, the best approach is to minimize windows that face east and west. *Landscaping features can be considered to increase comfort but cannot be used for compliance credit* [my italics]."[101]

Landscaping features (i.e., shrubs and trees) "increase comfort" but cannot be "inputted" into the compliance software, although they can now be simulated with a high degree of precision— a topic discussed in the next chapter, in the conversation with Michael Bruse, the creator of the ENVI-met microclimate-simulation software. Since the shade that they provide (or shadow they cast) is variable, it cannot be easily quantified and expressed numerically, as specified in the 2019 Residential Compliance Manual, Table 3-4, "Exterior Shades and Solar Heat Gain Coefficients," in which an array of devices (e.g., bug screens, sunscreens, awnings, etc.) is ranked according to the percentage of transmitted sunlight.[102] Even though, unlike vertical fins and bug screens, trees do not "degrade the quality of the view," they are not on the list. In the meantime, "all operable windows and skylights are assumed to have an insect screen, and this is the default condition against which other window/exterior shading device combinations are compared."[103] The insect screen is considered to be the default shading option. I permanently removed it on the day I moved into a Los Angeles house under Title 24 jurisdiction.

Vegetative Insulation: Manufacturers, Installers, and Ratings

While the CALGreen Code does suggest vegetative shade as a possible voluntary nonresidential measure (specifying that it may be used if documented to reach coverage within five years), no part of the code mentions vegetative insulation.[104] Until recently, it did not even mention straw, a traditional plant-based insulation, a topic discussed in the next chapter, in the conversation with Martin Hammer, the lead author of the straw-bale construction ICC model code appendix. It may be that the code never mentions vegetative insulation because it would not satisfy the provisions that regulate insulation materials in the Energy Code, in which the expression *documented* acquires a more absolute meaning: the insulation product must be rated by the manufacturer. Section 110.8, "Mandatory Requirements for Insulation, Roofing Products, and Radiant Barriers," explicitly states that insulation materials must be certified by the Department of Consumer Affairs.[105]

Reliance on a manufacturer's rating is confirmed in the 2019 Residential Alternative Calculation Method Reference Manual, which allows for nonlisted assemblies (e.g., insulation) to be used as long as their properties (e.g., R-value) have been rated by the manufacturer.[106] Last but not least, exceptions are permitted, but exceptional quality has also been normalized. It is a clearly standardized procedure described in Section 2.2.5, "Quality Insulation Installation (QII)," and it must be field verified, certified, and reported by a licensed installer following Home Energy Rating System (HERS) procedures.[107] As of today, no manufacturer can rate, and no licensed expert can verify, the quality of vegetative insulation. Unrated and unverified, vegetation, however exceptional its performance, cannot be considered a viable option when following the performance compliance path offered by the Energy Code.

Phyto-Air Purification: The Agency of the User

As stated in the previous section discussing the example of air-related regulations, the Residential Code, specifically Section R303.1, "Habitable Rooms," prescribes openable windows to guarantee natural ventilation. At the same time, the Mechanical Code, in the previously mentioned Section 402.2, "Natural Ventilation," makes ASHRAE Standard 62.2 requirements mandatory and imposes mechanical ventilation in addition to openable windows. The reason for this level of protectiveness can be found in one of the Energy Code reference manuals, which states, "Energy Commission–sponsored research has revealed that concentration of pollutants such as formaldehyde are higher than expected, and that many occupants do not open windows regularly for ventilation."[108] This explains why the code emphasizes that, while mandatory, "window operations are not a permissible method for providing whole-house ventilation."[109] However, while it is clearly stated that users cannot be trusted to regularly open windows, what is not made equally clear is that outdoor air can no longer be trusted to purify indoor air either. Although the code implicitly recognizes that outdoor air is polluted—inlets must be located ten feet away from outdoor air contaminants—nothing prohibits outdoor air intakes from being placed within one thousand feet of a freeway where cars incessantly emit hazardous pollutants.[110]

What is necessary, then, is not only a forced supply of air but, obviously, also a filter. In fact, a filter in domestic whole-fan systems and local exhausts is required by the Energy Code, Section 150.0 (m) 12, "Air Filtration."[111] Yet while the same code encourages compliance through performance approach, the way this and other prescriptions related to air purification are formulated does not leave space for "phyto-innovation." Neither a living wall, as discussed in the next chapter, in a conversation with Al Benner, the creator of Moss Walls, nor a NASA-developed phyto-purification system is a valid compliance option.[112] Since vegetation cannot be rated by a manufacturer, an experimental phyto-filter cannot comply with the section, which imposes MERV labeling, and cannot obtain a HERS certificate.[113] A phyto-purification system developed for the "airless" outer space is also not an acceptable option, although it requires neither supply nor filtering of outdoor air. When mentioned in the code by their name, plants are simply considered a hazard or a nuisance. While performative enough for the outer space, they are not a valid compliance option here in the down-to-earth residential construction. The code treats humans with well-founded skepticism, and it mistrusts organic life in general. Its nature—our nature—is too unstable.

Phyto-Wastewater Purification: The Liability of the Plan-Checker

One instance of rule makers welcoming plants is the previously discussed Stormwater LID Ordinance. Meant to mitigate the impact of urban runoff, the ordinance imposes such methods as bioretention and phyto-purification as mandatory prescriptions. While this federally imposed ordinance embraces the performative capacity of plants (retention and purification) and sets some objectives in exact terms (i.e., the amount of the runoff to be retained on-site), it also accepts that other aspects of phyto-performance will remain less well defined (i.e., the degree to which stormwater runoff is purified). The attitude toward plants is slightly different in the state-imposed, conservation-driven Model Water Efficient Landscape Ordinance and in the Plumbing Code that references it. In this case, vegetation becomes a passive object, if not a culprit partly responsible for water scarcity. It is referred to as "the receiving landscape," gets ranked according to water consumption using a numerical system, and must meet precise requirements.[114] Among prescriptions included in the MWELO, one reads:

> For residential areas, install climate adapted plants that require occasional, little or no summer water (average WUCOLS [Water Use Classifications of Landscape Species] plant factor 0.3) for 75 percent of the plant area excluding edibles and areas using recycled water.[115]

The attitude toward vegetation is even more distrustful when it comes to wastewater treatment. While the local authorities can authorize a private sewage-disposal system (i.e., septic tanks), such freedom is granted only in low-density (and low-risk) rural areas.[116] In these areas, they can also approve aerobic systems as an alternative to septic tanks:

> H101.11 Alternate Systems…Approved aerobic systems shall be permitted to be substituted for conventional septic tanks provided the Authority Having Jurisdiction is satisfied that such systems will produce results not less than equivalent to septic tanks, whether their aeration systems are operating or not.[117]

Due to the way these rules are expressed, aerobic treatment units are still rare, although standardized models are available on the market and often constitute the only alternative to a conventional septic tank.[118] Yet since they require continuous maintenance, they are considered even riskier than the risky septic tanks. More experimental systems, in which not only aerobic bacteria but also plants are used to treat water, are even less common. Ecological designer John Todd's Eco-Machines (as he refers to his pioneering wastewater treatment systems) mostly serve research or educational institutions.[119] As aforementioned, the code imposes connection to the public sewer in urban areas, and few municipal treatment plants rely for treatment on natural systems, such as constructed wetlands.[120] The potential liability is so high that without a dedicated insurance system, local authorities will continue testing and praising natural systems but insist on sending the treated water back to a conventional treatment facility to avoid responsibility.[121] Perhaps the early Victorian engineers embraced the convenience of water-borne waste removal because they, as observed by Eran Ben-Joseph, "believed in the purifying nature of water."[122] We no longer share this belief—although we still don't question water-borne sewage systems, but unfortunately, we also don't "believe" in the capacity of plants to purify wastewater and in our own capacity to take care of them.

The Plant-Minded Design

Organic systems, nonstandard technologies, and passive spatial solutions are penalized by the prescriptive code that favors manufacturer-rated products over custom-designed spatial configurations, a code that mistrusts users and "rebellious" vegetation.[123] Not only is the use of plants not prescribed by the building code— we are clearly far from that—but also it is not an acceptable option when satisfying the quasi-performance-driven regulations found in the Energy Code. As one might expect, the only section of the building code meant to protect vegetation can be found in the CALGreen Code. Nonetheless, in the 2019 edition of the green part of the building regulations, its adoption depends on the goodwill of the client and the architect. Restoring native vegetation species and patterns after construction remains a voluntary measure.[124]

As of today, plant-minded design can only be practiced as an uncredited expression of a genuine passion for the environment or a form of unrewarded, in E. O. Wilson's term, biophilia— a dangerous extravagance, considering the multitude of mandatory prescriptions that one must satisfy before engaging with the *otherness* of plants, the vital substrate of our own existence. Unfortunately, returning to Bateson's parable, the acrobatics of sustainability are so rigidly regulated by laws, that we, the acrobat-architects, risk not only falling off but also simply losing patience and stepping off the wire to apply our skill to a less standardized facet of the art of building.[125]

CHAPTER SIX

THE POWER OF PREDESIGN IN FOUR CONVERSATIONS

Clearly, the built environment is only in part shaped by architects and their designs. Many other professions indirectly influence what designers can or cannot do. Their work focuses on, among other things, regulations, construction standards, building products, and design tools. Their research, entrepreneurship, and advocacy precede design and construction and constitute what we might call the predesign phase of construction. Although these people make environmentally minded designs proposed by architects possible (or not), they often remain behind the scenes while architects' achievements are publicly celebrated (or criticized).

The following conversations focus on four predesign initiatives. Two of them directly challenge existing building codes and standards; the other two concentrate on design tools and

—
Disposing of obsolete construction standards—
the water closet

products that will hopefully, one day, allow environmentally minded code developers to challenge some of the currently accepted regulations. In the first conversation, architect and code developer Martin Hammer talks about legalizing straw-bale construction as an alternative to insulating materials made from synthetic fibers. In the second conversation, code advocate Mathew Lippincott shares his experience with developing standards for composting toilets as an alternative to centralized waterborne sewage systems. In the third conversation, geographer and software developer Michael Bruse recounts the latest advancements in digital simulation of urban microclimates and vegetation. In the closing conversation, entrepreneur Al Benner talks about commercializing living moss walls. While the first two initiatives address the need to normalize and standardize the use of by-products—be it straw as insulation material or human urine and feces as fertilizer—the other two suggest that vegetation could soon become a "permissible," in regulatory terms, alternative to mechanical climate- and air-quality-control methods. In a broader sense, they all confirm the importance of predesign as an overlooked area for environmental agency. What these initiatives suggest is that, perhaps, it is time to question what it means to be a designer.

6.1. Standardizing the Nonstandard. Focus: Straw-Bale Construction.

IN CONVERSATION WITH MARTIN HAMMER

Martin Hammer is a licensed architect based in Northern California and an internationally recognized expert in straw-bale construction.[1] A long-term member of the California Straw Building Association (CASBA) and the recipient of CASBA's Annual Award in 2006 and 2015, he has contributed to the global acceptance of straw-bale construction as a designer, builder, writer, instructor, and code developer. Hammer is the lead author of the straw-bale construction model code, first included in the 2015 International Residential Code (IRC) as Appendix S – Strawbale Construction, and of Appendix AU – Cob Construction (Monolithic Adobe), added to the IRC in 2021.[2] He is a coauthor of Appendix R – Light Straw-Clay Construction, first appearing in the 2015 IRC, and Appendix Q – Tiny Houses, in the 2018 IRC. He is currently working with a team on a proposed appendix for the 2024 IRC on Hemp-Lime (Hempcrete) Construction. In our conversation, we speak about straw-bale construction, his work on IRC Appendix S, and the importance of code development as a form of predesign.

Aleksandra Jaeschke: Your first straw-bale building was built in 1996. Most people start with a little shed in their backyard. You started with a three-thousand-square-feet workshop. At that time, there was no mention of straw-bale construction in the building code. How did you get it permitted?

Martin Hammer: First, some history. The first two straw-bale codes in the United States, and the world, were developed in parallel in the early 1990s and adopted in 1996 in New Mexico and in Tucson, Pima County, Arizona. While those codes were being developed, California was grappling with seasonal burning of rice straw, which caused significant air pollution and associated health effects. In 1995, to promote alternative uses of rice straw, state representative Byron Sher wrote a bill proposing the nascent Arizona code as voluntary guidelines for straw-bale buildings in California. Assembly Bill 1314 passed, and California's Guidelines for Straw-Bale Structures became effective January 1, 1996. So they *were* available for our project, and we did use them. However, these new guidelines didn't reside with all of the other California building codes—having originated in legislation, they were placed in the Health and Safety Code.[3]

AJ: Were you able to refer to these guidelines?

MH: Yes, we presented them to the county building department, and they said, "Okay, we'll use them." The guidelines and our project were appropriately scrutinized by the building official, since this was the first straw-bale building in the county, but he worked with us. As important as the guidelines were for legitimizing straw-bale building in California, they were flawed—too restrictive in some ways, too lenient in others—and important issues were not addressed at all.

AJ: What exactly were the problems?

MH: Internal "pinning" of successive courses with steel rebar was required, but in practice it was being abandoned. Though sensible for early iterations during the straw-bale-building revival, the practice was soon seen as costly and unnecessary.

Plastered straw-bale walls were assigned no capacity to resist wind and earthquake forces as "shear walls," though informal tests and field experience suggested they have significant capacity and are even ideal for absorbing these forces. This was a more important issue for high-seismic California compared with Arizona, and its absence highlighted the need for seismic testing.

Most importantly, by this time, 1996, straw-bale walls were commonly being built with plaster applied directly to the straw, with no exterior water-resistive barrier. This allows a superior plaster bond and causes little or no moisture problems in the straw. To the contrary, it allows any unwanted moisture in the bales to better escape. To untrained eyes, it appears problematic because a water-resistive barrier is a long-standing requirement in wood-frame construction. This difference was not addressed in the straw-bale guidelines, causing countless conflicts with building officials.

The straw-bale building community struggled for years with these and other deficiencies. We knew how straw-bale buildings should be designed and built, but the guidelines were not allowing it. So, together with architect Dan Smith and structural engineer Bruce King, I reached out to Representative Sher, who by then had become a state senator, to write a bill to revise the guidelines.[4] Senate Bill 332 (SB332), with our revisions, was signed into law in 2002.

During that process, state agencies that develop and adopt building codes became aware of SB332. They had never liked that the straw-bale guidelines were in the Health and Safety Code, outside of their control. "It needs to be in the normal building-code-development realm," they said. So, in 2001, we met with representatives from Housing and Community Development, the State Fire Marshal, and the Building Standards Commission. Though they wouldn't accept all of our revisions, we agreed on the important ones. They then said, "It will stay in the Health and Safety Code for now, but we want you to work with us to move it into the state building code."

AJ: So, the national straw-bale model code, Appendix S, is based on the provisions first developed for the California building code?

MH: Yes, but as I said, the California guidelines were based on the Arizona code. We discussed the idea of a national model code while working on the state code. California is highly seismic and contains almost every climate zone, so we thought approval in California would make approval in other states much easier. And by then, the US model codes had been consolidated into one set, overseen by the newly formed International Code Council [ICC]. However, while all other states accepted the ICC Codes, California was stuck on the 1997 Uniform Building Code, until 2006, due to a political conflict between stakeholders wanting the International Building Code [IBC] and others wanting the NFPA 5000, Building Construction and Safety Code.[5] Eventually, then Governor Schwarzenegger broke the logjam, and California transitioned to the IBC. This impasse interrupted the development of a straw-bale state code, but it caused me to look outside California to make progress.

At about that time, the ICC invited proposals for construction methods seen as green for the new International Green Construction Code [IgCC]. My colleague David Eisenberg, a member of the IgCC committee, enthusiastically showed me that straw-bale construction was on the list. So I took what we developed for California and submitted a proposal. We were surprised when it was denied in the IgCC hearings. Some who spoke in opposition said, "This belongs in the building code, not the green construction code."

We thought, "But what could be more green?" However, in a way I agreed. I felt, and still do, that there should not be a separate green construction code. The *building code should be green*. Period.

AJ: I could not agree more with you! Also, at that time, the State of California was developing the Green Building Standards Code [CALGreen Code], so if the straw-bale code was included in the IgCC as opposed to the residential code, it would have never been adopted in California because it has its own state-written green code.

MH: That's a good point. As it turned out, California and all other states have much better access to it in the IRC.[6] I'll add that when Appendix S was ultimately approved for the IRC, it made me very happy to simply see the word *straw* in the building code. It implies acceptance of straw as a building material.

AJ: The inclusion of this traditional nonstandard construction method in the code is a huge accomplishment. I imagine that it required a tremendous amount of effort. How was it funded?

MH: The California Straw Building Association covered expenses for all work on the California code. But I and other contributors worked as volunteers until 2012, when my primary code colleague, David Eisenberg, and I began being paid modestly by CASBA and associated organizations. Well-established materials and systems, like timber or concrete, have the support of large industries and trade associations, such as the International Wood Products Association and the American Concrete Institute.

AJ: How does this fact impact the code-development process?

MH: The process works reasonably well. When industry representatives submit a proposal or testify, it's obvious if they're advocating things that solely benefit their industry and not the public interest. In this sense, it's transparent and

is judged accordingly. Also, public servants, mostly building officials, have the final vote on code proposals. However, because it takes so much time to participate effectively, the process filters out many who should have a say. In practice, well-funded building industries and associations have the greatest influence on the ICC Codes.

AJ: You and your colleagues persisted and eventually your straw-bale-code proposal received ICC approval without support from a large trade association. Was there a list of tests that you were asked to perform to have Appendix S included in the IRC? These tests must be very expensive as well.

MH: We were able to rely on previous tests. Architects David Eisenberg and Matts Myhrman, the primary authors of the Arizona code, facilitated an ASTM E84 test for surface burning characteristics in 2000 and informal structural-wall tests in 1993. An out-of-plane load test had been conducted for a California project at the building official's request. The most important testing program occurred after 2001, when a team led by Bruce King and his Ecological Building Network [EBNet] obtained a $250,000 grant from a fund established by the California Air Resources Board to address air pollution caused by the rice-straw burning mentioned earlier. This included rigorous seismic testing, in particular, in-plane lateral-load tests at the University of Illinois, overseen by the late engineer Mark Aschheim.

Mark was a brilliant and dedicated civil-engineering professor, who later moved to Santa Clara University, where he continued to structurally test straw bale and other natural building systems. Other small-scale tests addressed moisture issues and plaster strength and durability. In 2006, EBNet received another grant, this time from a private foundation, which funded the first full-scale fire tests prescribed in the ASTM

E119 standard. We relied on all of these tests to write and justify the ICC code proposals.

AJ: Appendix S is included in the IRC, and so it can only be used for one- and two-family dwellings and townhouses. What if I want to build a nonresidential straw-bale structure?

MH: Appendix S can be proposed to the local building official for that project. The choice between a well-developed ICC code and a blank slate is usually an easy decision for a building official. In 2012, we tried, unsuccessfully, to incorporate straw-bale construction into the IBC because, although most straw-bale buildings are residential, nonresidential straw-bale buildings are common, including offices, retail stores, wineries, and even a US post office. The primary reason straw-bale construction is not in the IBC is the incomplete peer review of a seismic-safety computer analysis required by the Federal Emergency Management Agency for new construction systems to enter the IBC. The IRC has less stringent requirements. Recently, renewed interest in completing the peer review could result in straw-bale construction in the 2027 IBC.

AJ: What else, in your opinion, needs to be done to improve the acceptance of straw-bale construction, increase its applicability, and in general, promote its use in mainstream construction?

MH: Decrease the cost. Straw bales are inexpensive, US$3–5 each, but straw-bale wall assemblies are labor-intensive, and labor is about two-thirds of construction costs in industrialized countries.[7] So straw-bale buildings tend to cost the same as or more than wood-frame buildings, contrary to early claims, which is an obstacle to expanded use. One way to reduce cost is modular construction units prefabricated in a controlled environment.

AJ: Something like the prefabricated panels made by ModCell based in the UK?

MH: Yes, ModCell is a great system, but there are other examples.[8] Like the seven-story cross-laminated timber building in France, insulated with prefabricated straw-bale panels attached to its exterior structure.[9] And sustainable-building expert Chris Magwood has done significant work with prefabricated straw-bale walls in Canada.[10] However, the system I think still has the most potential is called Stak Block. It uses interlocking twelve-by-twelve-by-twenty-four-inch two-hole blocks of compressed straw. They can be reinforced similar to concrete blocks but interlock without mortar, like the new generation of compressed-earth blocks. They can receive conventional finishes, are uniform and load bearing, and are thinner than straw bales but with comparable insulation. Unfortunately, product development stalled.[11]

AJ: What else is preventing straw-bale construction from entering the mainstream?

MH: Appendix S has certainly made it easier to obtain a permit in most states. And straw's exceptional ability to store carbon has spurred new interest in straw-based building systems. But difficulty persists with the lending and insurance industries. We thought that once straw-bale construction was in the building codes, those industries would say, "Okay, this is a viable building system, and we'll provide loans and insurance." But comparatively few straw-bale buildings exist, so they are still seen as outliers. Also, you can't simply ask an average contractor to build or repair straw-bale walls.

AJ: And the bales are not available at your local Home Depot!

MH: Well, I'm happy to say that's not quite true. Several years ago, I discovered straw bales for sale at Home Depot! Advertised for erosion control, mulch, and seasonal decoration. I wouldn't trust those bales for building because their density and exposure to moisture are questionable. But maybe it's only a matter of time before construction-grade straw bales are as available as 2×4s are today!

6.2. Normalizing the Alternatives. Focus: Waterless Toilet.

IN CONVERSATION WITH MATHEW LIPPINCOTT

Mathew Lippincott studied arts and philosophy before becoming an expert in alternative water and sanitation technologies and a technical writer and editor in engineering and environmental monitoring. An active member of Recode, he is the lead author of the 2017 ANSI Water Efficiency and Conservation Standard [WE·Stand], a supplement to the Uniform Plumbing Code [UPC] published by the International Association of Plumbing and Mechanical Officials [IAPMO]. He was the chair of the 2013–15 IAPMO's UPC Green Supplement Composting Toilet Committee and is the author of the provisions on composting toilets included in the 2011 edition of the Oregon Reach Code. In our conversation, we speak about composting toilets, his work on WE·Stand, and the importance of standard setting for the diffusion of alternative technologies.

Aleksandra Jaeschke: What drew a visual artist into the world of composting toilets and standard setting?

Mathew Lippincott: When the 2008 housing crash happened, I had already been thinking about changing direction and decided to try to start a composting portable-toilet company with architectural designer Molly Danielsson, who had previously worked on a John Todd Living Machine. While traveling in Europe, we had learned that composting portable toilets were a normal business in France. So we decided to bring it to the United States. We thought, "What could possibly be hard about that? We could just modify a porta potty!" That was a very naive

dream. We quickly encountered an entire world of regulations that did not explicitly say we could not do it but had nothing that said that we could. We did some prototyping and encountered all of these problems, which led us to working with Recode, which focuses on access to and adoption of equitable and sustainable water systems and are based in Portland, Oregon.[12]

When we joined as volunteers in 2010, Recode was just finishing a three-year-long campaign organized by Brenna Bell, who had launched the organization. It focused on gray-water and rainwater reuse, but many people were interested in composting toilets because a composting toilet and a gray-water recycling system together form a complete alternative to a septic tank or sewer hookup. That's when we stopped focusing exclusively on the portable composting toilet and started to look at systemic reform instead. We submitted a proposal to the Bullitt Foundation, a regional foundation focused on conservation and sustainability, to fund it. The issue had little to do with their funding priorities, except that they were just about to build their new headquarters in Seattle, and they wanted it to become a demonstration building, so they decided to process all their water on-site. The Bullitt Center became the first office building to earn Living Building certification in 2015.

AJ: How did you end up working with the IAMPO on the WE·Stand standards?

ML: The existence of the Oregon Reach Code provision on composting toilets that we developed as Recode volunteers reached the IAPMO, and they invited us to work on the WE·Stand standards that were supposed to replace their Green Plumbing and Mechanical Code Supplement, which is a part of their Uniform Plumbing Code. In 2014, while we were focusing on the WE·Stand provisions, the Oregon Reach Code went through a revision, and someone asked for our section to be removed.[13]

AJ: Is it then again impossible to install a composting toilet in Oregon?

ML: Using the WE·Stand standards, variances are still possible. In Portland, several people have been successful going through the Alternative Technology Advisory Committee. People applied for a variance from their local jurisdiction, saying that their project was compliant with the IAPMO's supplement. But even if you can now install a composting toilet in Oregon, you still need a septic tank, although you usually get permission to reduce the septic field. If you are in a sewer district, your house will still need a water closet, and you will have to hook up to the sewer.

AJ: At least you can install it! And most importantly, in April 2021, the state decided to adopt the 2017 edition of WE·Stand and include it in the 2021 Oregon Residential Reach Code. So the composting toilet provisions made it back to Oregon, thanks to your work on the IAPMO's UPC supplement. How is this technology defined?

ML: The language gets tricky because when we normally think of a toilet, we mean the commode that does no treatment at all. The composting toilet refers to the entire treatment system: the commode and the compost processor. It can be a self-contained unit or a split system, in which the processor is located underneath the commode—for example, in the basement—and connected to it through a system of pipes. In terms of composting, the two main options are a continuous composter and a batch composter.

We also added a provision that allows for the composting chamber not to be directly connected to the commode. It's the simplest combination, which includes the composting portable toilet case. There are lots of situations, like a campground, where you have a concrete box and a pump-out system. The idea was to be able to do a version of that, except then you could move the waste to an appropriately sized composting chamber located nearby rather than taking it away to be discharged to the sewer network or a wastewater treatment plant.

And then there is a growing interest in urine-diverting toilets. People who already have a water-based sanitation system are often seeking nutrient recovery using urine diversion. Urine contains most of the nutrients found in human waste, but it is usually disease-free or of low risk.[14] It can be directly used as a fertilizer. By diverting urine, you also reduce the need for soaking and bulking material and ultimately decrease the volume of the composting chamber. So by adding this provision to the code, we were able to cover both composting toilets with urine diversion and urine-diverting flush toilets.

AJ: Humus, too, can be used on-site to fertilize ornamental plants and fruit trees. The alternative is to have it removed by an authorized professional. I wonder whether the need for professional removal services is not a potential obstacle. Most people will want it taken away, but the infrastructure is probably still missing.

ML: That's the big obstacle. A very small segment of the population wants to be engaged on a regular basis with their own excreta. Most people just want it flushed away, and our current system is very good at that whether or not there is proper treatment on the other end. Currently, we have septic tank pumpers, but they would need a slightly modified equipment and training to deal with composting toilets.

AJ: What are the main risks?

ML: I always think of risk in a comparative sense. According to the Environmental Protection Agency [EPA], 10 to 20 percent of septic tanks in the US are failing, and the EPA relies on the state's definitions of failure, which are usually limited to surface discharge of raw sewage. A lot of unprocessed or minimally processed sewage is being discharged underground.[15] Also, a well-maintained sewer system loses one in six toilet flushes to the soil in random locations that we don't know about, and yet you are convinced that your toilet is "working."[16] Still, thanks to the distance between the toilet and the processing plant, public health is largely protected.

The biggest problem with composting toilets is insect infestation. Flies are the real health risk because they can fly out of the toilet and land on your food. There are multiple ways to deal with that. Proper maintenance is key to preventing infestation, but you can also install a flytrap inside your composting toilet for additional protection. It works like a lobster trap; it prevents the flies from finding their way out. Also, if you put a light in the composting chamber, they will fly to the light. Still, flies are a potential disease transmission vector. That's the main risk.

AJ: Composting toilets are mainly used in rural areas. What is the situation in urban areas?

ML: A good example of a municipally supported rural system of composting toilets is in Skaneateles, New York, but we are starting to see localized wastewater treatment systems in cities.[17] The recently completed PAE Living Building in Portland is fitted with vacuum toilets connected to composting chambers, as well as urine-diversion urinals. The Hassalo on Eighth in Portland is a good case as well. This mixed-use development was built in an area served by a combined sewer system, already functioning at capacity, causing sewage to overflow into the river during heavy rain. The architects proposed to install a membrane bioreactor in the basement of one of the buildings to then discharge treated water for further treatment into an on-site artificial wetland. They did not install composting toilets, but there's no discharge to the municipal sewer. Another good example is the Flintenbreite eco-village in Lubec, Germany, where vacuum toilets are integrated with a biogas reactor. In this case, wastewater is treated on-site to generate electricity and heat for the community, but it could be composted as well.

AJ: When will we give up the "out of sight, out of mind" mindset? What needs to happen so that people recognize the advantages of these systems and adopt them as a mainstream standard in rural and urban areas?

ML: I am convinced that the water scarcity is going to drive it. The interest in composting toilets in water-stressed states, that is in California, Arizona, New Mexico, Colorado, and Texas, is constantly growing. When I was chairing the UPC Green Supplement Composting Toilet Committee, they put a man on the committee, who was the former plumbing inspector for the City of Dallas, to see if our proposal could stand up to heavy scrutiny. He was a very conservative fellow, but he loved the proposal. He said, "We need to get rid of flush toilets in Texas. There's no way we are going to be able to live in a city like Dallas if people continue flushing their toilets, because 25 percent of our city's water is used by one appliance. And we just don't have the water. Period."

AJ: For this to happen, we would have to change the terms used in the building code and stop referring to toilets as "water closets." It is a matter of language.

ML: You touched on a very interesting issue. When we were working on these codes, one of the biggest problems we have had is that urine and feces are not mentioned in the regulatory codes. There are many places in the US where nitrogen in sewage requires strict controls, but without a definition of urine, homeowners and municipalities can't meet control regulations by removing urine. Farmers also have difficulty using urine as a fertilizer because it doesn't fit neatly into the regulatory categories created for biosolids—in other words, sewage sludge—manure, et cetera. To combat this blind spot, the Gold Ribbon Commission on Urine Diversion was created in 2020. I am on the executive committee and our goal is to define urine and develop a national urine-reuse standard.[18]

AJ: Why is there only a handful of composting toilets on the market that are certified by the National Sanitation Foundation [NSF]? I believe that it is the only standard referenced in the ICC Codes.[19]

ML: It costs about $20,000 a year to keep the certification up. I don't want to denigrate any of the manufacturers of the NSF-certified toilets because some are great, but some of them have a very low user-acceptance rating. To give you an example, some of the smaller toilets have a tray underneath, supposedly for the finished compost, that will collect leachate if used at a higher-than-normal rate, even for a brief time."[20] This tray has a one-inch rim, so you have this contaminated liquid sloshing around while you are trying to empty it somewhere. This issue is not covered by the NSF standard. There is no relationship between good composting toilets and NSF-certified toilets. In the United States, everybody—including building officials—is trying to minimize their legal exposure, and so everything needs to be certified by an authorized body to assure legal protection.

AJ: What is the issue with the alarms in containers with less than five gallons? Is it also related to risk aversion?

ML: You can see the level of urine as you approach the toilet. Why would you need an alarm? It adds a provision in the US code, which is out of step with the developments elsewhere in the world. The United States is not a leader in these technologies, so it is important that we can use models produced elsewhere.

AJ: Do you think that the International Code Council will include WE·Stand in their model plumbing code?

ML: Although we were able to fund some paid work on code reform, for much of the six years I was a volunteer. Unfortunately, I did not have the time to work on the International Plumbing Code version of these provisions. I did negotiate one important thing with the IAPMO. The WE·Stand standards were developed from a Recode reference code, which is nearly identical, and were released into the public domain specifically to avoid the copyright issues between the ICC and the IAPMO and be able to have two independent processes going on in parallel. In the US, the states are forced to rely on these nongovernmental code-making organizations to fulfill federally imposed obligations—for example, regulating construction practices— that they cannot afford to execute. These organizations have their own agendas, and industries see it as an opportunity. Instead of a federally controlled system, you end up with an industry-driven system of regulation.

AJ: What else, other than state adoption of the appropriate standards, can potentially contribute to the success of these technologies?

ML: If you are an architect and have gone through the process of getting your special project approved, please contact Recode and let them know, so that they can add it to their code map and make it available to the others. Please document the details because the nuts and bolts of how designs get approved are easily lost. To develop the provisions, we often relied on examples of unpermitted systems built by a community of enthusiasts concerned about water scarcity and nutrient pollution and recovery. These people worked around the rules in order to develop the technologies that are now allowing us to change those same rules. We need to keep on building up on each other's experiences.

6.3. Coding the Uncertain. Focus: Environmental Simulation Software.

IN CONVERSATION WITH MICHAEL BRUSE

Michael Bruse is a geographer and professor of geoinformatics at Johannes Gutenberg University of Mainz in Germany. He specializes in climatology and urban microclimate with a focus on numerical simulation. SHADOW, the first software he launched in 1992, was one of the earliest urban shadow-casting simulation programs. In 1995, Bruse started working on ENVI met, a holistic microclimate model for the simulation of surface-plant-air interactions, and in 2014 founded ENVI_MET, a company that continues to develop the software used by cities, researchers, and designers across the world. In our conversation, we speak about his work on ENVI-met, modeling urban forests, simulating plant living processes, and the relationship between environmental simulation programs and the provisions that regulate the design of buildings.

Aleksandra Jaeschke: How did the ENVI-met project start? Was it meant for architects and urban designers from its inception?

Michael Bruse: No, at that time, architects were not interested in it, except for the shadow-analysis component, since there are these building-code provisions that regulate shadow casting on neighboring buildings. At that time, urban microclimate was a very specific area of physical geography and climatology. For me, it all started when I studied in Bochum [Germany]. We were dealing with urban climatology, heat island effect, ventilation, solar access, et cetera. At some point, we were in need of a program to calculate the shadow cast by a building that was

going to be erected in the town where I lived. There was no software available, so we programmed one for ourselves. We continued to expand it until it became a complete microclimate model. Sometime around 2000, Simon Yannas, the director of the Sustainable Environmental Design program at the Architectural Association in London, approached us—they were interested in working with these kinds of tools. Urban designers and, eventually, investors followed.

AJ: You have just mentioned shadow casting. ENVI-met and, by now, many other programs can simulate shadows cast by built objects. Your advantage is that you can model more than just man-made structures. Can ENVI-met simulate and assess shadows cast by vegetation? And if yes, what are the limitations?

MB: From the technical point of view, including the effect of vegetation is pretty easy if you know the geometry of the tree and you have an idea of the foliage and its distribution. Of course, for a full understanding of its shading, and also its thermal-shielding capacity throughout the year, you have to consider the leaf drop cycle, which makes a tree a bit different from an awning. At this point, the questions are: Do I want to consider the twigs and branches? Do I know where they are? The more detail you want to include, the more complicated it gets. In computer graphics, they call it the uncanny-valley effect. When your graphics are simple, like in Minecraft, no one complains that the characters do not look like they do in reality. But as you include more and more detail, suddenly there is a point—the uncanny-valley point—when the character is no longer compared to other computer simulations but to reality.

The same happens with trees. In the latest release of ENVI-met, trees are no longer cube-based.[21] They are modeled using the fractal-based L-system, which makes them look and behave so much more realistically that people now say, "The tree in front of my building looks different." So we have reached the uncanny-valley point. Still, it is now possible to actually capture these differences because with LIDAR [Light Detection and Ranging] technology, it is easy to get a high-resolution picture of real trees and transform it into a 3D model.

A slightly trickier thing is that trees convert some of the intercepted solar radiation into diffuse radiation, which creates this beautiful flickering effect, but this can also be modeled. Apart from that, cloud cover is an estimate, so the exact solar radiation is a guess. Still, as long as you accept these approximations, it is pretty easy to model the radiation part.

AJ: Recognizing that vegetation can be simulated with precision will hopefully allow architects to get credit for plant-based shading strategies in the future. Although a performance-oriented path, which opens the door to simulation-based decision-making, is offered in the California Energy Code, it only considers the effect of shading from awnings, fins, and screens. No credit is offered for shading from vegetation, although the same code recognizes that it has a positive impact on our health and welfare.

MB: The building officials probably want you to base your shading concept on the use of devices that are part of the building. The tree could be removed, and the shading strategy would no longer work.

AJ: That's most likely the reason, but one can also remove an awning or an insect screen.

MB: Yes, that's true.

AJ: The same code also excludes green walls from the list of potential insulation materials and systems. One can propose alternative solutions, but they must be rated in terms of R-value. Even though R-value offers a limited, if not distorted, understanding of thermal transfers, it is the main value considered in the code. ENVI-met can simulate energy-exchange processes in green walls and green roofs. Can it analyze the thermal performance in terms of R-value?

MB: It is a bit tricky. The R-value is a constant, but a green wall is part of an open system. Its state depends on many fluctuating factors—there is not much that is constant. The energy flux will depend on the changing solar angle and foliage. It will be affected by the watering pattern. With ENVI-met, we can construct a layer of vegetation in front of a wall or a roof. We can simulate the microclimate of this layer, the leaf temperature, vapor exchange, et cetera. We can also model the substrate, which can be composed of different sublayers depending on the plant species and the design of your building. We can model the air gap. And then, you can run your simulation to understand the energy flux between the inside and the outside to eventually reverse engineer an R-value for the entire wall system. But this R-value will change throughout the year. So, yes, we can give you an R-value, but this R-value will not be a constant anymore. It will vary within a certain range because your green wall is part of a dynamic system.

AJ: Any wall for that matter. Not just a green wall.

MB: Yes. Let's say that you have a very complex model of an indoor environment with all the AC units, walls, doors, people, and equipment precisely modeled. But then, when it comes to the outer wall, you consider one constant R-value independently of whether it is a south- or north-facing wall, if it is shielded by another building, or the wind speed is different at every corner. In addition, you take the weather data from the airport located fifteen miles away. You have this very detailed model of the indoor environment and a very forged model of the outside. There has always been this contradiction.

AJ: ENVI-met can be used to assess dispersion and deposition of urban pollutants. Can it be used to analyze the capacity of a living wall to absorb pollutants?

MB: This is a very hot topic. I think, and this is in line with the current research, that the filtering potential of plants in urban environments is not as much as we might have thought. If I have a forest of, let's say, twenty thousand trees, the amount of filtered particulate matter will be significant. But if you only have a green wall or a line of twenty trees, the effect tends to me insignificant. But, yes, you can simulate it. However, technically speaking, these plants do not absorb the particulate matter. Unlike some gaseous air pollution that can get absorbed by the stomata, the particles get deposited on the leaf surface. There are two main kinds of vascular plants: some plants retain the particles on the leaf surface until the leaves fall; in case of the other plants, for example, plane trees, the particles are washed off by rain.

AJ: How about an indoor environment?

MB: This is a completely different issue because in an indoor environment, you have a fixed volume of air. Even if you open the windows or operate an HVAC [heating, ventilation, and air-conditioning] system, you still have a chance to get all the molecules and particles in contact with the green wall. If it works at all, it will work better in the indoor environment for sure.

AJ: The grid resolution in the ENVI-met is one meter, approximately three feet. Is it detailed enough to capture indoor air dynamics?

MB: Many of the processes that we model are grid size dependent. When you go down in scale, some of the laws no longer apply, and the results are no longer correct. Still, you can easily go down to twenty centimeters, approximately eight inches, so this is not a problem. But the indoor environment is really a different game. You have a fine resolution in everything, not only in terms of spatial dimensions but also when it comes to, for example, turbulence. So other models might work better in this sense. You would simply need to calculate the influx of gaseous and particulate matter from the outdoor sources and add it to the indoor sources.

AJ: Do you know of a software that can simulate the deposition rate of pollution on plants in an indoor environment?

MB: Most of the people who work on these indoor living-wall systems take a simpler approach. They will rely on a laboratory experiment and use the data to design their living wall considering the anticipated room surface area, airflow rates, and type of air pollutants.

AJ: We will then need more and more accurate scientific data to understand plant performance. In your case, in order to model the plant and its life processes, you not only need the data but you also have to understand the processes to be able to simulate them. I imagine that you rely on models developed by botanists and ecologists. What are the challenges?

MB: We have already talked about the plant geometry. The upper part of the tree is less of a problem. The roots are a very big problem—we do not know anything about them, and they are fundamental, even if we only consider water uptake. They often get damaged by car traffic or during construction. The soil gets so compact that it limits root growth because air and water—even if there is water—cannot penetrate through it. Because soil is often replaced with a different type during construction, you simply don't know what soil you have until you excavate. The only currently available instrument is a soil radar, and it is very expensive. We decided to add the TreePass module—the part of ENVI-met that focuses on vegetation health—when our region lost 20 percent of its trees during a thunderstorm. We felt the need to create a simulation tool that would allow us to investigate this issue.

AJ: What about physiological processes?

MB: In terms of physiological processes, the science is there, and it has been used for crop-management purposes since the 1960s. Of course, most research focused on edible plants, but the fundamentals are the same. There are very good models to simulate CO_2 assimilation, evapotranspiration, leaf temperature, et cetera. Of course, the model is not enough. We still need the data for different species to be able to simulate their behavior. The CAM [Crassulacean acid metabolism] plants are not yet in ENVI-met, and it is something that we want to include in the next version because many xerophytes metabolize in this way and cannot be compared to conifers, deciduous trees, or grasses.[22] But once we have added this group, we will have models of everything from the little moss to the biggest tree. You will be able to design your own vegetation, as long as you use one of the provided models.

AJ: As long as I manage to find the data for the various species, I can build them the same way architects model a material or a wall assembly in CAD to then add it to the material library.

MB: Exactly. Many things, such as albedo value, are easily available and can be added to the database, but some processes, for example, the behavior of stomata, still lacks research. Once there is a new stomata model, we will revise this part of the software. Since one cannot predict all the needs, we decided to integrate ENVI-met V5 with the Python programming language.

6.4. Certifying the Living.
Focus: Live Moss Panel.

IN CONVERSATION WITH AL BENNER

Al Benner is a start-up consultant and a serial entrepreneur in the green industry. He has launched a dozen successful gardening and wellness start-ups. Benner is the founder of Moss Acres, the nation's leading supplier of live moss, and the president of its sister business, Moss Walls, the producer of Verdure Wellness Walls, the first self-contained and self-sustaining moss wall for interior spaces. In this conversation, we speak about moss and its air-purifying potential, the fundamental role of lab testing, and the importance of service providers for the diffusion of living products.

Aleksandra Jaeschke: You have launched a number of green start-ups, but the moss business stands out as a unique enterprise. You mention somewhere that you are very sensitive to air quality and that is why the Verdure Wellness Walls project has special meaning for you. There is also a family history behind it.

Al Benner: It's true. My father purchased a property in Bucks County, Pennsylvania, along the Delaware River, in the early 1960s. It was a wooded, terraced hillside, and the grass would not grow because there was too much shade. He didn't really know what to do, but he was a horticulturist, so he decided to kill the grass with, I think, a mix of sulfur and aluminum sulfate, which acidified the soil to the extent that the grass just died. And then he said, "I'm just going to wait and see what happens." And within a year, he started to see this green film. He became known as a pioneer for moss gardening.[23] For decades, he gave tours of the property. At some point, my brother and I started to help keep the property up, although it is pretty self-maintaining. And then, I guess twenty years ago, I started Moss Acres. We were the first and only supplier of live moss for gardening. Moss is a rapidly renewable resource on the wet and woodsy hillsides of northeastern Pennsylvania. It is sustainable to harvest it if it is done selectively; it grows back in a few years. And then, at some point, I branched off and started Moss Walls.

AJ: The simple modular moss panels sold by Moss Acres have no misters. I wonder how this moss can survive in an air-conditioned environment. Does it simply extract moisture from the air?

AB: Let me be clear about this product. It is actually a reindeer lichen, although everybody calls it reindeer moss. These simple wall moss panels are not alive. They are preserved with glycerin and a food-grade dye, since in nature, this lichen is creamy gray, not mossy green. Now, is this stuff still alive?! I am not quite sure. It might be dormant.

AJ: Yes, both lichens and mosses go dormant without water, so perhaps your reindeer moss could come back to life if it was not for the preservatives. How about your live moss products?

AB: Our original indoor moss walls had an automated misting system that went up and down the face of the wall. These things occasionally required service, and we were never set up as a service provider. We are a supplier, so we had to pull this product off the market and rethink what we were offering. We now use the reindeer moss, or the reindeer lichen, for the vertical portion of the Verdure Wellness Wall, and for the basin we still use cushion moss, *Leucobryum glaucum*, that is doing the work. It only needs a gallon or two of water every couple of months, much less than when we had the misting system. It is not ideal—we want to stop using the reindeer lichen, since we don't harvest it ourselves and can't control the process, but that is where we are for now when it comes to indoor moss walls.

AJ: Still, if there was a network of businesses dedicated to servicing these systems, you could, again, be making indoor living walls equipped with misters, which would significantly increase the surface area covered with live moss and possibly improve its chances to be accepted as an air-purifying device.

AB: That's correct. We could do that if there was such network in place.

AJ: After all, it is normal to call an HVAC company every six months to have your machines serviced. Why not do the same for a living wall? I believe that it is a cultural issue. We blindly trust these mechanical systems because they are everywhere, and what's fundamental to my argument is that they are legitimized as a safe and healthy solution by building regulations. And yet think how many people regularly forget to change their HVAC filters or service the machines.

AB: These machines do important work, when they work, in terms of air exchange and humidity control, but that is about it. Plants provide visual and therapeutic benefits as well. There are all these studies done in hospitals that prove the healing potential of plants, but people continue to underestimate the feeling one gets from being surrounded by greenery. Still, we have come a long way, and I feel like something is going to break.

Right now, we are focusing on the outdoor moss-wall system. We are very close to perfecting a way to mass-produce these vertical rain screens for buildings. Working outdoors has its own issues. Moss prefers to be watered from above, and when you go vertical, it becomes challenging because of gravity. Luckily, *Bryum caespiticium*, the species that we use for the outdoor walls, likes to grow where there are pockets of moisture beneath it. It is commonly referred to as sidewalk moss and is used to absorbing water in this way. What I am planning to do, and so far we have been successful, is to install a soaker line along the top of each panel and allow the water to drip down through the capillary mat system to be then absorbed by the moss from below.

AJ: These urban green walls are definitely comforting to the eye, but their air-purifying potential seems insignificant if you compare it to the amount of pollution generated each day by traffic. Strong winds also seem to limit the deposition of particulate matter. Perhaps moss walls are more beneficial indoors than outdoors?

AB: Yes, but indoors is difficult to manage. There are lighting issues, humidity issues…

AJ: Is that worse than the changing climate, unpredictable winds, sudden temperature swings, and torrential rains?

AB: There is no guarantee with living plants. The thing with outdoor living walls, if they're in a northern climate, is that the plants are going to die off if they freeze in winter. Replacing these plants is cost prohibitive. We are hoping to be able to offer these moss walls for a fraction of that cost. It is a very viable concept; it just needs to be perfected.

AJ: Speaking of guarantees, I have come across a study that states that moss can accumulate metal pollutants at a much higher rate than vascular plants.[24] I was wondering whether you have come across scientific studies that quantify the air-purifying potential of mosses. There are databases that classify plants in terms of water use, but I have not come across a database that would classify them in terms of their air-purifying potential.[25]

AB: This is tricky, but there are tangible proofs that moss has purifying qualities. *Sphagnum* moss, for example, was used for centuries by the military as a field wound dressing. Mosses produce secondary compounds, which protect them from viruses, fungi, and bacteria.[26] Unlike most vascular plants, they ingest pollutants as nutrients. Moss has no roots, so it gets its moisture and nutrients from the air. It absorbs everything. They have an incredible amount of surface area. If you look at *Bryum caespiticium*, the primary species we use in the outdoor walls, you will first think, "Oh, that doesn't have much surface area. It's just covering a small crack in the sidewalk." But if you look at it under a microscope, it is like a green lung.

The CityTree is an interesting project by a Berlin-based company called Green City Solutions. They did some tests on their moss biofilters that yielded promising results.[27] I also know of a study recently done by an undergraduate student at Columbia University,

under the mentorship of Dr. William R. Buck from the New York Botanical Garden, that looked at the effects four native mosses have on particulate matter, humidity, and temperature within a controlled microenvironment, a small test chamber.[28] I have not yet come across a study that would compare different mosses in an indoor environment.

In 2018, we did our own research with the early version of the Verdure Wellness Wall, when it was still equipped with misters and only used cushion moss. We set up a sealed room, used a Particles Plus meter, and ran a control test for two days before running the actual test. It was not an independent study, but it was very compelling. We observed an incredible decrease in particulate matter—approximately 95 percent compared to baseline—and a significant drop in CO_2—approximately 55 percent—over a period of three days. So I know for a fact that an indoor live-moss wall equipped with misters works.

AJ: The reason why I asked this question is that the building code tells you that plants are beneficial, but you do not get credit for using them. In terms of ventilation, every permissible filtering device must be labeled with a MERV [Minimum Efficiency Reporting Value] rating, which is a system that classifies air filters according to the size of intercepted particles.[29] As sad as it sounds, until we can actually certify how much pollution plants can absorb or retain, they will not be considered as a potential permissible alternative in the building code.

AB: I think that in this phase, we have to rely on the interest in their potential to beautify the cities. There's a lot of interest in that. The numbers will follow. My ambition is to get to a point in the next couple of years where I can have all these studies done.

AJ: Imagine if you could say, "Listen, I have tested it and can guarantee the results." You could compete against a MERV-rated filter!

AB: It would be the game-changer.

CONCLUSION

1. Plotting the Regulatory Circuits: From Ideas to Standards

The agendas that shaped the character of building regulations throughout their history also indirectly influenced the contemporary attitudes toward the environment and the ways in which we define and practice what is today called sustainable design. Many long-forgotten events, ideas, and programs had informed building regulations before the ecological thinking first gained currency among scientists, then received attention from the society, and eventually informed environmental legislation and the green building standards as presently applied to construction practices. While this fact in itself deserves notice—these events, ideas, and programs continue to indirectly predetermine our actions—an even deeper challenge also calls for attention. As Gregory Bateson acutely observed, ideas and programs interact and survive in circuits.[1]

While in nature the survival of ideas and programs depends on material, energetic, electrical, and chemical circuits, in human society they are further ingrained in language and eventually in socially accepted norms and legally binding codes. Hence, it is these multiple canalized pathways, or to use the term coined by C. H. Waddington, "epigenetic chreods," that in large part determine how we formulate ideas, devise programs, and eventually transform them into mandatory standards.[2] As Waddington observes, "many types of change going on in society have a more or less well-developed chreotic character; once they have got well started in a certain direction, it is very hard to divert them."[3]

Building regulations provide a perfect example of this characteristic. While standards can be changed (consider the predesign

173

initiatives presented in Chapter 6, "The Power of Predesign in Four Conversations"), once crystallized, the circuits of code making remain ingrained in the regulatory landscape. They continue to determine how we can think about new standards, and this is what makes the initiatives discussed in Chapter 6 so challenging. It is therefore a fallacy to assume that by changing ideas and programs, and by updating the standards, we can change our attitudes toward ecology. The design of the circuit itself constitutes a determinant aspect of the programs transferred along its pathways. Ideas and programs need to be regularly revised and standards accordingly updated, but the regulatory landscape from which they originate needs to be occasionally *recircuited* as well.

Since it is beyond the scope of a single study to provide an answer to such a colossal challenge, my intention was to trace some of the processes that have informed the circuits of code making, sculpted the topography of the regulatory landscape, affected our thinking about the environment, and ultimately determined the ecological character of America's houses. The path from welfare and safety to green building standards led through the era of ecology, but economic interests determined its precise trajectory. The recognition of this simple, and in part, obvious fact is crucial for the understanding of the current regulatory landscape and the circuits along which green building standards continue to be propagated.

Part One – Agendas revealed how the original ambitions of code makers evolved under the pressure of competing ecological and economic interests. It provided an account of pre-ecological agendas that influenced the American house throughout the century and in part continue to exert influence today, albeit disguised as green building standards. It also emphasized when the environmentally driven regulations actually addressed the state of the environment—its protection as opposed to shortsightedly focusing on human climate comfort and natural-resource management.

The events, ideas, and programs that gradually connected the knowing of nature (the science of ecology) with the making of domestic architecture (the art of building) also exposed the troublesome nature of technology. More than just an interface between the economies of nature and man, technology—both the artifacts and the techniques that support them—is a profit-making hinge. Rather than curbing environmentally harmful economic growth, by supporting certain technologies, green standards indirectly support economic growth. Market-driven interests have influenced environmental action in the same way in which they once influenced the social reform. Back then, by co-opting the health and welfare discourse, and recently, under the green banner of sustainability, policy makers and standard setters used all available means and methods to promote green technologies to perpetuate economic growth. As a result, a study of the impact of green building standards would be incomplete if it only addressed coercive methods (building regulations and their internal structure and language) without paying attention to the techniques of incentivizing (various rebates and write-offs, and the types of green appliances and construction systems that they promote). If the "unsustainable" remains difficult to locate, it is because it resides at a deeper level and is also more dispersed. It is together that technological artifacts, subsidies, and regulations determine the environmental impact of architecture, and this issue was explored in the three chapters that make Part Two – Means and Methods.

2. Recircuiting the Code Landscape: Topics for Predesign Research

Architect Cedric Price once said, "Technology is the answer—but what was the question?"[4] The question, most of us now think, should be concerned with the preservation of living communities and the restraint in the use of natural resources. However, the ecological question, if we wish to call it that, cannot only scrutinize how we use technology and cannot be separated from the questions regarding the standards used to regulate its development and use. In other words, the codes are definitely not the answer, but they are part of the question that designers must finally engage with.

The crystallized structure of the building code and the circuits from which it originates affect our capacity to transform the emerging environmental ideas and programs into more ecologically minded forms of spatial practice. Code making is a form of predesign. Not only does the core of the regulatory apparatus, the building code, determine the limits of environmental mindedness, but it also indirectly supports many of the products promoted with economic incentives—instruments conceived from within the same market claimed responsible for environmental degradation. Ultimately, predesigned in the code-making circuits and expressions of the market-preferred technologies, American houses continue to be frenetically built, demolished, and flipped, but the American house resists change.

Several possible themes for future research emerge from this analysis of the greening of building codes. First, there is an interrogation of the impact of construction that goes beyond the operational efficiency to address the embodied energy, water footprint, toxicity of materials, and the politics of material extraction, transportation, and disposal of construction waste. While some of these issues are the subjects of current research, practice, and, to a limited degree, regulatory reform, the topic—when addressed as a matter of code making—requires a telescopic lens capable of capturing both the metacode of the regulations and the mega-landscape of the material ecology.[5] Rather than merely quantitative, such research should also be linguistic and cartographic (involve rethinking definitions and making maps). Second, there is an examination of the excessive permissiveness toward material and financial obsolescence as affected by, on the one hand, tax depreciation rates and mortgage terms and, on the other hand, the lifespan of materials as defined in manufacturer's warranties.[6] Third, there is an inquiry into the impact of zoning ordinances on the ways individual house lots affect the structure and functioning of urban landscapes as potential support for biodiversity and wildlife. Last but not least, what awaits to be addressed in creative and joyful terms is the status of vegetation. As it became clear in the last section of Chapter 5 and the conversations that make up Chapter 6, this type of inquiry will have to address the regulatory language, its metacode, and (sadly) require that plant performance be quantified in numerical terms.

Still, regardless of how positive the outcomes of such research projects might be, only a massive event can truly reconfigure the rigidly canalized pathways of the regulatory landscape and project the American house out of the profit-driven market realm and into a more ecologically minded circuit. The trouble is that it is hard to tell whether one should fear or hope for such a revolutionary quake. The risk is that it will be an effect of a life-threatening environmental catastrophe.

Meanwhile, in this book, I tried to expose how the "ecofascism" that André Gorz saw hidden in the basic premises of *The Limits to*

Growth has redefined our relationship with the environment through an interface called green technology and, ultimately, how this redefinition has been subsidized with federal incentives and legitimated by green building standards—standards that consider trees, users, and passive design inconvenient, unpredictable, and inefficient. The fact that neither a tree nor a form-driven design solution proposed by an architect will receive a tax write-off is simply because neither the latter nor the former stimulates economic growth the way a solar panel does. Neither a tree nor an ingenious building envelope can generate enough megawatts of renewable energy to compete with it.

"Shading shall not cast a shadow," a prescription found in the California Green Building Standards Code, best reflects this bias.[7] It exemplifies how construction standards support a specific technological interface powered by active mechanical devices and driven by a reductionist quest for energy efficiency and now carbon neutrality. In *Tools for Thought*, Waddington succinctly stated, "Reductionism is a recipe for action…it is the belief that if you are confronted with a complex situation, for instance a living system, your best bet to get some sort of pay-off or other is to look for the physical or chemical factors which can influence the phenomenon in question." He then added, "Undoubtedly, the 'thing' view 'works,' up to a point."[8] In this book, I tried to expose how the technological "thing" imperative—the one embraced by Western societies—distorts our understanding of ecology and our place in it, affects our judgment of what is, to echo George Parkin Grant, environmentally appropriate, good, and beautiful, and how it transforms a priceless union with the environment into an act of monetary valuation of the environment as a source.[9]

3. Breaking the Green Circuit Open: Sustainable Morality versus Ecological Consciousness

While environmentalists continue to denounce the devastating impacts of free trade and a fossil fuel–based economy, governments keep on fine-tuning green building standards concentrating on incentives for ecotechnologies to guarantee demand among potential consumers. Georges Canguilhem once said, "Certainly, the logic of normalization can be pushed as far as the normalization of needs by means of the persuasion of advertising."[10] While entire ecosystems disappear, we advertise sustainability in terms of net-zero technologies and smart cities.

The vision of sustainability that underlines most of today's voluntary and mandatory green building standards selectively isolates certain quantifiable aspects of ecological dynamics. Simultaneously, it fails to address the open and interconnected character of ecological systems. Decades of delay in response to global warming legitimize what philosopher Giorgio Agamben calls (after jurist Carl Schmitt) a "state of exception."[11] Now extremely urgent, climate bills justifiably focus on minimizing energy use and curbing carbon emissions. But are they exceptional enough?

The protestant ethic that sociologist and historian Max Weber identified as one of the major forces behind the spirit of capitalism can now be perceived in the contemporary attitudes toward the natural environment.[12] The mechanisms that coupled the protestant ethic with the capitalist ethos of accumulation of wealth has also aligned the environmental consciousness, if we want to call it that, with the spirit of consumerism. The puritan ethos of the daily duty and the utilitarian attitude toward virtues resonate in the contemporary pursuit of environmental efficiency and translate environmental consciousness into sustainable morality. Cities adopt the practice of bookkeeping of environmental conduct; environmentally minded citizens track good deeds against ecological sins. The spirit of sustainable development has conquered the last uncharted territory: the American household, *oikos*.

Unfortunately, like the puritan ethic, which from a calling turned into an "iron cage," in Weber's words, we increasingly find ourselves in a green cage of sustainable capitalism that imposes a rigid conduct while successfully neutralizing the underlying desire for a joyful and contemplative communion with nature. In fact, like the protestant ethic, sustainable morality prefers the individual daily discipline to collective action. It transforms the oppressiveness of scientific management into a daily environmental heroism. Sustainable morality requires a similar form of discipline, "a regulation of the whole of conduct," and relies on a panoptical apparatus of control of all aspects of individual life.[13] Once again, as Michael Hardt and Antonio Negri pointed out, capitalism manages to transform the desire to resist into a useful mechanism.[14] It absorbs, celebrates, and manages resistances and differences to successfully couple the global-warming imperative with the micropolitics of sustainability.

Alternative visions of ecology, such as Félix Guattari's "ecosophy," which combine multiple ecological registers—the environment, social relations, and human subjectivity—struggle to compete with the concept of sustainability that underlies mandatory green building standards.[15] Guattari's ethico-political position remains in stark contrast with the prevailing technocratic attitudes, as he advocates against standardization, normalization, and commodification of relations and subjectivities. Guattari opens *The*

Three Ecologies with a quotation from Bateson: "There is an ecology of bad ideas, just as there is an ecology of weeds."[16] The ideas and programs generated by interconnected human minds and eventually propagated in a standardized format across the regulatory circuits inform these ecologies. Whether the circuitry of code making supports an impoverished ecology of weed-notions—think of the net-zero dogma—or a true diversity of healthy ideas is of vital importance. Unfortunately, an expanded ecological consciousness will continue to be globally "over-encoded," in Guattari's words, by weed-notions that spread fast and easily adapt to new market "habitats," if we insist on thinking about the environment as an outside from which to extract and isolate ourselves.[17]

As Hardt and Negri state in *Empire*, "Capital [depends] on its outside."[18] It will generate it (the outside) from within itself if it goes missing. Driven by a technoscientific rationality and a puritan set of ethical values, our economic and regulatory systems thrive on the concept of a strategically externalized—vilified at times and sanctified at others—nature, a thing to exploit and simultaneously close ourselves off from, preferably in a green-rated building.

What is the best way out of this impasse considering the rigid rules that we operate within? Once again, I turn to Bateson, and this is what he has to say: "The question is not what is the best thing to do within the rules as they are at the moment. The question is how can we get away from the rules within which we have been operating."[19] The greening of an old game won't do it. It is time to get away from the rules that put us humans outside of nature. The first step toward this vital shift is to recircuit our mindsets.

NOTES

PREFACE

1. Charles A. Reich, *The Greening of America* (New York: Random House, 1970). For more information about how Reich's project transformed in reaction to the events of 1968, see "Interview with Charles Reich," *Salient* 34, no. 16 (September 8, 1971), http://nzetc.victoria.ac.nz/tm/scholarly/tei-Salient34161971-t1-body-d12.html.

INTRODUCTION

1. For a discussion of Michel Foucault's use of the term *apparatus (dispositif)*, see, for example, Giorgio Agamben, *What Is an Apparatus?* in *What is an Apparatus? and Other Essays* (Stanford, CA: Stanford University Press, 2009), 2. According to Agamben, the following is one of the few working definitions offered by Foucault in an interview: "What I'm trying to single out with this term is, first and foremost, a thoroughly heterogeneous set consisting of discourses, institutions, architectural forms, regulatory decisions, laws, administrative measures, scientific statements, philosophical, moral, and philanthropic propositions—in short, the said as much as the unsaid. Such are the elements of the apparatus. The apparatus itself is the network that can be established between these elements."
2. Because the events and ideas mentioned in these introductory passages are discussed at length in Part One – Agendas, the sources are provided later.
3. Rachel Carson, *Silent Spring* (Boston: Houghton Mifflin, 1962).
4. Donella H. Meadows, Dennis L. Meadows, Jørgen Randers, and William W. Behrens III, *The Limits to Growth: A Report for the Club of Rome's Project on the Predicament of Mankind* (New York: Universe Books, 1972).
5. United Nations World Commission on Environment and Development, *Report of the World Commission on Environment and Development: Our Common Future* (Oxford: Oxford University Press, 1987). The report was produced by a team led by political leader Gro Harlem Brundtland and is also known as the *Brundtland Report*.
6. Ha-Joon Chang, *23 Things They Don't Tell You about Capitalism* (London: Penguin Books, 2010), Thing 16.
7. In the 2015 edition of the *Housing Market Analysis Report* (Los Angeles: Housing and Community Investment Department, 2015), 151, the City of Los Angeles identified the introduction of the green building standards as a potential barrier to affordable housing; Naomi Klein, *This Changes Everything: Capitalism vs. the Climate* (New York: Simon & Schuster, 2015), 79.
8. The difficulties encountered by the code developers who helped legalize straw-bale construction and composting toilets are discussed in Chapter 6, "The Power of Predesign in Four Conversations," of this book.
9. Michael Hardt and Antonio Negri, *Empire* (Cambridge, MA: Harvard University Press, 2000), 313.
10. Félix Guattari, *Molecular Revolution: Psychiatry and Politics* (New York: Penguin, 1984), 229.
11. Guattari, *Molecular Revolution*, "The Micro-Politics of Fascism," 217–32.
12. Georges Canguilhem, *A Vital Rationalist: Selected Writings*, ed. Francois Delaporte (New York: Zone Books, 1994), 370.
13. California Building Standards Commission, 2019 California Green Building Standards Code, California Code of Regulations, Title 24, Part 11 (Washington, DC: International Code Council, 2019).
14. Chang, *23 Things*, Thing 1.
15. In *Questioning Architectural Judgment: The Problem of Codes in the United States* (New York: Routledge, 2014), Steven A. Moore and Barbara B. Wilson discuss two important instances of market limitation achieved through code making: the Americans with Disabilities Act and the case of the Affordable Housing Act introduced by the City of Austin, TX.
16. Eran Ben-Joseph, *The Code of the City: Standards and the Hidden Language of Place Making* (Cambridge, MA: MIT Press, 2005), 104.
17. Ibid., 168.
18. Jane Jacobs, "The Kind of Problem a City Is," in *The Death and Life of Great American Cities* (New York: Vintage Books, 1992), 428–48.
19. William C. Baer, "Customs, Norms, Rules, Regulations and Standards in Design Practice," in *Companion to Urban Design*, ed. Tridib Banerjee and Anastasia Loukaitou-Sideris (New York: Routledge, 2011), 277.
20. Herbert A. Simon, *The Science of the Artificial* (Cambridge, MA: MIT Press, 1996), 479.
21. See, for example, Moore and Wilson, *Questioning Architectural Judgment*, 131–36.
22. Possibly (but sadly), plants will only gain the acceptance of the building industry if they can be represented as "predictable" CAD blocks and if their performance—as discussed in Chapter 6, "The Power of Predesign in Four Conversations," of this

book—can be digitally simulated or lab tested.

23. Simon, *The Science of the Artificial*, 44.

24. Canguilhem, *A Vital Rationalist*, 353–54.

25. See, for example, Ben-Joseph, *The Code of the City*, 43.

26. "Potential harmful environmental impacts as a consequence of material and system specifications, installation, and operations in current U.S. green building practices." Tamera L. McCuen and Lee A. Fithian, *Green Buildings and the Law*, ed. Julie Adshead (New York: Spon Press, 2011), 38.

27. Reyner Banham, *Los Angeles: The Architecture of Four Ecologies*, 2nd ed. (Berkeley: University of California Press, 2009).

PART ONE – INTRODUCTION

1. Gregory Bateson, *Steps to an Ecology of Mind* (Chicago: University of Chicago Press, 2000), 489.

CHAPTER ONE

1. Some of the oldest standard-setting organizations were created just before the turn of the century. Underwriters Laboratories was founded in 1894, and the American Society of the International Association for Testing and Materials (ASTM: now ASTM International) began in 1898. Eventually, in 1918, a group of leading engineering societies supported by the federal government established what is now called the American National Standards Institute (ANSI), an organization that oversees standard-setting efforts and accredits standard-setting organizations.

2. Frederick Winslow Taylor, *Principles of Scientific Management* (New York: Harper and Brothers, 1911).

3. In chronological order: the 1867 San Francisco Zoning Ordinance; the 1885 Modesto Zoning Ordinance, CA; the 1899 Height of Buildings Act, Washington, DC; the 1908 Los Angeles Land Use Zoning Ordinance; and the 1913 New Jersey Subdivision Regulation.

4. *American Sewerage Practice, Vol. 1: Design of Sewers* (New York: McGraw-Hill, 1914) by Leonard Metcalf and Harrison P. Eddy was published a year after Mulholland's controversial Owens Valley Aqueduct started pumping water to Los Angeles.

5. Ebenezer Howard, *Garden Cities of To-Morrow: (Being the Second Edition of "To-morrow: A Peaceful Path to Real Reform")* (London: Swan Sonnenschein, 1902). Although few garden cities were built, Howard's ideas influenced urban design. An example can be found in Raymond Unwin's *Nothing Gained by Overcrowding! How the Garden City Type of Development May Benefit Both Owner and Occupier* (London: Garden Cities and Town Planning Association, 1912).

6. See Keller Easterling, "Subdivision Products" and "Function and Template: War-town Subdivision Science," in *Organization Space: Landscapes, Highways, and Houses in America* (Cambridge, MA: MIT Press, 1999), 129–35, 136–60.

7. Eran Ben-Joseph, *The Code of the City: Standards and the Hidden Language of Place Making* (Cambridge, MA: MIT Press, 2005), 58.

8. National Board of Fire Underwriters, Building Code Recommended by the National Board of Fire Underwriters (New York: James Kempster Printing, 1905).

9. Frank Lloyd Wright, *The Natural House* (New York: Horizon Press, 1982), 14.

10. Catherine Beecher's function-driven approach was first made known to the public in *A Treatise on Domestic Economy, For the Use of Young Ladies at Home, and At School* (Boston: T. H. Webb, 1841) and then more fully in *The American Woman's Home, Principles of Domestic Science* (New York: J .B. Ford, 1869), written with Harriet Beecher Stowe.

11. For examples, see Witold Rybczynski, "Light and Air" and "Efficiency," in *Home: A Short History of an Idea* (New York: Penguin Books, 1987), 123–43, 145–71.

12. Between 1908 and the beginning of World War II, the California-based Pacific Ready-Cuts sold thousands of ready-to-assemble homes based on almost two thousand plan variations. See Rosemary Thornton and Dale Patrick Wolicki, *California's Kit Homes: A Reprint of the 1925 Pacific Ready-Cut Homes Catalog* (Alton, IL: Gentle Beam Publications, 2004).

13. An attitude openly expressed in such popular books as *House Architecture* (London: Macmillan, 1880) by British architect John J. Stevenson. See Rybczynski, *Home*, 146–47.

14. In 1862, Canadian engineer Henry Ruttan published *Ventilation and Warming of Buildings* (New York: Putnam), in which he discussed many systems designed for railroad cars, such as double glazing, that were still waiting to be applied to house construction. For further details, see Rybczynski, *Home*, 146.

15. Wright, *The Natural House*, 15.

16. In 1892, John Muir founded the Sierra Club, one of the first large-scale environmental-preservation organizations, and prior to that successfully campaigned for the creation of Yosemite National Park in 1890. Through his preservationist efforts, he expressed the same holistic attitude encapsulated in Henry David Thoreau's "Walking," *Atlantic Monthly*, June 1862, https://www.theatlantic.com/magazine/archive/1862/06/walking/304674/.

17. Gifford Pinchot served under Theodore Roosevelt as Chief Forester. Notably, the U.S. Forest Service was part of the Department of Agriculture, where plants were perceived as crops.

18. Although German zoologist Ernst Haeckel coined the term *oekologie* in 1866, it was not used by scientists and naturalists until the 1890s. One of the first influential studies in ecology was *Oecology of Plants: An Introduction to the Study of Plant Communities*, written by Eugenius Warming in 1895 (Oxford: Clarendon Press, 1909).

19. George Perkins Marsh, *Man and Nature: Or, Physical Geography as Modified by Human Action* (Seattle: University of Washington Press, 2003), 465.

20. Ibid., 320.

21. Village of Euclid, Ohio v. Ambler Realty Co., 272 U.S. 365 (1926). For a brief description of Euclidean zoning (and other more recent forms of land-use regulation), see Donald L. Elliott, *A Better Way to Zone: Ten Principles to Create More Livable Cities* (Washington, DC: Island Press, 2008).

22. A set of guidelines for legislators entitled Standard State Zoning Enabling Act was published by the Advisory Committee on City Planning and Zoning in 1924 (rev. 1926). The Standard City Planning Enabling Act was published in 1928. Many states and cities since then adopted zoning acts and ordinances. Among the first, California Planning Act was approved in 1927, and the Los Angeles Zoning Ordinance was eventually passed in 1930.

23. Lewis Mumford, "Regionalism and Irregionalism," *Sociological Review* 19, no. 4 (October 1927): 277.

24. See Patrick Geddes, *Cities in Evolution: An Introduction to the Town Planning Movement and to the Study of Civics* (London: Williams and Norgate, 1915).

25. The New York State Housing and Regional Planning Commission was the first body to develop a state-level land-use plan in 1925. The plan was developed under the supervision of Clarence Stein, one of the founders of the Regional Planning Association of America (RPAA). See Thomas Daniels, "A Trail Across Time: American Environmental Planning from City Beautiful

to Sustainability," *Journal of the American Planning Association* 75, no. 2 (Spring 2009): 183. Clarence Stein and Henry Wright (both founders of RPAA) worked on Sunnyside Gardens in Queens, NY, and Radburn, NJ (never fully completed), which became models for planned unit developments.

26. See Benton MacKaye, *The New Exploration: A Philosophy of Regional Planning* (New York: Harcourt, Brace, 1928). For a detailed discussion of MacKaye's work on the TVA project, see Easterling, *Organization Space*, 54–56.

27. For the published version of the lectures, see Alfred North Whitehead, *Science and the Modern World* (New York: Free Press, 1997). Among other pioneering works, see C. Lloyd Morgan, *Emergent Evolution: The Gifford Lectures, Delivered in the University of St. Andrews in the Year 1922* (New York: Henry Holt, 1923). In his lectures, Morgan introduced the concept of emergence and discussed the issue of unpredictability in nature.

28. The importance of energy flow in nature was first studied by Alfred J. Lotka. See Lotka, "Contribution to the Energetics of Evolution," *Proceedings of the National Academy of Sciences* 8, no. 6 (June 1, 1922): 147–51.

29. See Charles Elton, *Animal Ecology* (New York: Macmillan, 1927).

30. Wright, *The Natural House*, 39. In the Hollyhock House, for example, the landscape literally crossed the house, water flew through it, occasionally inundating it. In his textile-block houses, on the other hand, Wright pushed this organic union to another level: he "introduced decomposed granite from the site into the mix so as to achieve an intrinsic, not to say mystical, union between nature and culture." Kenneth Frampton, *American Masterworks: Houses of the 20th and 21st Centuries*, rev. ed. (New York: Rizzoli, 2008), 14.

31. Already at that time, for reasons of simple common sense and economy rather than matters of national energy security or climate change, the *American Society of Heating and Ventilating Engineers (ASHVE) Guide* made the following recommendation: "The installation of automatic temperature regulation, or system for prevention of excess temperature, is a justifiable investment for all heating systems inasmuch as it very positively contributes to: 1. Conservation of fuel; 2. Improvement in health; 3. Gain in personal efficiency." ASHVE, *ASHVE Guide* (New York: American Society of Heating and Ventilating Engineers, 1922), 34. The ASHVE was established in 1894 and became the American

Society of Heating, Refrigerating and Air-Conditioning Engineers (ASHRAE) in 1959.

32. Rudolf Schindler's Lovell Beach House was completed in 1926, and Richard Neutra's Lovell Health House in 1929. In both houses, the integration of the natural landscape into the domestic space and careful treatment of natural and artificial light promoted aspects of healthy living, although in dramatically distinct ways.

33. Christine Frederick, *Household Engineering: Scientific Management in the Home* (Chicago: American School of Home Economics, 1923).

34. Rybczynski, *Home*, 168–71.

35. Christine Frederick, *Selling Mrs. Consumer* (New York: Business Bourse, 1929). For a discussion of feminism in the household design, see Dolores Hayden, *The Grand Domestic Revolution: A History of Feminist Designs for American Homes, Neighborhoods, and Cities* (Cambridge, MA: MIT Press, 1981).

36. In 1918, the Department of Labor supported the Own Your Own Home campaign organized by the National Association of Real Estate Brokers, and the Department of Commerce supported the Architects' Small House Service Bureau, created in 1920. See Jonathan Massey, "Risk and Regulation in the Financial Architecture of American Houses," in *Governing by Design: Architecture, Economy, and Politics in the Twentieth Century*, ed. Timothy Hyde and Aggregate Group (Pittsburgh: University of Pittsburgh Press, 2012), 21–46.

37. See Easterling, *Organization Space*, 138–39.

38. U.S. Department of Commerce, Recommended Minimum Requirements for Small Dwelling Construction: Report of Building Code Committee, July 20, 1922 (Washington, DC: U.S. Government Printing Office, 1923).

39. Easterling, *Organization Space*, 143. In 1918, the Emergency Fleet Corporation and the U.S. Housing Corporation was created to provide adequate housing for wartime workers. It served as a testing ground for the future organization of the US housing economy and influenced urban developments in the United States in the decades to come.

40. U.S. Department of Commerce, Recommended Minimum Requirements for Small Dwelling Construction (Washington, DC: U.S. Government Printing Office, 1932).

41. For a discussion of the impact of President Hoover's Conference on the future of land planning and development, see Marc A. Weiss, *The Rise of the Community Builders: The American Real Estate Industry and Urban Land Planning* (New York: Columbia University Press, 1987), 67.

42. Caroline Bartlett Crane, *Everyman's House* (Garden City, NY: Doubleday, Page, 1925).

43. Iñaki Ábalos, *The Good Life: A Guided Visit to the Houses of Modernity* (Barcelona: Editorial Gustavo Gili, 2001), 142–43. One Week, directed by Buster Keaton and Edward F. Cline (New York: Comique Film Corporation, 1920).

44. Lillian Gilbreth authored several books on domestic engineering, among them *The Home Maker and Her Job* (New York: D. Appleton, 1927). As a mother of twelve, she applied many of the ideas developed together with her husband (an expert in scientific management and an industrial engineer) in the running of her own household and family.

45. Georges Canguilhem, *A Vital Rationalist: Selected Writings*, ed. Francois Delaporte (New York: Zone Books, 1994), 352.

46. Massey, "Risk and Regulation," 36.

47. Although the Federal Housing Administration (FHA) did not directly provide support in financing subdivisions, complying with their land subdivision guidelines reduced the risk of mortgage insurance being refused to individual home buyers due to poor planning. For a discussion of subdivision guidelines and their impact on development patterns, see Weiss, *The Rise of the Community Builders*, 148–49.

48. Easterling, *Organization Space*, 134.

49. U.S. FHA, Circular 2, Property Standards: Requirements for Mortgage Insurance, under Title II of the National Housing Act (Washington, DC: U.S. Government Printing Office, 1936); U.S. FHA, Minimum Construction Requirements for New Dwellings (Washington, DC: U.S. Government Printing Office, 1942).

50. See National Institute of Building Sciences (NIBS), *Part 1 of a Study of the HUD Minimum Property Standards for One- and Two-Family Dwellings and Technical Suitability of Products Programs* (Washington, DC: NIBS, 2003), 4, https://www.huduser.org/Publications/pdf/mps_report.pdf.

51. Two important examples in the Los Angeles area were the Westside Village built in 1939 and Homes at Wholesale in Westchester, developed between 1941 and 1944, both by developer Marlow-Burns. For a discussion of construction methods and design principles applied in these massive prewar (and pre-Levittown) developments, see Greg Hise, *Magnetic Los Angeles: Planning the Twentieth-Century Metropolis* (Baltimore, MD: Johns Hopkins University Press, 1997), 137–49.

52. Wright, *The Natural House*, 54.

53. See Temple Hoyne Buell Center for the Study of American Architecture at Columbia University, *House Housing: An Untimely History of Architecture and Real Estate* (research conducted 2013–2016), accessed December 28, 2021, https://househousing.buellcenter. columbia.edu.

54. Except for Buckminster Fuller's Dymaxion House designed in 1927, technological innovation drove the design of such projects as Neutra's 1934 Beard House (which even won a Better Homes in America award) and Keck & Keck's 1933 House of Tomorrow and 1934 Crystal House (the latter two designed for Chicago's Century of Progress exhibition). Many less radical prefabricated solutions, such as Motohome by White & Co. (1935) or Thermo-Namel House by Higgins Incorporated of New Orleans (1946), were developed before the postwar boom. For an overview of the prefabricated system, see Easterling, *Organization Space*, 187. For a brief discussion of both Neutra's and Keck & Keck's prototypes, see Frampton, *American Masterworks*, 72–73. For an account of Neutra's experimentation, see Barbara Lamprecht, *Richard Neutra: Complete Works* (Cologne: Taschen 2000), 22–32.

55. Albert Farwell Bemis, *Rational Design*, vol. 3 of *The Evolving House* (Cambridge, MA: Technology Press MIT, 1936). The first edition of Neufert's *Architects' Data* was published in 1936 as *Bauentwurfslehre* [Building Design Guide] (Berlin: Bauwelt-Verlag, 1936).

56. Reyner Banham, *The Architecture of the Well-Tempered Environment*, 2nd ed. (Chicago: University of Chicago Press, 1984), 213–16. Banham discusses suspended ceiling kits on the example of the Acousti-Vent Ceiling System developed by Burgess Laboratories in 1936.

57. Hise, *Magnetic Los Angeles*, 63–64.

58. Wright, *The Natural House*, 34.

59. Mumford, "Regionalism and Irregionalism," 277.

60. Paul B. Sears, *Deserts on the March* (Washington, DC: Island Press, 1988), 73–74.

61. Donald Worster, *Nature's Economy: A History of Ecological Ideas*, 2nd ed. (Cambridge: Cambridge University Press, 1996), 253. For a discussion of Frederic Clements's and Arthur G. Tansley's contributions to the science of ecology, see Chapter 11, "Clements and the Climax Community," 205–20, and Chapter 12, "Dust Follows the Plow," 221–53.

62. Arthur G. Tansley, "The Use and Abuse of Vegetational Terms and Concepts," *Ecology* 16, no. 3 (July 1935): 284–307. Tansley rejected use of such emotionally charged terms as *community* in relation to animals and plants and replaced them with the term *ecosystem*, which allowed him to describe processes in terms of material and energetic flows and exchange.

63. Worster, *Nature's Economy*, 305. Worster refers to Chancey Juday, "The Annual Energy Budget in an Inland Lake," *Ecology* 21, no. 4 (October 1940): 438–50.

64. The world *became* a system, an intelligible and controllable one, thanks to computers developed for military needs. Among many different disciplines, which emerged in that period, one can mention Wiener's cybernetics, Shannon's information theory, and von Neumann and Morgenstern's game theory, and, in general, the operations research methods. Although initially the goal was analytical and consisted in simulating to predict, eventually it became normative and consisted in writing "recipes" to generate new artificial systems.

65. In his groundbreaking study of Cedar Bog Lake, Raymond L. Lindeman expressed all processes in terms of energy storage and flow, providing a clear analysis of the metabolic efficiency of organisms across various trophic levels. See Lindeman, "The Trophic-Dynamic Aspect of Ecology," *Ecology* 23, no. 4 (October 1942): 399–417. Lindeman was clearly inspired by his professor Evelyn Hutchinson, whose concept of the "niche" provided a numerically controlled mathematical model describing an organism as an n-dimensional system (of needs) interlinked with n-independent dimensions of its habitat (reduced to conditions and resources). Eugene P. Odum was another pioneer in ecosystem ecology. Together with Howard T. Odum, they wrote the popular ecology textbook *Fundamentals of Ecology* (Philadelphia: Saunders, 1953).

66. Aldo Leopold, "The Land Ethic," in *A Sand County Almanac, and Sketches Here and There* (Oxford: Oxford University Press, 1989). For an account of Leopold's personal transformation from the Progressive conservationism to a biocentric approach to nature, see Worster, *Nature's Economy*, 284–88.

67. The union was formed by a group of ecologists who were previously part of the Ecological Society of America formed in 1915. Unlike other members of this society, the founders of the union believed that scientists should support conservation efforts. The union was renamed Nature Conservancy in 1951. Although criticized for its close links with businesses, it remains the leading nonconfrontational environmental organization in the world. See "Our History," Nature Conservancy, accessed December 28, 2021, http://www.nature.org/ about-us/vision-mission/history/index. htm?intc=nature.tnav.about.

68. This was the Air Pollution Control Act of 1955. For a history of air-pollution acts, see Kate C. Shouse and Richard K. Lattanzio, *Clean Air Act: A Summary of the Act and Its Major Requirements*, CRS Report No. RL30853 (Washington, DC: Congressional Research Service, 2020), https://crsreports.congress. gov/product/pdf/RL/RL30853.

69. For a history of clean-water acts, see Claudia Copeland, *Clean Water Act: A Summary of the Law*, CRS Report No. RL30030 (Washington, DC: Congressional Research Service, 2016), https://crsreports. congress.gov/product/pdf/RL/RL30030.

70. D. J. Waldie, *Holy Land: A Suburban Memoir* (New York: W. W. Norton, 1996), 100.

71. Ibid., 48.

72. Among other modernist architects, Joseph Eichler worked with architects Jones and Emmons, who were involved in John Entenza's Case Study House Program. However, Eichler quickly realized that he had to find ways to innovate without dramatically changing construction methods; his houses were all wooden post-and-beam structures, rarely featuring completely flat roofs or fully glazed walls. His success was in the capacity to find balance between profit and quality.

73. For a firsthand account of "the startling results" of simple organizational (rather than technological) improvements introduced by merchant builders in the 1950s, see Ned Eichler, *The Merchant Builders* (Cambridge, MA: MIT Press, 1982), 77–78.

74. Easterling, *Organization Space*, 188.

75. For an overview of these acts, see Congressional Research Service (CRS), *A Chronology of Housing Legislation and Selected Executive Actions, 1892–2003* (Washington, DC: CRS, 2004), https://www.govinfo.gov/ content/pkg/CPRT-108HPRT92629/pdf/ CPRT-108HPRT92629.pdf.

76. Published in modified form by local FHA offices.

77. U.S. FHA, Minimum Property Standards for Properties of One or Two Living Units (Washington, DC: U.S. Government Printing Office, 1958). See National Institute of Building Sciences, *Part 1 of a Study of the HUD Minimum Property Standards*, 5–6. The following article from a 1952 edition of standards can serve as an example: "Provide each bedroom with at least one closet having a minimum: Depth: 2 feet. Floor area: 6 square feet. Height: 6 feet above closet

floor. One shelf, rod, and hooks." See U.S. FHS, Minimum Property Requirements for Properties of One or Two Living Units Located In the Northern California District (Washington, DC: FHA, San Francisco and Sacramento Insuring Offices, 1952): 302–C.4.b.

78. See Alliance Commission on National Energy Efficiency Policy, *The History of Energy Productivity*, January 2013, 9, https://www.ase.org/sites/ase.org/files/resources/Media%20browser/ee_commission_history_report_2-1-13.pdf.

79. See Banham, *The Architecture of the Well-Tempered Environment*, 186; the previously mentioned 1952 editions of the Minimum Property Standards for Northern California contain the following articles: 402-A. Insulation, which defines the maximum allowable heat losses, and 501-C. Heat Loss Calculations, which refers to the 1922 *ASHVE Guide* for calculations on maintaining 70°F. (As mentioned in section 1.2, "Building the Real-Estate Market: 1920s," of this book, the guide already recommended automatic temperature control for reasons of common sense and economy.)

80. Henry Dreyfuss's first edition of *The Measure of Man: Human Factors in Design* (New York: Whitney Library of Design, 1959) closed a long period of studies in efficiency and ergonomics; in reference to Sloan Wilson, *The Man in the Gray Flannel Suit* (New York: Simon & Schuster, 1955).

81. Ábalos, *The Good Life*, 69.

82. Ibid., 165.

83. See Eichler, *The Merchant Builders*, 138–39.

84. Three types of products prevailed: patio houses (5–7 per acre), townhouses (7–12 units per acre), and quads (12–15 units per acre). Significantly denser than the patio houses, quads and townhouses became the predominant products in the 1960s and 1970s. See Eichler, ibid., 142–43.

85. See Esther McCoy, *Case Study Houses, 1945–1962*, 2nd ed. (Los Angeles: Hennessey & Ingalls, 1977), 189.

86. The last edition of Minimum Property Standards was published in 1982. From then onward, HUD would provide mortgage insurance based on the compliance with the local building codes only. See National Institute of Building Sciences, *Part 1 of a Study of the HUD Minimum Property Standards*, 10.

87. By launching Operation Breakthrough, the government hoped to develop advanced construction technologies to build five thousand lower-cost dwellings, in part on federal land. See Congressional Research

Service, *A Chronology of Housing Legislation*, 119–20.

88. See Banham, *The Architecture of the Well-Tempered Environment*, 73.

89. In *American Masterworks*, Frampton separates this 1964 project from all the other "late-modern houses" (post-1964) and includes it in the "Blueprints for Modern Living: The American House and the Pax Americana 1945–65." The Sea Ranch Condominium (designed by architects Joseph Esherick and MLTWC—Charles Moore, Donlyn Lyndon, William Turnbull Jr., Richard Whitaker—and landscape architect Lawrence Halprin) stands out as a beautiful blueprint for many (less spectacular) examples of "sustainable vernacular" that fill the pages of magazines such as *Dwell* to this day.

90. See Victor Olgyay, *Design with Climate: Bioclimatic Approach to Architectural Regionalism*, ed. Aladar Olgyay (Princeton, NJ: Princeton University Press, 1963); Baruch Givoni, *Man, Climate, and Architecture* (Oxford: Elsevier, 1969); and Ralph Knowles, *Energy and Form: An Ecological Approach to Urban Growth* (Cambridge, MA: MIT Press, 1974).

91. American Society of Heating, Refrigerating and Air-Conditioning Engineers, ASHRAE Standard 55-1966 Thermal Environmental Conditions for Human Occupancy (New York: American Society of Heating, Refrigerating and Air-Conditioning Engineers, 1966).

92. American Society of Heating, Refrigerating and Air-Conditioning Engineers, *ASHRAE Handbook of Fundamentals* (New York: American Society of Heating, Refrigerating and Air-Conditioning Engineers, 1967).

93. The ancient Greek word *oikos* means "house" or "household."

94. See Worster, *Nature's Economy*, 346–47.

95. Samuel E. Wood and Alfred E. Heller, *California Going, Going: Our State's Struggle to Remain Beautiful and Productive* (Sacramento: California Tomorrow, 1962).

96. Rachel Carson, *Silent Spring* (Boston: Houghton Mifflin, 1962). For an important book that slightly predates Carson's book, see Lewis Herber, *Our Synthetic Environment* (New York: Alfred A. Knopf, 1962).

97. Discoveries published in Edward Lorenz, "Deterministic Nonperiodic Flow," *Journal of the Atmospheric Sciences* 20 (March 1963): 130–41.

98. Jay Forrester first applied system dynamics methods to simulate industrial business cycles. The results were published in Forrester, *Industrial Dynamics* (Cambridge, MA: MIT Press, 1961).

99. For example, in *The Destruction of California* (New York: Macmillan, 1965), conservation biologist Raymond F. Dasmann questioned projects focusing on isolated islands of wildlife and recognized the need for a more holistic approach.

100. Stewart L. Udall, *The Quite Crisis* (New York: Holt Rinehart and Winston, 1963).

101. Ezra J. Mishan, *The Costs of Economic Growth* (London: Penguin Books, 1969).

102. Jeremy L. Caradonna, *Sustainability: A History* (New York: Oxford University Press, 2014), 127.

103. For example, Kenneth Boulding called for a new economy seen as a closed system that includes the natural environment. See his seminal essay, "The Economics of the Coming Spaceship Earth," in *Environmental Quality in a Growing Economy*, ed. H. Jarrett (Baltimore, MD: Johns Hopkins University Press, 1966), 3–14.

104. Gregory Bateson, *Steps to an Ecology of Mind* (Chicago: University of Chicago Press, 2000), 492.

CHAPTER TWO

1. Aldo Leopold, "The Land Ethic," in *A Sand County Almanac, and Sketches Here and There* (1949; Oxford: Oxford University Press, 1989), 214.

2. Their respective ideas were published in William H. Drury and Ian C. T. Nisbet, "Succession," *Journal of the Arnold Arboretum* 54, no. 3 (July 1973): 331–68; Robert M. May, "Biological Populations with Nonoverlapping Generations," *Science* 186 (November 15, 1976): 645–47; Herbert Bormann and Gene Likens, "Catastrophic Disturbance and the Steady State in Northern Hardwood Forests," *American Scientist* 67, no. 6 (November–December 1979): 660–69; Daniel Simberloff, "A Succession of Paradigms in Ecology: Essentialism to Materialism and Probabilism," *Synthese* 43, no. 1 (January 1980): 3–39.

3. "Only One Earth" was the motto of the Stockholm conference. In his book *Sustainability: A Cultural History* (Devon: Green Books, 2012), 161–64, Ulrich Grober describes the interests that conflicted during the conference and how they shaped the future notions of sustainable development.

4. See United Nations, *Report of the United Nations Conference on the Human Environment, Stockholm, 5–16 June 1972*, A/CONF.48/14/REV.1 (New York: United Nations, 1973), 5, https://www.un.org/ga/search/view_doc.asp?symbol=A/CONF.48/14/REV.1.

5. For James E. Lovelock's Gaia Theory, see Lovelock, "Gaia as Seen Through the Atmosphere," *Atmospheric Environment* 6, no. 8 (1972): 579–80.

6. Paul R. Ehrlich, *The Population Bomb* (New York: Sierra Club–Ballantine Books, 1968).

7. For a critical discussion of Jay Forrester's "seductive" system models, see C. H. Waddington, *Tools for Thought* (London: Jonathan Cape, 1977), 225–30. Some of the limitations were recognized by the authors. See Donella H. Meadows, Dennis L. Meadows, Jørgen Randers, and William W. Behrens III, *The Limits to Growth: A Report for the Club of Rome's Project on the Predicament of Mankind* (New York: Universe Books, 1972), 21.

8. Meadows et al., *The Limits to Growth*, 22, 86.

9. Herman E. Daly, *Steady-State Economics*, 2nd ed. (Washington, DC: Island Press, 1991), 69.

10. Tim Jackson and Robin Webster, *Limits Revisited: A Review of the Limits to Growth Debate* (April 2016): 6, https://limits2growth.org.uk/publication/limits-revisited.

11. E. F. Schumacher, *Small Is Beautiful: Economics as if People Mattered* (New York: Harper & Row, 1975), 60–61.

12. Fred Hirsch, *Social Limits to Growth* (Cambridge, MA: Harvard University Press, 1976).

13. Ezra J. Mishan, *The Costs of Economic Growth* (London: Penguin Books, 1969), 20.

14. Daly, *Steady-State Economics*, 3.

15. Ibid., 9. According to Jeremy L. Caradonna, the 1989 Exxon Valdez oil spill boosted the US GDP by at least $2 billion. Caradonna, *Sustainability: A History* (New York: Oxford University Press, 2014), 130.

16. Howard T. Odum, *Ecological and General Systems: An Introduction to Systems Ecology*, rev. ed. (Niwot: University Press of Colorado, 1994), 86.

17. Howard T. Odum, *Environment, Power, and Society* (New York: John Wiley & Sons, 1971), 21.

18. Howard T. Odum, "Energy, Ecology and Economics," *AMBIO: A Journal of the Human Environment* 2, no. 6 (1973): 224.

19. Amory B. Lovins, *Soft Energy Paths: Towards a Durable Peace* (New York: Harper Colophon, 1977).

20. In *The Coal Question; An Inquiry Concerning the Progress of the Nation, and the Probable Exhaustion of Our Coal Mines* (London: Macmillan, 1865), British economist William Jevons observed that an increase in efficiency of engines (lower energy use) triggered an increase in demand (and consequently an increase in the rate of consumption of the energy originally saved thanks to technological progress).

21. Odum, "Energy, Ecology, and Economics," 223. Herman Daly supports Odum's statement with the following example: "For each calorie of food produced in the United States in 1970, about seven calories of nonfood fuels were consumed by agriculture and related activities." Daly, *Steady-State Economics*, 10.

22. See the Solar Heating and Cooling Demonstration Act and the Solar Energy Research, Development, and Demonstration Act, both passed in 1974.

23. Brookhaven House was a collaborative project that involved private and public actors: the project was funded by the Department of Energy (DOE), designed by Total Environmental Action architects, and built, monitored, and tested on the premises of the Brookhaven National Laboratory. See the following DOE websites for current initiatives, accessed December 28, 2021, https://www.solardecathlon.gov, https://www.energy.gov/eere/buildings/zero-energy-ready-homes.

24. California Public Resources Code, Division 15, "Energy Conservation and Development" (1974), Sections 25402 and 25402.1.

25. American Society of Heating, Refrigerating and Air-Conditioning Engineers, ASHRAE Standard 90-1975 Energy Conservation in New Building Design (New York: American Society of Heating, Refrigerating and Air-Conditioning Engineers, 1975).

26. California Energy Commission, Energy Conservation Standards for New Residential and New Nonresidential Buildings, California Administrative Code Title 24, Part 6, Article I (Sacramento, CA: CEC, 1977). The 1977 Model Code for Energy Conservation in New Buildings was jointly developed by the Building Officials and Code Administrators International, the International Conference of Building Officials, and the Southern Building Code Congress International, for the National Conference of States on Building Codes and Standards, with funding from the U.S. Department of Energy.

27. Alliance Commission on National Energy Efficiency Policy, *The History of Energy Productivity*, January 2013, 7, https://www.ase.org/sites/ase.org/files/resources/Media%20browser/ee_commission_history_report_2-1-13.pdf. The Energy Tax Act was part of the 1978 National Energy Act (NEA). Another NEA act, the National Energy Conservation Policy Act, established the Residential Conservation Service program designed to improve energy efficiency of the residential sector.

28. The Council of American Building Officials One- and Two-Family Dwelling Code was introduced in 1971 to unify residential construction standards across the country. It was a joint effort of the three model code makers: the Building Officials and Code Administrators International, the International Conference of Building Officials, and the Southern Building Code Congress International.

29. Ned Eichler, *The Merchant Builders* (Cambridge, MA: MIT Press, 1982), 166.

30. Unfortunately, environmental regulations were not always used for the right reasons. In *City of Quartz: Excavating the Future in Los Angeles* (New York: Verso Books, 2006), 173, Mike Davis discusses how Los Angeles homeowner associations used environmental-protection laws to their advantage: "The 'greening' of the Santa Monicas…was widely seen as a hypocritical attempt by the rich to use ecology to detour Vietnam-era growth around their luxury enclaves."

31. Eichler, *The Merchant Builders*, 233.

32. Dan Immergluck, *Foreclosed: High-Risk Lending, Deregulation, and the Undermining of America's Mortgage Market* (Ithaca, NY: Cornell University Press, 2009), 35.

33. See D'Arcy W. Thompson, *On Growth and Form* (Cambridge: Cambridge University Press, 1992). Thompson's explanation of morphogenesis was highly influential among a generation of architects (equipped with computers) who approached design as a (computational) process in which a geometric system (a pattern of spatial relations) defined by a set of interconnected variables (or parameters) gradually evolves into a built form in response to internal (e.g., programmatic) requirements and external (e.g., environmental) conditions.

34. Ralph Knowles, *Energy and Form: An Ecological Approach to Urban Growth* (Cambridge, MA: MIT Press, 1974), 1.

35. American Institute of Architects Research Corporation, *Solar Dwelling Design Concepts* (Washington, DC: U.S. Government Printing Office, 1976).

36. Richard Crowther, *Sun Earth: How to Use Solar and Climatic Energies* (Denver, CO: Crowther/Solar Group, 1977).

37. Mariel Wolfson, "The Ecology of a Healthy Home: Energy, Health, and Housing in America, 1960–1985" (PhD diss., Harvard University, 2012), http://nrs.harvard.edu/urn-3:HUL.InstRepos:10368127. In this unpublished dissertation, Wolfson discusses

the story of the Mendocino County owner-built houses and the struggle of the owners to defend their right to healthy and affordable housing despite the violation of building codes. For an account of the early active and passive solar systems, see Phillip Tabb and A. Senem Deviren, *The Greening of Architecture: A Critical History and Survey of Contemporary Sustainable Architecture and Urban Design* (Burlington, VT: Ashgate, 2013), 52–68.

38. In the mid-1970s, the Farallones Institute of Berkeley, California, converted a Victorian mansion into an urban homestead. It promoted self-reliance through urban gardening, meat raising, aquaculture, waste management, and passive solar heating. See The Farallones Institute, *Integral Urban House: Self-Reliant Living in the City* (New York: Random House, 1982).

39. Baruch Givoni expanded the Comfort Diagram by indicating zones of comfort that could be achieved by adopting various passive strategies, such as natural ventilation, or thermal inertia.

40. Dolores Hayden, *Redesigning the American Dream*, rev. ed. (New York: Norton, 2002), 67; Reyner Banham, *The Architecture of the Well-Tempered Environment*, 2nd ed. (Chicago: University of Chicago Press, 1984), 288.

41. See, respectively, Christopher Alexander, *Notes on the Synthesis of Form* (Cambridge, MA: Harvard University Press, 1964); and Christopher Alexander, Sara Ishikawa, and Murray Silverstein, *A Pattern Language: Towns, Buildings, Construction* (New York: Oxford University Press, 1977).

42. While criticized by academia, *Pattern Language* had a strong influence on New Urbanists. Highly successful developments such as Seaside, Florida (the setting for *The Truman Show*), and other trademarked historicizing communities were built (and generated profit) in the 1980s in an attempt to "replicate" what worked in the past.

43. This is how Alexander referred to the work developed by postmodernists and structuralists in his famous debate with Peter Eisenman, which took place at the Harvard Graduate School of Design in 1982. See Christopher Alexander and Peter Eisenman, "The Debate: Contrasting Concepts of Harmony in Architecture," *Lotus International* 40 (1983): 60–68.

44. Kenneth Frampton, *American Masterworks: Houses of the 20th and 21st Centuries*, rev. ed. (New York: Rizzoli, 2008), 164.

45. In *A Field Guide to American Houses*, rev. ed. (New York: Alfred A. Knopf, 2015), Virginia Savage McAlester painstakingly analyzes the many historical styles of American domestic architecture, often pointing at how styles were "launched" by singular masterpieces: Americans owe Craftsman houses to the brothers Greene and Prairie houses to Frank Lloyd Wright, and when it comes to the International Style, the European exiles are the culprits.

46. For a brief story of the show and a conversation with creators and participating homeowners, see Francis Storrs, "This Old House: An Oral History," *Boston*, January 21, 2009, http://www.bostonmagazine.com/2009/01/this-old-house.

47. The descriptions relate to the following episodes: *This Old House*, "The Newton House," season 2, episode 7: "The Newton House," created, produced, and directed by Russel Morash, aired March 1, 1981, on WGBH, https://www.thisoldhouse.com/newton-house/21053092/the-newton-house-episode-7; and *This Old House*, "The Dorchester House," season 1, episode 4: "Insulation and Plumbing," created, produced, and directed by Russel Morash, aired February 28, 1979, on WGBH, https://www.thisoldhouse.com/dorchester-house/21053173/dorchester-house-insulation-and-plumbing.

48. In the revised edition of her *Field Guide to American Houses*, 725–26, 708, McAlester names a new style: the New Traditional, a revival of anything but the International Style—in short, the house preferred by the majority of American homeowners and the New Urbanists, and, as she points out, ignored by the American Institute of Architects and the architectural press. McAlester is careful to distinguish the New Traditional from what she calls the Millennium Mansions, an aberration that she defines as "oversized in comparison with adjacent homes or disjointed in style."

49. For a brief account of how these phenomena influenced the real-estate market in the 1980s, see Tyson Freeman, "The 1980s: (Too) Easy Money Fuels a New Building Boom!" *National Real Estate Investor*, September 30, 1999, https://www.nreionline.com/mag/1980s-too-easy-money-fuels-new-building-boom.

50. Immergluck, *Foreclosed*, 41–46.

51. Immergluck, "Mortgage Market Disparities and the Dual Regulatory System in the Twentieth Century," in *Foreclosed*, 47–67; the report was prepared for HUD by the National Association of Home Builders Research Foundation and entitled *Solutions to Permit Compatible Use of the One- and Two-Family Code and the Minimum Property Standards*. For a discussion, see National Institute of Building Sciences (NIBS), *Part 1 of a Study of the HUD Minimum Property Standards for One- and Two-Family Dwellings and Technical Suitability of Products Programs* (Washington, DC: NIBS, 2003), 7–9, https://www.huduser.gov/Publications/pdf/mps_report.pdf.

52. The issue of affordability is a question of funding, but it is also inseparable from the planning and design of American neighborhoods and homes. One possible, although highly criticized, way to decrease the cost is to allow for the construction of accessory dwelling units in neighborhoods zoned as single family. The issue was the subject of a research project carried out by the UCLA Luskin School of Public Affairs and cityLAB. See Vinit Mukhija, Dana Cuff, and Kimberly Serrano, *Backyard Homes and Local Concerns: How Can These Concerns Be Better Addressed?* (Los Angeles: cityLAB, UCLA Department of Architecture + Urban Design, 2014). In "Coding Affordable Housing," in *Questioning Architectural Judgment: The Problem of Codes in the United States* (New York: Routledge, 2014), Steven A. Moore and Barbara B. Wilson discuss the issue of accessory dwelling units in the example of the Austin-based Alley Flat initiative.

53. The act had far-reaching repercussions in architecture as it imposed standards related to physical accessibility. See Department of Justice, *2010 ADA Standards for Accessible Design*, September 15, 2010, https://www.ada.gov/regs2010/2010ADAStandards/2010ADAStandards.pdf.

54. The New Alchemy Institute pioneered research into organic agriculture, aquaculture, and bioshelter design between 1971 and 1991. It evolved into the Green Center. In 1981, the founders, John and Nancy Todd, established another organization called Ocean Arks, which concentrates on the design of natural wastewater treatment systems, among them the so-called Eco-Machines.

55. See the Rocky Mountain Institute website, accessed December 28, 2021, https://rmi.org/about.

56. In "The Ecology of a Healthy Home," Wolfson provides a detailed analysis of Lawrence Berkeley Lab's program of research into indoor environmental quality in relation to residential energy-conservation research and legislation in the United States after the 1973 oil crisis.

57. *The Bubble Policy* allowed industries to decide how and where to reduce air pollution to comply with EPA standards. The policy—designed to reduce cleanup costs and stimulate technological innovation—

was criticized for its excessive focus on cost-effectiveness for the polluters rather than environmental impact of specific facilities on their immediate surroundings. For a brief critical discussion, see Steven J. Marcus, "Bubble Policy: Pros and Cons," *New York Times*, June 30, 1983, http://www.nytimes.com/1983/06/30/business/technology-bubble-policy-pros-and-cons.html.

58. See Linda-Jo Schierow and David M. Bearden, *Federal Programs Related to Indoor Pollution by Chemicals*, CRS Report No. RL42620 (Washington, DC: Congressional Research Service, 2012), https://fas.org/sgp/crs/misc/R42620.pdf.

59. See Claudia Copeland, *Clean Water Act: A Summary of the Law*, CRS Report No. RL30030 (Washington, DC: Congressional Research Service, 2016), https://fas.org/sgp/crs/misc/RL30030.pdf.

60. Superfund is the common name used in reference to the Comprehensive Environmental Response, Compensation, and Liability Act of 1980. With time, the impact of the program decreased due to funding issues and costs of litigation. In a book entitled *Drosscape: Wasting Land in Urban America* (New York: Princeton Architectural Press, 2007), 65–66, landscape architect Alan Berger discusses how the program has been subject to real-estate speculation around contaminated and blighted sites. A map included in Berger's book shows approximately 1,600 Superfund sites among the total of 480,000 contaminated sites identified in the US.

61. Charles Perrow, *Normal Accidents: Living with High-Risk Technologies* (Princeton, NJ: Princeton University Press, 1984).

62. While California's last nuclear plant, the Diablo Canyon facility, has announced that it will shut down in the mid-2020s, the casks with spent fuel will remain on the Diablo Canyon site until the federal government finds a place for a repository. The casks accumulated around approximately one hundred US nuclear reactors concentrated in the Midwest and on the East Coast are waiting to be permanently stored as well. The question that comes to mind is whether "normal accidents" can be prevented during storage, over many millennia of peak risk.

63. See, for example, Martin Rees, *Our Final Hour* (New York: Basic Books, 2003); and his more recent and hopeful book *On the Future: Prospects for Humanity* (Princeton, NJ: Princeton University Press, 2018).

64. Langdon Winner, *Autonomous Technology: Technics-out-of-Control as a Theme in Political Thought* (Cambridge, MA: MIT Press, 1977), 302.

65. This idea was later popularized by biologist and environmental activist Daniel Botkin. In *Discordant Harmonies: A New Ecology for the 21st Century* (New York: Oxford University Press, 1990), Botkin discusses the clash between change, which is inherent in nature, and a vision of stability, which underlies environmental policies, resource management, and conservation programs. In his book, Botkin advocated for flexible regulatory and management frameworks, which respect randomness and variability of environmental phenomena.

66. Margaret B. Davis, "Climatic Instability, Time Lags, and Community Disequilibrium," in *Community Ecology*, ed. Jared M. Diamond and Ted J. Case (New York: Harper and Row, 1986). For a discussion, see Donald Worster, *Nature's Economy: A History of Ecological Ideas*, 2nd ed. (Cambridge: Cambridge University Press, 1996), 295–96.

67. Ilya Prigogine and Isabelle Stengers, *Order Out of Chaos: Man's New Dialogue with Nature* (New York: Bantam Books, 1984).

68. Eileen Crist, "Beyond the Climate Crisis: A Critique of Climate Change Discourse," *Telos* 141 (Winter 2007): 35.

69. According to E. O. Wilson, our deeply rooted affiliation with nature is an effect of the evolutionary history of human species, which has lived in close contact with other animals and plants for most of its natural history. Technological advancements that have allowed humans to survive and thrive in isolation from nature have increasingly weakened this connection. Wilson hoped that it was possible to build a new conservation project on the basis of this "biophilia," an innate "love of life." See Wilson, *Biophilia* (Cambridge, MA: Harvard University Press, 1985).

70. The problem of spatial patterns gained a lot of attention in the 1980s. Landscape ecologists, among them Richard T. T. Forman and Michael Godron in *Landscape Ecology* (New York: Wiley, 1986), addressed the importance of spatial heterogeneity (patterns and their scales) for the functioning of ecosystems, emphasizing the interconnectedness of biophysical and socioeconomic processes. A large-scale and long-term perspective on how stable states are achieved, maintained, and restored in form of resilience, variability, persistence, and resistance can be found in Stuart Pimm's *The Balance of Nature? Ecological Issues in the Conservation of Species and Communities* (Chicago: University of Chicago Press, 1991).

71. Eran Ben-Joseph, *Rethinking a Lot: The Design and Culture of Parking* (Cambridge, MA: MIT Press, 2012). Ben-Joseph argues that since cars are parked 95 percent of the time, there is little difference between the environmental impact of a hybrid Prius and a Hummer.

72. Mark J. Perry, "New U.S. Homes Today are 1,000 Square Feet Larger Than in 1973 and Living Space Per Person Has Nearly Doubled," *American Enterprise Institute*, June 5, 2016, http://www.aei.org/publication/new-us-homes-today-are-1000-square-feet-larger-than-in-1973-and-living-space-per-person-has-nearly-doubled. The article reports statistics provided by the U.S. Census Bureau.

73. For an annotated list of notable international conferences and programs that defined the concept of sustainability and shaped the international politics between 1969 and 2012, see Caradonna, *Sustainability*, 145–51.

74. International Union for Conservation of Nature (IUCN), *World Conservation Strategy* (Gland: IUCN, 1980), VI, https://portals.iucn.org/library/efiles/documents/wcs-004.pdf.

75. Ibid., 1.4.

76. Grober, *Sustainability*, 175–77. The term underwent its first modern transformation in 1969, when the IUCN embraced the concept of "quality of life" as a focal issue in its program. The 1980 report marks a further evolution and opening toward issues of economic development.

77. IUCN, *World Conservation Strategy*, 1.11.

78. Independent Commission on International Development, *North–South: A Program for Survival* (Cambridge, MA: MIT Press, 1980).

79. Quoted in Grober, *Sustainability*, 179–80.

80. James Bernard Quilligan, *The Brandt Equation: 21st Century Blueprint for the New Global Economy* (Philadelphia: Brandt 21 Forum, 2002), 60–62, http://www.brandt21forum.info/brandtequation-19sept04.pdf.

81. United Nations World Commission on Environment and Development, *Report of the World Commission on Environment and Development: Our Common Future* (Oxford: Oxford University Press, 1987), I. 2. III. 7. 79.

82. Ibid., I. 2. IV. 81; Gregory Bateson, *Steps to an Ecology of Mind* (Chicago: University of Chicago Press, 2000), 506.

83. According to these two planning experts, most scientific problems are "tame": "For any given tame problem, an exhaustive formulation can be stated containing all the information the problem-solver needs for understanding and solving the

problem—provided he knows his 'art,' of course." Meanwhile, "the formulation of a wicked problem is the problem!" Horst W. J. Rittel and Melvin M. Webber, "Dilemmas in a General Theory of Planning," *Policy Sciences* 4, no. 2 (June 1973), 160–61.

CHAPTER THREE

1. Ulrich Grober, *Sustainability: A Cultural History* (Devon: Green Books, 2012), 184.
2. Herman Daly, *Beyond Growth: The Economics of Sustainable Development* (Boston: Beacon Press, 1996), 5–10.
3. In *Beyond Growth*, Daly lists "Four Parting Suggestions for the World Bank," 92. One of them reads: "Move away from the ideology of global economic integration by free trade, free capital mobility, and export-led growth." Unfortunately, sympathizing with economist John Maynard Keynes was not fashionable in the era of neoliberal economy. See the WTO website, accessed December 28, 2021, https://www.wto.org/english/thewto_e/whatis_e/tif_e/bey2_e.htm.
4. United Nations Conference on Environment and Development (UNCED), *Agenda 21: Earth Summit: The United Nations Programme of Action from Rio* (Rio de Janeiro: UNCED, 1992), 2.1–2.2, https://sustainabledevelopment.un.org/content/documents/Agenda21.pdf.
5. Earth Charter commission, *The Earth Charter* (Paris: Earth Charter Commission, 2000), Preamble, https://earthcharter.org/wp-content/uploads/2020/03/echarter_english.pdf?x10401.
6. Herman E. Daly, *Steady-State Economics*, 2nd ed. (Washington, DC: Island Press, 1991), 47.
7. David Pearce, "Green Economics," *Environmental Values* 1 (1992): 3.
8. Ibid., 7.
9. Daly, *Steady-State Economics*, 280. Daly applied Alfred North Whitehead's notion on many occasions, recognizing that it was Nicholas Georgescu-Roegen who first used it in reference to economics.
10. David Pearce, Anil Markandya, and Edward Barbier, *Blueprint for a Green Economy* (London: Earthscan Publications, 1989), 154–56.
11. Ibid., 21.
12. Ibid., 135–37.
13. In 2006, the state of California enacted the Global Warming Solutions Act (Assembly Bill 32). Among various measures the act introduced a cap-and-trade system targeting energy sold in California.

14. Lara J. Cushing, Madeline Wander, Rachel Morello-Frosch, Manuel Pastor, Allen Zhu, and James Sadd, "A Preliminary Environmental Equity Assessment of California's Cap-And-Trade Program," Research Brief, September 2016, https://dornsife.usc.edu/PERE/enviro-equity-CA-cap-trade. While the risk of CO_2 hot spots is low—it mixes in the upper atmosphere and distributes globally—many unregulated copollutants tend to concentrate locally. The possibility of offsetting emissions with out-of-state credits aggravates this problem by further concentrating pollution. Also, big polluters often tend to be located near underprivileged neighborhoods, which raises issues of social equity.
15. Daniel A. Faber, "Pollution Markets and Social Equity: Analyzing the Fairness of Cap and Trade," *Ecology Law Quarterly* 39, no. 1 (2012): 1–56.
16. In chronological order: Hurricane Andrew (1992), Great Flood (1993), Superstorm (1993), Louisiana flood (1995), Chicago heat wave (1995), Great Ice Storm (1998), Oklahoma tornado (1999). These were followed by a series of storms and hurricanes: Allison (2001), Charlie, Frances, Ivan (2004), and eventually Katrina (2005). In 1998, an organization called the Oregon Institute of Science and Medicine published the *Oregon Petition*, trying to undermine the consensus around the science underlying the international climate-change action. The report, formatted to resemble a scientific article published by the National Academy of Sciences, was disowned by the Academy. See National Academy of Sciences, "Statement of the Council of the NAS Regarding Global Change Petition," April 20, 1998, https://www.nationalacademies.org/news/1998/04/statement-of-the-council-of-the-nas-regarding-global-change-petition.
17. In March 2014, the Sierra Club, together with the Mexican Action Network on Free Trade, the U.S.-based Institute for Policy Studies, and the Council of Canadians, released a report entitled *NAFTA: 20 Years of Costs to Communities and the Environment*, https://content.sierraclub.org/creative-archive/sites/content.sierraclub.org.creative-archive/files/pdfs/0642-NAFTA%20Report_05_low.pdf. The report discussed the effects of large-scale, export-oriented farming methods, the explosion of mining in Mexico, the exploitation of Canadian tar sands, and the increase in traffic-triggered air pollution. The authors also discussed the corporate power influencing environmental policy making. It is meaningful that

while NAFTA itself was binding, the independent North American Agreement on Environmental Cooperation only provided nonbinding recommendations.
18. It is probably safe to say that the US-Mexico-Canada Agreement that replaced NAFTA in July 2020 does not drastically differ from its predecessor. In fairness, the agreement does contain a "promising" addition, Chapter 24, "Environment," which addresses environmental protection, acknowledges the sovereignty of each individual state with regards to handling its own environmental policy, and refers to a number of international multilateral environmental agreements (including the *Montreal Protocol*). Although the pact recognizes "the importance of resource efficiency," the critics (including the Sierra Club) point out that it does not impose adoption of specific environmental-protection laws or clean technologies meant to mitigate climate change and greenhouse gas emissions. See "Trump's NAFTA Deal Threatens Our Air, Water, and Climate; Environmental Groups Oppose this Deal, Given Failure to Meet Basic Criteria," Sierra Club website, accessed December 28, 2021, https://www.sierraclub.org/sites/www.sierraclub.org/files/NAFTA-environment-statement.pdf.
19. See the WTO website, accessed December 28, 2021, https://www.wto.org/english/thewto_e/whatis_e/what_stand_for_e.htm.
20. Naomi Klein, *This Changes Everything: Capitalism vs. the Climate* (New York: Simon & Schuster, 2015), 60. See also Paolo Davide Farah and Cima Elena, "World Trade Organization, Renewable Energy Subsidies and the Case of Feed-In Tariffs: Time for Reform toward Sustainable Development?" *Georgetown International Environmental Law Review* 27, no. 1 (2015): 515–37, https://papers.ssrn.com/sol3/papers2.cfm?abstract_id=2704398.
21. In 1995, the Environmental Protection Agency (EPA) published Municipal Waste Combustors, a measure meant to reduce emissions from waste combustion. In 1997, the New Air Quality Standards and, in 1996, the Safe Drinking Water Act Amendments (Public Law 104-182) were passed. In 2006, the EPA also introduced the Ground Water Rule, a set of measures against contamination of groundwater.
22. Environmental Protection Agency, "International Methane to Markets Partnership to Enhance Clean Energy Sources and Reduce Greenhouse Gas

Emissions," July 28, 2004, https://archive.epa.gov/epapages/newsroom_archive/newsreleases/ad2f332a8d79d39885256edf005253f6.html.

23. Jeremy L. Caradonna, *Sustainability: A History* (New York: Oxford University Press, 2014), 163.

24. Paul Hawken, Amory Lovins, and L. Hunter Lovins, *Natural Capitalism: Creating the Next Industrial Revolution* (Boston: Little, Brown, 1999), 3.

25. Ibid., 6–8.

26. Michael Hardt and Antonio Negri, *Empire* (Cambridge, MA: Harvard University Press, 2000), 361.

27. See, for example, Janine Benyus, *Biomimicry: Innovation Inspired by Nature* (New York: William Morrow, 1997). In this book and at the Biomimicry Institute, Benyus promotes innovation inspired by nature, convinced that understanding the richness of design solutions hidden in natural systems will make entrepreneurs, designers, and policy makers more inclined to protect it.

28. See William McDonough and Michael Braggart, *Cradle to Cradle: Remaking the Way We Make Things* (New York: North Point Press, 2002).

29. See John Elkington, *Cannibals with Forks: The Triple Bottom Line of 21st Century Business* (Mankato, MN: Capstone, 1997).

30. For an annotated list of sustainability rating systems, including various eco-labels, see Caradonna, *Sustainability*, 180–88. For building specific systems, see Stephanie Vierra, "Green Building Standards and Certification Systems," *Whole Building Design Guide*, August 5, 2019, https://www.wbdg.org/resources/green-building-standards-and-certification-systems.

31. See the Overshoot Day website, accessed December 28, 2021, http://www.overshootday.org/about-earth-overshoot-day.

32. The slightly more optimistic result registered in 2020, as compared to July 29, 2019, can only be attributed to the global halt imposed by COVID-19. See the Overshoot Day website.

33. Daly, *Steady-State Economics*, 89.

34. William McDonough Architects and Michael Braungart, *The Hannover Principles: Design for Sustainability* (Charlottesville, VA: William McDonough Architects, 1992), http://www.mcdonough.com/wp-content/uploads/2013/03/Hannover-Principles-1992.pdf.

35. Building Design & Construction, "White Paper on Sustainability," *Building Design & Construction* 11, no. 3 (November 2003): 7.

36. It is noteworthy that the founder of the USGBC, Rick Fedrizzi, has recently published a book entitled *Greenthink: How Profit Can Save the Planet* (Austin, TX: Disruption Books, 2015).

37. See Drew Johnson, "LEED Standards Fail Taxpayers," *Newsmax*, April 3, 2013, http://www.newsmax.com/DrewJohnson/LEED-Standards-Taxpayers-Environment/2013/04/03/id/497706. Johnson, a senior fellow of Taxpayers Protection Alliance, described LEED as "a flawed standard that lines the pockets of a private organization with tax dollars." Obtaining a LEED certification is obviously not free. For a comprehensive list of the cities that adopted LEED as a mandatory measure, see Michael Lewyn and Kristoffer Jackson, "How Often Do Cities Mandate Smart Growth or Green Building?" (Mercatus working paper, Mercatus Center at George Mason University, October 2014).

38. When grouped under the FHA umbrella during the 1930s, builders, mortgage lenders, insurers, and realtors indirectly shaped and standardized local land-planning and building standards. Their agendas were informed by the ideals promoted a decade earlier by Better Homes in America, a grassroots movement indirectly supported by the federal government. In the 1990s, the construction industry successfully organized itself to establish a set of market-friendly green building standards before another (possibly less convenient) option appeared as an alternative.

39. Living Future Institute, *Living Building Challenge 3.0, A Visionary Path to a Regenerative Future* (Seattle, WA: Living Future Institute, 2014), 62, https://living-future.org/wp-content/uploads/2016/12/Living-Building-Challenge-3.0-Standard.pdf.

40. Sarah Stanley, "USGBC Announces Vision for LEED Positive," USGBC website, November 20, 2019, https://www.usgbc.org/articles/usgbc-announces-vision-leed-positive.

41. The Living Building Institute groups the imperatives into "petals": Place, Water, Energy, Health + Happiness, Materials, Equity, Beauty.

42. Mathis Wackernagel and William Rees, *Our Ecological Footprint: Reducing Human Impact on the Earth* (Gabriola Island, BC: New Society Publisher, 1996). For examples, see Global Footprint Network, *State of the States* (Oakland, CA: Global Footprint Network 2015), http://www.footprintnetwork.org/content/images/article_uploads/USAFootprintReport_final_lores.pdf. Although it is questionable whether independent footprints of such intricately related economic and administrative entities as US states are meaningful, the method revealed their political, ecological, and economic vulnerability. It also exposed international imbalances. According to the Global Footprint Network, the state of California leads in the national ranking—its economy is the strongest, its biocapacity very low, and hence its ecological footprint is the largest. This might explain why its environmental bills are (and should be) among the most progressive.

43. M. J. McDonnell, "The History of Urban Ecology: An Ecologist's Perspective," in *Urban Ecology: Patterns, Processes and Applications*, ed. Jari Niemelä, Jürgen H. Breuste, Thomas Elmqvist, Glenn Guntenspergen, Philip James, and Nancy E. McIntyre (Oxford: Oxford University Press, 2011), 8. Ecological studies of urban regions experienced a boom in the 1990s. Use of terms *urban/urbanization* dramatically increased in the mid-1990s, and, next to *fragmentation* and *conservation*, these issues continue to be among the most frequently addressed in articles published in the journal *Landscape Ecology*. See Jianguo Wu, Chunyang He, Ganlin Huang, and Deyong Yu, "Urban Landscape Ecology: Past, Present, and Future," in *Landscape Ecology for Sustainable Environment and Culture*, ed. B. Fu and K. B. Jones (Dordrecht: Springer Netherlands, 2013), 40.

44. IBM Corporation, *A Vision of Smarter Cities*, 2009, https://www.ibm.com/downloads/cas/2JYLM4ZA. The trademark "smart cities" has belonged to IBM since 2011; Selina Holmes, "LEED v4.1 launches for cities and communities," USGBC website, April 2, 2019, https://www.usgbc.org/articles/leed-v41-launches-cities-and-communities. Launched in 2016, LEED for Cities and Communities was expanded into a complete certification program in 2019.

45. Mark DeKay and G. Z. Brown, *Sun, Wind, and Light: Architectural Design Strategies* (Hoboken, NJ: John Wiley and Sons, 1985).

46. See the RESNET website, accessed December 28, 2021, https://www.resnet.us/about/history-of-resnet/. RESNET was established in 1995.

47. For more details, see the HPDC website, accessed December 28, 2021, http://www.hpd-collaborative.org/about.

48. See RESNET, "State of California Incorporates RESNET Air Tightness Testing Provisions into Revised Energy Code," RESNET website, June 4, 2012, http://www.resnet.us/blog/

state-of-california-incorporates-resnet-air-tightness-testing-provisions-into-revised-energy-code.

49. See EPACT92, Title I, A, Section 101. Building Energy Efficiency Standards, (a), https://www.govinfo.gov/content/pkg/STATUTE-106/pdf/STATUTE-106-Pg2776.pdf.

50. See EPACT92, Title I, A, Section 104. Manufactured Housing Energy Efficiency, (c).

51. See EPACT92, Title I, C, Section 125. Energy Efficiency Information for Commercial Office Equipment, (a).

52. See Alliance for Water Efficiency, *The Status of Legislation, Regulation, Codes & Standards on Indoor Plumbing Water Efficiency*, January 2016, 3, https://www.allianceforwaterefficiency.org/sites/www.allianceforwaterefficiency.org/files/highlight_documents/AWE_White-Paper-on-Water-Efficiency_01-2016.pdf.

53. The International Code Council (ICC) consolidated the Building Officials and Code Administrators International, the International Conference of Building Officials, and the Southern Building Code Congress International. The International Building Code was first published in 1997 and the International Residential Code in 2000.

54. California's Title 24, which consists of thirteen parts, is composed of three state-developed parts, four parts based on the ICC model codes, two parts based on the International Association of Plumbing and Mechanical Officials models, and one on the National Electrical Code.

55. California, for example, was the first state to introduce an Energy Code and then the Green Building Standards Code. Respective ICC model codes followed.

56. Evan McKenzie, *Privatopia: Homeowner Associations and the Rise of Residential Private Government* (New Haven, CT: Yale University Press, 1994), 23.

57. Although abandoned after a decade in 1995, the project became an incubation of formal and spatial ideas, design techniques, and technological solutions for future buildings. As a side note, an option developed in 1993 was discarded, as it failed to meet energy codes. See Aurelien Lemonier and Frederic Migayrou, eds., *Frank Gehry* (New York: Prestel, 2015), 131.

58. Dan Immergluck, *Foreclosed: High-Risk Lending, Deregulation, and the Undermining of America's Mortgage Market* (Ithaca, NY: Cornell University Press, 2009), 74.

59. Ibid., 33–34.

60. Ibid., 83.

61. Adam Davidson and Alex Blumberg, "The Giant Pool of Money," *This American Life*, episode 355, aired May 9, 2008, on NPR, https://www.thisamericanlife.org/radio-archives/episode/355/the-giant-pool-of-money. The amount of global savings (that is capital ready to be invested) doubled after the year 2000 due to the rapid growth of new economic powers, such as China and India.

62. Luke Mullins, "America's 4 Nastiest Regional Housing Busts," *U.S. News*, June 19, 2009, https://money.usnews.com/money/blogs/the-home-front/2009/06/19/americas-4-nastiest-regional-housing-busts-2.

63. Immergluck, *Foreclosed*, 85. Immergluck also explains that subprime loans experienced its first boom already in the mid-1990 in the form of "cash-out" refinancing (see page 68.) Later, during the housing bubble, they were used toward mortgage payments to prevent foreclosures.

64. Ibid., 112.

65. Jonathan Massey, "Risk and Regulation in the Financial Architecture of American Houses," in *Governing by Design: Architecture, Economy, and Politics in the Twentieth Century*, ed. Timothy Hyde and Aggregate Group (Pittsburgh: University of Pittsburgh Press, 2012), 41.

66. Immergluck, *Foreclosed*, 136–37.

67. In the seventeenth century, the Netherlands experienced a speculative frenzy of buying and selling tulips, "tulipomania." At the height of speculation, single flowers, bulbs, or even promissory notes were sold for sums that could buy a house.

68. Immergluck, *Foreclosed*, 81, 102. Subprime lending was disproportionally high among minorities, especially African Americans, who had historically a reduced access to prime-mortgage channels. It was also higher among older, divorced, and female borrowers.

69. Although the 2008 Housing and Economic Recovery Act was followed by the American Recovery and Reinvestment Act and the Preventing Mortgage Foreclosures and Enhancing Mortgage Credit Act, in late 2008, the US Congress passed the Emergency Economic Stabilization Act, the controversial bailout act that included the Troubled Asset Relief Program. One of the aims of the 2010 Dodd-Frank Wall Street Reform and Consumer Protection Act was, in part, to put an end to this type of bailout.

70. In addition to obvious financial distress, relocating due to a foreclosure forces families to abandon social networks that support them, including friends, family, community centers, churches, child care, and education. It also weakens these structures for those who remain in the neighborhoods.

71. Joel Kurth and Christine MacDonald, "Volume of Abandoned Homes 'Absolutely Terrifying,'" *Detroit News*, June 24, 2015, http://www.detroitnews.com/story/news/special-reports/2015/05/14/detroit-abandoned-homes-volume-terrifying/27237787. The article reports 139,699 total homes foreclosed since 2005 (1 in 3), with 56 percent of all mortgage foreclosures blighted, and requiring properties to be either demolished or foreclosed again for nonpayment of taxes.

72. Barry Bergdoll, Peter Christensen, Ron Broadhurst, and the Museum of Modern Art, *Home Delivery: Fabricating the Modern Dwelling* (New York: Museum of Modern Art, 2008).

73. The Solar Decathlon program was launched by the U.S. Department of Energy in 2002 and is now in its ninth edition. With few exceptions (e.g., the 2005 MiSo House, designed by the University of Michigan team, or the 2011 CHIP House, built by the team from SCI-Arc/Caltech), projects tend to embrace the simplicity of the prefab green construction. For a preview of the current contest, see the program website, accessed December 28, 2021, https://www.solardecathlon.gov/past-build-challenge.html.

74. See Greg Hise, *Magnetic Los Angeles: Planning the Twentieth-Century Metropolis* (Baltimore, MD: Johns Hopkins University Press, 1997), 71–79. Hise discusses the failed attempts to replace stick frame with prefabricated products in the 1930s. A similar argument is made by Ned Eichler in reference to the postwar period, in Eichler, *The Merchant Builders* (Cambridge, MA: MIT Press, 1982), 67, 77.

75. Kaufmann's mkLotus house was advertised around 2009 at $125,000 ($181 per square foot). Once relaunched by Blu Homes in 2016, the almost identical 640-square-foot LotusMini started at $275,000 ($430 per square foot). See, respectively, the Prefabs website, accessed December 28, 2021, http://www.prefabs.com/PrefabHomes/MichelleKaufmannDesigns/mkLotus.htm; and Patrick Sisson, "Prefab Tiny Homes a Highlight of New Blu Homes Product Launch," *Curbed*, April 15, 2016, https://www.curbed.com/2016/4/15/11437688/prefab-tiny-homes-blu-new-models. Considering that the average cost of construction, as reported by National Association of Home Builders, was $103 per square foot (average construction cost: $289,415; average footage: 2,802.), in 2015, neither of them is an affordable alternative. See Carmel Ford, "Cost of Constructing a Single-family

Home in 2015," NAHB website, November 4, 2015, https://eyeonhousing.org/2015/11/cost-of-constructing-a-single-family-home-in-2015-2/.

76. Ann Brenoff, "Downsizing: Could You Live in a Tiny Home in Retirement?" *Huffington Post*, October 22, 2012, http://www.huffingtonpost.com/2012/10/22/downsizing-for-retirement_n_1961961.html. This article refers to data collected by the National Association of Realtors.

77. Laura Mordas-Schenkein, "How Tiny House Villages Could Solve America's Homeless Epidemic," *Inhabitat*, August 22, 2014, https://inhabitat.com/how-tiny-house-villages-could-solve-americas-homeless-epidemic.

78. The ICC model residential code only specifies the size of habitable rooms. This used to be 120 square feet (for one room at least) and is now 70, regardless of the number of rooms. According to the ICC model code, a habitable space can consist of a 70-square-foot room and a bathroom.

79. Mark J. Perry, "New U.S. Homes Today are 1,000 Square Feet Larger Than in 1973 and Living Space Per Person Has Nearly Doubled," *American Enterprise Institute*, June 5, 2016, http://www.aei.org/publication/new-us-homes-today-are-1000-square-feet-larger-than-in-1973-and-living-space-per-person-has-nearly-doubled.

80. Henry David Thoreau lived near Walden Pond in a 150-square-foot cabin while writing *Walden* (Boston: Ticknor & Fields, 1854) in the 1840s.

81. For the 2020 edition of the 20K project, see the Rural Studio website, accessed December 28, 2021, http://ruralstudio.org/project/2020-20k-home.

82. In addition to Kappe's Zeta 6, seven other single-family houses have won the award. Among them there were three private residences: Yin Yang House by Brooks + Scarpa (2011, Top Ten 2013); Solar Umbrella House by Pugh + Scarpa (2005, Top Ten 2006); Wine Creek Road Home by Siegel & Strain Architects (2002, Top Ten 2003). The other four were "demonstration" projects: A New Norris House, designed by the University of Tennessee College of Architecture & Design (2011, Top Ten 2013); OS House by Johnsen Schmaling Architects (2010, Top Ten 2011); Special No. 9 House by John C. Williams Architects and KieranTimberlake (2008, Top Ten 2010); and Factor 10 House by Esherick Homsey Dodge & Davis (2003, Top Ten 2004). The last time a single-family house won this award was in 2013.

83. *This Old House*, "The Austin House," season 28, episode 19: "Where Green Building Was Born," created by Russel Morash, produced and directed by David Vos, aired February 2, 2007, on WGBH, https://www.thisoldhouse.com/austin-house/21052956/austin-where-green-building-was-born. This eco-friendly season was dedicated to an Austin, Texas, craftsman bungalow. Austin's Energy Green Building Program, introduced in the early 1990s, was the first rating system in the US.

84. The goal of this act was to bring the state's greenhouse gas emissions to 1990 levels by the year 2020. The target levels were met in 2018, and the new 2030 target level (as specified in the 2016 set in Senate Bill 32) is 40 percent below 1990.

85. Alliance Commission on National Energy Efficiency Policy, *The History of Energy Productivity*, January 2013, 9, https://www.ase.org/sites/ase.org/files/resources/Media%20browser/ee_commission_history_report_2-1-13.pdf.

86. California Building Standards Commission, Guide to the 2019 California Green Building Standards Code Nonresidential (Washington, DC: International Code Council, 2019), viii. The then governor vetoed the initial legislation and specified that the state should not rely on a model code written by a private entity to set the standards.

87. California Building Standards Commission, 2019 California Green Building Standards Code, California Code of Regulations, Title 24, Part 11 (Washington, DC: International Code Council, 2019), 1.

88. Stuart Kaplow, "2018 IgCC Is Not in Use Anywhere. A Detailed Analysis of Why?" *Green Building Law Update*, December 1, 2019, https://www.greenbuildinglawupdate.com/2019/12/articles/igcc/2018-igcc-is-not-in-use-anywhere-a-detailed-analysis-of-why. According to the author, the 2018 IgCC heavily relies on "the 2017 edition of ANSI/ASHRAE/ICC/USGBC Standard 189.1 for the Design of High-Performance Green Buildings Except Low-Rise Residential Buildings," which according to the author gained little market acceptance. The 2018 IgCC contains an appendix that can be applied to single-family dwellings, but low-rise residential buildings continue to be outside of the main scope of the IgCC. See also Stuart Kaplow, "2018 IgCC Poised to Be Adopted for the First Time," *Green Building Law Update*, August 9, 2020, https://www.greenbuildinglawupdate.com/2020/08/articles/igcc/2018-igcc-poised-to-be-adopted-for-the-first-time.

89. The White House, Office of the Press Secretary, "FACT SHEET: Obama Administration Announces Public and Private Sector Efforts to Increase Community Resilience through Building Codes and Standards," the White House President Obama website, May 10, 2016, https://obamawhitehouse.archives.gov/the-press-office/2016/05/10/fact-sheet-obama-administration-announces-public-and-private-sector.

90. For example, 350.org, founded by Bill McKibben, organizes climate-focused campaigns against fossil-fuel projects and promotes community-owned low-carbon initiatives. This, and many other organizations (e.g., Greenpeace, Earth First!), were actively involved in the wake of such events as the 2010 BP oil spill and in actions against such projects as the Keystone XL tar sands pipeline and the Dakota Access fracked-oil pipeline in 2016. Examples of environmental impact of free-trade agreements were reported in the previously mentioned Sierra Club et al., *NAFTA: 20 Years of Costs*.

91. This is one of the questions that open *The Economics of Happiness* (Gabriola Island, BC: New Society Publisher, 2007), in which Mark Anielski presents an alternative economic model called "genuine wealth."

92. Peter Victor, *Managing without Growth: Slower by Design, Not Disaster* (Northampton, MA: Edward Elgar Publishing, 2008).

93. Tim Jackson, *Prosperity without Growth*, 2nd ed. (New York: Routledge, 2016), 2.

94. Richard Heinberg, *The End of Growth: Adapting to Our New Economic Reality* (Gabriola Island, BC: New Society Publisher, 2011), 6. The previously mentioned report *Limits Revisited* (commissioned by the UK-based All-Party Parliamentary Group on Limits to Growth) cited a number of studies reporting that our civilization is following the "standard run." The question, however, is how these new findings will be used by those who commissioned the report this time, or better, whether any government has enough power to change these trends. Tim Jackson and Robin Webster, *Limits Revisited: A Review of the Limits to Growth Debate* (April 2016): 6, https://limits2growth.org.uk/publication/limits-revisited.

95. James F. Peltz, "Q&A: Why Home Prices in Southern California Keep Climbing," *Los Angeles Times*, July 14, 2016, http://www.latimes.com/business/la-fi-qa-home-prices-20160713-snap-story.html.

96. Among them are the first National Standards for Mercury Pollution from Power

Plants, published by the EPA in 2011, and the Air Pollution Standards for Oil and Natural Gas, updated by the EPA in 2012.

97. Peter Victor, "Managing Without Growth: Slower by Design, Not Disaster" (lecture, York University, Toronto, Canada, April 4, 2013), https://www.youtube.com/watch?v=pZI2RDNvd6M. Jim MacNeill was Secretary General of the World Commission on Environment and Development (Brundtland Commission) and one of the main authors of *Our Common Future*. United Nations World Commission on Environment and Development, *Report of the World Commission on Environment and Development: Our Common Future* (Oxford: Oxford University Press, 1987).

98. Christopher Hight, "Designing Ecologies," in *Projective Ecologies*, ed. Chris Reed and Nina-Marie E. Lister (Cambridge, MA: Harvard Graduate School of Design; ACTAR, 2014); Félix Guattari, *Molecular Revolution: Psychiatry and Politics* (New York: Penguin, 1984), 263.

PART TWO — INTRODUCTION

1. George Parkin Grant, "Thinking about Technology," in *Technology and Justice* (Toronto: Anansi, 1986), 12.

2. Lewis Mumford dedicated an entire chapter to this issue in *The Pentagon of Power*, vol. 2 of *The Myth of the Machine* (New York: A Harvest/HBJ Book, Harcourt Brace Jovanovich, 1970), 106. In the section entitled "Science as Technology," he writes while talking about the seventeenth-century polymath Sir Francis Bacon: "Bacon brought science to earth. He linked science to technique recognizing in this union a way to fulfill 'the immediate human desire for health, wealth, and power.'" Alfred North Whitehead writes in *Science of the Modern World* (New York: Free Press, 1997), 96–97, about Bacon's prophecy realized in the nineteenth century: "Science, conceived not so much in its principles as in its results, is an obvious storehouse of ideas for utilization. But, if we are to understand what happened during the century, the analogy of a mine is better than that of a storehouse… One element in the new method is just the discovery of how to set about bridging the gap between the scientific ideas, and the ultimate product."

George Parkin Grant, on the other hand, observed in "Thinking about Technology," 14, that "applied" (science) means "folded toward," insisting: "Why that foldedness toward potentialities of new makings has

been implicit in modern science since its origin is extremely difficult to understand, and indeed has not yet been understood."

CHAPTER FOUR

1. André Gorz, *Ecology as Politics* (Boston: South End Press, 1980), 79.

2. Gorz, "Socialism or Ecofascism," in *Ecology as Politics*, 77–90.

3. Gorz, *Ecology as Politics*, 18–19.

4. Ivan Illich, *Tools for Conviviality* (New York: Harper and Row, 1973), 11, 22, 51.

5. An example of this fallacy can be found in the rhizomatic patterns of post-Fordian landscapes. Decentralized control and fragmentation, which brought some of the anticipated autonomy to smaller communities, also resulted in previously underestimated environmental consequences (i.e., extensive networks of storage and transport infrastructure). See Alan Berger, *Drosscape: Wasting Land in Urban America* (New York: Princeton Architectural Press, 2007), 54. According to Berger, "flexible modes of production create more waste landscape."

6. E. F. Schumacher, *Small Is Beautiful: Economics as if People Mattered* (New York: Harper & Row, 1975), 65–66.

7. Witold Rybczynski, *Paper Heroes, Appropriate Technology: Panacea or Pipe Dream?* (New York: Penguin Books, 1991), 148–49. Rybczynski emphasizes these structural issues when discussing examples of Appropriate Technology programs introduced in India, Pakistan, Mexico, and the United States.

8. Lewis Mumford, "Authoritarian and Democratic Technics," *Technology and Culture* 5, no. 1 (Winter 1964): 6. In this essay, Mumford briefly discusses the perils hidden in the subtle power mechanisms embedded in the economy of abundance. The same argument was further explored in his tour de force *The Pentagon of Power*, vol. 2 of *The Myth of the Machine* (New York: A Harvest/HBJ Book, Harcourt Brace Jovanovich, 1970), 330, where he writes, "On megatechnic terms complete withdrawal is heresy and treason, if not evidence of unsound mind. The arch-enemy of the Affluent Economy would not be Karl Marx but Henry Thoreau."

9. Mumford referred to Jacques Ellul as a fatalist refusing, with typical trust in humanity, to accept that the current trends cannot be reversed. See *The Pentagon of Power*, 291. Thomas P. Hughes also distanced himself from his determinism. See Hughes, "Technological Momentum," in *Does Technology Drive History?*, ed. Merritt Roe

Smith and Leo Marx (Cambridge, MA: MIT Press, 1994), 103. George Parkin Grant, on the other hand, positioned Ellul's book among the greatest commentaries on advanced societies. See "The Civilization of Technique," in *The Grant Reader*, ed. William Christian and Sheila Grant (Toronto: University of Toronto Press, 1998), 394–98. Jacques Ellul, *The Technological Society* (New York: Vintage Books, 1964), 110. For Ellul's ideas about technological autonomy and its self-directing movement toward the greatest efficiency, see Chapter 11, "The Characterology of Technique," 79–84.

10. Ellul, *The Technological Society*, 81.

11. For Thomas Hughes's concept of "reverse salient," see Hughes, "Evolution of Large Technological Systems," in *The Social Construction of Technological Systems*, ed. Wiebe E. Bijker, Hughes, and Trevor J. Pinch (Cambridge, MA: MIT Press, 1987).

12. Ellul, *The Technological Society*, 82.

13. Ibid., 194.

14. Mumford, "Authoritarian and Democratic Technics," 5.

15. The idea of technological determinism was strongly contested in the 1980s by a school of scholars who focused on the importance of social shaping of technology. The following two volumes offer a good representation of various approaches within this school: Wiebe E. Bijker, Thomas P. Hughes, and Trevor J. Pinch, eds., *The Social Construction of Technological Systems* (Cambridge, MA: MIT Press, 1987); and Donald MacKenzie and Judy Wajcman, eds., *The Social Shaping of Technology* (Philadelphia: Open University Press, 1999). The method developed by these scholars, the Social Construction of Technology (SCOT), helped analyze technological artifacts as context dependent and as culturally constructed and interpreted phenomena. Related to the SCOT method, the Actor Network Theory (ANT), developed by philosopher Bruno Latour and sociologist Michel Callon, attempted to go a step further, giving equal agency to human and nonhuman actors that together shape technological networks. In "Technological Momentum," Hughes argued that technological development is not only shaped by science but also by economic decisions (and regulatory frameworks), which in turn are socially (and politically) determined. While less radical than Ellul's determinism, he believed that certain assemblages originally shaped by the social and natural environment "gather enough momentum" to eventually start shaping them. Last but not least, the SCOT method describes the immediate "how" but not the distant "why." Sociologist Trevor J. Pinch and theorist of technology Wiebe E. Bijker recognize this limitation noting, "The sociocultural and political situation of a social group shapes its norms and values, which in turn influence the meaning given to an artifact." See Bijker et al., *The Social Construction of Technological Systems*, 46.

16. Lewis Mumford, *Technics and Civilization* (Chicago: University of Chicago Press, 2010), 41.

17. Ellul, *The Technological Society*, 4.

18. Carl Circo, "Using Mandates and Incentives to Promote Sustainable Construction and Green Building Projects in the Private Sector: A Call for More State Land Use Policy Initiatives." *Penn State Law Review* 112, no. 3 (2008): 731–82. This article was published when the first (voluntary) version of Green Building Standards Code was being introduced in California.

19. Ibid., 737.

20. Ibid., 744. For common origins of market failures, see Molly F. Sherlock, *Energy Tax Policy: Historical Perspectives on and Current Status of Energy Tax Expenditures*, CRS Report No. R41227 (Washington, DC: Congressional Research Service, 2011), https://crsreports. congress.gov/product/pdf/R/R41227.

21. Sherlock, *Energy Tax Policy*, 10.

22. Although this process varies across states, the Green Building Standards Codes and Energy Codes in California are becoming increasingly stringent. California's New Residential Zero Net Energy Action Plan imposes that all new residential buildings achieve zero net energy status beginning in 2020. This means producing enough renewable energy on site to satisfy the building's operational needs. See "Net Zero Energy," California Public Utility Commission website, accessed December 28, 2021, https://www.cpuc.ca.gov/industries-and-topics/electrical-energy/demand-side-management/energy-efficiency/zero-net-energy.

23. Ulrich Beck, *World at Risk* (Cambridge: Polity Press, 2009), 9–10.

24. Steven Nadel, *Energy Efficiency Tax Incentives in the Context of Tax Reform*, American Council for an Energy-Efficient Economy website, July 16, 2012, 3, https://www.aceee.org/content/energy-efficiency-tax-incentives-context-tax-reform. Oftentimes, levels of efficiency achieved by an incentivized product will later be adopted as a minimum-efficiency standard.

25. The following statement is worth a pause: "By 2050, energy efficiency measures and practices could reduce U.S. energy use by 42–59 percent relative to current projections, and in the process, save consumers and businesses billions of dollars, raise gross domestic product in 2050 by $100–200 billion, and support 1.3–1.9 million jobs in 2050." Nadel, *Energy Efficiency Tax Incentives*, 8. In order to support the promoted measure, the author makes sure to emphasize the "selfish" gains: growth of domestic product, and an increase in job numbers.

26. Sherlock, *Energy Tax Policy*, 27–28.

27. See Bryan Pfaffenberger, "Technological Dramas," *Science, Technology, & Human Values* 17, no. 3 (Summer 1992): 285–86. In this essay, historian of technology Pfaffenberger defines the process of creation, interpretation, appropriation, and assimilation of technological artifacts and systems as a form of recursive discourse in which often unrelated actors gradually form common frames of meaning to achieve their cultural, social, and political goals. It is when these initial "dramas" gradually get forgotten and a technological artifact becomes an unquestioned part of daily routines that it reaches its "greatest social penetration."

28. Nadel, *Energy Efficiency Tax Incentives*, (iii). Although not free, these incentives do offer a savings and hence risk attracting "free riders," buyers who were already planning to purchase an energy-saving technology regardless of any associated subsidies.

29. Sherlock, *Energy Tax Policy*, 10.

30. The Funding Wizard lists grants, rebates, and incentives for sustainable projects. The service is supported by the Air Resources Board, a part of the California Environmental Protection Agency. Most funding is available to select residents (based on income), depending on geographic location or the power and water utility that serves it. The data for this analysis was collected on March 8, 2017. For the currently available programs, see the Funding Wizard website, accessed December 28, 2021, https://fundingwizard.arb.ca.gov.

31. Established in 1995, Database of State Incentives for Renewables & Efficiency is operated by the North Carolina Clean Energy Technology Center at North Carolina State University and is funded by the U.S. Department of Energy. The data for this analysis was collected on March 8, 2017. For currently available programs, see the database website, accessed December 28, 2021, http://www.dsireusa.org.

32. Charles Kubert and Mark Sinclair, *State Support for Clean Energy Deployment: Lessons Learned for Potential Future Policy* (Golden, CO: National Renewable Energy Laboratory, 2011), http://www.nrel.gov/docs/fy11osti/49340.pdf. See Chapter 3, "Financing Tools," which, next to rebates and tax credits, also describes various forms of loans.

33. For an analysis of the socially discriminative effects of tax-based tools, see Margot L. Crandall-Hollick and Molly F. Sherlock, *Residential Energy Tax Credits: Overview and Analysis*, CRS Report No. R42089 (Washington, DC: Congressional Research Service, 2018), 9, https://fas.org/sgp/crs/misc/R42089.pdf.

34. Kubert and Sinclair, *State Support for Clean Energy Deployment*, 29.

35. See Lynn J. Cunningham, *Renewable Energy and Energy Efficiency Incentives: A Summary of Federal Programs*, CRS Report No. R40913 (Washington, DC: Congressional Research Service, 2021), 9, https://crsreports.congress.gov/product/pdf/R/R40913.

36. Kubert and Sinclair, *State Support for Clean Energy Deployment*, 28–29.

37. Ibid., 77–82. According to the report, these are: 1) renewable portfolio standards; 2) interconnection standards (connection of distributed generators to utility distribution lines); and 3) net metering (methods in which distributed generators are compensated for surplus energy they feed into the distribution grid).

38. Ordinance No. 184,802, passed by the Los Angeles City Council on March 1, 2017, https://planning.lacity.org/ordinances/docs/R1VariationZones/SingleFamily.pdf.

39. For an overview of these programs, see Cunningham, *Renewable Energy and Energy Efficiency Incentives*. The Department of Housing and Urban Development and the Department of Health and Human Services also run their own programs.

40. Cunningham, *Renewable Energy and Energy Efficiency Incentives*, 13.

41. A similar program is run by the Department of Health and Human Services as the Low-Income Home Energy Assistance Program. Ibid., 39.

42. See Chapter 2.1, "Regulating Environmental Degradation: 1970s," of this book.

43. Cunningham, *Renewable Energy and Energy Efficiency Incentives*, 30. This incentive is called the Residential Energy Conservation Subsidy Exclusion, 26 U.S. §136.

44. Ibid., 30–31, 33. The EPACT 2005 authorized two tax credits. The first 10 percent credit was the Residential Energy Efficiency Tax Credit, 26 U.S. §25C. The second one was the Residential Renewable Energy Tax Credit, 26 U.S. §25D. This 30

percent credit applied to the following types of equipment: solar water heat, photovoltaics, wind, fuel cells, geothermal heat pumps, other solar electric technologies. In 2007, the US Congress passed another tax credit, the Energy-Efficient New Homes Tax Credit for Home Builders, 26 U.S. §45L (authorized by the Tax Technical Corrections Act).

45. Nadel, *Energy Efficiency Tax Incentives*, 6. An increase in tax expenditures after 2009 is also discussed in Sherlock, *Energy Tax Policy*, 19.

46. The 1958 edition of the FHA Minimum Property Standards for Properties of One or Two Living Units addressed energy efficiency and defined allowable heat losses. See Chapter 1.4, "Prospering by Expansion: 1945–1950s," of this book. However, as mentioned in Chapter 1.2, "Building the Real-Estate Market: 1920s," also in this book, financial risks associated with building performance in general were already addressed in the precursor of the FHA mortgage-issuance standards, the 1922 Recommended Minimum Requirements for Small Dwelling Construction, prepared by the Department of Commerce's Bureau of Standards.

47. See Cunningham, *Renewable Energy and Energy Efficiency Incentives*, 39. The FHA PowerSaver Loan Program (no statutory authority, developed by HUD in 2009) applies to "energy efficient improvements, including installation of insulation, duct sealing, replacement doors and windows, HVAC systems, water heaters, home automations systems and controls (e.g., smart thermostats), solar panels, solar thermal hot water systems, small wind power, and geothermal systems."

48. Sherlock, *Energy Tax Policy*, Summary.

49. Ibid.

50. See Alliance Commission on National Energy Efficiency Policy, *The History of Energy Productivity*, January 2013, 4, https://www.ase.org/sites/ase.org/files/resources/Media%20browser/ee_commission_history_report_2-1-13.pdf. The report further specifies: "In 1970 Americans consumed the energy equivalent of about 2,700 gallons of gasoline per person for all uses of energy. That rate of consumption extrapolated to our current economy would have come to the equivalent of about 5,400 gallons per person. Instead, 2010 consumption was the equivalent of 2,500 gallons per person." According to the U.S. Census Bureau, the US population was 203.1 million in 1970 and 308.7 million in 2010. Considering the per capita consumption provided above, the absolute consumption of energy by all

Americans in 1970 was 548,370 gallons (2,700 × 203.1 million) and 771,750 gallons in 2010 (2,500 × 308.7 million). The absolute use of energy increased by 40 percent. The Alliance report mentions an even higher increase in demand: 50 percent.

51. Kubert and Sinclair, *State Support for Clean Energy Deployment*, 9.

52. Ibid., 4. Outsourcing of heavy industries is mentioned as one of the factors that drive energy productivity.

53. Ulrich Beck, *Risk Society* (London: SAGE Publications, 1992), 41.

54. While Beck's first extensive discussion of democratization of risk can be found in *Risk Society*, this statement comes from his book *Ecological Enlightenment* (Amherst, NY: Prometheus Books, 1995), 27.

55. Kubert and Sinclair, *State Support for Clean Energy Deployment*, 8.

56. Ibid., 20–22.

57. Nadel, *Energy Efficiency Tax Incentives*, 13.

58. In September 2016, surprising news made international headlines: the Swedish government decided to offer tax breaks for repairs to reduce waste due to planned obsolescence built into most household appliances and also to create jobs for unskilled workers. See, for example, Richard Orange, "Waste Not Want Not: Sweden to Give Tax Breaks for Repairs," *Guardian*, September 19, 2016, https://www.theguardian.com/world/2016/sep/19/waste-not-want-not-sweden-tax-breaks-repairs.

59. Ralph Knowles, *Energy and Form: An Ecological Approach to Urban Growth* (Cambridge, MA: MIT Press, 1974).

60. Ralph Knowles, "The Solar Envelope: Its Meaning for Energy and Buildings," *Energy and Buildings* 35 (2003): 15–25. In this paper, Knowles defined maximum urban densities that allow for the application of his solar-envelope concept.

61. Although very progressive, the previously mentioned California New Residential Zero Net Energy Action Plan expresses the same emphasis on operational efficiency. Unfortunately, while homes become more efficient, the average household consumption has been increasing due to the size of and equipment used in homes. See Stephen Lacey, "The Growing Size of New U.S. Homes Is Offsetting Residential Efficiency Gains," *Greentech Media*, February 13, 2013, https://www.greentechmedia.com/articles/read/the-growing-size-of-new-us-homes-is-offsetting-residential-efficiency-gains.

62. According to the rules established in the aforementioned New Residential Zero Net Energy Action Plan, the obligation to

produce renewable energy on-site may be waived if the new building is shaded by other structures or by trees.

63. Ideally, a roof-mounted solar energy system should be at an angle that is equal to the latitude of the location. A completely horizontal surface offers most flexibility but, assuming that the orientation is correct, surfaces inclined up to forty-five degrees will work in most situations equally well.

64. Project Sunroof analyzes roof exposure using Google Maps and computes hours of usable sunlight per year and square feet available for solar panels. It couples this data with projected savings. See the project website, accessed December 28, 2021, https://www.google.com/get/sunroof#p=0.

65. Illich, *Tools for Conviviality*, 49.

66. Ibid., 51.

67. The Los Angeles Zoning Code is part of the Municipal Code, accessed December 28, 2021, https://codelibrary.amlegal.com/codes/los_angeles/latest/lamc/0-0-0-118269#JD_12.42. See Chapter I, "General Provisions and Zoning"; Article 2, "Specific Planning – Zoning, Comprehensive Zoning Plan"; Section 12.42, "Landscape"; Subsection A, "Conservation of Energy"; Point 2, "Tree Plainting."

68. Reyner Banham, "A Home Is Not a House." *Art in America* 2 (1965): 70–79.

69. California Building Standards Commission, 2019 California Green Building Standards Code, California Code of Regulations, Title 24, Part 11 (Washington, DC: International Code Council, 2019), 100.

70. Ibid. See Appendixes 4, "Residential Voluntary Measures," and A4.106.7, "Reduction of Heat Island Effect or Nonroof Areas," 1.

71. California Public Resources Code, Division 15, "Energy Conservation and Development"; Chapter 12, "Solar Shade Control," December 28, 2021, https://leginfo.legislature.ca.gov/faces/codes_displayText.xhtml?lawCode=PRC&division=15.&title=&part=&chapter=12.&article=. For a review of the provisions included in the act, see Scott Anders, Kevin Grigsby, Carolyn Adi Kuduk, and Taylor Day, *California's Solar Shade Control Act: A Review of the Statutes and Relevant Cases*, Energy Policy Initiatives Center, University of San Diego School of Law, 2010, https://www.sandiego.edu/law/documents/centers/epic/100329_SSCA_Final_000.pdf.

72. See Scott Anders, Kevin Grigsby, Carolyn Adi Kuduk, Taylor Day, Allegra Frost, and Joe Kaatz, *California's Solar Shade Control Act: A Review of the Statutes and Relevant Cases*, Energy Policy Initiatives Center, University of San

Diego School of Law, 2014, https://www. sandiego.edu/law/documents/centers/epic/ Solar%20Rights%20Act-A%20Review%20 of%20Statutes%20and%20Relevant%20 Cases.pdf.

73. George Parkin Grant, "Thinking about Technology," in *Technology and Justice* (Toronto: Anansi, 1986), 32.

74. EnergySage, "Should You Cut Down Trees to Go Solar?" EnergySage website, last updated October 13, 2020, https://news.energysage.com/ should-you-cut-down-trees-to-go-solar/.

75. Grant, "Thinking about Technology," 32.

76. Ellul, *The Technological Society*, 79–80.

77. See Mumford, "Authoritarian and Democratic Technics," 2. In this essay, Mumford makes a series of statements that help determine whether distributed solar technologies can be considered a democratic technic. Although small-scale, distributed, and in part controlled by homeowners, solar panels depend on technological know-how that is controlled by a few large corporations, they must be installed by certified contractors, and in most cases, they "feed" the energy into the municipal grid (first, because storing energy is still very expensive; second, because that is how homeowners receive some of the incentives). Eventually, yes, they provide some autonomy and control, but most importantly, they are potentially democratic while many other systems are not compatible with democracy at all.

78. See, for example, Philip J. Craul, *Urban Soils: Applications and Practices* (New York: John Wiley, 1992); Lisa Gartland, *Heat Islands: Understanding and Mitigating Heat in Urban Areas* (London: Earthscan, 2008), 109–38; Cecil C. Konijnendijk, Kjell Nilsson, Thomas B. Randrup, and Jasper Schipperijn, eds., *Urban Forests and Trees* (New York: Springer, 2005), 81–110, 149–85; Kjell Nilsson, Thomas B. Randrup, and Barbara L. M. Wandall, "Trees in the Urban Environment: Some Practical Considerations," in *The Forests Handbook*, ed. Julian Evans, vol. 1 (Oxford: Wiley-Blackwell, 2001), 260–74; and Jianguo Wu, "Towards a Landscape Ecology of Cities: Beyond Buildings, Trees, and Urban Forests," in *Ecology, Planning, and Management of Urban Forests*, ed. M. M. Carreiro, Y. C. Song, and J. Wu (New York: Springer, 2008).

79. Beck, *World at Risk*, 83.

80. Illich, *Tools for Conviviality*, 51; and Ellul, *The Technological Society*, 82.

CHAPTER FIVE

1. California Building Standards Commission (CBSC) and International Code Council (ICC), 2019 California Residential Code, California Code of Regulations, Title 24, Part 2.5 (Washington, DC: ICC, 2019). Unless otherwise specified, all referenced codes are part of the 2019 California Building Standards Code, California Code of Regulations, Title 24.

2. See CBSC and ICC, 2019 California Residential Code, 3. Section 1.1.2, "Purpose," states: "The purpose of this code is to establish the minimum requirements to safeguard the public health, safety and general welfare through structural strength, means of egress facilities, stability, access to persons with disabilities, sanitation, adequate lighting and ventilation, and energy conservation; safety to life and property from fire and other hazards attributed to the built environment."

3. CBSC and ICC, 2019 California Residential Code, 35–36. While a complete "dwelling unit" is one that provides permanent provisions for living, sleeping, eating, cooking, and sanitation, the term *habitable* is reserved for individual spaces within the unit, excluding those used for sanitation, storage, and utilities.

4. California Building Standards Commission (CBSC), 2019 California Energy Code, California Code of Regulations, Title 24, Part 6 (Washington, DC: International Code Council, 2019); CBSC, 2019 California Green Building Standards Code, California Code of Regulations, Title 24, Part 11 (Washington, DC: International Code Council, 2019).

5. CBSC and ICC, 2019 California Residential Code, 419.

6. Ibid., 113.

7. Expanded polystyrene (EPS) and extruded polystyrene (XPS) insulations are so commonly used that most people don't question them. As an example, the following safety data sheet (SDS) lists no hazards related to use, but recognizes that the "degradation component styrene is listed as a possible carcinogen." Under Section 12, "Ecological Information," one also reads, "Non-biodegradable, insoluble in water, low potential for bioaccumulation." Under Section 13, "Disposal Considerations," "Reuse or dispose via sanitary landfill or adequate incinerator…Do not discharge into waterways or sewer system." Insulation Corporation of America, ICA-LITE EPS SDS, prepared on May 23, 2016, https://insulationcorp.com/wp-content/ uploads/2016/05/ICA-LITE-SDS.pdf.

8. Michael Bernstein, "Plastics in Oceans Decompose, Release Hazardous Chemicals, Surprising New Study Says," American Chemical Society website, August 19, 2009, https://www.acs.org/content/acs/en/ pressroom/newsreleases/2009/august/ plastics-in-oceans-decompose-release- hazardous-chemicals-surprising-new-study- says.html. The article reports that, contrary to previous beliefs, plastics (including polystyrene, used in insulation boards) are not indestructible. They do (and quite quickly) decompose in contact with seawater and become toxic. In 2014, hexabromocyclo- dodecane was added to the Annex A (Elimination) of the *Stockholm Convention on Persistent Organic Pollutants*. The Annex A specifies: "Parties must take measures to eliminate the production and use of the chemicals listed under Annex A. Specific exemptions for use or production are listed in the Annex and apply only to Parties that register for them." Unfortunately, the exemptions include EPS and XPS insulation. (The convention has not been ratified by the US.) See the website of the convention, accessed December 28, 2021, http://chm.pops.int/Implementation/ Alternatives/AlternativestoPOPs/ ChemicalslistedinAnnexA/tabid/5837/ Default.aspx.

9. Convenience Products, Clayton Corporation, Touch 'n Foam Pro Foam Kit 15 Part A Safety Data Sheet, SDS revised September 3, 2015, https:// images.homedepot-static.com/catalog/ pdfImages/6d/6d19cfab-7af7-48a7-8068- b9eb972cecbb.pdf.

10. For more detail, see, for example, Wnceqing Yang, Qingyin Dong, Shili Liu, Henghua Xie, Lili Liu, and Jinhui Li, "Recycling and Disposal Methods for Polyurethane Foam Wastes," *Procedia Environmental Sciences* 16 (2012): 167–75.

11. See the Home Depot website, accessed December 28, 2021, http://www. homedepot.com/p/Thermasheath-Rmax- Thermasheath-3-2-in-x-4-ft-x-8-ft-R-13-1- Polyisocyanurate-Rigid-Foam-Insulation- Board-613010/100573703.

12. Many researchers question the value of R-value as an indicator of thermal insulation performance. See, for example, Ken Wells, "R-values: Controversy and Performance Values," *Construction Specifier*, November 12, 2013, https://www.constructionspecifier. com/r-values-controversy-and-performance- values-cont/. In this article, the author observes, "The R-value can be an extremely misleading value due to the laboratory

guarded–hot plate apparatus test methods used in attaining these numbers. These procedures are conducted under ideal conditions, and the real-world performance has absolutely no bearing on such tests. As a result, the listed R-values can be higher than what actually occurs. These tests obviously favor fibrous insulations whose performance drastically drops with temperature fluctuations."

13. Trisphosphate, another halogenated flame retardant, has been scrutinized by governments and third-party organizations but has not been banned yet. Prior to 2013, the USGBC's LEED awarded pilot points for not using materials that contain it.

14. U.S. Environmental Protection Agency (EPA), "Flame Retardant Alternatives for Hexabromocyclododecane (HBCD)," June 2014, 5–9, 5–12, https://www.epa.gov/sites/production/files/2014-06/documents/hbcd_report.pdf.

15. See Paula Melton, "Polyiso Impacts Are High, but Performance May Make Up for Them," BuildingGreen website, April 21, 2015, https://www.buildinggreen.com/news-analysis/polyiso-impacts-are-high-performance-may-make-them. The author questions the objectivity of the environmental product declaration released by the Polyisocyanurate Insulation Manufacturers Association in 2015.

16. See the product page on the Home Depot website, accessed December 28, 2021, https://www.homedepot.com/p/Schluter-Kerdi-Board-1-2-in-x-32-in-x-48-in-Building-Panel-KB121220812/202967605. "Proposition 65 requires businesses to provide warnings to Californians about significant exposures to chemicals that cause cancer, birth defects or other reproductive harm." Proposition 65 website, accessed December 28, 2021, https://www.p65warnings.ca.gov.

17. An expression commonly used in the building code.

18. Vytenis Babrauskas, Donald Lucas, David Eisenberg, Veena Singla, Michel Dedeo, and Arlene Blum, "Flame Retardants in Building Insulation: A Case for Re-evaluating Building Codes," Building Research & Information 40, no. 6 (2012): 738–55.

19. CBSC, 2019 California Green Building Standards Code, 1.

20. Ibid., 175. Here only a voluntary standard is suggested for health facilities, yet exactly the same prescription is imposed in Section 110.8 (b) of the Energy Code to all interiors. See CBSC, 2019 California Energy Code, 47.

21. See the California Proposition 65 website, accessed December 28, 2021, https://www.p65warnings.ca.gov/fact-sheets/formaldehyde.

22. For a list of similar products, see Alex Wilson, "Formaldehyde-Based Foam Insulation Back from the Dead," BuildingGreen website, October 30, 2013, https://www.buildinggreen.com/blog/formaldehyde-based-foam-insulation-back-dead. Some experts think that the precaution was excessive. Canada's oldest and largest home inspection company, Carson Dunlop, claims, "UFFI is one of the most thoroughly investigated and most innocuous building products we have used." Alan Carson and John Caverly, "Urea Formaldehyde Foam Insulation," Carson Dunlop website, February 4, 2014, http://www.carsondunlop.com/resources/articles/urea-formaldehyde-foam-insulation.

23. CBSC and ICC, 2019 California Residential Code, 113.

24. Two issues arise here. First, most individual standards, such as ASTM E84, rate a specific aspect of performance without reference to environmental concerns. Second, overlaps and redundancies between standards—such as imposition of specific material-burning characteristics and a physical thermal barrier—often increase environmental impact without improving human safety.

25. The UN formally recognized water and sanitation as vital human rights only in 2010. See Resolution 64/292: The Human Right to Water and Sanitation, United Nations General Assembly, July 28, 2010, https://undocs.org/A/RES/64/292.

26. Most environmental acts apply to residential construction via state regulations and municipal ordinances, often only under certain circumstances, depending on lot size, location, or level of hazard. For example, construction in the proximity of protected waters is regulated by the Clean Water Act of 1972, and certain types of hazardous construction waste (which does not include sewage or sludge) are federally regulated by the Resource Conservation and Recovery Act of 1976.

27. In California, water rights are based on the riparian and appropriative doctrines. The former originates from the English common law and was adopted from the Eastern states. It is based on the adjacency of owned land to a source of water, gives a right to use a *reasonable* quantity, and prohibits diversion or storage. The latter originates in the American West, where the right to unlimited use, diversion, and storage of water was claimed by early settlers, gold miners, and entrepreneurs, regardless of the distance from the land on which the water was used. Since the passage of the Water Commission Act of 1914, appropriation requires a permit. For more details, see "The Water Rights Process," California State Water Resources Control Board website, updated August 20, 2020, https://www.waterboards.ca.gov/waterrights/board_info/water_rights_process.html. For a fascinating account of the events that led to the construction of the water projects that turned the inhospitable West into the present powerhouse, see Marc Reisner, Cadillac Desert: The American West and Its Disappearing Water (New York: Penguin Books, 1993). The potential profits and dreams were so big that both the local magnates and the federal government participated in the frenzy. While the magnates invested to secure the value of their real-estate assets in Los Angeles (e.g., by orchestrating the quasi-legal land takeovers necessary for the construction of the LA aqueduct), the federal government provided subsidies and often the final word in disputes over water and land rights.

28. The Los Angeles Basin's economic output accounts for half of the state's economy. California has the strongest economy in the nation, and in 2018, it was ranked the fifth-largest economy in the world. "CA Solidifies Position as World's 5th Largest Economy," Center for Continuing Study of the California Economy website, July 2019, https://www.ccsce.com/PDF/Numbers-July2019-California-Economy-Rankings.pdf. Except for a small amount of water extracted from local wells (the average for the fiscal years 2011–2015 was 12 percent) and an even smaller amount of recycled water (2 percent), Los Angeles relies on three major sources of water. The municipally owned, 240-mile-long Los Angeles Aqueduct (LAA) inaugurated in 1913 delivers water from the Owens Valley (29 percent). The 242-mile-long Colorado River Aqueduct inaugurated in 1939 delivers water from the Colorado River and originates at Lake Havasu. It is operated by the Metropolitan Water District (MWD). The most recent of the three, the California Aqueduct (part of the State Water Project), originates in the San Joaquin Valley and delivers water from Northern California and the Sierra Nevada Mountains (total length of canals and pipes is approximately 700 miles). Its West Branch was inaugurated in 1973. Los Angeles provisions are supplied by the MWD (57 percent, from the Colorado River and the California Aqueduct). Supplies from the LAA have gradually diminished due

to drought and environmental regulations, which impose environmental mitigation (the LAA provided only 7 percent of supplies in 2014). The deficit is compensated by water from the MWD sources, locally sourced water (gray water recycling, stormwater reuse), and drastic conservation measures. City of Los Angeles Department of Water and Power (LADWP), Urban Water Management Plan (Los Angeles: LADWP, 2015), ES-21, ES-25, https://www.ladwp.com/ladwp/faces/ladwp/aboutus/a-water/a-w-sourcesofsupply?_adf.ctrl-state=qwesjwct1_4&_afrLoop=104171301574783.

29. County of Los Angeles Department of Public Works (LACDPW), *Water Resilience Plan: Rapid Assessment* (Alhambra, CA: LACDPW, 2017), 2, https://dpw.lacounty.gov/wrp/docs/Rapid-Needs-Assessment.pdf.

30. California Code of Regulations, Title 23, Division 2, Chapter 2 (23 CCR § 490–495), accessed December 28, 2021, https://govt.westlaw.com/calregs/Browse/Home/California/CaliforniaCodeofRegulations?guid=I55B69DB0D45A11DEA95CA4428EC25FA0&transitionType=Default&contextData=%28sc.Default%29#IF088C67ECF9946E09B6A989B1CB24A80. Although, in 1996, the city of Los Angeles passed a landscape ordinance (Ord. No. 170,978), which is now a part of the Zoning Code (Sections 12.40–12.43), the water-management prescriptions did not apply to one-family dwellings. The state-authored Model Water Efficient Landscape Ordinance (MWELO, implementation of the AB 1881, adopted in 2010, revised in 2015) imposed, among other measures, water budgets. Initially only applied to single-family dwellings if the landscaped area exceeded 2,500 square feet when developer-built and 5,000 square feet when built by the homeowner, the ordinance is now mandatory for residential landscaped areas that exceeded 500 square feet. The CALGreen Code references the MWELO in Section 4.304, "Outdoor Water Use." CBSC, 2019 California Green Building Standards Code, 25.

31. City of Los Angeles Department of Water and Power (LADWP), Stormwater Capture Master Plan (Los Angeles: LADWP, 2015), 19, https://www.ladwp.com/cs/idcplg?IdcService=GET_FILE&dDocName=OPLADWPCCB421767&RevisionSelectionMethod=LatestReleased.

32. LADWP, Urban Water Management Plan, ES-23. Of course, not all rainwater can be captured for human use. A large portion is

reserved for "environmental uses," which surprisingly means both maintaining gardens and allowing it to flow into water bodies or be used by plants and animals. Also, only approximately half of the water that is captured is recharged to an aquifer; the remaining half infiltrates soils separated from the aquifer by an impermeable layer. See LADWP, Stormwater Capture Master Plan, ES-7.

33. In California, in 2000, which was an average year, only 11 percent of water use was urban (it was 8 percent in the wet in 1998, and 13 percent in the dry in 2001), 42 percent was agricultural (28 percent in 1998, 52 percent in 2001), and the remaining 47 percent (35 percent in 1998, 64 percent in 2001) was reserved for "nature." Since most farmland is concentrated in the central and northern parts of the state, Los Angeles's water use is urban: on average in the period between 2011 and 2014, 66 percent of use was residential (37 percent single family, 29 percent multifamily), 17 percent commercial, 14 percent governmental and nonrevenue (e.g., firefighting, leakage), and only 3 percent industrial. Of all water use, 40 percent was employed outdoors. LADWP, Urban Water Management Plan, ES-09, ES-10.

34. The 1936 Flood Control Act was a "victory" for Los Angeles developers and realtors. It provided the legal basis and funding for the channelizing of the LA River (1938–60). While the project made the city safer, and, of course, denser and wealthier, it isolated the river from its watershed. To mention a couple of side effects, it sent rain to the ocean rather than the aquifer and deprived soil of vital nutrients.

35. LADWP, Stormwater Capture Master Plan, ES-10. The LADWP estimates that the annual groundwater recharge can increase twofold by 2035 (68,000 acre-feet/year), thanks to the construction of new stormwater-spreading facilities and distributed stormwater-infiltration methods. The city considers less than approximately a quarter of it (15,000 acre-feet/year) as a future source of supply. The rest is supposed to counteract the effects of overconsumption. LADWP, Urban Water Management Plan, 7–29.

36. The Safe Drinking Water Act of 1974 imposes the maximum contaminant levels in the supplies of drinking water. Although it focuses on the quality of water at the supply end, it also indirectly protects groundwater through a 2006 regulation commonly called the Ground Water Rule. In coastal areas, the Ocean Dumping Act of 1972 partly overlaps with the Clean Water Act.

37. Since 1990, the National Pollutant Discharge Elimination System (NPDES) permit issued by the California State Water Resources Control Board (Los Angeles Region) to the Los Angeles County Flood Control District sets the allowable pollutant loads that can be discharged from their Municipal Separate Storm Sewer Systems to the ocean (Santa Monica Bay). It primarily targets indicator bacteria and total aluminum, copper, lead, zinc, diazinon, and cyanide but also aquatic toxicity during wet weather and discharges of debris and trash. California Regional Water Quality Control Board Los Angeles Region, NPDES PERMIT NO. CAS004001, November 23, 2016, 10, https://www.waterboards.ca.gov/losangeles/water_issues/programs/stormwater/municipal/losangeles.html.

38. Donald L. Elliott, *A Better Way to Zone: Ten Principles to Create More Livable Cities* (Washington, DC: Island Press, 2008), 17. Municipalities and counties (in unincorporated areas) were granted the right to control land based on state zoning-enabling acts. It is the municipal zoning code that indirectly determines the amount of stormwater runoff when it defines floor-area ratios and the impervious cover limitations.

39. City of Los Angeles Sanitation (LASAN), Planning and Land Development Handbook for Low Impact Development (LID), 5th ed. (Los Angeles: LASAN, 2016), 3–4, https://www.lacitysan.org/cs/groups/sg_sw/documents/document/y250/mde3/~edisp/cnt017152.pdf. The 2011 ordinance (Ord. No. 181899), updated in 2015 (Ord. No. 183833), is a part of the Planning and Land Development Program and of the Standard Urban Stormwater Mitigation Plan, both requirements of the NPDES permit.

40. The permit (ORDER R4-2017-0045) is available on the EPA website, accessed December 28, 2021, https://www.epa.gov/npdes-permits/city-los-angeles-hyperion-treatment-plant-playa-del-rey-ca-ca0109991.

41. LADWP, Urban Water Management Plan, 2–5. According to the authors, 46 percent of water consumed by single-family households is used indoors. According to a 2011 report prepared for the California Board of Water Resources, it was 47 percent in the entire state. Aquacraft Water Engineering and Management, *California Single-Family Water Use Efficiency Study*, December 6, 2011, 25, http://www.irwd.com/images/pdf/save-water/CaSingleFamilyWaterUseEfficiencyStudyJune2011.pdf.

42. Aquacraft Water Engineering and Management, *California Single-Family Water Use Efficiency Study*, 274.

43. First open in 1894, Hyperion was modernized and expanded in the 1990s. In 2001, the American Public Works Association named it one of the ten most outstanding public works projects of the twentieth century.

44. Aquacraft Water Engineering and Management, *California Single-Family Water Use Efficiency Study*, 260; California Building Standards Commission (CBSC) and International Association of Plumbing and Mechanical Officials (IAPMO), 2019 California Plumbing Code, California Code of Regulations, Title 24, Part 5 (Ontario, CA: IAPMO, 2019), 64. Section 419.1 of the Plumbing Code specifies that disposers must comply with standard UL 430, and ASSE 1008.

45. Since the Ocean Dumping Act prohibits dumping of the wastewater sludge into the ocean, at the Hyperion plant, sludge is transformed into biosolids and transported by road to be used as fertilizer on a city-owned farm in Kern County. Compost from single-family households can be used directly by the owner as fertilizer or collected by a service contractor to be used elsewhere.

46. CBSC and ICC, 2019 California Residential Code, 84.

47. CBSC, 2019 California Green Building Standards Code, 84.

48. CBSC and IAPMO, 2019 California Plumbing Code, Appendix L, "Sustainable Practices," 460.

49. Ibid., 58.

50. CBSC and ICC, 2019 California Residential Code, Chapter 44, "Referenced Standards," 535–54. Standards related to water closets are authored by the American Society of Mechanical Engineers, American Society of Sanitary Engineering, American Water Works Association, CSA Group, IAPMO, International Organization for Standardization, and NSF International.

51. The 2018 International Residential Code (on which the California 2019 Residential Code is based) contains the following provision: "P2725.1 General. Materials, design, construction, and performance of nonliquid saturated treatment systems shall comply with NSF 41." See the ICC website, accessed December 28, 2021, https://codes. iccsafe.org/content/IRC2018/chapter-27-plumbing-fixtures#IRC2018_Pt07_Ch27_SecP2725.

52. Only two manufacturers meet the standard as of December 28, 2021. See the NSF website, http://info.nsf.org/Certified/wastewater/Listingsasp?TradeName=&Standard=041.

53. Except for the requirements for composting toilets, WE·Stand also includes a new method for water-demand calculation, which should help reduce oversizing of plumbing. See the IAPMO website, accessed December 28, 2021, https://www.iapmo.org/we-stand/.

54. CBSC and ICC, 2019 California Residential Code, 84.

55. States adopt, amend, and repeal regulations following directives from a number of state agencies depending on the building occupancy. The main agencies that develop and propose building standards related to residential construction are the Office of the State Fire Marshal (for fire and panic safety) and the Department of Housing and Community Development (for structural, construction, mechanical, plumbing, electrical standards and green building standards). The California Energy Commission develops, proposes, and adopts standards contained in the Energy Code, which are also developed by the state. See California Building Standards Commission, 2019 Guide to Title 24, 4th ed., August 2019, 8, https://www.dgs.ca.gov/BSC/Resources/Page-Content/Building-Standards-Commission-Resources-List-Folder/Guidebooks---Title-24.

56. CBSC and IAPMO, 2019 California Plumbing Code, 48. Section 303.0, "Disposal of Liquid Waste," includes the following amendment: "Exception: [HCD 1] Limited-density owner-built rural dwellings. A water closet shall not be required when an alternate system is provided and has been approved by the local health official."

57. Federal programs such as WaterSense are directly referenced in building codes. They couple environmental regulation with incentivization of green technologies, in this case, low-flow water closets and faucets.

58. See Jean C. Buzby, Hodan F. Wells, and Jeffrey Hyman, "The Estimated Amount, Value, and Calories of Postharvest Food Losses at the Retail and Consumer Levels in the United States," U.S. Department of Agriculture, February 2014, Summary, https://www.ers.usda.gov/webdocs/publications/43833/43680_eib121.pdf. According to this report: "In the United States, 31 percent…of the available food supply at the retail and consumer levels in 2010 went uneaten. Retail-level losses represented 10 percent (43 billion pounds) and consumer-level losses 21 percent (90 billion pounds) of the available food supply." The statistics come from the website of the Water Footprint Network, accessed December 28, 2021, https://waterfootprint.org/en/resources/waterstat/product-water-footprint-statistics.

59. While everyone agrees that water should be managed more wisely, the need to do so goes beyond water security. First, importing water via open channels is wasteful, but it is also harmful for the ecosystems disrupted in the process of its extraction and transportation. Second, waterborne disposal of wastewater should be limited to minimize use of water but also to limit disruption of nutrient cycles. We mine the rock to make phosphate fertilizers and we use the energy-intensive Haber process to artificially fix nitrogen, while we release excessive amounts of both nitrogen and phosphorus to the environment by not recycling organic waste. Third, stormwater runoff should be captured to recharge aquifers but also to limit overheating and pollution of water bodies with hundreds of contaminants.

60. Herman E. Daly, *Steady-State Economics*, 2nd ed. (Washington, DC: Island Press, 1991), 89.

61. The adoption of the Ocean Dumping Act forced the Hyperion in LA to modernize: treat water before dumping it and transform sludge into biosolids. The passage of this act was triggered by an international agreement, the 1972 London Convention on the Prevention of Marine Pollution by Dumping of Wastes and Other Matter. (The stricter 1996 London Protocol, which amends the 1972 convention and prohibits all dumping by removing most of the previous exceptions, remains unratified in the United States.) See the website of the International Maritime Organization for details, accessed December 28, 2021, https://www.imo.org/en/KnowledgeCentre/IndexofIMOResolutions/Pages/LDC-LC-LP.aspx.

62. See Kate C. Shouse and Richard K. Lattanzio, *Clean Air Act: A Summary of the Act and Its Major Requirements*, CRS Report No. RL30853 (Washington, DC: Congressional Research Service, 2020), 8, https://crsreports.congress.gov/product/pdf/RL/RL30853. While the federal Air Pollution Act recognized that air (like the US waters) needed to be protected from local speculation, the issue of airborne transport of pollutants was not addressed until the 1990 amendment to the Clean Air Act of 1963. This particular amendment introduced provisions meant to protect downwind states.

63. Ibid. Some of the most important provisions gradually introduced as Clean Air Act amendments include the National Ambient Air Quality Standards for six main air pollutants (see page 3); provisions targeting mobile sources, which tightened the nexus between ambient pollution and clean-energy sources and provided federal funds for electric car incentives (see page 8); hazardous air pollutants, which addressed the importance of small but numerous "area sources," such as gas stations or dry cleaners (see page 11); pollution generated by solid-waste incinerators; prevention of significant deterioration in areas where air quality is above minimum standards (e.g., national parks); acid deposition control (see pages 13–14), which addressed acid rain and introduced the cap-and-trade method; and stratospheric ozone protection, which implements the *Montreal Protocol* (see page 16).

64. The mandatory provisions are included in Section 4.106.4, "Electric Vehicle (EV) Charging for New Construction." Additional voluntary measures can be found in Section A4.106.8, while the voluntary Section A4.106.9 regulates bicycle parking spaces. See CBSC, Green Building Standards Code, 20, 100–101.

65. The City of Los Angeles Council District, "Freeway Adjacent Advisory Notice for Sensitive Uses," Z.I. NO. 2427, November 8, 2012, https://planning.lacity.org/StaffRpt/InitialRpts/Freeway%20Adjacent%20Residential-%20ZI2427.pdf. The notice explicitly stated that it was not a moratorium on development but an instrument meant to assist developers in decision-making. It advised the applicants to: 1) install high-efficiency air filters; 2) consider building orientation, screening with vegetation, and nonresidential uses; and 3) reduce operable windows. The notice was updated in September 2018, http://zimas.lacity.org/documents/zoneinfo/ZI2427.pdf. It now contains other alternative design suggestions. For a general overview of the problem, see Tony Barboza and Jon Schleuss, "L.A. Keeps Building Near Freeways, Even Though Living There Makes People Sick," *Los Angeles Times*, March 2, 2017, http://www.latimes.com/projects/la-me-freeway-pollution.

66. While Sections 4.508 and A4.508, "Outdoor Air Quality," both part of the residential measures, remain a "reserved" placeholder, the nonresidential mandatory measures already address the issue. Sections 5.508 and A5.508 address, among other issues, ozone depletion and greenhouse gas reductions as impacted by HVAC and other types of equipment that uses chlorofluorocarbons and halons. See CBSC, 2019 California Green Building Standards Code, 32, 112, and 53, 151, respectively.

67. The EPA does not regulate indoor air quality but offers advice on how to improve it. For details, see the EPA website, accessed December 28, 2021, https://www.epa.gov/regulatory-information-topic/regulatory-information-topic-air#indoorair.

68. See Chapter 1.1, "Standardizing Human Welfare: Before the 1920s," of this book.

69. See Chapter 2.2, "Aligning Sustainability with Global Economic Expansion: 1980s," of this book.

70. Ulrich Beck, *Ecological Enlightenment* (Amherst, NY: Prometheus Books, 1995), 60.

71. CBSC and ICC, 2019 California Residential Code, 565. The Residential Code contains Appendix F, "Radon Control Methods," but it has not been adopted by California.

72. This is until a federal law is enacted, and depending on its nature, states are either forced, or encouraged with financial incentives, to adjust their regulations accordingly.

73. An expression used by Eran Ben-Joseph in *The Code of the City: Standards and the Hidden Language of Place Making* (Cambridge, MA: MIT Press, 2005), 168.

74. This and many other aspects of land-use control and environmental protection are considered examples of "police powers"—powers, as suggested in the Tenth Amendment to the U.S. Constitution, reserved to the states.

75. CBSC and ICC, 2019 California Residential Code, 82.

76. Unless one happens to live within one thousand feet of a freeway.

77. CBSC and ICC, 2019 California Residential Code, 83.

78. California Building Standards Commission (CBSC) and International Association of Plumbing and Mechanical Officials (IAPMO), 2019 California Mechanical Code, California Code of Regulations, Title 24, Part 4 (Ontario, CA: IAPMO, 2019), 63.

79. CBSC and ICC, 2019 California Residential Code, 83. See Section R303.10, "Required Heating."

80. CBSC and ICC, 2019 California Residential Code, 43.

81. Ibid., 83. ANSI/ASHRAE Standard 62.2 Ventilation and Acceptable Indoor Air Quality in Residential Buildings is referenced in Section 402.1.2, "Dwelling." Those are then listed in Table 402.1, "Minimum Ventilation Rates in Breathing Zone." In residential construction, the two important parameters are: People Outdoor [ventilation] Air Rate—5 cfm/person per dwelling Unit; and Area Outdoor [ventilation] Air Rate—0.06 cfm/ft 2 for each occupant. CBSC and IAPMO, 2019 California Mechanical Code, 63, 80.

82. CBSC and IAPMO, 2019 California Mechanical Code, 38. The definition is as follows: "Natural Ventilation. Ventilation provided by thermal, wind, or diffusion effects through doors, windows, or other intentional openings in the building. [ASHRAE 62.1:3]."

83. CBSC and IAPMO, 2019 California Mechanical Code, 63.

84. In part, what precludes the entire set of codes from being a fully hyperlinked text available online is the fact that it references model codes. Although the model code enters the public domain when it is incorporated into the state code, the online access to each part depends on the publisher.

85. CBSC, 2019 California Energy Code, 47.

86. Ibid., 143–44.

87. Ibid., 145.

88. CBSC and ICC, 2019 California Residential Code, 137.

89. CBSC, 2019 California Green Building Standards Code, 29.

90. Ibid., 111. Ways to reduce VOC emissions from insulation materials are suggested in Section A4.504.3, "Thermal Insulation."

91. Ibid., 30. The VOC limits imposed by the California Air Resources Board are listed in Tables 4.504.1–3.

92. CBSC, 2019 California Green Building Standards Code, 32. Appendix E, "Sustainable Practices" contained in the Mechanical Code (see page 365) is not adopted by California, most likely because its objectives overlap with those included in the CALGreen code. Other numerous sections, for example, 311.0, "Heating Or Cooling Air System" (see page 53), could be simply amended by the state authorities to include the provision listed in the CALGreen Code. Yet sections such as 402.5, "Bathroom Exhaust," are added to the Mechanical Code by California agencies specifically to refer back to the CALGreen Code (see page 64).

93. CBSC, 2019 California Green Building Standards Code, 31.

94. CBSC and ICC, 2019 California Residential Code, 189, 229. Wood framing in floors and walls is addressed in Section R502 and R602, respectively. Both Section R502.1.1 and R602.1.1, "Sawn Lumber," address lumber grading. One of the designations stamped on lumber is "KD," which stands for "kiln dry." It indicates that lumber was dried in a heated kiln to a moisture content less than 19

percent. Specifying the grade in this section would make the provision currently included in the CALGreen Code unnecessary.

95. Stefan Timmermans and Steven Epstein, "A World of Standards but Not a Standard World: Toward a Sociology of Standards and Standardization," *Annual Review of Sociobiology* 36 (2010): 82. Timmermans and Epstein discuss the signaling function of standards on the example of ISO 9000. They point out that many companies obtain the certificate for marketing reasons without actually changing their approach to quality management.

96. William C. Baer, "Customs, Norms, Rules, Regulations and Standards in Design Practice," in *Companion to Urban Design*, ed. Tridib Banerjee and Anastasia Loukaitou-Sideris (New York: Routledge, 2011), 277–78.

97. For example, "405.3 Miscellaneous Fixtures…No dry or chemical closet (toilet) shall be installed in a building used for human habitation, unless first approved by the Health Officer." The following section provides an example of another prohibitive, although more flexible proscription: "411.2 Water consumption. The effective flush volume of all water closets shall not exceed 1.28 gallons (4.8 L) per flush." CBSC and IAPMO, 2019 California Plumbing Code, 58, 62. The section provides an example of a positive prescription: "411.2.3 Performance [HCD 1 & HCD 2]. Water closets installed in residential occupancies shall meet or exceed the minimum performance criteria developed for certification of high-efficiency toilets under the WaterSense program." CBSC and IAPMO, Plumbing Code, 62. While this prescriptive regulation is expressed in positive terms, its ultimate meaning is similar to the one cited in the above note. The former prohibits performance below a precise numeric value; the latter prescribes a standard.

98. CBSC, 2019 California Green Building Standards Code, 111.

99. A certain degree of freedom is inscribed into the previously cited Section R316.4, "Thermal Barrier." While it refers to a specific standard of performance, the expression "or a material that is tested in accordance with and meets the acceptance criteria of" leaves some space for innovation and allows for use of new materials. CBSC, 2019 California Energy Code, 153. A performance-oriented approach is defined in Section 150.1, "Performance and Prescriptive Compliance Approaches for Low-Rise Residential Building"; under b) "Performance Standards," one reads: "A building complies

with the performance standards if the energy consumption calculated for the proposed design building is no greater than the energy budget calculated for the standard design building using Commission-certified compliance software as specified by the Alternative Calculation Methods Approval Manual."

100. California Energy Commission (CEC), 2019 Residential Alternative Calculation Method (ACM) Reference Manual for the 2019 Building Energy Efficiency Standards (May 2019), 1, https://www.energy.ca.gov/sites/default/files/2020-10/2019%20Residential%20ACM%20Reference%20Manual_ada.pdf. The Energy Code relies on a number of additional manuals. The Residential ACM Reference Manual "establishes the rules for creating a building model, describing how the proposed design (energy use) is defined, how the standard design (energy budget) is established, and ending with what is reported on the Certificate of Compliance (CF1R)." Other sources include the 2019 Reference Appendices for the 2019 Building Energy Efficiency Standards, the 2019 Residential Compliance Manual, and the 2019 California Building Energy Code Compliance User Manual, which provides guidelines for software users.

101. California Energy Commission (CEC), 2019 Residential Compliance Manual for the 2019 Building Energy Efficiency Standards (Sacramento, CA: CEC, December 2018), 3–25, https://www.energy.ca.gov/sites/default/files/2021-07/2019_Residential_Compliance_Manual-Complete_without_forms_ada.pdf.

102. CEC, 2019 Residential Compliance Manual, 3–22. The rest of the building code either does not mention vegetation or mentions it to prevent damage from it. In Residential Code, Section R337, "Materials and Construction Methods for Exterior Wildfire Exposure" (see page 128) protects from "vegetation fire"; in Section R408.5, "Removal of Debris" (see page 185), plants are referred to as litter.

103. CEC, 2019 Residential Compliance Manual, 3–23.

104. CBSC, 2019 California Green Building Standards Code, 131. Vegetation as a shading device is mentioned as a voluntary nonresidential measure in Section A5.106.7, "Exterior Wall Shading." It suggests that in the future vegetation might become a shading option. It simply needs to be standardized first.

105. CBSC, 2019 California Energy Code, 47.

106. CEC, 2019 Residential ACM Reference Manual, 21.

107. CEC, 2019 Residential ACM Reference Manual, 14.

108. CEC, 2019 Residential Compliance Manual, 4–74.

109. CBSC and ICC, 2019 California Residential Code, 83.

110. CEC, 2019 Residential Compliance Manual, 4–110. See Section 4.6.8.9, "Air Inlets."

111. CBSC, 2019 California Energy Code, 145.

112. See Robert M. Carver, Jianshun (Jensen) S. Zhang, and Zhiqiang Wang, *Air Cleaning Technologies for Indoor Air Quality (ACT-IAQ): Growing Fresh and Clean Air*, Report 11-10 (New York: New York State Energy Research and Development Authority, 2010). This NASA-developed system uses Golden Pothos and root microbes in an irrigated bed of activated carbon and shale pebbles and is fitted with an induction fan.

113. CBSC, 2019 California Energy Code, 146. See Section 150.0 (m) 12E, "Air Filter Product Labeling."

114. CBSC and IAPMO, Plumbing Code, 41.

115. California Code of Regulations, Title 23, Appendix D, "Prescriptive Compliance Option." See University of California Cooperative Extension California Department of Water Resources, "A Guide to Estimating Irrigation Water Needs of Landscape Plantings in California: The Landscape Coefficient Method and WUCOLS III," August 2000, https://cimis.water.ca.gov/Content/PDF/wucols00.pdf.

116. CBSC and IAPMO, 2019 California Plumbing Code, 427. See Appendix H, "Private Sewage Disposal Systems."

117. Ibid., 429–30.

118. "Aerobic Treatment Units: An Alternative to Septic Systems," West Virginia University National Environmental Services Center website, *Pipeline* 16, no. 3 (2005), https://www.nesc.wvu.edu/files/d/2a62a149-f578-4509-ad97-fdf32d2c0101/pl_summer05.pdf. The article reports that two-thirds of all the land area in the US is not suitable for septic systems due to the lot size, soil conditions, high water table, or proximity to a body of water.

119. For example, in the Omega Center Eco-Machine, Rhinebeck, NY, "treatment is accomplished through a combination of septic and equalization tanks and anoxic tanks, aerated aquatic cells, outdoor wetland and a recirculating sand filter." For details, see the John Todd Ecological Design website, accessed December 28, 2021, https://www.toddecological.com/projects.

120. The Arcata Wastewater Treatment Plant and Wildlife Sanctuary, located in Northern California, combines conventional wastewater treatment with the natural processes of constructed wetlands and serves a city of approximately eighteen thousand inhabitants.

121. Ben-Joseph, *The Code of the City*, 96–97. This was the case with a project built in South Burlington, VT, in 1995. The system was funded and tested by the EPA, but although the results met the federal standards, the agency and the municipal authorities insisted the cleaned water be sent back to the local treatment facility to avoid liability.

122. Ibid., 91.

123. While vegetation is still not standardized enough in terms of building performance, it is highly controlled in other fields—turf grasses and most agricultural products have been engineered for decades. Possibly, organic systems will be accepted by the building industry only when it becomes possible to represent them as CAD blocks and therefore integrate them into the BIM system. They will be integral to the project once the process of their scientific management is complete all the way through to representation.

124. CBSC, 2019 California Green Building Standards Code, 99.

125. See Chapter 2.2, "Aligning Sustainability with Global Economic Expansion: 1980s," of this book.

CHAPTER SIX

1. Straw-bale construction, originating in the late 1800s in Nebraska and reborn in the 1980s in the American Southwest, uses blocks of baled straw, stacked and plastered to create highly insulating walls. Straw-bale buildings now exist in all fifty US states and in more than fifty countries worldwide.

2. Appendix S was relabeled in the 2021 edition of the International Residential Code (IRC) and is now called Appendix AS – Strawbale Construction.

3. The 1995 Assembly Bill 1314 authorized all California jurisdictions to adopt building codes for houses whose walls are constructed of straw bales. See CA Health and Safety Code § 18944.30, 2020, for the current "Guidelines for Straw-Bale Structures."

4. Bruce King is the founder/director of the Ecological Building Network (EBNet) and primary author of *Design of Straw Bale Buildings: The State of the Art* (San Rafael, CA: Green Building Press, 2006). He was the co-organizer (with Ann Edminster) of the First International Straw Building Conference held by the California Straw Building Association in Marin County, CA, in 1999.

5. The Uniform Building Code (UBC) was developed and published by the International Conference of Building Officials between 1927 and 1997. In 2000, as discussed in Chapter 3.1, "Greening the Markets: 1990s–mid-2000s," of this book, the UBC and two other regional model-building codes were replaced by the International Code Council's International Building Code. The NFPA 5000, Building Construction and Safety Code, on the other hand, was developed and published by the National Fire Protection Association.

6. Forty-nine of the fifty US states use the IRC as the basis for their residential code, whereas only one in three states have adopted the International Green Construction Code (IgCC).

7. Labor costs are the inverse in developing countries, accounting for one-third or less of construction costs. So while low material and high labor costs can be a disadvantage in industrialized countries, they are an advantage in developing countries.

8. For more information about ModCell prefabricated panels, see the company website, accessed December 28, 2021, https://www.modcell.co.uk/.

9. This residential building is located in Saint-Dié-des-Vosges, France. It was designed by Antoine Pagnaux and completed in 2013.

10. See Chris Magwood, *Essential Prefab Straw Bale Construction: The Complete Step-by-Step Guide* (Gabriola Island, BC: New Society Publishers, 2016).

11. Stak Block was developed by Oryzatech, Inc., founded by Ben Korman and Jay Ruskey and based in Goleta, CA. The company has granted and pending patents on the manufacturing process, but the project has been stalled since 2009 due to insufficient funding.

12. For more information about Recode and its activities, visit its website, accessed December 28, 2021, https://www.recode now.org/.

13. The Oregon Reach code is based on the IgCC, but the provision on composting toilets was added by the state, so it was only available in Oregon as a local amendment. International Association of Plumbing and Mechanical Officials standards and supplements can be adopted by any state.

14. See Franziska Meinzinger and Martin Oldenburg, "Characteristics of Source-Separated Household Wastewater Flows: A Statistical Assessment," *Water Science & Technology* 59, no. 9 (February 2009): 1785–91. The authors state that urine contains 87 percent of the nitrogen and 66 percent of the phosphorus found in human waste. See World Health Organization, *WHO Guidelines for the Safe Use of Wastewater, Excreta and Greywater*, vol. IV, *Excreta and Greywater Use in Agriculture*, specifically section 3.2.2, "Pathogens in Urine" (Geneva: World Health Organization, 2006), 34–36, https://apps.who.int/iris/handle/10665/78265.

15. U.S. Environmental Protection Agency, "Onsite Wastewater Treatment Systems Manual," EPA/625/R-00/008 (Washington, DC: U.S. EPA, 2002), 1-4-1-5.

16. See Robert S. Amick and Edward H. Burgess, "Exfiltration in Sewer Systems," EPA/600/R-01/034 (Cincinnati: U.S. EPA, 2000), 18–20.

17. See Rick Abbott, "Skaneateles Lake Watershed Composting Toilet Project," *Small Flows Quarterly* 5, no. 2 (Spring 2004).

18. See Julia Cavicchi, "Launching the Gold Ribbon Commission," Rich Earth Institute website, September 25, 2020, accessed December 28, 2021, https://richearthinstitute.org/launching-the-gold-ribbon-commission/.

19. See Chapter 5.2, "Where Are the Rule Makers? Focus: Water," of this book, specifically the section dedicated to sanitary sewage.

20. The Envirolet®/Santerra Green Composting Toilet is equipped with such a soil-collecting tray.

21. ENVI-met V5 was released on November 1, 2021. For more information, see the ENVI_MET website, accessed Decemeber 28, 2021, https://www.envi-met.com/.

22. Crassulacean acid metabolism is a carbon-fixation pathway that allows a plant to photosynthesize during the day but only exchange gases at night to reduce water loss. It is a form of adaptation to arid conditions.

23. David E. Benner's work is featured in *Made in the Shade*, directed by Richard T. Slade (Silver Spring, MD: Audio Visual Artists' Productions, 2007).

24. See, for example, Yanbin Jiang, Miao Fan, Ronggui Hu, Jinsong Zhao, and Yupeng Wu, "Mosses Are Better than Leaves of Vascular Plants in Monitoring Atmospheric Heavy Metal Pollution in Urban Areas," *International Journal of Environmental Research and Public Health* 15 (6), no. 1105 (May 2018).

25. See Chapter 5.4, "What About Agency? Focus: Vegetation," of this book, specifically the section dedicated to phyto-wastewater purification, for a brief mention of the

Water Use Classifications of Landscape Species system.

26. The secondary compound produced by *Spagnum* mosses in response to external pressures is the phenolic compound.

27. According to the company website, Green City Solutions mosses "can filter up to 82 percent of the fine dust from the air flowing through it. This leads to a fine dust reduction of 53 percent at a distance of one and a half meters." For more information, see the company website, accessed December 28, 2021, https://greencitysolutions.de/en/solution/#.

28. Sophia Elena BenJeddi, "The Effects of Native Mosses on Indoor PM 2.5 and Humidity" (BSc diss., Columbia University, 2021). As the author explains,

> This study examines the effects native mosses *Hypnum cupressiforme*, *Pleurozium schreberi*, *Climacium americanum*, and *Plagiomnium cuspidatum* have on fine particulate matter $PM_{2.5}$ and humidity… The results demonstrate that fine particulate $PM_{2.5}$ concentrations decayed at a greater rate in chambers containing moss than control chambers. While both *P. schreberi* and *H. cupressiforme* are frequently used in bioremediation studies, *P. schreberi* demonstrated faster characteristic $PM_{2.5}$ decay times than *H. cupressiforme* at 13 mins, while the control chamber had a characteristic decay time of 44 mins. In contrast, *H. cupressiforme* had a characteristic time of decay of 20 mins. *P. schreberi* also had the largest cell widths (6–8µm) and highest cell surface area (732µm$_2$) out of all four species, which could account for its high decay time. Humidity levels in the control chambers also decreased across all six experiments, while average humidity tended to increase in the experimental chambers containing panels of moss. Temperature had an overall cooling effect inside chambers containing moss.

29. Minimum Efficiency Reporting Value is a measurement scale designed in 1987 by the American Society of Heating, Refrigerating and Air-Conditioning Engineers. See Chapter 5.4, "What About Agency? Focus: Vegetation," of this book, specifically the section on air purification, for a brief mention of the use of the MERV system in the building code.

CONCLUSION

1. Gregory Bateson, *Steps to an Ecology of Mind* (Chicago: University of Chicago Press, 2000), 489.

2. C. H. Waddington, *Tools for Thought* (London: Jonathan Cape, 1977).

3. Ibid., 106.

4. Quoted in John Frazer, "Computing without Computers," in "The 1970s Is Here and Now," ed. Samantha Hardingham, *Architectural Design* 75 (April 2005): 43.

5. Among recent scholarship that follows in Howard T. Odum's footsteps and addresses energy systems in architecture, one should mention William W. Braham, *Architecture and Systems Ecology: Thermodynamic Principles of Environmental Building Design in Three Parts* (New York: Routledge, 2016); and Ravi Srinivasan and Kiel Moe, *The Hierarchy of Energy in Architecture: Emergy Analysis* (New York: Routledge, 2015). The 2019 CALGreen Code, on the other hand, contains Division 4.4, "Material Conservation and Resource Efficiency," which lists voluntary measures meant to reduce material use and increase recycling. See California Building Standards Commission, 2019 California Green Building Standards Code, California Code of Regulations, Title 24, Part 11 (Washington, DC: International Code Council, 2019), 107-10.

6. Daniel M. Abramson's book *Obsolescence: An Architectural History* (Chicago: University of Chicago Press, 2017) tackles this issue, also in relation to sustainability, but without addressing the role of building regulations.

7. See Chapter 4.4, "Artifacts Versus Plants. Paradoxes," of this book.

8. Waddington, *Tools for Thought*, 23.

9. See George Parkin Grant, "Thinking about Technology," in *Technology and Justice* (Toronto: Anansi, 1986), 32; and Chapter 4.4, "Artifacts Versus Plants. Paradoxes," of this book.

10. Georges Canguilhem, *A Vital Rationalist: Selected Writings*, ed. Francois Delaporte (New York: Zone Books, 1994), 373.

11. Giorgio Agamben, *State of Exception* (Chicago: University of Chicago Press, 2005).

12. Max Weber, *The Protestant Ethic and the Spirit of Capitalism* (New York: Routledge, 2005).

13. Ibid., 4; see Michel Foucault, *Discipline and Punish: The Birth of the Prison* (New York: Vintage Books, 1995).

14. See Michael Hardt and Antonio Negri, *Empire* (Cambridge, MA: Harvard University Press, 2000), 360. See also page 198 of *Empire*. The authors observe, "Each imperial action is a rebound of the resistance of the multitude that poses a new obstacle for the multitude to overcome."

15. Félix Guattari, *The Three Ecologies* (London: Athlone Press, 2000).

16. Ibid., 27. For the original text, see Bateson, *Steps to an Ecology of Mind*, 492.

17. See Félix Guattari, *Molecular Revolution: Psychiatry and Politics* (New York: Penguin, 1984), 288. This is how Guattari defines the term *over-encoding* in the Glossary: "The idea of code is used in a very wide meaning. It could apply to semiotic systems as well as to social fluxes and material fluxes…The term of over-encoding corresponds to a coding at the second degree. For example: primitive territorialized agrarian societies functioning according to their own system of coding are over-encoded by a relatively de-territorialized imperial system imposing on them its military, religious, fiscal hegemony etc."

18. Hardt and Negri, *Empire*, 270-72. The authors attribute this statement to political activist Rosa Luxemburg.

19. Bateson, *Steps to an Ecology of Mind*, 484-85. Bateson made this statement in 1966 while discussing use of game theory in international policy making.

SELECTED BIBLIOGRAPHY

BOOKS, ESSAYS, PAPERS, AND ENVIRONMENTAL REPORTS
—

Ábalos, Iñaki. *The Good Life: A Guided Visit to the Houses of Modernity*. Barcelona: Editorial Gustavo Gili, 2001.

Agamben, Giorgio. "What Is an Apparatus?" In *What Is an Apparatus? and Other Essays*. Stanford, CA: Stanford University Press, 2009.

Anielski, Mark. *The Economics of Happiness*. Gabriola Island, BC: New Society Publisher, 2007.

Baer, William C. "Customs, Norms, Rules, Regulations and Standards in Design Practice." In *Companion to Urban Design*, edited by Tridib Banerjee and Anastasia Loukaitou-Sideris. New York: Routledge, 2011.

Banham, Reyner. *The Architecture of the Well-Tempered Environment*. 2nd ed. Chicago: University of Chicago Press, 1984.

———. "A Home Is Not a House." *Art in America* 2 (1965): 70–79.

Bateson, Gregory. *Steps to an Ecology of Mind*. Chicago: University of Chicago Press, 2000.

Beck, Ulrich. *Risk Society*. London: SAGE Publications, 1992.

———. *World at Risk*. Cambridge: Polity Press, 2009.

Ben-Joseph, Eran. *The Code of the City: Standards and the Hidden Language of Place Making*. Cambridge, MA: MIT Press, 2005.

Bijker, Wiebe E., Thomas P. Hughes, and Trevor J. Pinch, eds. *The Social Construction of Technological Systems*. Cambridge, MA: MIT Press, 1987.

Canguilhem, Georges. *A Vital Rationalist: Selected Writings*, edited by Francois Delaporte. New York: Zone Books, 1994.

Caradonna, Jeremy L. *Sustainability: A History*. New York: Oxford University Press, 2014.

Carson, Rachel. *Silent Spring*. Boston: Houghton Mifflin, 1962.

Chang, Ha-Joon. *23 Things They Don't Tell You about Capitalism*. London: Penguin Books, 2010.

Circo, Carl. "Using Mandates and Incentives to Promote Sustainable Construction and Green Building Projects in the Private Sector: A Call for More State Land Use Policy Initiatives." *Penn State Law Review* 112, no. 3 (2008): 731–82.

Crist, Eileen. "Beyond the Climate Crisis: A Critique of Climate Change Discourse." *Telos* 141 (Winter 2007): 29–55.

Daly, Herman E. *Beyond Growth: The Economics of Sustainable Development*. Boston: Beacon Press, 1996.

———. *Steady-State Economics*. 2nd ed. Washington, DC: Island Press, 1991.

Daniels, Thomas L. "A Trail Across Time: American Environmental Planning from City Beautiful to Sustainability." *Journal of the American Planning Association* 75, no. 2 (Spring 2009): 178–92.

Earth Charter Commission. *The Earth Charter*. Paris: Earth Charter Commission, 2000. https://earthcharter.org/wp-content/uploads/2020/03/echarter_english.pdf?x10401.

Easterling, Keller. *Organization Space: Landscapes, Highways, and Houses in America*. Cambridge, MA: MIT Press, 1999.

Eichler, Ned. *The Merchant Builders*. Cambridge, MA: MIT Press, 1982.

Ellul, Jacques. *The Technological Society*. New York: Vintage Books, 1964.

Foucault, Michel. *Discipline and Punish: The Birth of the Prison*. New York: Vintage Books, 1995.

Frampton, Kenneth. *American Masterworks: Houses of the 20th and 21st Centuries*. Rev. ed. New York: Rizzoli, 2008.

Gorz, André. *Ecology as Politics*. Boston: South End Press, 1980.

———. "Thinking about Technology." In *Technology and Justice*. Toronto: Anansi, 1986.

Grober, Ulrich. *Sustainability: A Cultural History*. Devon: Green Books, 2012.

Guattari, Félix. *Molecular Revolution: Psychiatry and Politics*. New York: Penguin, 1984.

———. *The Three Ecologies*. London: Athlone Press, 2000.

Hardt, Michael, and Antoni Negri. *Empire*. Cambridge, MA: Harvard University Press, 2000.

Heinberg, Richard. *The End of Growth: Adapting to Our New Economic Reality*. Gabriola Island, BC: New Society Publisher, 2011.

Hight, Christopher. "Designing Ecologies." In *Projective Ecologies*, edited by Chris Reed and Nina-Marie E. Lister. Cambridge, MA: Harvard Graduate School of Design; Actar, 2014.

Hise, Greg. *Magnetic Los Angeles: Planning the Twentieth-Century Metropolis*. Baltimore, MD: Johns Hopkins University Press, 1997.

Hughes, Thomas. "Technological Momentum." In *Does Technology Drive History?*, edited by Merritt Roe Smith and Leo Marx. Cambridge, MA: MIT Press, 1994.

Illich, Ivan. *Tools for Conviviality*. New York: Harper and Row, 1973.

Immergluck, Dan. *Foreclosed: High-Risk Lending, Deregulation, and the Undermining of America's Mortgage Market*. Ithaca, NY: Cornell University Press, 2009.

Independent Commission on International Development. *North-South: A Program for Survival*. Cambridge, MA: MIT Press, 1980.

International Union for Conservation of Nature (IUCN). *World Conservation Strategy*. Gland: IUCN, 1980. https://portals.iucn.org/library/efiles/documents/wcs-004.pdf.

Jackson, Tim. *Prosperity without Growth*. 2nd ed. New York: Routledge, 2016.

Jacobs, Jane. "The Kind of Problem a City Is." In *The Death and Life of Great American Cities*, 428–48. New York: Vintage Books, 1992.

Klein, Naomi. *This Changes Everything: Capitalism vs. the Climate*. New York: Simon & Schuster, 2015.

Knowles, Ralph. *Energy and Form: An Ecological Approach to Urban Growth*. Cambridge, MA: MIT Press, 1974.

———. "The Solar Envelope: Its Meaning for Energy and Buildings." *Energy and Buildings* 35 (2003): 15–25.

Leopold, Aldo. *A Sand County Almanac, and Sketches Here and There*. New York: Oxford University Press, 1989.

MacKenzie, Donald, and Judy Wajcman, eds. *The Social Shaping of Technology*. Philadelphia: Open University Press, 1999.

Massey, Jonathan. "Risk and Regulation in the Financial Architecture of American Houses." In *Governing by Design: Architecture, Economy, and Politics in the Twentieth Century*, edited by Timothy Hyde and Aggregate Group. Pittsburgh: University of Pittsburgh Press, 2012. http://muse.jhu.edu.ezp-prod1.hul.harvard.edu/books/9780822977896/.

McKenzie, Evan. *Privatopia: Homeowner Associations and the Rise of Residential Private Government*. New Haven, CT: Yale University Press, 1994.

Meadows, Dennis, Donella Meadows, Jørgen Randers, and William W. Behrens III. *The Limits to Growth: A Report of Rome's Project on the Predicament of Mankind*. New York: Universe Books, 1972.

Mishan, Ezra J. *The Costs of Economic Growth*. London: Penguin Books, 1969.

Moore, Steven A., and Barbara B. Wilson. *Questioning Architectural Judgment: The Problem of Codes in the United States*. New York: Routledge, 2014.

Mumford, Lewis. "Authoritarian and Democratic Technics." *Technology and Culture* 5, no. 1 (Winter 1964): 1–8.

———. *The Pentagon of Power: The Myth of the Machine*, vol. 2. New York: A Harvest/HBJ Book, Harcourt Brace Jovanovich, 1970.

———. *Technics and Civilization*. Chicago: University of Chicago Press, 2010.

Odum, Howard T. "Energy, Ecology and Economics." *AMBIO: A Journal of the Human Environment* 2, no. 6 (1973): 220–27.

———. *Environment, Power, and Society*. New York: John Wiley & Sons, 1971.

Pearce, David. "Green Economics." *Environmental Values* 1 (1992): 3–13.

Pearce, David, Anil Markandya, and Edward Barbier. *Blueprint for a Green Economy*. London: Earthscan Publications, 1989.

Perrow, Charles. *Normal Accidents: Living with High-Risk Technologies*. Princeton, NJ: Princeton University Press, 1984.

Pfaffenberger, Bryan. "Technological Dramas." *Science, Technology, & Human Values* 17, no. 3 (Summer 1992): 282–312.

Quilligan, James Bernard. *The Brandt Equation: 21st Century Blueprint for the New Global Economy*. Philadelphia: Brandt 21 Forum, 2002. http://www.brandt21forum.info/brandtequation-19sept04.pdf.

Rittel, Horst W. J., and Melvin M. Webber. "Dilemmas in a General Theory of Planning." *Policy Sciences* 4, no. 2 (June 1973): 155–69.

Rybczynski, Witold. *Home: A Short History of an Idea*. New York: Penguin Books, 1987.

———. *Paper Heroes: Appropriate Technology: Panacea or Pipe Dream?* New York: Penguin Books, 1991.

Schumacher, E. F. *Small Is Beautiful, Economics as if People Mattered*. New York: Harper & Row, 1975.

Simon, Herbert A. *The Science of the Artificial*. Cambridge, MA: MIT Press, 1996.

Timmermans, Stefan, and Steven Epstein. "A World of Standards but Not a Standard World: Toward a Sociology of Standards and Standardization." *Annual Review of Sociobiology* 36 (2010): 69–89.

United Nations. *Report of the United Nations Conference on the Human Environment, Stockholm, 5–16 June 1972.* A/CONF.48/14/REV.1. New York: United Nations, 1973. https://www.un.org/ga/search/view_doc.asp?symbol=A/CONF.48/14/REV.1.

United Nations Conference on Environment and Development. *Agenda 21: Earth Summit: The United Nations Programme of Action from Rio.* Rio de Janeiro: UNCED, 1992. https://sustainabledevelopment.un.org/content/documents/Agenda21.pdf.

United Nations World Commission on Environment and Development (UNCED). *Report of the World Commission on Environment and Development: Our Common Future.* Oxford: Oxford University Press, 1987.

Victor, Peter. *Managing without Growth: Slower by Design, Not Disaster*. Northampton, MA: Edward Elgar Publishing, 2008.

Wackernagel, Mathis, and William Rees. *Our Ecological Footprint: Reducing Human Impact on the Earth*. Gabriola Island, BC: New Society Publisher, 1996.

Waddington, C. H. *Tools for Thought*. London: Jonathan Cape, 1977.

Waldie, D. J. *Holy Land: A Suburban Memoir*. New York: W. W. Norton, 1996.

Weber, Max. *The Protestant Ethic and the Spirit of Capitalism*. New York: Routledge, 2005.

Weiss, Marc A. *The Rise of the Community Builders: The American Real Estate Industry and Urban Land Planning*. New York: Columbia University Press, 1987.

Whitehead, Alfred North. *Science of the Modern World*. New York: Free Press, 1997.

Winner, Langdon. *Autonomous Technology: Technics-out-of-Control as a Theme in Political Thought*. Cambridge, MA: MIT Press, 1977.

Worster, Donald. *Nature's Economy: A History of Ecological Ideas*. 2nd ed. Cambridge: Cambridge University Press, 1996.

LEGISLATIVE REPORTS
—

Alliance Commission on National Energy Efficiency Policy. *The History of Energy Productivity*. January 2013. https://www.ase.org/sites/ase.org/files/resources/Media%20browser/ee_commission_history_report_2-1-13.pdf.

Alliance for Water Efficiency (AWE). *The Status of Legislation, Regulation, Codes & Standards on Indoor Plumbing Water Efficiency*. Chicago: AWE, January 2016. https://www.allianceforwaterefficiency.org/sites/www.allianceforwaterefficiency.org/files/highlight_documents/AWE_White-Paper-on-Water-Efficiency_01-2016.pdf.

Congressional Research Service (CRS). *A Chronology of Housing Legislation and Selected Executive Actions, 1892–2003*. Washington, DC: CRS, 2004. https://www.govinfo.gov/content/pkg/CPRT-108HPRT92629/pdf/CPRT-108HPRT92629.pdf.

Copeland, Claudia. *Clean Water Act: A Summary of the Law*. CRS Report No. RL30030. Washington, DC: Congressional Research Service, 2016. https://crsreports.congress.gov/product/pdf/RL/RL30030.

County of Los Angeles Department of Public Works (LACDPW). *Water Resilience Plan: Rapid Assessment*. Alhambra, CA: LACDPW, 2017. https://dpw.lacounty.gov/wrp/docs/Rapid-Needs-Assessment.pdf.

Crandall-Hollick, Margot L., and Molly F. Sherlock. *Residential Energy Tax Credits: Overview and Analysis*. Congressional Research Service (CRS) Report No. R42089. Washington, DC: CRS, 2018. https://fas.org/sgp/crs/misc/R42089.pdf.

Cunningham, Lynn J. *Renewable Energy and Energy Efficiency Incentives: A Summary of Federal Programs*. Congressional Research Service (CRS) Report No. R40913. Washington, DC: CRS, 2021. https://crsreports.congress.gov/product/pdf/R/R40913.

Kubert Charles, and Mark Sinclair. *State Support for Clean Energy Deployment: Lessons Learned for Potential Future Policy*. Golden, CO: National Renewable Energy Laboratory, 2011. http://www.nrel.gov/docs/fy11osti/49340.pdf.

Nadel, Steven. *Energy Efficiency Tax Incentives in the Context of Tax Reform*. American Council for an Energy-Efficient Economy website, July 16, 2012. https://www.aceee.org/content/energy-efficiency-tax-incentives-context-tax-reform.

National Institute of Building Sciences (NIBS). *Part 1 of a Study of the HUD Minimum Property Standards for One-and Two-Family Dwellings and Technical Suitability of Products Programs*. Washington, DC: NIBS, 2003. https://www.huduser.gov/Publications/pdf/mps_report.pdf.

Schierow, Linda-Jo, and David M. Bearden. *Federal Programs Related to Indoor Pollution by Chemicals*. Congressional Research Service (CRS) Report No. RL42620. Washington, DC: CRS, 2012. https://fas.org/sgp/crs/misc/R42620.pdf.

Sherlock, Molly F. *Energy Tax Policy: Historical Perspectives on and Current Status of Energy Tax Expenditures*. Congressional Research Service (CRS) Report No. R41227. Washington, DC: CRS, 2011. https://crsreports.congress.gov/product/pdf/R/R41227.

Shouse, Kate C., and Richard K. Lattanzio. *Clean Air Act: A Summary of the Act and Its Major Requirements.* Congressional Research Service (CRS) Report No. RL30853. Washington, DC: CRS, 2020. https://crsreports.congress.gov/product/pdf/RL/RL30853.

CODES, STANDARDS, AND ASSOCIATED MANUALS
—

California Building Standards Commission. 2019 California Energy Code. California Code of Regulations, Title 24, Part 6. Washington, DC: International Code Council, 2019.

California Building Standards Commission. 2019 California Green Building Standards Code. California Code of Regulations, Title 24, Part 11. Washington, DC: International Code Council, 2019.

California Building Standards Commission and International Association of Plumbing and Mechanical Officials (IAPMO). 2019 California Mechanical Code. California Code of Regulations, Title 24, Part 4. Ontario, CA: IAPMO, 2019.

California Building Standards Commission and International Association of Plumbing and Mechanical Officials (IAPMO). 2019 California Plumbing Code. California Code of Regulations, Title 24, Part 5. Ontario, CA: IAPMO, 2019.

California Building Standards Commission and International Code Council (ICC). 2019 California Residential Code. California Code of Regulations, Title 24, Part 2.5. Washington, DC: ICC, 2019.

California Energy Commission (CEC). 2019 Reference Appendices for the 2019 Building Energy Efficiency Standards. Sacramento, CA: CEC, December 2018. https://www.energy.ca.gov/sites/default/files/2021-06/CEC-400-2018-021-CMF.pdf.

California Energy Commission (CEC). 2019 Residential Alternative Calculation Method Reference Manual for the 2019 Building Energy Efficiency Standards. Sacramento, CA: CEC, May 2019. https://www.energy.ca.gov/sites/default/files/2020-10/2019%20Residential%20ACM%20Reference%20Manual_ada.pdf.

California Energy Commission (CEC). 2019 Residential Compliance Manual for the 2019 Building Energy Efficiency Standards. Sacramento, CA: CEC, December 2018. https://www.energy.ca.gov/sites/default/files/2021-07/2019_Residential_Compliance_Manual-Complete_without_forms_ada.pdf.

City of Los Angeles Department of Water and Power (LADWP). Stormwater Capture Master Plan. Los Angeles: LADWP, 2015. https://www.ladwp.com/cs/idcplg?IdcService=GET_FILE&dDocName=O PLADWPCCB421767&RevisionSelectionMethod=LatestReleased.

City of Los Angeles Department of Water and Power (LADWP). Urban Water Management Plan. Los Angeles: LADWP, 2015. https://www.ladwp.com/cs/idcplg?IdcService=GET_FILE&dDocName=QOELLADWP005416&RevisionSelectionMethod=LatestReleased.

City of Los Angeles Sanitation (LASAN). Planning and Land Development Handbook for Low Impact Development. 5th ed. Los Angeles: LASAN, 2016. https://www.lacitysan.org/cs/groups/sg_sw/documents/document/y250/mde3/~edisp/cnt017152.pdf.

National Board of Fire Underwriters. Building Code Recommended by the National Board of Fire Underwriters. New York: James Kempster Printing, 1905.

U.S. Bureau of Standards. Recommended Minimum Requirements for Small Dwelling Construction. Report of Building Code Committee, July 20, 1922. Washington, DC: U.S. Government Printing Office, 1923.

U.S. Department of Commerce. Recommended Minimum Requirements for Small Dwelling Construction. Washington, DC: U.S. Government Printing Office, 1932.

U.S. Federal Housing Administration. Minimum Property Standards for Properties of One or Two Living Units. Washington, DC: U.S. Government Printing Office, 1958.

U.S. Federal Housing Administration. Property Standards: Requirements for Mortgage Insurance, under Title II of the National Housing Act. Washington, DC: U.S. Government Printing Office, 1936.

INDEX

Ábalos, Iñaki, 59, 64
Acid Rain for Sale Program, 86–87
Act to Amend the Federal Water Pollution Control Act (1965), 67
Act to Provide for A Metropolitan Water Supply, An (1895), 54
ADA Standards for Accessible Design, 92
aerobic treatment units, 154–55
Agamben, Giorgio, 176
Age of Ecology, 62
Agenda 21, 85–86
Agosta House (Patkau Architects), 93
AIA/COTE, 91, 96, 97
air, 78–79, 143–49, 153–54
Air Pollution Act (1955), 143
Air Pollution Control Act (California; 1947), 63
Air Quality Act (1967), 67
air-filtering devices, 147, 153–54
Alexander, Christopher, 75
Alliance to Save Energy, 64
Alternative Technology Advisory Committee, 163
American City Planning Institute, 54
American Forestry Association, 129
American Institute of Architects (AIA), 89
American Institute of Architects (AIA) Research Corporation, 74, 91
American Masterworks (Frampton), 76, 93, 96
American Recovery and Reinvestment Act (ARRA; 2009), 97, 98, 122
American Society for Testing and Materials (renamed ASTM International), 89, 134
American Society of Heating and Ventilating Engineers (ASHVE), 57–58
American Society of Heating, Refrigerating and Air-Conditioning Engineers (ASHRAE), 32, 66, 73, 91, 147
Americans with Disabilities Act (ADA; 1990), 78
Anielski, Mark, 98
ANSI Water Efficiency and Conservation Standard (WE•Stand), 162–63, 165
ANSI/ASHRAE Standard 62.2 Ventilation and Acceptable Indoor Air Quality in Residential Buildings, 147
ANSI/ASHRAE Standard 90.2 Energy Efficient Design of Low-Rise Residential Buildings, 91
Anthropocene, 80–81
Appalachian Trail, 57
Appropriate Technology (AT) movement, 112, 116
Arcosanti, 65
Aschheim, Mark, 160
ASHRAE Standard 55 Thermal Comfort Conditions for Human Occupancy, 58, 66, 73
ASHRAE Standard 90 Energy Conservation in New Building Design, 73
ASHVE Guide, 66
ASTM E84, 134
ASTM International, 134
Atelier Wylde-Oubrerie, 76

Baer, Steven, 75
Baer, William, 37, 149
Balcomb House (Lumpkins), 74–75
"band-aiding" (Ben-Joseph), 37
Banham, Reyner, 39, 61, 75, 127
Bateson, Gregory, 43, 67, 69, 82–83, 90, 173, 177
Beard House (Neutra), 61
Beck, Ulrich, 114–15, 124, 129, 144, 148
Beecher, Catherine, 55
Bell, Brenna, 162
Bemis, Albert, 61
Bemis Industries, 61
Ben-Joseph, Eran, 37, 155
Benner, Al, 109, 154, 157, 169–71
Bercy Chen Studio, 97
Better Homes in America (BHA) campaign, 58, 60
Better Homes Week program, 58
"Beyond the Climate Crisis" (Crist), 80
Bhopal pesticide plant, 83
biodepletion, 80
biogas reactors, 164
Blu Homes, 96
Blue Marble photograph, 70
Blueprint for a Green Economy (Pearce), 86
Bormann, Herbert, 69
Boyar, Louis, 63
Brandt, Willy, 82
Brandt Commission, 82, 85
Brandt Equation, The (Quilligan), 82
Brookhaven House, 73
Brown, G. Z., 91
Brundtland, Gro Harlem, 82, 83
Brundtland Report (Our Common Future), 81, 99
Bruse, Michael, 109, 152, 157, 166–69
Bubble Policy, 78, 79
Buck, William R., 171
Building Code Recommended by the National Board of Fire Underwriters (1905), 58
building codes, adoption of, 54
Building Officials and Code Administrators International, 55, 64
Building Research Establishment Environmental Assessment Method (BREEAM), 89
BuildingGreen, 91
BuildingGreen Approved product database, 91
Bullitt Foundation, 162
Bush, George H. W., 85

California, Going, Going (Wood and Heller), 66
California Air Resources Board, 160
California Building Standards Code (California Code of Regulations, Title 24), 38, 131–32
California Building Standards Commission, 97
California Energy Code, 167
California Energy Commission, 73, 91, 152
California Green Building Standards Code (CALGreen), 32, 36, 97–98, 127, 132, 134, 142, 143, 145, 148, 152, 160
California Health and Safety Code, 96
California Residential Code, 131–32, 133–34
California Solar Initiative, 124
California Straw Building Association (CASBA), 158, 160
California Tomorrow, 66
California Water Quality Control Board, 141
CAM (Crassulacean acid metabolism) plants, 169

Canguilhem, Georges, 35, 37–38, 59, 176
cap-and-trade mechanisms, 34, 86–88
Capehart Act (National Housing Act; 1934), 59–60
Caradonna, Jeremy, 67, 88
Carson, Rachel, 33, 66, 67, 140
Carter administration, 72–73
Case Study houses, 63, 64, 65
Case Study House, 76
Cellophane House (Kieran Timberlake), 96
Chang, Ha-Joon, 36
Chemosphere (Lautner), 65
Chernobyl nuclear disaster, 83
Chicago City Club competition, 59
Church Rock nuclear waste spill, 79
Circo, Carl, 114
City Beautiful movement, 54
CityTree, 171
Civil Rights Act (1968), 66
Clean Air Act (1963), 67, 143
Clean Air Act amendment (1970), 72
Clean Air Act amendment (1990), 86
Clean Air Nonroad Diesel Rule of the Environmental Protection Agency (EPA), 87
Clean Water Act (1972), 72, 140–41
Clean Water Act amendment (1987), 79, 140
Clements, Frederic, 62
climate change, 32, 80, 86–87, 98, 123
Climate Change Bill (California; AB 4420), 80
climate control
    efficiency and, 55
    health-driven, 44
Clinton administration, 87
Club of Rome, 70, 71, 111
code architecture, 108
code-making circuits, 43, 103, 175
coercion, forms of, 106, 114–16, 174
Comfort Zone diagram, 58, 66
command-and-control policies, 87, 114, 123
Committee for Nuclear Information, 66
common interest developments (CIDs), 92–93
Commoner, Barry, 66
community, focus on, 65
composting/waterless toilets, 141, 142–43, 157, 162–65
Conference on Home Building and Home Ownership, 59
conservation, understanding of term, 81
conservation efforts, 63
construction
    nonstandard, 109
    resilient, 98
    stick frame, 113
    straw-bale, 157, 158–61
Corrugated Cardboard Pod (Rural Studio), 96
Council of American Building Officials, 78, 91
Crane, Caroline Bartlett, 59
Cranston-Gonzalez National Affordable Housing Act (1990), 78
Crist, Eileen, 80
Crowther, Richard, 74
Cubical Module Method (Bemis), 61

Daly, Herman, 33, 70, 72, 85, 86, 89, 98, 106, 116, 123
Danielsson, Molly, 162
Database of State Incentives for Renewables & Efficiency (DSIRE), 117, 121
Davis, Margaret, 80
Death and Life of Great American Cities, The (Jacobs), 65

decentralization, 113
Deconstructivist Architecture (MoMA exhibition), 76
DeKay, Mark, 91
demonstration houses/cottages, 58–59
Department of Commerce, 33, 53, 58
Department of Energy (DOE), 72–73, 75, 78, 91–92, 121, 122, 124
Department of Housing and Urban Development (HUD), 65, 74, 77, 123
Department of the Treasury, 122
Department of Veteran Affairs, 77
"depletion quota" (Daly), 116
Desert on the March (Sears), 61
Design with Climate (Olgyay and Olgyay), 91
digital modeling/simulation, 109, 157, 166–69
Digitally Fabricated House for New Orleans (Sass), 96
Dirty Thirties, 44, 61–62
Douglas House (Meier), 75–76
Drury, William, 69
Dursban, 87

Earth Charter, 86, 88
Earth Day, 33, 70
Earth First! 81–82
Earth Overshoot Day, 89
Earthship, 97
Easterling, Keller, 63
"ecofascism" (Gorz), 111, 129, 175–76
Ecological Building Network (EBNet), 160
Ecologists' Union, 63
ecology, 43, 57, 62, 99
Ecology as Politics (Gorz), 112
Eco-Machine (John Todd), 155.
    see also Living Machine
economic models, 106
Economic Recovery Act (1981), 77
"ecosophy" (Guattari) 177
ecosystem ecology, 62
ecotoxicity, 133–34
Edgeland House (Bercy Chen Studio), 97
efficiency, focus on, 55
"efficient ordering" (Ellul), 112–13
Ehrlich, Paul, 70
Eichler, Joseph, 63, 64
Eichler, Ned, 65
Eichler Homes, 63, 65
Einstein, Albert, 88
Eisenberg, David, 159, 160
Eisenman, Peter, 76
Ellul, Jacques, 103, 112–14, 128
Elton, Charles, 57, 62
emissions reduction, 34
Emmons, Frederick E., 65
Empire (Hardt and Negri), 35, 177
End of Growth, The (Heinberg), 99
Endangered Species Act (1973), 72
Endangered Species Preservation Act (1966), 67
end-user incentives, 115, 116
"Energy, Ecology, and Economics" (Odum), 71
Energy and Form (Knowles), 74, 124
Energy Code, 36–37, 147, 148, 152
Energy Conservation and Production Act (1976), 73, 122
Energy Conservation Standards, 144–45
energy consumption, 64
Energy Efficient Mortgages, 123
Energy Independence and Security Act (2007), 97

Energy Policy Act (2005), 122
Energy Policy Act (EPACT92; 1992), 91–92, 97, 122
Energy Policy and Conservation Act (1975), 33, 73, 122
energy security, 123–24
Energy Star program, 91–92
Energy Tax Act (1978), 73, 122
Energy Tax Policy (Sherlock), 116, 123
energy-conservation standards, 32, 44, 78
EnergySage, 128
ENVI_MET, 166
ENVI-met, 109, 152, 166–69
environmental awareness, 33
Environmental Building News (BuildingGreen), 91
environmental comfort, 55
environmental movement, 66–67, 69–70
Environmental Protection Agency (EPA), 72, 117, 133
environmental protection framework, creation of, 72
Environmental Resource Guide (AIA/COTE), 91
environmental simulation software, 166–69
epigenetic chreods, 173
Era of Loneliness/Emptiness, 80
Euclidean zoning, 56
Everyman's House (Better Homes in America), 59
Evolving House, The (Bemis), 61
Existenzminimum, 61
expanded polystyrene (EPS), 133
extruded polystyrene (XPS), 133
Exxon Valdez, 83

Fair Housing Provision, Title VIII, Civil Rights Act (1968), 66
Fallingwater (Wright), 61
Farallones Institute, 75
"fear business," 114–15
Federal Housing Administration (FHA), 32–33, 44, 59–60, 64, 65, 77, 123
Federal Water Pollution Control Act (1948), 63
Fedrizzi, Rick, 89
feed-in tariffs, 121
First National Conference on City Planning, 54
Fithian, Lee, 38
Flintenbreite eco-village, 164
foam plastics, 132–33. see also insulation
Ford Model T, 53
Forrester, Jay, 66, 70, 71
Foucault, Michel, 32
Frampton, Kenneth, 76–77, 93, 96
Frederick, Christine, 58
free-trade agreements, 34
Fuller, Buckminster, 61, 112
Fuller House (Predock), 76
Funding Wizard, 117, 121

Gandhi, Indira, 81
Garden Cities of To-morrow (Howard), 54
gardening, 34
Geddes, Patrick, 57
Gehry, Frank, 76, 93
Gehry Residence (Gehry), 76
"Giant Pool of Money, The," 94
Gilbreth, Lillian, 59
Gilman, Charlotte Perkins, 58
Givoni, Baruch, 65, 75, 91
Glide House (Kaufman), 95
global warming. see climate change

Global Warming Solutions Act (California; 2006), 97
Gold Ribbon Commission on Urine Diversion, 164
Good Life, The (Ábalos), 64
Gorz, André, 111, 129, 175–76
Gottfried, David, 89
government-sponsored enterprises (GSEs), 93
Grant, George Parkin, 103, 106, 112, 128, 176
Graves, Michael, 77
gray water, 141, 162
Great Depression, 44, 59
green building floor-area bonus, 122, 125
Green Building Standards Code (CALGreen Code; California). see California Green Building Standards Code (CALGreen)
Green Buildings and the Law (McCuen and Fithian), 38
Green City Solutions, 171
green economy, 32
Green House (television show), 97
Green House, The (exhibit), 95
Greenberg House (Legorreta), 76
green/living walls, 154, 167–68.
    see also moss walls
green prefab, 32
Grober, Ulrich, 81
Gropius, Walter, 61
Guattari, Félix, 35, 99, 177

Hammer, Martin, 109, 153, 157, 158–61
Handbook of Fundamentals (ASHRAE), 66
Hannover Principles, The, 89, 90
Hardt, Michael, 35, 88, 177
Hassalo on Eighth, 164
Hawken, Paul, 88
Hayden, Dolores, 75
Heinberg, Richard, 99
Hertz, David, 97
hexabromocyclododecane (HBCD), 133
Hight, Christopher, 99
Hirsch, Fred, 71
Hise, Greg, 61
Hockney, David, 64
Holl, Steven, 93
Holy Land (Waldie), 63
Home Delivery (MoMA exhibition), 95–96
Home Energy Rating System (HERS) procedures/index, 91, 153
"Home is Not a House, A" (Banham), 127
homeownership
    migration control and, 59
    promotion of, 33, 58–59
Hoover, Herbert, 57, 59, 60
House and Studio (Graves), 77
House and Studio (Myers and Myers), 93
house flipping, 77, 94
house size, increase in, 96
House VI (Eisenman), 76
household manuals, 58
Housing Act (1948), 63
Housing Act (1949), 64
Housing and Economic Recovery Act (2008), 95
Housing Division of the Pierce Foundation, 61
Howard, Ebenezer, 54
Hubbard Brook studies, 69
Hughes, Thomas P., 113
hurricanes, 79–80
Hutchinson, G. Evelyn, 62
Hyperion treatment plant, 141

Illich, Ivan, 108, 112, 115, 125, 127, 129
Immergluck, Dan, 74
incentives
    end-user, 115, 116
    market-based, 86–88, 91, 174
    nonfinancial, 122
    performance-based, 121
    rebates, 121–22
    tax-based, 121, 122
incentivization, 106, 108, 114–16, 117, 174
indoor air pollution, 78–79, 144
indoor air quality, 147–48
Indoor Radon Abatement Act (1988), 79, 144
insect infestation, 164
insulation
    foam plastic, 132–33
    thermal barriers against, 132
    urea formaldehyde foam, 134
    vegetative, 153
Integral Urban House (Farallones Institute), 75
intergovernmental actions, 34
Intergovernmental Panel on Climate Change, 80
International Association of Plumbing
    and Mechanical Officials (IAPMO),
    142, 145, 162–63, 165
International Building Code (IBC),
    55, 57, 159, 161
International Code Council (ICC),
    36, 55, 92, 98, 145, 159–61, 165
International Conference of Building Officials
    (ICBO), 57
International Green Construction Code (IgCC),
    36, 98, 159–60
International Residential Code (IRC), 158
International Union for Conservation of
    Nature, 81
Italiano, Mike, 89

Jackson, Bohlin Cywinski, 93
Jackson, Tim, 99
Jacobs, Jane, 37, 65
Jevons, William, 72
Jevons paradox, 72, 88
Johnson, Philip, 76
Jones, Quincy, 65
Joy, Rick, 93

Kappe, Ray, 96
Kaufman, Michelle, 95, 96
Keaton, Buster, 59
Keck & Keck, 61
Kerdi-Board, 133
Kieran Timberlake, 96
King, Bruce, 159, 160
kitchen waste, 141
Klein, Naomi, 34, 87
Knowles, Ralph, 65, 74, 75, 124–25
Krueck & Olson, 76
Kyoto Protocol on Climate Change, 86, 87, 98

Lake|Flato, 97
Lakewood, 63
Land and Water Conservation Fund Act
    (1965), 67
"Land Ethic, The" (Leopold), 62
land management, 56
Lautner, John, 65
Le Corbusier, 76
Lead-Based Paint Poisoning Prevention Act
    (1971), 72

Leadership in Energy and Environmental
    Design (LEED), 35–36, 90, 91, 92, 96,
    97, 122, 125
Ledge House (Jackson), 93
Legorreta, Ricardo, 76
Leopold, Aldo, 62, 69
Lewis Residence (Gehry), 93
LIDAR (Light Detection and Ranging)
    technology, 167
Likens, Gene, 69
Limits to Growth, The (Meadows et al.),
    33, 70, 71, 82, 85, 99, 111, 176
Lindeman, Raymond L., 62
Lippincott, Mathew, 109, 142, 157, 162–65
Living Building Challenge (LBC), 90, 116, 162
Living Future Institute, 35, 90
living/green walls, 154, 167–68.
    see also moss walls
Living Machine (John Todd), 162.
    see also Eco-Machine
LivingHomes, 96
Lorenz, Edward, 66
Los Angeles, 38–39
Lotka, Alfred J., 62, 71
Lovell, Philip, 58
Lovelock, James, 70
Lovins, Amory, 71–72, 78, 88
Lovins, L. Hunter, 88
Lucy Carpet House (Rural Studio), 96
Lumpkins, William, 74–75

machine
    Mumford on, 113
MacKaye, Benton, 57
MacNeill, Jim, 99
Magwood, Chris, 161
Man, Climate and Architecture (Givoni), 91
Man in the Gray Flannel Suit, The (Wilson), 64
Managing without Growth (Victor), 98–99
market-based incentives, 86–88, 91, 174
Marsh, George Perkins, 56
Massey, Jonathan, 60, 94
Master Draft of Proposed Minimum Property
    Requirements for Properties of One or Two
    Living Units, 64
materials, 109, 131–34, 137
May, Robert, 69
McCuen, Tamera, 38
McKenzie, Evan, 93
Mechanical Code, 145, 147, 148, 153
mechanical ventilation, 145, 147
"megatechnics" (Mumford), 112, 114
Meier, Richard, 75–76
MERV (Minimum Efficiency Reporting Value)
    rating, 154, 171
meta-code, 109
Methane to Markets Partnership, 88
"micro-fascism" (Guattari), 35
"middle position" (Pearce), 86
Miller House (Atelier Wylde-Oubrerie), 76
Minimum Construction Requirements for New
    Dwellings, 60
Minimum Property Standards (1958), 123
Minimum Property Standards for One and Two
    Family Dwellings, 77–78
Minimum Property Standards for Properties of
    One or Two Living Units, 32–33, 64, 73
Mishan, Ezra J., 67, 71, 123
Mockbee, Samuel, 96
ModCell, 161

Model Code for Energy Conservation in New
    Buildings, 73, 78
Model Energy Code, 78, 91
Model Tenement House Law (1910), 54
Model Water Efficient Landscape Ordinance
    (MWELO), 140–41, 154
modular building components, 61
MoMA, 76, 95–96
Mon Oncle, 64
Montreal Protocol, 83
mortgages
    defaults on, 64, 122
    disintegration/deregulation of industry for,
    77, 93–94
    HUD and, 123
    mortgage-backed securities and, 94–95
    securitization of, 74
    subprime mortgage crisis and,
    44, 74, 94–95
Moss Acres, 169
moss walls, 109, 157, 169–71.
    see also green/living walls
Moss Walls (company), 154, 169
Mother's House (Venturi), 65
Muir, John, 33, 56
Mumford, Lewis, 56, 61, 113–14, 116
Myers, Barton and Vicki, 93
Myhrman, Matts, 160

National Appliance Energy Conservation Act
    (1987), 78
National Board of Fire Underwriters, 54–55
National Building Code, 64
National Bureau of Standards (NBS), 53, 73
National Conference of States on Building
    Codes and Standards (NCSBCS), 73
National Energy Act (1978), 78
National Energy Conservation Policy Act
    (1978), 73
National Energy Plan, 72–73
National Environmental Policy Act (1970),
    33, 67
National Fire Protection Association, 134, 145
National Housing Act (1934), 59–60
National Housing Association, 54
National Park Service, 56
National Pollutant Discharge Elimination System
    (NPDES) permits, 140
National Renewable Energy Laboratory (NREL),
    73, 121–22, 123, 124
National Sanitation Foundation (NSF),
    142, 165
National Wildlife Reserve System, 56
Natural Capitalism (Hawken, Lovins, and
    Lovins), 88
Natural House, The (Wright), 55
natural materials, minimally processed, 109
Nature Conservancy, 63
NBSIR 74-452 Design and Evaluation
    Criteria for Energy Conservation in
    New Buildings, 73
Negri, Antonio, 35, 88, 177
net zero concept, 35, 125, 127, 176
Neufert, Ernst, 61
Neutra, Richard, 58, 61
New Alchemy Institute, 78
New Deal, 44, 57, 59
New Ecology, 57, 62
New York State Tenement House Act, 54
New York Tenement House Act (1901), 54
New York Workmen's Home, 54

New York Zoning Resolution, 54
NFPA 5000, Building Construction and Safety Code, 159
Nisbet, Ian, 69
nonfinancial incentives, 122
nongovernmental organizations (NGOs), 35
nonstandard construction systems, 109
"normal accidents" (Perrow), 79, 83
North American Free Trade Agreement (NAFTA), 34, 87
North-South: A Program for Survival (Independent Commission on International Development), 82, 85
NSF International, 142
Nuclear Test Ban Treaty (1963), 66
Nuclear Waste Policy Act (1982), 79

Obama administration, 32, 98, 99, 122
obsolescence, 175
Ocean Dumping Act (1972), 143
Odum, Eugene, 62
Odum, Howard T., 62, 66–67, 71, 72
Oikos, 66
Oil Pollution Act (1990), 83
Olgyay, Victor and Aladar, 65, 75, 91
Olmsted, Frederick Law, 54
One Week, 59
Open Standard Health Product Declaration Collaborative, 91
Operation Breakthrough, 65
operational efficiency, 116
Oregon Reach Code, 162
Oregon Residential Reach Code, 163
organicist approach, 57
organization, techniques of, 106
Our Common Future, 82, 83, 85
outdoor air quality, 143–44
ozone-depleting compounds, 83

Pacific Ready-Cut Homes, 55
PAE Living Building, 164
passive design strategies/methods, 37, 121, 124
passive solar, 32, 75, 112, 125. *see also* solar panels/energy systems
Patkau Architects, 93
Pearce, David, 86, 91, 115, 129
Peccei, Aurelio, 111
"pentagon of power" (Mumford), 116
Pentagon of Power, The (Mumford), 113–14
performance-based incentives, 121
Perrow, Charles, 79
phyto-air purification, 153–54. *see also* plant-based systems, vegetation
Pinchot, Gifford, 33, 56, 62, 88
Plan of Chicago, 54
plant-based systems, 109. *see also* phyto-air purification, vegetation
Plumbing Code, 142, 154
point source pollution, 141
Pollution Prevention Act (1990), 83
Population Bomb, The (Ehrlich), 70
Porch Houses (Lake | Flato), 97
PowerSaver Loans, 123
predesign, 39, 109, 157–58, 175
Predock, Antoine, 76
prefabrication, 95–96
preservation projects, 56
Price, Cedric, 175
Prickly Mountain (Sellers), 65
Prigogine, Ilya, 80

Principles of Scientific Management (Taylor), 53
Privatopia (McKenzie), 93
Progressive Era, 53–54, 55, 62, 64
Project Sunroof (Google), 125
Property Standards, 60
Property Standards and Minimum Construction Requirements, 60
Prosperity without Growth (Jackson), 99
puritan ethic, 176–77

Quiet Crisis, The (Udall), 67
Quilligan, James, 82

racial bias, 77
Radon Abatement Act, Indoor (1988), 79, 144
rainwater, 140
rating systems, 89–90
Rational Design (Bemis), 61
Reagan administration, 33, 73–74, 78, 82
rebates, 121–22. *see also* incentives
Recode, 142, 162, 165
Recommended Minimum Requirements for Small Dwelling Construction, 58–59
regimentation, 113–14
Regional Planning Association of America (RPAA), 56–57
Reich, Robert, 93
Report of the World Commission on Environment and Development: Our Common Future, 34
Residential Alternative Calculation Method Reference Manual, 153
Residential Conservation Service program, 73–74
Residential Energy Services Network (RESNET), 91
resilience
    current usage of, 33
    need for, 32
resilient construction, 98
Rio Earth Summit, 83, 85
Rittle, Horst, 83
Rmax Thermasheath-3, 133
Roaring Twenties, 44
Rockwood, David, 76
Rockwood House (Rockwood), 76
Rocky Mountain Institute, 78
Roosevelt, Franklin D., 57, 59
Roosevelt, Theodore, 88
Rural Studio, 65, 96–97
Ruth, D. K., 96
R-value, 167. *see also* insulation
Rybczynski, Witold, 58

Safe Drinking Water Act (1974), 72, 140
Santa Monica Residence (Gehry), 76
Sass, Lawrence, 96
Scarpa, Carlo, 93
Schindler, Rudolf, 58
Schmitt, Carl, 176
Schumacher, E. F., 70–71, 72, 112
Schwarzenegger, Arnold, 159
Science and the Modern World (Whitehead), 57
Science of the Artificial, The (Simon), 37
scientific management, 53–54, 55
Sea Ranch Condominium, 65
Sears, Paul, 61
Sellers, David, 65
Selling Mrs. Consumer (Frederick), 58

septic tanks, 154–55, 163
sewage, 141–43, 154, 162–65
SHADOW, 166
shadow-casting simulation software, 166
Sher, Byron, 158, 159
"Should You Cut Down Trees to Go Solar?" (EnergySage), 128
Silent Spring (Carson), 33, 66, 140
Simberloff, Daniel, 69
Simon, Herbert, 37, 113
Small Is Beautiful (Schumacher), 70, 112
Smart House, 97
SmartWrap (Kieran Timberlake), 96
Smith, Dan, 159
Soft Energy Paths (Lovins), 71
Solar Decathlon, 73, 96
Solar Dwelling Design Concepts (American Institute of Architects Research Corporation), 74, 91
"solar envelope" project (Knowles), 124–25, 127
solar panels/energy systems, 34–35, 38, 72, 74–75, 88, 113, 121–22, 124–25, 127–29
Solar Rights Act (AB 3250, 1978), 128
Solar Shade Control Act (1978), 127
Soleri, Paolo, 65
Solid Waste Disposal Act (1965), 67
speculation, 94
Stak Block, 161
standardization, 53–56, 58–59, 63, 64
standard-setting efforts, 89–90, 91–93
State Energy Program, 122, 124
State Support for Clean Energy Deployment (Kubert and Sinclair), 121
Steady-State Economics (Daly), 70, 98
Steel & Glass House (Krueck & Olson), 76
stick frame construction, 113
Stockholm Conference on the Human Environment, 33
Stockholm Convention on Persistent Organic Pollutants, 87, 133
Stockholm Declaration, 70
Stormwater Capture Master Plan, 140
stormwater discharge/runoff, 79, 140–41, 154
Stormwater Low Impact Development (LID) Ordinance, 140–41, 154
straw-bale construction, 157, 158–61
subprime mortgage crisis, 44, 74, 94–95
subsidies, 115, 117
suburban expansion, promotion of, 44
sulfur dioxide, 86
Sun, Wind and Light (DeKay and Brown), 91
Sun Earth: How to Use Solar and Climatic Energies (Crowther), 74
Superfund Program, 79
survivalism, 72
sustainable development
    development efforts for, 81–83
    introduction of concept of, 34
    misinterpretation of, 99
    Rio Earth Summit and, 85–86
Sustainable Development Concepts (World Bank), 85
systems ecology, 57

Tansley, Arthur G., 62
Tati, Jacques, 64
tax-based incentives, 73, 121, 122
Taylor, Frederick Winslow, 53
TCPP (trisphosphate), 133
technique (Ellul), 112–13

technology, Gorz on, 112
tenements, 54
Tennessee Valley Authority (TVA), 57
Terrani, Giuseppe, 76
Thatcher, Margaret, 82
thermal barrier, 132
"Thinking about Technology" (Grant), 128
third-party rating systems, 44
This Changes Everything (Klein), 87
This Old House, 77, 97
Thompson, d'Arcy, 74
Thoreau, Henry David, 56
Three Ecologies, The (Guattari), 177
Three Mile nuclear meltdown, 79
tiny-house movement, 96
Todd, John, 155
toilets
    composting/waterless, 141, 142–43,
        157, 162–65
    urine-diversion, 109, 163, 164
    vacuum, 164
"tools" (Illich), 112
Tools for Thought (Waddington), 176
Touch 'n Foam, 133
Toxic Substances Control Act (1976), 79
trees
    ecological functions of, 128–29
    planting, 127
    see also vegetation
Truman, Harry S., 63–64
20K project (Rural Studio), 97
Tyller House (Joy), 93

Udall, Stewart L., 67
UN Scientific Conference on the Conservation
    and Utilization of Resources, 62
uncanny-valley effect, 166–67
Uniform Building Code, 57, 159
Uniform Plumbing Code (UPC), 162
United Nations (UN), 34
United Nations Conference on the Human
    Environment, 70
United Nations Environment Program, 81
United States Forest Service, 56
Unwin, Raymond, 54
UPC Green Supplement Composting
    Toilet Committee, 162, 164
urban stormwater pollution, 79
urea formaldehyde foam insulation, 134
urine-diversion toilets, 109, 163, 164
U.S. Department of Commerce, 33, 53, 58
U.S. Department of Energy, 72–73, 75, 78,
    91–92, 121, 122, 124
U.S. Department of Housing and Urban
    Development (HUD), 65, 74, 77, 123
U.S. Department of the Treasury, 122
U.S. Department of Veteran Affairs, 77
U.S. Green Building Council (USGBC),
    35–36, 89–90, 98
U.S. Housing Authority, 61
U.S. National Urban Runoff Program, 79
Usonian houses (Wright), 60, 61

VA lending programs, 123
vacuum toilets, 164
vegetation
    air purification and, 153–54
    ecological functions of, 128–29
    encouraging use of, 127
    exclusion of, 108–9

focus on, 149–55
    insulation from, 153
    shade from, 152–53
    shadow-casting simulation software and,
        166–67
ventilation, 144–48, 153–54. *see also* air
Venturi, Robert, 65
Verdure Wellness Wall (Moss Walls),
    169–70, 171
Victor, Peter, 98–99
Village of Euclid Zoning Ordinance, 56
volatile organic compounds (VOCs), 144

Waddington, C. H., 173, 176
Waldie, D. J., 63
Washington National Building Museum, 95
wastewater. see sewage; water supply and
    drainage systems
Water Conservation in Landscaping Act
    (2006), 140
water consumption, 143
Water Efficiency and Sanitation Standard
    (WE•Stand), 142
water pollution, 79
water supply and drainage systems,
    137–43, 154
WateReuse, 92
waterless/composting toilets, 141,
    142–43, 157, 162–65
WaterSense standards, 92
weatherization, 97, 117, 144
Weatherization Assistance Program,
    73, 121, 122
Webber, Melvin, 83
Weber, Max, 176, 177
Weiss, Marc, 60
Whitehead, Alfred North, 57, 86
Whole Earth Catalog, 112
Wigley, Mark, 76
Wilderness Act (1964), 67
Wilson, Alex, 91
Wilson, E. O., 80, 155
Wilson, Sloan, 64
Wing House (Hertz), 97
Winner, Langdon, 79, 94
Winton Guest House (Gehry), 76
women in the workforce, 74, 75
World at Risk (Beck), 114–15
World Bank, 85
World Climate Conference, 80
World Commission on Environment and
    Development, 82
World Conference on the Changing
    Atmosphere, 34
World Conservation Strategy (International
    Union for Conservation of Nature), 81
World Meteorological Organization, 80
World Trade Organization (WTO),
    34, 85–86, 87
World Wildlife Fund, 81
World's Columbian Exposition, 54
Worster, Donald, 62
Wright, Frank Lloyd, 55, 57, 60, 61

Yannas, Simon, 166
Yestermorrow, 65

Zero Emission Vehicle program, 143
Zero Energy Ready Homes, 73, 91
Zeta 6 House (Kappe), 96
Zome House (Baer), 75

Published by
Princeton Architectural Press
70 West 36th Street
New York, NY 10018
www.papress.com

© 2022 Aleksandra Jaeschke

All rights reserved.
Printed and bound in China
25 24 23 22 4 3 2 1 First edition

ISBN 978-1-64896-008-6

No part of this book may be used or
reproduced in any manner without written
permission from the publisher, except in the
context of reviews.

Every reasonable attempt has been made
to identify owners of copyright. Errors or
omissions will be corrected in subsequent
editions.

Editors: Holly La Due, Kristen Hewitt,
Linda Lee
Designer: Natalie Snodgrass
All images © Aleksandra Jaeschke

Library of Congress Control Number:
2022936461